WOOD

ARCHITECTURE NOW!

IMPRINT

PROJECT MANAGEMENT
Florian Kobler, Cologne

COLLABORATION
Harriet Graham, Turin

PRODUCTION
Ute Wachendorf, Cologne

DESIGN
Sense/Net Art Direction,
Andy Disl and Birgit Eichwede,
Cologne

GERMAN TRANSLATION
Nora von Mühlendahl,
Ludwigsburg

FRENCH TRANSLATION
Jacques Bosser, Paris

© VG BILD-KUNST
Bonn 2011, for the works of
Piet Hein Eek

PRINTED IN ITALY
ISBN 978–3–8365–2329–5

© 2011 TASCHEN GMBH
Hohenzollernring 53
D–50672 Cologne
www.taschen.com

WOOD

ARCHITECTURE NOW!

HOLZ-*Architektur heute!*
L'architecture EN BOIS *d'aujourd'hui!*
Philip Jodidio

TASCHEN

CONTENTS

INTRODUCTION

WOOD IS FOR NOW

Within these plantations of God, a decorum and sanctity reign, a perennial festival is dressed, and the guest sees not how he should tire of them in a thousand years. In the woods, we return to reason and faith. There I feel that nothing can befall me in life,—no disgrace, no calamity, (leaving me my eyes,) which nature cannot repair. Standing on the bare ground,—my head bathed by the blithe air, and uplifted into infinite space,—all mean egotism vanishes. I become a transparent eye-ball; I am nothing; I see all; the currents of the Universal Being circulate through me; I am part or particle of God.

Ralph Waldo Emerson, *Nature*, 1836

Wood is, first of all, the forest, the "plantations of God." It is in the moonlit woods that the characters of Shakespeare's *A Midsummer Night's Dream* play out their transformative comedy; it is again in the forest that architecture itself, in disguises ranging from the simple column, to the temple and the cathedral, finds much of its inspiration. A canopy of branches, stacked trunks to provide shelter from the storm, wood is a quintessential element of the earliest built habitations, most of which returned to the earth in time. Architecture in wood is often reputed to be ephemeral. Indeed, depending on such factors as climate and maintenance, wooden structures may not last very long. And yet, to take just one example, the five-story pagoda at Daigoji Temple, built in 951, is the oldest building in Kyoto. And so wood, properly turned, can stand a thousand years even as the earth shakes and the generations pass. Before they are cut and formed, trees live, depending on the species, longer than any other organism on earth. A Great Basin bristlecone pine aptly named Methuselah (White Mountains, California) is estimated to be more than 4800 years old. Clonal trees like the so-called Pando, a quaking aspen located in Utah, send up shoots from a single massive root system thought in this instance to be 80 000 years old. A tree far older than human civilization. Trees, both figuratively and literally, are the origin of built form, shelter, and inspiration; the stuff of the earth.

Stories of the rape of the forests carried forward in Indonesia and elsewhere abound, and few would defend such practices as having anything to do with an ecological approach to building, yet wood, properly managed and harvested, is living a new life in the early 21st century as a material of predilection in architecture. Because a managed forest can be renewed, wood that is not transported over too great a distance is surely one of the most ecologically sound building materials available. Organizations such as the United States Green Building Council (USGBC) have established standards (LEED, or Leadership in Energy and Environmental Design) that can serve to certify lumber for environmentally sustainable construction. In this case, the USGBC works with the Forest Stewardship Council (FSC). The FSC "is an independent, non-governmental, not-for-profit organization established to promote the responsible management of the world's forests. Established in 1993 as a response to concerns over global deforestation, FSC is widely regarded as one of the most important initiatives of the last decade to promote responsible forest management worldwide."[1] In December 2008, 107 million hectares of forest in 78 countries were certified to the FSC's "Principles and Criteria."

1
BETON, Church in Tarnów,
Tarnów on the Vistula,
Poland, 2007–10

1

Because its use has been so widespread over time, and by no means only in inventive architecture, wood carries with it something of a reputation. Why have a wooden house when concrete and aluminum seem so much more modern and solid? *Wood Architecture Now!* is about an entirely new generation of buildings, surely inspired in part by traditions, but also by the "green" building vogue. As strict modernism or the even more arid minimalism slip out of fashion, so, too, many architects and clients have sought the warmth that wood conveys, its natural feeling. Being an "old" building material, wood can nonetheless be fashioned using the most contemporary CNC (computer numerical control) milling techniques, making complex forms or unique pieces economically feasible. Then, too, many architects represented in this volume use wood for specific purposes and areas of their buildings. A building may be clad in wood but built of concrete or steel. The point of this book, as indeed of the rest of the *Architecture Now!* series, is to give an overview of what is being done in different styles and techniques from as many locations as possible. By no means exhaustive, *Wood Architecture Now!* focuses on buildings of the 21st century, and indeed mainly on work of the past two or three years—proof that wood is back as a contemporary building material.

NATURE CALLING

Examples of wooden churches, chapels, or simple places of meditation in wood abound, almost throughout the history of architecture, thus it is natural that some should continue to turn their attention in this direction. Although they named their firm BETON (French for concrete), Marta Rowińska and Lech Rowiński (both born in 1976) have taken an obvious pleasure in erecting a small (60-square-meter) wooden church in Tarnów on the Vistula River (Poland, 2007–10, page 108). Set on a concrete slab foundation, the structure was built largely by unskilled workers, a procedure that is obviously easier using wood than more complex building materials. The architects sought to achieve "a certain quality of space with the use of rudimentary technical simplicity." At a cost of just €20 000, the church in Tarnów does indeed assume an uplifting quality, particularly when seen from the interior—an apt metaphor for spirituality.

Half a world away in Chile, the young architects Alejandro Dumay Claro, Nicolás Fones, and Francisco Vergara Arthur, all born in Santiago in 1977, built an even smaller (21-square-meter) wooden chapel that has a similar pointed form. Their Fuente Nueva Chapel (2006, page 184) looks directly out on Lake Rupanco in southern Chile. Indeed, the full-height opening behind the altar makes it clear that here nature is the message. The architecture is reduced to its strict minimum and yet the structure retains a stripped-down modernity that in fact reinforces the natural setting in its impact on the 12 people who can gather in this space. Although religious architecture has often relied heavily on ornamentation or the complex development of spatial effects, such small structures bereft of all superfluous detail are witness to a certain return to fundamental values—both in form and function.

Beatriz Meyer, born in São Paulo in 1977, is a collaborator of the architect Marcio Kogan, but she has designed a number of her own structures, such as the wooden chapel located in Tatuí (São Paulo, Brazil, 2006, page 310). Little more than a sloped roof with fully glazed walls on three sides, the chapel does make use of stone for the wall behind the altar, and more sophisticated materials such as an Alwitra

2
*Rodrigo Sheward, Pinohuacho
Observation Deck, Pinohuacho,
Villarrica, Chile, 2006*

2

membrane for the roof. The overall impression here is nonetheless one of great simplicity and elegance. Nearby trees emphasize the impression of a chapel in the forest, returning in some sense to the points of origin of worship in more sense than one.

Though it is not a religious structure, Rodrigo Sheward's Pinohuacho Observation Deck (Pinohuacho, Villarrica, Chile, 2006, page 374) certainly does encourage meditation. Located in the midst of a former logging area, it participates in an attempt to consider the damage done by indiscriminate logging. Made of wood left over from the logging, in good part by a worker who had been a member of the team that brought the forest down, the Observation Deck, measuring 78 square meters at a cost of just $3000, faces the Villarrica Volcano. Born in 1979, Sheward, like the other architects cited here all under 40 years of age, seems to have heeded the call of the forest, past or present, embodied in wood, a worthy subject of meditation and the need to build anew.

COME RAIN, COME SHINE

Houses are clearly one the most fertile areas of investigation for architects using wood today. Although larger-scale structures can of course be fashioned from wood, the generally small scale of residential architecture makes the material attractive from many points of view. These include the obvious ecological benefits of properly harvested and transported wood, the relative ease of woodworking as opposed to the mechanical processes required for metal or other construction materials, and quite simply the warmth that wood confers in a natural way in both exterior and interior use.

Jular is a firm based in Azambuja, near Lisbon in Portugal, that specializes in sustainable modular housing in wood. Although transportable housing does not often seem to be compatible with good design, the Treehouse System (Azambuja, Portugal, 2008–09, page 35), developed in this instance with the architects João Appleton and Isabel Domingos, is both attractive and practical. The 3.3 x 6.6-meter modules of the Treehouse System can be assembled in various different ways, allowing for either modest or more substantial dwellings. At a cost of €900 per square meter, the system is also economically reasonable. Created with limited window surfaces in order to make the structures well suited to a Mediterranean climate, the Treehouse System brings wood into the areas of modular and transportable architecture in a most convincing way. Jular duly notes that houses of this type may have existed in the past, but that they were not conceived for climates like that of Portugal (on the Atlantic, but also influenced by the Gulf Stream) or Mediterranean countries from Spain to Greece.

Neither transportable nor modest, the RW House (Búzios, Rio de Janeiro, Brazil, 2006–09, page 100) measures no less than 4900 square meters in size. Low-lying and designed in an H-form, the house is lifted 50 centimeters off the beach site. Despite the obvious luxury that such a residence entails, the architects Bernardes + Jacobsen have made use of laminated, untreated eucalyptus wood from reforested areas in the structure. Natural ventilation also emphasizes the proximity of the house to its setting and reduces energy consumption. From a 21-square-meter chapel to a 4900-square-meter house, it would seem that wood is the material of choice, a fact that also serves to reconcile modernity with the warm feeling that wood procures, even when it is laid out in geometric fashion. It can be said in this instance that the architects, known for large, luxurious houses amongst other types of projects, make the best of what cannot be considered a fundamentally "green" realization. Without any prejudice to the wealthy clients, it is difficult to imagine a 4900-square-meter house that is ecologically responsible on the whole, whether or not use of wood is made.

WHAT WAS MADE OF WOOD SWAYED AND REMAINED

Marco Casagrande, born in 1971 in Turku, Finland, says that a ruin emerges when something "man-made has become part of nature. I am looking forward," he says, "to designing ruins." His small (62-square-meter) Chen House (Sanjhih, Taipei, Taiwan, 2007–08, page 138) was built of mahogany and concrete. More than a ruin, this house looks like a place to brave the elements, no matter what they may be. Indeed, the site in the Datun Mountains is subject to flooding, typhoons, and earthquakes. Wooden slats allow breezes to cool the interior, while a fireplace is used for winter heating. This is certainly not high-end design in the usual sense, but there is a rugged accuracy in the design of Marco Casagrande that almost makes it a symbol for hard times, with wood as the mainstay of survival. He quotes a short poem called "Iron" by Bertolt Brecht (1898–1956) that can readily be applied to this design: "In a dream last night, I saw a great storm. It seized the scaffolding. It tore the cross-clasps, the iron ones, down. But what was made of wood, swayed and remained."

Nicolás del Río (born in 1975) and Max Núñez (born in 1976) in Santiago (dRN Architects) are used to harsh conditions where they build; a number of their buildings (Skibox, 2006; Mountain Refuge Chalet C6, 2006; and Mountain Refuge Chalet C7, 2008, all in Portillo, Chile) are built at an altitude of about 2800 meters above sea level. La Baronia House (Quintero, Valparaíso, Chile, 2009, page 172) is not set so high, but it is on a hill facing the ocean. Because of the corroding power of the salt carried in the waves, the architects selected pre-corroded Cor-ten steel and glass to face its fury. And yet within, the structure of the house is made up of bolted wood frames. A wooden skeleton with a skin of steel, the Baronia House shows the appeal of wood as a structural material even in circumstances of climatic extremes. dRN is one of the more inventive young firms working in Chile and this house surely confirms their reputation. The fact that Cor-ten is frequently used in purely sculptural works like those of Richard Serra increases the appeal of the Baronia House, making it a kind of sculptural shelter against the elements.

HAPPY CAMPERS

There is an air of practicality or even frugality in wood that appeals to many clients and a good number of architects. Shin Ohori of Tokyo's General Design was approached by a client who really wanted nothing more than a good place to set up a tent. The result of this unusual collaboration was a "residence" called Mountain Research (Minamisaku, Nagano, Japan, 2007–08, page 208). A larch deck and spaces for cooking, storage, and bathroom facilities shelter a space for a two-meter dome tent. Shin Ohori says: "I hope that architecture will be a place where people discover something new and make innovations in their lifestyles." In this instance, wood is an obvious choice given the mountain location and the extreme frugality of the plans of the client. Naturally other materials could have been employed for this 97-square-meter structure, but wood seems to be very much in keeping with both the place and the program. This stated, might there not be a fundamental contradiction between the purely mobile style of life suggested by a tent and the more fixed nature of the Mountain Research? Let us say that it is an intermediate creation, neither a full house, nor a real place for camping. The use of wood definitely integrates the structure more into its mountain site than other materials.

Wood is an essential element in a number of the most far-reaching attempts to render architecture itself ecologically responsible. The Smart Air House (2010, page 11) by the German architects GRAFT is a prototype for a stacked, two-unit residence that makes use of cross-laminated timber for its structure and wood floors inside. Naturally other materials are used but the principles behind this house are rooted in the latest thinking on how to make "intelligent and efficient building technology symbiotically interact with the eco-friendly material composition without technically dominating the habits of the users." In a way, ecologically responsible architecture is in its formative phase, without clear directions yet established. Indeed, many apparently "eco-friendly" materials reveal themselves to be somewhat less responsible when their entire production chain is examined in detail. An exception to this danger is of course wood, to the extent that it is harvested in a responsible way.

The Trojan House (Melbourne, Victoria, Australia, 2005, page 240) by the architects Jackson Clements Burrows disproves the notion that wooden architecture cannot have a thoroughly modern appearance. Making use of a "seamless timber skin covering roof, windows, and walls," and operable timber shutters, the Trojan House is in fact an extension of an existing house, distinguishable by its blank forms when the shutters are closed. Again, wood, allowing a transition from an older structure to a contemporary one without conflict, shows itself to be adaptable and practical. Jackson Clements Burrows are clearly not the only architects to give thoroughly modern forms to wooden structures, but the Trojan House clearly states the appropriateness of this material in the context of willful modernity.

One house published in this volume, the Lilypad (Point Roberts, Washington, USA, 2008–09, page 286) is unusual because it is not at all the work of an architect, but of a photographer, Nic Lehoux, together with Jacqueline Darjes. At just 24 square meters and a cost calculated at $4500 this is also not an ambitious project in terms of size or price. Cedar decks, reclaimed old Douglas fir for the windows, and glulam beams are the essential elements of the house that is lifted off the ground on sonotubes (a product used to make forms for concrete). Clearly, more complex materials would have rendered this project, at least at its actual cost, less practical. Wood is a material that can be recuperated and worked by people who do not have elaborate equipment or training. Clearly steel, or even concrete, requires superior means and expertise to make a solid structure.

3
GRAFT, Smart Air House,
2010

3

PLYWOOD APARTMENTS AND MOUNTAIN HUTS

Where wood can readily be employed for individual houses, it is also being used frequently for larger residential structures, some of which are quite unusual. The first published here is the Hameau de Plantoun (Bayonne, France, 2008–09, page 132) by the Bordeaux architect Bernard Bühler. Working with the Bayonne public housing authority (OPHLM), this group of 39 residences stands out because the main cladding material is plywood, and the houses themselves are lifted off the ground on wood pilotis and thin metal posts. Many would equate plywood with decidedly temporary uses such as worksite hoarding, and its visible aging may not make for the most readily acceptable appearance. The Hameau de Plantoun is thus unusual both in appearance and in its use of materials, though its ecological "footprint" is surely smaller than that of other more traditionally conceived structures.

Where wood is the most obvious structural material of the Hameau de Plantoun, it seems, at first glance, not to be present at all in the New Monte Rosa Hut SAC (Zermatt, Switzerland, 2008–09, page 196), fully clad in aluminum. And yet the work on this project (ETH-Studio Monte Rosa / Bearth & Deplazes) selected to mark the 150th Anniversary Jubilee of the ETH Zurich was carefully conceived to have the lowest possible energy requirements and also, in its use of materials, to have the minimum conceivable environmental impact. Set at an altitude of 2883 meters, the structure was built using helicopters, which might not seem the least carbon-friendly approach, but it was rendered necessary by the site. The greater part of the interior of this very modern building is made of wood. All of the building materials can be recovered from the site when it is eventually demolished, and on the whole the new hut consumes far less energy than its predecessor. As those who occasionally frequent mountain huts in Switzerland know, wood is a standard element of interiors, surely because it was easier to transport in earlier times than prepared stone for example. The aluminum skin of the Monte Rosa hut represents a technological response to extreme climatic conditions. Wood for the interiors surely has a structural logic but it also responds to the tradition of this building type. The net result is thorough modernity, energy efficiency, and practicality. No material other than wood could have been used to greater benefit inside such a building.

FINNISH FINERIES

As might be expected, the Scandinavian countries are in the forefront of contemporary wood architecture because of local traditions that include such important modern figures as Alvar Aalto who frequently used wood. Emma Johansson (born in 1985 in Turku, Finland) and Timo Leiviskä (born in 1981 in Oulu, Finland) were called on by the Anttolanhovi Hotel in Mikkeli to demonstrate that contemporary houses in wood could be at the cutting edge of architecture, design, and art. Their Lakeside (Johansson) and Hillside (Leiviskä) Villas (2007–08; 2006–08, page 246) are luxury serviced houses made with timber, natural stone, and textiles (indoors). Seeing these villas might make one wonder why architects ever design without using wood. The youth of the architects concerned and the emphasis on "art and design" in the promotion of the site by the Anttolanhovi Hotel place wood in the midst of the most contemporary thinking on resort or hotel architecture.

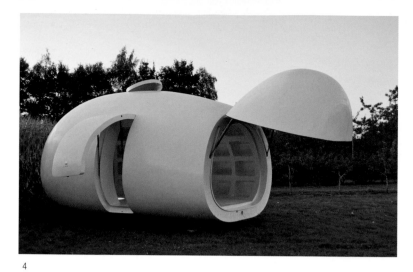

4

Two older Finnish architects, Kirsi Korhonen (born in 1958) and Mika Penttinen (born in 1951) designed the three-story Huvitus Terraced Housing (Helsinki, Finland, 2007–08, page 280). Set on a sandy, pine-covered hill, this structure was built using laminated veneer lumber (LVL) ribs and red-and-black-painted wood façade cladding. The configuration of this housing, with repetitive yet individual volumes, makes for a feeling of modernity that is nonetheless at ease with local tradition. Fire regulations required the architects to build the ground floor of the 1986-square-meter building out of concrete. This said, it has been shown in many circumstances that materials such as steel may resist fire less well than properly treated wood. The ample use of fair wood for interior elements ranging from cladding to furniture makes it clear, in any case, that wood is the essential element of the structure—with the concrete being far less in evidence.

A BLOB AND A TEAHOUSE

Perhaps because it is a notably malleable material, wood is often used for small, unorthodox structures. A number of examples of this kind of architecture are shown in this book. One of the most curious is the Tree Trunk House (Hilversum, The Netherlands, 2009, page 190) conceived by the noted designer Piet Hein Eek. Eek is known for the scrap wood furniture he started making in the early 1990s, but his office also engages in architectural projects. It is at the request of the Dutch musical and comedy performer Hans Liberg that he created a 9.3-square-meter office that looks very much like a simple stack of logs, particularly in its fully closed position. Actual oak logs were used on the sides and tops of the moveable structure, while five-centimeter-thick trunk sections form the cladding elsewhere. This is the kind of trompe l'oeil design that has on occasion been used for military structures, but here it is imbued with a certain humor. In any case, the significance of the wood motif can hardly be denied in this instance.

The Belgian architects dmvA had another take on mobile wooden construction in their Blob VB3 (2008–09, page 164) designed for XfactorAgencies. Intended as an extension to an existing house and an office, the Blob was designed to "skirt around" strict local building codes. Containing a bathroom, kitchen, bed, and storage areas, the structure is, indeed, quite flexible for use for other purposes. Made with a wood frame covered by a polyester skin, the Blob surely does not look like many wood buildings of the past—indeed, its wood structure is not perceptible from the exterior. Although the word "blob" took on some rather negative connotations in the early years of computer-assisted design, dmvA seem perfectly amenable to using this name for their egg-shaped building.

In the fullest sense One Main (Cambridge, Massachusetts, USA, 2009, page 158), designed by Mark Goulthorpe (deCOi), is not architecture, but office refurbishment. The 1000-square-meter shell was made of computer-cut wooden elements. As the architect points out, not only the raw materials (spruce) but also the sophisticated manufacturing techniques used are low-energy alternatives. The price of wood may vary but new techniques for designing and cutting architectural elements have made undeniable gains in efficiency that can be measured not only in terms of cost but also of energy usage, for example.

5
A1Architects, Teahouse,
Prague, Czech Republic, 2008

The tiny Teahouse (7 square meters) built by A1Architects in Prague (Czech Republic, 2008, page 56) is an example of the unexpected things that can be done with wood. The architects call it "a minimal place to gather," and it certainly brings to mind the tradition of the Japanese teahouse, a fact confirmed by the interest shown in this little building by the noted Japanese wood architect Terunobu Fujimori. Built on top of stones from a nearby pond, the building is made of oak, charred larch, clay, plaster, and paper. Its dimensions and disposition are in harmony with the tea ceremony, but the structure also has underlying Western modernity that makes this culture-crossing design interesting.

Terunobu Fujimori, a professor at the University of Tokyo's Institute of Industrial Science, conceived a number of such widely published buildings as the Charred Cedar House (Nagano City, Nagano, Japan, 2006–07). He likens the interior of this house to a cave—the place of origin in many senses, the first sheltered "home" of men, as in Lascaux, the specific example cited by Fujimori. Known for his quirky and usually tiny teahouses, Fujimori has come onto the Japanese architectural scene like a breath of fresh air, reinterpreting tradition in essentially modern ways despite the "rustic" appearance of his work as seen from many angles. There is a teahouse perched at one end of Charred Cedar House in a way that might be likened to humor, just as the three hiroki tree trunks that emerge from the ceiling of the residence have a comical side, even as they speak in a figurative sense of the roots of architecture. Fujimori can be considered emblematic of a certain use of wood that harkens back to the origins of architecture even as it speaks very clearly to the most contemporary thoughts. The Prague Teahouse by A1 might seem a bit out of context in the Czech Republic, and yet it is also a statement that prolongs and redirects the essentially Japanese influence of Fujimori.

SPIRIT OF NATURE

A number of official organizations, convinced of the virtues of wood construction, have endeavored to publicize such buildings through financial or technical assistance. This was the case of the small (147 square meters) Piano Pavilion built in Lahti (Finland, 2007–08, page 406) by the firm Wingårdhs for the Wood in Culture Association. The Wood in Culture Association, founded in 1998 to promote culture and forestry companies, is behind the Spirit of Nature Wood Architecture Award given in the early part of this decade to the likes of Peter Zumthor (2006) and Kengo Kuma (2002). Finnforest provided construction materials while the UPM Lahti Mill offered the special plywood used for interior cladding, as well as the ProFi wood plastic composite employed for the terrace. Aspen staves were used in the façade and ash furniture in the café. Sitting on the water on a steel platform, the Piano Pavilion is intended as an homage to the work of Renzo Piano, who won the 2000 Spirit of Nature Wood Architecture Award, and, indeed, its boldly racked roof does bring to mind certain gestures of the Italian master.

As Terunobu Fujimori and other leading Asian architects have demonstrated, the use of wood in contemporary architecture is very much a living practice. Nor is this use confined to small private houses. Three recent golf club projects in Korea demonstrate the affinity of Japanese and Korean architects for wood, but also the possibilities of this material when used for relatively large-scale projects. Shigeru Ban may be best known for his use of a wood product—in the form of structural paper tubes—but in the case of the Haesley Nine Bridges Golf

6
*Shigeru Ban with Kyeong Sik Yoon,
Haesley Nine Bridges Golf Clubhouse,
Yeoju, South Korea, 2008–10*

6

Clubhouse (Yeoju, South Korea, 2009, page 88; in collaboration with Kyeong Sik Yoon, KACI International Inc.) it is the treelike timber columns that attract the most attention, in a building that measures 36 meters in width and 72 meters in length. Rising up three stories, these columns give a forest like feeling to the structure. Here, as in some other cases, the architects were obliged to use a stone podium for the building because Korean regulations do not allow purely timber buildings to exceed 6000 square meters in area.

The Seoul-based architects SKM have recently completed two other golf facilities where wood is a significant element in the design and construction. Surprisingly enough, the Kumgang Ananti Golf & Spa Resort (Gangwon-do, North Korea, 2008, page 314) is set just to the north of the border separating the two Koreas. The 13 210-square-meter structure is located near Kumgang Mountain and the master plan for the facility privileged the preservation of the natural environment. A wooden post-and-beam system and glulam arches for the exterior canopy and interior lobby are visible elements in the overall design and, indeed, give the tone to the architecture. Also by SKM, the Lake Hills Sun-cheon Country Club (Suncheon, JeollaNam-do, South Korea, 2008, page 320) uses a buried concrete base and a glulam post-and-beam system that is meant as an echo of traditional Korean architecture. This is by no means a pastiche of old forms however, as the ample use of skylights and full glazing and metal cladding make clear. The reference to Korean architecture may be most evident in the sweeping curves of the roofs of this 16 311-square-meter complex.

24 HOURS

Larger buildings that are used for purposes ranging from visitor centers to hotels or restaurants have also called more and more frequently on wood. One of the more striking recent buildings in wood, the Wisa Wooden Design Hotel (Helsinki, Finland, 2009, page 82), is not actually a hotel in the traditional sense. It is an 80-square-meter structure that was the result of a 2009 competition. Pieta-Linda Auttila was chosen to design "a bold and iconic work from Finnish pine and spruce." Participants in the competition organized by UPM, an energy, pulp, paper, and engineered materials company, were given just 24 hours to complete their designs. The designer sought to "blow the wooden block" to pieces, combining open and closed spaces or geometric and organic forms. Given the nature of this design, it may not be completely indicative of trends in wood architecture, and yet it does show how unexpected wooden forms can be combined in a thoroughly contemporary way.

More "solid" and less experimental, the Grand Teton Discovery and Visitor Center (Moose Junction, Grand Teton National Park, Wyoming, USA, 2007, page 114) by the architects Bohlin Cywinski Jackson was built with log timber frames and laminated wood beams. Where wood could not be used because of climatic conditions, the designers employed board-formed concrete that preserves the grain of wood. Broad, high glazing allows the building to communicate fully with its spectacular natural setting, where forests and mountains are the rule. The architects are familiar with building and design in the wooded west of the United States and this is tangible in the Visitor Center, a building that combines a distinctly modern feeling with a respect for its function and environment.

7
Pieta-Linda Auttila,
Wisa Wooden Design Hotel,
Helsinki, Finland, 2009

The architect José Cruz Ovalle had the unusual experience of designing a hotel on Easter Island (Rapa Nui Explora Hotel, Miro O'one Sector, Chile, 2005–07, page 154). Conceived like an archipelago of islands and inland seas, the structure is tied together by wooden decks. This is an interesting concept in this location since it is speculated that one reason for the demise of the civilization that erected the famous sculptures of Easter Island was the over-harvesting of the trees that existed there. The Explora Hotel is carefully integrated into the landscape and takes full advantage of views of the horizon through generous glazing. Aside from the rough stone base of the structures, wood is present throughout the facility. The earlier Perez Cruz Winery (Paine, Chile, 2001–02, page 146) also by Cruz Ovalle makes spectacular use of wood in a large (5433-square-meter) building. It is interesting to note that wood was selected in that instance to provide proper temperature conditions inside the building for the wine.

AN UMBRELLA AND A TREE TRUNK

The French architect Edouard François is well known for his ecologically minded designs. His latest project the Club Med-Aldiana (Nianing, Senegal, 2010–, page 202) is an ambitious, 100 000-square-meter hotel complex that will include 250 rooms and suites, as well as all necessary facilities for restaurants and sports. François makes ample reference to local traditions such as African masks and calls on wood throughout, including the restaurant that is shaped like "reversed umbrellas." Edouard François situates himself somewhat outside the currents in architectural design that might be considered "ordinary" and does not mind shaking up expectations a bit, as he does in this Club Med project. Wood, with its flexibility and multiple uses, fits in well with his green and surprising design.

Tusen Restaurant (Ramundberget, Sweden, 2007–08, page 324) by Murman Arkitekter is a 340-square-meter structure that is intended to be in a permanent state of "harmony with nature." The architects used full birch tree trunks to frame the structure and protect the actual façade, since these are the only trees that grow at the altitude of the restaurant and because they can be easily replaced. "By choosing wooden construction," say the architects, "we achieved low weight. It is a prefabricated building with a small impact on the ground and this was also a way to minimize the building time." Light weight is, indeed, an important factor in the choice of wood in architecture, as it was throughout the centuries in the seismic areas of Japan, for example. The Tusen Restaurant is an environmentally friendly structure that uses heat pumps and its own sewage treatment system. It is true that it might well be assumed today that a new wooden building would be ecologically responsible in other aspects of its design than the simple choice of materials.

GERMAN AND GREEN

Wood is used for almost all building types as a number of examples published here demonstrate. The German architect Jörg Aldinger used wood as a visible part of his Cafeteria and Day Care Center for the Waldorf School (Stuttgart, Germany, 2005–07, page 62), but the basic three-story structure concerned is made of reinforced concrete. Clad in larch, with wood window frames and furniture and a green roof, this design is indicative of another substantive trend in contemporary architecture—the use of wood as a secondary or cladding element.

8

Nothing new, this method has taken on added popularity particularly in exterior use, more often given over to concrete or metals in the recent past. Other German architects, Auer+Weber+Assoziierte, employed a trellis-like larch external façade on their Central Facilities on the Martinsried Campus of the Ludwig-Maximilians University (Munich, Germany, 2004–09, page 78). As with the Waldorf School structure, wood is not the main structural material at Martinsried, but larch is nonetheless a key to the design. The modernist Gut Siggen Seminar Building (Siggen, Germany, 2006–07, page 72) by the same architects makes use of moveable larch shades and wood ceilings or oak floors to emphasize the connection to nature seen in views from the building. Emphasizing what might appear to be a German trend, the architects Kauffmann Theilig & Partner used a good deal of apparent wood in their Boehringer Ingelheim Employee Restaurant (Biberach an der Riss, Germany, 2003–04, page 258). This 3000-square-meter facility built for a pharmaceuticals firm has a "spatial folded-plate structure" that is clad in wood. These plates form the interior ceiling of the restaurant and protrude from the roof like so many shards of wood.

WORKING IN WOOD

Two recent buildings by the Finnish architect Seppo Häkli (born in 1951) demonstrate the utility and appropriateness of wood in the context of work environments. The Seurasaari Building Conservation Center (Helsinki, Finland, 2007–09, page 16) built for the National Board of Antiquities is part of the Seurasaari Open-Air Museum. The timber-columned structure contains a woodworking shop. Laminated timber beams or black-tarred pine board cladding are used according to the principles of local wood construction in a project that remains modern and above all efficient. The Metla Office and Laboratory Building (Haapastensyrjä, Finland, 2007–08, page 216) by the same architect is a 550-square-meter building that is inspired by the form of Finnish farmhouses. It contains laboratories and technical spaces walled in spruce, and offices clad in alder wood, with a total of 12 different woods used in a structure that is, again, intended to display Finnish know-how in this area. Another building for Metla, the Finnish Forest Research Institute (Joensuu, Finland, 2004, page 368), was designed by SARC Architects. At 7400 square meters in area, this structure is much larger than those previously cited. It is intended for research on materials in wood that can be used for construction and other purposes. Wood is visible throughout the building, from the post-and-beam structural system to the outside cladding, while living pines mark the courtyard. It may be that Finland is the country that most emphasizes its tradition and innovation in wood architecture, a fact that surely privileges a certain number of its architects in a time when this material has gained popularity around the world.

Switzerland also has a long tradition of building in wood, particularly in mountainous areas. Although fires in time carried away a number of old towns built entirely in wood, numerous traces of this tradition remain in areas such as the Engadine valley near Saint Moritz and elsewhere in the Graubunden region. One architect who has taken up this tradition, while considerably modernizing it, is Valerio Olgiati, born in Chur in 1958. His family house, however, is located in the town of Flims, where Olgiati has his offices. In 2007 he undertook the construction of a new office building here on the site of a former barn (page 336). Located in the Dado section of Flims, the office, itself made of dark wood, is set up on concrete pillars and maintains the basic outline of local barns. In this and other projects, Olgiati has made use of the form

9
Enrique Browne,
Pedestrian Bridge, Zapallar,
Chile, 2008

of older buildings, while changing their function. Given that the original function is no longer required, this permits the villages where Olgiati has worked to maintain their basic outlines while entering contemporary life. Elsewhere, Valerio Olgiati has shown a decidedly contemporary, if rather unexpected style, although wood is only occasionally his main material.

FROM A BAR TO A PARASOL

In a completely different context, Niall McLaughlin designed a Café-Bar on Deal Pier (Deal, Kent, UK, 2008, page 298). Built in the late 1950s in concrete, the pier is somewhat weathered, and the architect sought a material that would "weather and improve with age." Laminated iroko wood was used with large windows offering a sea view to patrons. Though wooden piers were long ago the rule, it is interesting to note that in this instance, wood was chosen precisely because of its ability to age with some grace in the face of the elements. It might well be assumed that concrete weathers better than wood, and yet here it is the age of the concrete that inspired the choice of the architect.

Though materials such as steel have long been favored for the construction of bridges, the architect Enrique Browne chose laminated wood as the material for his small, elegant Pedestrian Bridge (Zapallar, Chile, 2008, page 126). Though metal netting and LED lights are also part of the scheme, the image of a boat was in the mind of Enrique Browne when he designed it. Wood clearly can be fashioned using less elaborate means than equivalent quantities of steel or other modern materials. Although examples published in this volume occasionally reach substantial size, it is clear that wood may be best adapted to relatively small projects where cost is an important factor.

So as to prove that the contrary is also entirely possible, another project published here, though not quite finished, will literally cover an area of 12 670 square meters at a cost of €51 million. The work of the German architect Jürgen Mayer H., the Metropol Parasol (Seville, Spain, 2005–11, page 18) is part of a redevelopment of the Plaza de la Encarnacion in Seville. Called a "new icon" for the city, the structure is meant to cover and shade bars, restaurants, and other public spaces. These large parasols are simply made of timber with a polyurethane coating—proof, if need be, that very contemporary forms can be made essentially out of wood, and at that, in this instance, on a large scale.

WOOD IN A SHINY NEW DRESS

A selection of about 60 recent structures designed partially or completely in wood may not be sufficient to give a real overview of what is happening across the world, but it is clear that wood is a very contemporary material, being used in innovative ways that include the very latest technology. Though making use of rare woods has long been considered a taboo, systems to certify wood from renewable forest sources are spreading rapidly, making it clear that wood is already one of the foremost "green" building materials when correctly employed. Though some go to the extent of protecting a wood skeleton in Cor-ten steel or shiny aluminum, wood can resist most environments as long as more "modern" materials, taking on a patina with age that is surely more attractive than an eroded concrete wall. Then too, with a polyurethane skin as in the Seville project by Jürgen Mayer H., wood can step out on the current architecture scene in a shiny new dress that suits it

10

well. Some projects published here make use of wood that has been reclaimed from other uses—a situation that certainly augments the ecological sustainability of a structure, if not necessarily its lifespan. In any case, the demolition of a wood structure would most probably entail fewer environmental consequences than the average asbestos insulated steel building, to be slightly facetious about it. More seriously, as this book should make clear, wood is very much a product for an economically uncertain future, but one in which the protection of the environment has become an important factor, to be taken into consideration by all. Wood is figuratively as "green" as building materials come to the extent that it is cut and fashioned in a responsible way. It ages when not protected, but that is the case of other materials as well. It can be thoroughly modern in the hands of an architect who wants it that way. In short, wood is for now.

Philip Jodidio, Grimentz, Switzerland, May 15, 2010

EINLEITUNG

HOLZ IST FÜR DAS HIER UND JETZT

„In diesen Pflanzungen Gottes herrscht Würde und Heiligkeit, eine immerwährende Festlichkeit wird bereitet, und kein Gast vermag zu erkennen, wie er in tausend Jahren ihrer überdrüssig werden sollte. In den Wäldern kehren wir zur Vernunft und zum Glauben zurück. Dort fühle ich, dass mich im Leben nichts treffen kann – keine Schande, kein Unheil (solange mir die Augen erhalten bleiben), was nicht die Natur heilen kann. Wenn ich auf dem kahlen Erdboden stehe – meinen Kopf in die heitere Luft getaucht und in den unendlichen Raum erhoben –, schwindet alle eitle Selbstgefälligkeit dahin. Ich werde zu einem durchsichtigen Augapfel; ich bin nichts; ich sehe alles; die Ströme des universellen Wesens durchwogen mich; ich bin ein Teil oder Splitter Gottes.“

Ralph Waldo Emerson, *Natur* (1836, deutsche Ausgabe: Zürich 1982)

Bei Holz denken wir in erster Linie an den Wald, an die „Pflanzungen Gottes". In den vom Mond beschienenen Wäldern lässt Shakespeare in seinem Stück *Ein Sommernachtstraum* die Gestalten ihre Verwandlungskomödie spielen, und aus dem Wald bezieht auch die Architektur eine Vielzahl von Inspirationen in übertragener Form: vom einfachen Pfeiler über den Tempel bis zur Kathedrale. Holz in Form eines Daches aus Zweigen und übereinandergestapelter Baumstämme zum Schutz vor Stürmen bildete das entscheidende Element der frühesten gebauten Unterkünfte, die nach einer gewissen Zeit meist wieder zu Erde wurden. Architektur aus Holz wird häufig als ephemer bezeichnet. Die Lebensdauer von Holzkonstruktionen hängt in der Tat von Faktoren ab wie Klima und Wartung. Und dennoch, um nur ein Beispiel zu nennen, ist die fünfstöckige, im Jahre 951 errichtete Pagode des Daigoji-Tempels das älteste Gebäude in Kyoto. So kann Holz, wenn man es richtig behandelt, tausend Jahre Bestand haben, auch wenn die Erde bebt und Generationen vergehen. Bäume leben, ihrer jeweiligen Art entsprechend, länger als alle anderen Organismen auf der Erde, bis sie gefällt und verarbeitet werden. Das Alter einer Great Basin Bristlecone Kiefer mit dem bezeichnenden Namen Methusalem (White Mountains, California) wird auf über 4800 Jahre geschätzt. Klonale Bäume wie der sogenannte Pando, eine in Utah heimische Zitterpappel, treibt Zweige aus einem einzigen, massiven Wurzelsystem, das in diesem Fall auf 80 000 Jahre geschätzt wird. Ein Baum, der viel älter ist als die menschliche Kultur! Bäume also, im übertragenen wie im buchstäblichen Sinn als Ursprung der gebauten Form, als Schutz und Inspiration: der Stoff, der aus der Erde kam.

Berichte über den Raubbau der Wälder in Indonesien und anderswo häufen sich, und kaum jemand würde derartige Praktiken in irgendeiner Weise mit ökologischem Bauen verbinden. Und dennoch erlebt Holz, das sachgemäß gewonnen und verarbeitet wird, am Anfang des 21. Jahrhunderts eine neue Blüte als bevorzugtes Material in der Architektur. Weil ein bewirtschafteter Forst sich erneuert, ist Holz, wenn es nicht über allzu große Entfernungen transportiert werden muss, mit Sicherheit eines der umweltfreundlichsten aller verfügbaren Baumaterialien. Organisationen wie der United States Green Building Council (USGBC) haben Standards (LEED = Leadership in Energy and Environmental Design) festgelegt, die zur Zertifizierung von Holz für umweltfreundliches, nachhaltiges Bauen dienen können. In diesem Bereich arbeitet der USGBC mit dem Forest Stewardship Council (FSC) zusammen. Der FSC „ist eine gemeinnützige und unabhängige Non-Profit-Organisation, die zur Förderung verantwortungsvoller Waldwirtschaft gegründet wurde. Er gilt weltweit als eine der wichtigsten Initiativen des vergangenen Jahrzehnts."[1] Im Dezember 2008 wurden 107 Millionen Hektar Wald in 78 Ländern nach den „Prinzipien und Kriterien" des FSC zertifiziert.

Weil die Verwendung von Holz im Verlauf der Zeit – und nicht nur für besondere Architekturaufgaben – so stark zugenommen hat, ist es auch im Ansehen gestiegen. Warum aber sollte man ein Holzhaus bauen, wenn Beton und Aluminium so viel moderner und solider erscheinen? *Wood Architecture Now!* behandelt eine völlig neue Generation von Bauten, die zweifellos zum Teil von der Tradition, aber auch von der „grünen" Welle im Bauen beeinflusst wurden. Da die strenge Moderne und vor allem der puristische Minimalismus aus der Mode gekommen sind, bevorzugen viele Architekten und Bauherren die vom Holz ausgehende Wärme und natürliche Wirkung. Obgleich es sich um ein „altes" Baumaterial handelt, lässt sich Holz mit neuster CNC (Computer Numerical Control)-Technik verarbeiten, wodurch komplexe und einmalige Formen und Teile wirtschaftlich hergestellt werden können. Außerdem nutzen auch viele der in diesem Buch vorgestellten Architekten diesen Baustoff für spezielle Zwecke und Bereiche ihrer Bauten. Ein Gebäude kann aus Beton oder Stahl errichtet, aber mit Holz verkleidet werden. Ziel dieses Buches, wie auch der gesamten Reihe *Architecture Now!*, ist es, einen möglichst umfangreichen – aber in keiner Weise erschöpfenden – Überblick darüber zu geben, was in unterschiedlichen Stilen und Techniken an verschiedenen Standorten entstanden ist. *Wood Architecture Now!* konzentriert sich auf Bauten des 21. Jahrhunderts, vorzugsweise aus den letzten zwei oder drei Jahren, um zu beweisen, dass Holz wieder zu einem zeitgemäßen Baumaterial geworden ist.

DER RUF DER NATUR

Beispiele für hölzerne Kirchen, Kapellen oder schlichte Meditationsräume gibt es reichlich aus fast allen Perioden der Architekturgeschichte. Daher ist es nur natürlich, dass einige Architekten sich auch heute weiterhin in diese Richtung orientieren. Obgleich Marta Rowińska und Lech Rowiński (beide 1976 geboren) ihr Büro BETON nennen, haben sie, offenbar mit großem Vergnügen, eine kleine (60 m² große) Holzkirche in Tarnów am Fluss Vistula (Polen, 2007–10, Seite 108) errichtet. Das auf einer Betonplatte gegründete Gebäude wurde überwiegend von Hilfsarbeitern erbaut – was bei der Verwendung von Holz gewiss einfacher ist als bei komplizierteren Baumaterialien. Die Architekten bemühten sich um „eine gewisse Raumqualität bei Anwendung rudimentärer, einfacher Technik". Bei Baukosten von nur 20 000 Euro zeichnet sich die Kirche in Tarnów in der Tat durch hohe Qualität vor allem im Innenbereich aus – als eine angemessene Metapher für Spiritualität.

Auf der anderen Seite des Erdballs, in Chile, haben die (alle 1977 in Santiago geborenen) jungen Architekten Alejandro Dumay Claro, Nicolás Fones und Francisco Vergara Arthur eine noch kleinere (21 m² große) Holzkapelle in ähnlich spitzer Form errichtet. Ihre Kapelle Fuente Nueva (2006, Seite 184) ist direkt zum Rupanco-See im Süden Chiles orientiert. Die Öffnung hinter dem Altar in voller Höhe deutet in der Tat darauf hin, dass hier die Botschaft Natur lautet. Die Architektur ist auf das strikte Minimum reduziert, und dennoch wahrt das Gebäude eine nüchterne Modernität, die die Wirkung der natürlichen Umgebung auf die zwölf Personen, welche dieser Raum fasst, noch verstärkt. Obgleich sakrale Architektur häufig das Schwergewicht auf Dekorationen oder die Bildung komplexer räumlicher Effekte legt, sind solche

11
Beatriz Meyer, Chapel,
Tatuí, São Paulo, Brazil, 2006

11

kleinen Bauwerke ohne jedes überflüssige Detail Zeugen einer gewissen Rückkehr zu grundlegenden Werten – sowohl in der Form als auch in der Funktion.

Die 1977 in Sao Paulo geborene Beatriz Meyer arbeitet mit dem Architekten Marcio Kogan zusammen, hat aber auch einige eigene Bauten geplant, zum Beispiel die hölzerne Kapelle in Tatuí (Sao Paulo, Brasilien, 2006, Seite 310). Das aus wenig mehr als einem geneigten Dach mit dreiseitig voll verglasten Wänden bestehende Gebäude hat eine Natursteinwand hinter dem Altar und verwendet anspruchsvollere Materialien, zum Beispiel eine Alwitra-Membrane für das Dach. Die Gesamtwirkung ist trotzdem von großer Schlichtheit und Eleganz. Die umgebenden Bäume betonen den Eindruck einer Waldkapelle und in gewissem Sinne eine Rückkehr zu den Ursprüngen der Andacht.

Rodrigo Shewards Aussichtsterrasse in Pinohuacho (Villarrica, Chile, 2006, Seite 374) regt, obgleich es sich um kein religiöses Bauwerk handelt, zweifellos zur Meditation an. Sie liegt mitten in einem früheren Holzeinschlag und soll zum Nachdenken über den Schaden anregen, den der verantwortungslose Raubbau der Wälder angerichtet hat. Die Aussichtsterrasse wurde aus Restbeständen des Holzeinschlags überwiegend von einem Arbeiter errichtet, der zum Team der Holzfäller gehörte. Die 78 m² große Terrasse für nur 3000 US Dollar Baukosten gewährt Ausblick auf den Vulkan Villarrica. Der 1979 geborene und, wie alle hier genannten Architekten, unter 40 Jahre alte Sheward scheint den früheren oder jetzigen Ruf des Waldes vernommen und in Holz verkörpert zu haben – als angemessenes Thema zum Nachdenken über die Notwendigkeit zum Umdenken im Bauen.

AUF REGEN FOLGT SONNE

Wohnhäuser sind eindeutig die ertragreichsten Versuchsobjekte für Architekten, die heute mit Holz bauen. Obgleich natürlich auch Großbauten aus Holz errichtet werden können, macht der im Allgemeinen kleine Maßstab von Wohnhäusern das Material in vieler Hinsicht attraktiv. Dazu zählen die offenkundigen ökologischen Vorzüge von richtig geschlagenem und transportiertem Holz, die relativ einfache Bearbeitung im Gegensatz zu den für Metallbau oder andere Bauweisen erforderlichen technischen Verfahren und einfach die Wärme, die Holz auf natürliche Weise bei der Anwendung im Innen- wie im Außenbereich ausstrahlt.

Die in Azambuja bei Lissabon in Portugal ansässige Firma Jular ist auf die Produktion nachhaltiger, modularer Wohnhäuser aus Holz spezialisiert. Obgleich Fertighäuser oft nicht den Ansprüchen an qualitative Gestaltung entsprechen, ist dieses von den Architekten João Appleton und Isabel Domingos entwickelte System Treehouse (Azambuja, Portugal, 2008–09, Seite 35) sowohl attraktiv als auch praktisch. Die 3,3 x 6,6 m großen Module des Systems Treehouse können in sehr unterschiedlicher Weise zu bescheidenen ebenso wie zu großzügigeren Wohnhäusern zusammengestellt werden. Bei Kosten von 900 Euro pro Quadratmeter ist das System auch verhältnismäßig preiswert. Mit relativ kleinen Fensterflächen, um die Bauten dem mediterranen Klima anzupassen, nutzt das System Treehouse Holz in überzeugender Weise für den Bereich des modularen und transportablen Bauens. Jular weist entsprechend darauf hin, dass dieser Bautyp zwar schon in der Vergan-

12

12
dRN Architects. La Baronia House,
Quintero, Valparaíso, Chile, 2009

genheit existiert hat, aber nicht für das vom Atlantik und dem Golfstrom bestimmte Klima Portugals oder der mediterranen Länder von Spanien bis Griechenland vorgesehen war.

Das weder transportable noch bescheidene Haus RW (Búzios, Rio de Janeiro, Brasilien, 2006–09, Seite 100) hat eine Nutzfläche von nicht weniger als 4900 m². Als H-förmiger Flachbau geplant, wurde das Haus 50 cm vom Strandboden angehoben. Obgleich es sich um ein eindeutig luxuriöses Wohnhaus handelt, verwendeten die Architekten Bernardes + Jacobsen für die Konstruktion laminiertes, unbehandeltes Eukalyptusholz aus aufgeforsteten Gebieten. Natürliche Belüftung betont die Nähe des Hauses zu seiner Umgebung und reduziert den Energieverbrauch. Für Bauten wie eine 21 m² große Kapelle bis zu einem 4900-m²-Haus hat man Holz als geeignetes Material gewählt – und moderne Architektur mit der warmen Wirkung des Holzes verbunden, selbst wenn es in geometrischen Formen gestaltet wird. Von diesem Beispiel kann man sagen, dass die durch verschiedene andere Bautypen und auch große, luxuriöse Wohnhäuser bekannt gewordenen Architekten sich um eine – wenn auch nicht durchweg – „grüne" Ausführung bemüht haben. Auch ohne Vorurteile gegenüber den potenten Bauherren zu hegen, ist es jedoch nur schwer vorstellbar, dass ein 4900-m²-Haus, ob aus Holz oder nicht, durchweg umweltfreundlich geplant werden kann.

DOCH WAS DA AUS HOLZ WAR BOG SICH UND BLIEB

Der 1971 in Turku, Finnland, geborene Marco Casagrande sagt, dass eine Ruine entstehe, wenn etwas „von Menschen Gemachtes Teil der Natur wird. Ich freue mich darauf, Ruinen zu entwerfen." Sein kleines (nur 62 m² großes) Haus Chen (Sanjhih, Taipeh, Taiwan, 2007–08, Seite 138) wurde aus Mahagoni und Beton errichtet. Dieser eher einer Ruine ähnelnde Bau wirkt wie ein Ort, der allen Elementen trotzen kann. Tatsächlich ist das Grundstück in den Datun-Bergen von Überschwemmungen, Taifunen und Erdbeben bedroht. Hölzerne Lamellen lassen kühle Luft ins Innere ein, im Winter dient ein Kamin zur Heizung. Dies ist natürlich kein anspruchsvolles Design im üblichen Sinne, doch die Gestaltung von Marco Casagrande zeichnet sich durch eine raue Sorgfalt aus, die sie fast zu einem Symbol für schwierige Zeiten macht – mit Holz als tragendes Element zum Überleben. Er zitiert ein kurzes Gedicht von Bertolt Brecht (1898–1956) mit dem Titel „Eisen", das auf diesen Entwurf zutreffen könnte: „Im Traum heute Nacht/ Sah ich einen großen Sturm./ Ins Baugerüst griff er/ Den Bauschragen riss er/ Den eisernen, abwärts./ Doch was da aus Holz war/ Bog sich und blieb."

Nicolás del Río (geboren 1975) und Max Núñez (geboren 1976) in Santiago (dRN Architects) sind bei ihren Projekten an schwierige Bedingungen gewohnt – mehrere ihrer Bauten (Skibox, 2006; Mountain Refuge Chalet C6, 2006, und Mountain Refuge Chalet C7, 2008, alle in Portillo, Chile) wurden etwa 2800 m über Meereshöhe errichtet. Das Haus La Baronia (Quintero, Valparaíso, Chile, 2009, Seite 172) liegt nicht so hoch, aber auf einem Hügel mit Blick auf den Ozean. Wegen der Korrosionsgefahr durch den hohen Salzgehalt des Meerwassers entschieden sich die Architekten für widerstandsfähigen, vorab bewitterten Corten-Stahl und Glas. Und dennoch ist das Tragwerk des Hauses im Innern eine verschraubte Holzkonstruktion. Mit einem hölzernen Skelett und einer Stahlhaut zeigt das Haus La Baronia die ansprechende Wirkung von Holz als tragendes Material sogar unter extremen klimatischen Bedingungen. dRN ist eins der kreativen, jungen Büros in Chile und dieses Haus ein Beweis für sein Renommee. Die Tatsache, dass Corten-Stahl häufig für rein bildhauerische Werke verwendet wird, zum Beispiel von Richard Serra, erhöht die Wirkung des Hauses La Baronia und macht es zu einer Art skulpturalem Schutzbau vor den Elementen.

FRÖHLICHE CAMPER

Holz strahlt etwas Praktisches oder sogar Sparsames aus, das viele Bauherren und auch zahlreiche Architekten anspricht. Shin Ohori vom Büro General Design in Tokyo wurde von einem Klienten beauftragt, der eigentlich nichts anderes als einen guten Platz suchte, um ein Zelt aufzustellen. Das Ergebnis dieser ungewöhnlichen Zusammenarbeit war ein „Wohnort" mit Namen Mountain Research (Minamisaku, Nagano, Japan, 2007–08, Seite 208). Eine Plattform aus Lärchenholz sowie Einrichtungen zum Kochen, Abstellen und Baden schützen einen Bereich für ein Zwei-Meter-Kuppelzelt. Shin Ohori sagt: „Ich hoffe, dass die Architektur einen Ort erzeugt, wo Menschen etwas Neues entdecken und ihre Lebensweise erneuern können." In diesem Fall, bei einem Standort in den Bergen und der extremen Bescheidenheit der Pläne des Bauherrn, war Holz eine naheliegende Entscheidung. Natürlich hätten für dieses 97 m² große Bauwerk auch andere Materialien verwendet werden können, aber Holz erscheint durchaus geeignet für diesen Ort und dieses Programm. Doch besteht, davon abgesehen, nicht trotzdem ein grundlegender Widerspruch zwischen der völlig mobilen Lebensweise, die ein Zelt nahelegt, und der statischen Form des Mountain Research? Man könnte es als Zwischenprodukt Schöpfung betrachten, weder als eigentliches Wohnhaus noch als eigentlichen Ort zum Zelten. Zweifellos ist das Gebäude durch die Verwendung von Holz besser in die Berglandschaft integriert als es mit anderen Materialien wäre.

Holz spielt eine wichtige Rolle bei zahlreichen weitergehenden Versuchen, Architektur umweltfreundlich zu gestalten. Das Haus Smart Air (2010, Seite 11) der deutschen Architekten Graft ist ein Prototyp für ein zweigeschossiges Zweifamilienhaus, bei dem das Tragwerk und die Böden innen aus Kreuzlagenholz (cross-laminated timber, CLT) bestehen. Natürlich wurden auch andere Materialien verwendet, aber dem Prinzip dieses Hauses liegen neueste Erkenntnisse darüber zugrunde, wie „intelligente und effiziente Bautechnologie symbiotisch mit umweltfreundlichem Material interagieren kann, ohne das Verhalten der Nutzer technisch zu dominieren". In gewisser Weise befindet sich umweltfreundliche Architektur nach wie vor in ihrer Entwicklungsphase, da es noch keine klaren Vorschriften dafür gibt. Tatsächlich erweisen sich viele scheinbar „umweltfreundliche" Materialien als etwas weniger freundlich, wenn man ihre gesamte Produktionskette im Detail überprüft. Eine Ausnahme bildet natürlich das Holz, sofern es verantwortlich gewonnen wird.

Das von Jackson Clements Burrows geplante Trojan House (Melbourne, Victoria, Australien, 2005, Seite 240) macht Schluss mit der Vorstellung, dass sich mit Holz kein wirklich modernes Erscheinungsbild bilden ließe. Mit einer „ Holzhaut, die Dach, Fenster und Wände nahtlos überzieht", und verstellbaren Holzläden ist das Trojan House tatsächlich die Erweiterung eines bestehenden Wohnhauses, dessen klare Formen bei geschlossenen Läden ablesbar sind. Auch hier ermöglicht das Holz einen konfliktfreien Übergang von einem Altbau zu einem zeitgenössischen Neubau und erweist sich als anpassbar und praktikabel. Jackson Clements Burrows sind sicher nicht die einzigen Architekten,

13
ETH-Studio Monte Rosa / Bearth &
Deplazes, New Monte Rosa Hut SAC,
Zermatt, Switzerland, 2008–09

13

die ganz moderne Holzbauten planen; das Trojan House beweist jedoch die Eignung dieses Materials für den Kontext einer bewusst angestrebten Modernität.

Eins der in diesem Band veröffentlichten Gebäude, das Haus Lilypad (Point Roberts, Washington, USA, 2008–09, Seite 286), ist insofern ungewöhnlich, als es nicht von einem Architekten, sondern von einem Fotografen namens Nic Lehoux in Zusammenarbeit mit Jacqueline Darjes geplant wurde. Mit nur 24 m² Wohnfläche und Baukosten von 4500 US Dollar ist es auch kein ambitioniertes Projekt in Bezug auf Größe oder Preis. Plattformen aus Zedernholz, Fensterrahmen aus wiederverwendeter Douglastanne und Schichtholzbalken bilden die wesentlichen Elemente des Hauses, das auf Sonotubes (einem Produkt, das für Betonschalungen verwendet wird) vom Boden abgehoben ist. Anspruchsvollere Materialien wären für dieses Projekt, zumindest was die Baukosten betrifft, eindeutig weniger geeignet gewesen. Holz ist ein erneuerbarer Baustoff, der von Personen verarbeitet werden kann, die über keine speziellen Vorrichtungen oder eine entsprechende Ausbildung verfügen. Stahl und sogar Beton erfordern ausgereiftere Methoden und Erfahrungen, um ein stabiles Bauwerk zu erstellen.

WOHNUNGSBAU UND BERGHÜTTEN AUS SPERRHOLZ

Während Holz durchaus für Einfamilienhäuser geeignet ist, wird es häufig auch für größere – unter anderem auch einige ganz ungewöhnliche – Wohnanlagen verwendet. Das erste hier veröffentlichte Beispiel dieser Art ist das Hameau de Plantoun (Bayonne, Frankreich, 2008–09, Seite 132) vom Architekten Bernard Bühler aus Bordeaux. In Zusammenarbeit mit dem Amt für öffentlich geförderten Wohnungsbau von Bayonne (OPHLM) entstand diese durch ihre Verkleidung aus Sperrholz hervorstechende Gruppe von 39 Wohneinheiten; die Häuser sind vom Boden abgehoben und stehen auf Holzpilotis und dünnen Metallstützen. Sperrholz wird üblicherweise als temporäres Material betrachtet, zum Beispiel zur Abschottung von Baustellen, und sein sichtbarer Alterungsprozess lässt es im Allgemeinen wenig attraktiv erscheinen. Das Hameau de Plantoun ist ungewöhnlich im Erscheinungsbild wie auch in der Anwendung der Materialien, obgleich sein ökologischer „Fußabdruck" sicher kleiner ist als der anderer, konventionell geplanter Gebäude.

Während Holz das überwiegende Baumaterial beim Hameau de Plantoun darstellt, scheint es bei der ganz mit Aluminium verkleideten Neuen Monte-Rosa-Hütte des Schweizer Alpen-Club SAC (Zermatt, Schweiz, 2008–09, Seite 196) auf den ersten Blick überhaupt nicht vorhanden zu sein. Und doch wurde dieses zum 150-jährigen Bestehen der Eidgenössischen Technischen Hochschule Zürich ausgeführte Projekt (ETH-Studio Monte Rosa / Bearth & Deplazes) sorgfältig geplant, um geringstmöglichen Energieverbrauch und in Bezug auf die Materialwahl ein Minimum an Auswirkungen auf die Umwelt zu erreichen. Der Bau in einer Höhe von 2883 m erfolgte mithilfe von Hubschraubern, was kaum umweltfreundlich erscheint, aber durch die Höhe des Geländes bedingt war. Das Innere dieses sehr modernen Gebäudes besteht überwiegend aus Holz. Das gesamte Baumaterial ist vor Ort recyclebar, wenn das Gebäude später einmal abgerissen wird, und die neue Berghütte verbraucht insgesamt viel weniger Energie als ihr Vorgänger. Wie gelegentliche Besucher von Schweizer Berghütten wissen, ist Holz hier das Standardmaterial für den Innenausbau, sicher weil es früher einfacher zu transportieren war als zum Beispiel behauene Steine. Die

14
Piet Hein Eek, Tree Trunk House,
Hilversum, The Netherlands, 2009

Aluminiumhülle der Monte-Rosa-Hütte ist eine technologische Reaktion auf die extremen klimatischen Bedingungen. Die Verwendung von Holz für den Innenausbau ist konstruktiv logisch; sie entspricht aber auch der Tradition dieses Gebäudetyps. Das Endergebnis ist durchweg modern, energieeffizient und praktisch. Kein anderes Material als Holz hätte für den Innenausbau eines solchen Gebäudes geeigneter sein können.

FINNISCHE FEINHEITEN

Wie zu erwarten, stehen die skandinavischen Länder in vorderster Front der zeitgenössischen Holzarchitektur aufgrund ihrer örtlichen Tradition, zu der so bedeutende Vertreter gehören wie Alvar Aalto, der häufig Holz verwendete. Emma Johansson (geboren 1985 in Turku, Finnland) und Timo Leiviskä (geboren 1981 in Oulu, Finnland) erhielten vom Hotel Anttolanhovi in Mikkeli den Auftrag zu zeigen, dass moderne Wohnhäuser aus Holz führend in Architektur, Design und Kunst sein können. Ihre Seevillen Lakeside (Johansson) und Bergvillen Hillside (Leiviskä) (2007–08 resp. 2006–08, Seite 246) sind großzügig ausgestattete Häuser aus Holz, Naturstein und Textilien (im Innenbereich). Beim Betrachten dieser Villen fragt man sich, warum Architekten nicht immer mit Holz planen. Diese jungen Architekten machen den Baustoff Holz durch ihre Betonung von „Kunst und Design" zur Aufwertung des Anttolanhovi-Geländes zu einem der modernsten Materialien für die Freizeit- und Hotelarchitektur.

Zwei ältere finnische Architekten, Kirsi Korhonen (geboren 1958) und Mika Penttinen (geboren 1951) planten die dreigeschossigen Reihenhäuser Huvitus (Helsinki, Finnland, 2007–08, Seite 280). Für diese Bauten auf einem sandigen, mit Kiefern bestandenen Hügel wurden Rippen aus Furnierschichtholz (laminated veneer lumber, LVL) sowie rot und schwarz gestrichene Fassadenverkleidung verwendet. Die Gestaltung dieser Wohnanlage mit sich wiederholender, aber trotzdem individueller Massenverteilung wirkt durchaus modern und dennoch im Einklang mit der örtlichen Bautradition. Die Brandschutzvorschriften forderten die Ausführung des Erdgeschosses in dem 1986 m² großen Komplex aus Beton. Aber wie schon gesagt, hat es sich in vielen Fällen gezeigt, dass Materialien wie zum Beispiel Stahl weniger feuerbeständig sind als richtig behandeltes Holz. Die reichliche Verwendung von fair gewonnenem Holz im Innern, von der Verkleidung bis zum Mobiliar, zeigt jedenfalls Holz als wesentliches Element der Häuser – der Beton tritt weit weniger in Erscheinung.

EIN BLOB UND EIN TEEHAUS

Weil Holz bekanntlich ein formbares Material ist, wird es oft für kleine, ausgefallene Bauwerke verwendet. Verschiedene Beispiele dieser Art werden im vorliegenden Buch gezeigt. Eins der merkwürdigsten ist das vom anerkannten Designer Piet Hein Eek geplante Tree Trunk House (Hilversum, Niederlande, 2009, Seite 190). Eek ist für seine Möbel aus Abfallholz bekannt geworden, die er seit den frühen 1990er-Jahren produziert, aber sein Büro plant auch Architekturprojekte. Auf Bitte des holländischen „Musikkomödianten" Hans Liberg entwarf er ein 9,3 m² großes Bürohaus, das eher einem schlichten Holzstapel ähnelt, vor allem wenn es geschlossen ist. Tatsächlich wurden für die Seiten und die obere Abdeckung dieses mobilen Gebäudes Eichenstämme verwendet, während die restliche Verkleidung aus 5 cm dicken

15

Stammscheiben besteht. Dies ist eine Art Trompe-l'œil-Gestaltung, wie sie gelegentlich für militärische Bauwerke genutzt wurde, doch hier mit einem gewissen Sinn für Humor. Auf jeden Fall lässt sich bei diesem Beispiel die Bedeutung des Themas Holz nicht leugnen.

Die belgischen Architekten dmvA gingen den Holzbau auf andere Weise an bei ihrem Blob VB3 (2008–09, Seite 164), den sie für die Firma XfactorAgencies entwarfen. Er wurde als Erweiterung eines bestehenden Wohnhauses und Büros geplant und sollte die strengen örtlichen Bauvorschriften „umgehen". Der Bau, der auch ein Bad, eine Küche sowie Schlaf- und Abstellräume enthält, ist tatsächlich flexibel und auch für andere Zwecke nutzbar. Er hat ein hölzernes Tragwerk, das mit einer Polyesterhaut verkleidet ist, und sieht in keiner Weise aus wie viele frühere Holzbauten – die Holzkonstruktion ist von außen nicht ablesbar. Obgleich der Begriff „Blob" aus den frühen Jahren des computerunterstützten Entwerfens noch negativ belastet ist, haben dmvA offenbar keine Probleme damit, ihr eiförmiges Gebäude so zu benennen.

Im eigentlichen Sinne ist das von Mark Goulthorpe (deCOi) geplante One Main (Cambridge, Massachusetts, USA, 2009, Seite 158) kein neues Architekturprojekt, sondern die Modernisierung eines Bürogebäudes. Die 1000 m² große Schale besteht aus computergeschnittenen Holzelementen. Der Architekt weist darauf hin, dass nicht nur das raue Material (Fichte), sondern auch die anspruchsvolle Produktionstechnik auf Niedrigenergie beruhten. Der Preis für Holz kann variieren, aber die neuen Techniken zum Entwerfen und Zuschneiden von Architekturelementen sind zweifellos viel effizienter geworden und sollten zum Beispiel nicht nur nach den Kosten, sondern auch nach dem Energieaufwand bewertet werden.

Das kleine (7 m² große) Teehaus von A1Architects in Prag (Tschechische Republik, 2008, Seite 56) ist ein Beispiel für die unerwarteten Dinge, die sich mit Holz machen lassen. Die Architekten nennen es „einen kleinen Ort zum Zusammenkommen", und es erinnert in der Tat an die Tradition des japanischen Teehauses, was das Interesse des bekannten japanischen Holzarchitekten Terunobu Fujimori an diesem kleinen Gebäude bestätigt. Der auf Steinen aus einem nahe gelegenen Teich errichtete Bau besteht aus Eiche, angekohlter Lärche, Lehm, Putz und Papier. Seine Maße und Aufteilung befinden sich im Einklang mit der Teezeremonie, aber das Gebäude zeigt auch eine westliche Modernität, die diesen kulturüberschreitenden Entwurf interessant macht.

Terunobu Fujimori ist Professor am Institute of Industrial Science an der Universität Tokyo und plante eine ganze Reihe weithin publizierter Bauten wie zum Beispiel das Charred Cedar House (Nagano Stadt, Nagano, Japan, 2006–07). Er vergleicht das Innere dieses Hauses mit einer Höhle – in vieler Hinsicht der Ursprungsort der ersten geschützten „Wohnung" der Menschheit, etwa in Lascaux, das Fujimori als spezifisches Beispiel nennt. Er selbst ist durch seine eigenwilligen und meist kleinen Teehäuser bekannt geworden und hat frischen Wind in die japanische Architekturszene gebracht, indem er die Tradition auf überwiegend moderne Weise neu interpretiert, trotz des aus verschiedenen Blickwinkeln „rustikal" wirkenden Erscheinungsbilds seiner Bauten. An einer Seite des Charred Cedar House ist ein Teehaus angefügt, fast wie ein Scherz, ebenso wie die drei aus dem Dach des Hauses ragenden Stämme des Hiroki-Baumes auch eine komische Seite haben, selbst wenn sie im übertragenen Sinne die Wurzeln der Architektur ausdrücken sollen. Fujimori kann als Vertreter einer bestimmten Anwendung von Holz betrachtet werden, die auf die Ursprünge der Architektur zurückgeht, auch wenn sie eindeutig moderner Auffassung entspricht. Das Prager Teehaus von A1 mag im tschechischen Kontext etwas ausgefallen erscheinen, aber es ist auch eine Aussage, die den weit reichenden, großen Einfluss des Japaners Fujimori bestätigt.

DER GEIST DER NATUR

Eine Reihe offizieller Organisationen, die von den Vorzügen des Holzbaus überzeugt sind, haben sich bemüht, solche Bauten mit finanzieller oder technischer Hilfe zu propagieren. Das war beim kleinen (147 m² großen) Piano-Pavillon der Fall, der in Lahti (Finnland, 2007–08, Seite 406) vom schwedischen Architekturbüro Wingårdhs für die Wood in Culture Association errichtet wurde. Dieser 1998 zur Förderung von Kultur- und Forstbetrieben gegründete Verband verleiht den Spirit of Nature Wood Architecture Award, mit dem Anfang dieses Jahrzehnts zum Beispiel Peter Zumthor (2006) und Kengo Kuma (2002) ausgezeichnet wurden. Finnforest lieferte die Baumaterialien und UPM Lahti Mill das spezielle Sperrholz für die Innenverkleidung sowie das ProFi Holz-Kunststoff-Verbundmaterial für die Terrasse. Für die Fassade wurden Espenstäbe verwendet, das Mobiliar des Cafés ist aus Eschenholz. Der Piano-Pavillon steht auf einer Stahlplattform über dem Wasser; er ist eine Hommage an Renzo Piano, der 2000 den Spirit of Nature Wood Architecture Award erhielt, und sein eindrucksvoll ausgebreitetes Dach erinnert in der Tat an gewisse Formelemente des italienischen Meisterarchitekten.

Wie Terunobu Fujimori und andere führende asiatische Architekten bewiesen haben, ist die Verwendung von Holz in der zeitgenössischen Architektur tatsächlich aktuelle Praxis und nicht nur für kleine Privathäuser geeignet. Drei neuere Entwürfe für Golfklubs in Korea zeigen die Vorliebe japanischer oder koreanischer Architekten für Holz, aber auch das Potenzial dieses Materials für relativ großmaßstäbliche Projekte. Shigeru Ban ist wohl am bekanntesten für seine Verwendung eines Holzprodukts – in Form von tragenden Papprohren –, aber beim Vereinshaus des Golfklubs Haesley Nine Bridges in Yeoju (Yeoju, Südkorea, 2008, Seite 88; in Zusammenarbeit mit Kyeong Sik Yoon, KACI International Inc.) sind es die baumähnlichen Holzstützen, die bei einem 36 m breiten und 72 m langen Bau das größte Aufsehen erregen. Diese drei Geschosse hohen Stützen verleihen dem Gebäude die Wirkung eines Waldes. Hier, wie auch in anderen Fällen, mussten sich die Architekten für einen Unterbau aus Stein entscheiden, weil die koreanischen Bauvorschriften keine reinen Holzbauten von über 6000 m² Flächeninhalt zulassen.

Die in Seoul ansässigen Architekten SKM haben kürzlich zwei weitere Golfbauten fertiggestellt, bei denen Holz ein wichtiges Entwurfs- und Ausführungselement bildet. Erstaunlicherweise liegt der Kumgang Ananti Golf & Spa Resort (Gangwon-do, Nordkorea, 2008, Seite 314) unmittelbar nördlich der Grenze, die beide koreanischen Staaten trennt. Das 13 210 m² große Gebäude steht am Berg Kumgang, und der Masterplan für diese Anlage legte besonderen Wert auf den Schutz der natürlichen Umwelt. Ein hölzerne Ständerkonstruktion sowie Schichtholzbogen für das äußere Vordach und die innere Lobby sind sichtbare Elemente der Gesamtplanung und bestimmten tatsächlich das

Erscheinungsbild. Der Country Club Lake Hills in Suncheon (Suncheon, JeollaNam-do, Südkorea, 2008, Seite 320), ebenfalls von SKM, hat ein versenktes Betonfundament und eine Ständerkonstruktion aus Schichtholz, die an die traditionelle koreanische Architektur erinnern soll. Es handelt sich jedoch keineswegs um eine Nachbildung alter Formen, wie der großzügige Einsatz von Oberlichtern, geschosshoher Verglasung und Metallverkleidung zeigt. Der Bezug zur koreanischen Architektur ist eher an dem schwungvoll gekrümmten Dach dieses 16 311 m² großen Komplexes erkennbar.

24 STUNDEN

Auch größere Gebäude, die als Besucherzentren, Hotels oder Restaurants dienen, werden immer häufiger mit Holz gebaut. Einer der eindrucksvollsten Neubauten aus Holz, das Wisa Wooden Design Hotel (Helsinki, Finnland, 2009, Seite 82) ist allerdings kein Hotel im üblichen Sinne. Es handelt sich um ein 80 m² großes Gebäude, das Ergebnis eines Wettbewerbs aus dem Jahre 2009. Pieta-Linda Auttila erhielt den Auftrag, „ein gewagtes und einprägsames Bauwerk aus finnischer Kiefer und Fichte" zu entwerfen. Die Teilnehmer an dem von der Firma UPM, einem Produzenten von Energie, Pulpe, Papier und Baumaterialien, ausgelobten Wettbewerb hatten ganze 24 Stunden Zeit, um ihre Entwürfe fertigzustellen. Die Architektin versuchte, „den hölzernen Block in Stücke zu zerlegen", offene und geschlossene Bereiche oder geometrische und organische Formen miteinander zu verbinden. Dieser Entwurf ist nicht unbedingt wegweisend für Trends in der Holzarchitektur, zeigt jedoch, wie ungewöhnliche Formen aus Holz in durchaus zeitgemäßer Weise zusammengestellt werden können.

„Solider" und weniger experimentell ist das Grand Teton Discovery and Visitor Center (Moose Junction, Grand Teton National Park, Wyoming, USA, 2007, Seite 114) der Architekten Bohlin Cywinski Jackson, das mit einem Balkentragwerk und Schichtholzträgern errichtet wurde. Wo Holz aufgrund der klimatischen Verhältnisse nicht verwendet werden konnte, kam brettverschalter Beton zum Einsatz, der die Maserung des Holzes bewahrt. Großzügige, hohe Verglasung ermöglicht die Kommunikation des Gebäudes mit seiner spektakulären Umgebung von Wäldern und Bergen. Diese Architekten beherrschen das Planen und Bauen im waldreichen Westen der Vereinigten Staaten, was im Visitor Center spürbar ist – einem Gebäude mit deutlich modernem Erscheinungsbild sowie Respekt vor seiner Funktion und der Umwelt.

Dem Architekten José Cruz Ovalle bot sich die ungewöhnliche Erfahrung, ein Hotel auf der Osterinsel (Rapa Nui Explora Hotel, Miro O'one Sector, Chile, 2005–07, Seite 154) zu planen. Das wie ein Archipelagos aus Inseln und Binnenmeer konzipierte Gebäude wird durch hölzerne Decks zusammengehalten. Es ist ein interessantes Konzept für diesen Standort, da man vermutet, dass die Gründe für den Untergang der Kultur, in der die berühmten Skulpturen der Osterinsel entstanden, auch im Raubbau an den seinerzeit vorhandenen Wäldern zu suchen sind. Das Hotel Explora wurde sorgfältig in die Landschaft integriert und bietet durch großzügige Verglasung herrliche Ausblicke zum Horizont. Von der Bruchsteinbasis abgesehen, ist Holz in der ganzen Anlage präsent. Beim früheren, ebenfalls von Cruz Ovalle geplanten Weingut Perez Cruz (Paine, Chile, 2001–02, Seite 146) wird Holz auf eindrucksvolle Weise für ein 5433 m² großes Gebäude verwendet. Interessant ist der Hinweis, dass man sich in diesem Fall für Holz entschied, um für den Wein geeignete Temperaturverhältnisse im Innern zu erzielen.

16
Ken Sungjin Min, Lake Hills
Suncheon Country Club, Suncheon,
JeollaNam-do, South Korea, 2008

16

EIN SCHIRM UND EIN BAUMSTAMM

Der französische Architekt Edouard François ist für seine ökologisch orientierten Entwürfe bekannt. Sein neuestes, ehrgeiziges Projekt, der Club Med-Aldiana (Nianing, Senegal, 2010–, Seite 202), ist ein 100 000 m² großer Hotelkomplex mit 250 Zimmern und Suiten sowie allen dafür notwendigen Einrichtungen zur Bewirtung und für sportliche Betätigung. François bezieht sich reichlich auf örtliche Traditionen, wie etwa afrikanische Masken, und verwendet überall Holz, auch im Restaurant, das in Form von „umgekehrten Schirmen" gestaltet wurde. Er versteht sich selbst als Architekt, der nicht dem sogenannten „üblichen" Weg folgt, und stimuliert gern Erwartungen, wie auch beim Club Med. Holz mit seiner Flexibilität und seinen vielfachen Nutzungsmöglichkeiten passt gut zu dieser „grünen" und überraschenden Architektur.

Das Restaurant Tusen (Ramundberget, Schweden, 2007–08, Seite 324) von Murman Arkitekter ist ein 340 m² großes Gebäude, das sich in anhaltender „Harmonie mit der Natur" befinden soll. Der Architekt verwendete ganze Birkenstämme für das Tragwerk und für die Fassade, da dies die einzigen Bäume sind, die in der Höhe dieses Standorts wachsen und leicht ersetzt werden können. „Durch die Wahl einer Holzkonstruktion", sagt der Architekt, „erreichten wir ein geringes Gewicht. Es handelt sich um ein vorgefertigtes Gebäude mit geringen Auswirkungen auf den Boden, und das war auch ein Weg, um die Bauzeit zu reduzieren." Das geringe Gewicht ist in der Tat ein entscheidender Faktor für die Wahl von Holz in der Architektur, wie zum Beispiel über die Jahrhunderte in den erdbebengefährdeten Gebieten Japans. Das Restaurant Tusen ist ein umweltfreundliches, mit Wärmepumpen und eigener Kläranlage ausgestattetes Gebäude. Natürlich erwartet man heutzutage von neuen Holzbauten Umweltfreundlichkeit auch in anderen Bereichen als in der Wahl der Materialien.

DEUTSCH UND GRÜN

Wie viele der hier gezeigten Beispiele beweisen, wird Holz für fast alle Bautypen verwendet. Der deutsche Architekt Jörg Aldinger nutzte Holz für den sichtbaren Teil seiner Cafeteria und Tagesstätte der Waldorfschule (Stuttgart, 2005–07, Seite 62); das dreigeschossige Gebäude besteht jedoch eigentlich aus Stahlbeton. Es ist aber mit Lärchenholz verkleidet, hat hölzerne Fensterrahmen und Möbel und ein begrüntes Dach – ein Hinweis auf einen weiteren wichtigen Trend in der gegenwärtigen Architektur: die Verwendung von Holz als sekundäres oder Verkleidungsmaterial. Diese Methode hat an Beliebtheit gewonnen, vor allem im Außenbereich, für den bisher oft Beton oder Metall gewählt wurden. Andere deutsche Architekten, Auer+Weber+Assoziierte, planten eine gitterartige Außenfassade aus Lärchenholz für ihre Cafeteria auf dem Campus Martinsried der Ludwig-Maximilians-Universität (München, 2004–09, Seite 78). Wie bei dem Gebäude für die Waldorfschule ist auch hier Holz nicht das hauptsächliche Baumaterial, aber dennoch ein entscheidendes Gestaltungselement. Das moderne Seminargebäude Gut Siggen (Ostholstein, 2006–07, Seite 72) von denselben Architekten hat steuerbare Jalousien und Decken aus Lärchenholz sowie Fußböden aus Eiche, um die Verbindung zu der vom Gebäude aus sichtbaren Umgebung zu betonen. Aus dem gleichen Grund, offenbar ein deutscher Trend, setzten die Architekten Kauffmann Theilig & Partner viel sichtbares Holz bei ihrem Mitarbeiterrestaurant der Firma Boehringer Ingelheim (Biberach an der Riss, 2003–04, Seite 258) ein. Dieser 3000 m² große Bau für eine Pharmafirma hat ein „räumliches

Faltwerk", das mit Holz verkleidet ist. Diese Elemente bilden die Innendecke des Restaurants und ragen, wie viele andere Holzteile, aus dem Dach heraus.

ARBEITEN IN HOLZ

Zwei neuere Bauten des finnischen Architekten Seppo Häkli (geboren 1951) demonstrieren die Brauchbarkeit und Zweckdienlichkeit von Holz im Bereich von Arbeitsstätten. Das für die staatliche Denkmalpflege errichtete Seurasaari Building Conservation Center (Helsinki, Finnland, 2007–09, Seite 16) ist Teil des Freilichtmuseums Seurasaari. Dieses mit Holzstützen versehene Gebäude enthält eine Schreinerwerkstatt. Schichtholzbalken oder schwarz geteerte Bretterverkleidung wurden nach lokalen Holzbaumethoden für einen Bau verwendet, der modern und vor allem funktional ist. Das Büro- und Laborgebäude Metla (Haapastensyrjä, Finnland, 2007–08, Seite 216) von demselben Architekten ist ein 550 m² großer Bau im Stil finnischer Bauernhäuser. Er enthält mit Fichte verkleidete Laboratoriums- und Technikräume sowie ebenfalls mit Holz verschalte Büros und ist ein Bauwerk aus insgesamt zwölf Holzarten, das auch vom finnischen Know-how auf diesem Gebiet zeugt. Ein weiterer Bau für die Firma Metla, das Finnish Forest Research Institute (Joensuu, Finnland, 2004, Seite 368) wurde von SARC Architects geplant. Mit 7400 m² Fläche ist dieses Gebäude viel größer als das vorher genannte. Es dient der Erforschung von Materialien aus Holz für den Bau und andere Zwecke. Holz ist im ganzen Gebäude sichtbar, von der Ständerkonstruktion bis zur Außenverkleidung, lebende Kiefern schmücken dagegen den Innenhof. Finnland ist wohl das Land, das seine Traditionen und Innovationen auf dem Gebiet der Holzarchitektur am meisten pflegt – eine Tatsache, die auch manche seiner Architekten auszeichnet, die dieses Material in der ganzen Welt populär gemacht haben.

Auch die Schweiz hat eine lange Holzbautradition, vor allem in den alpinen Regionen. Obgleich in der Vergangenheit einige ganz aus Holz errichtete Altstädte Bränden zum Opfer fielen, ist viel von dieser Tradition erhalten geblieben, zum Beispiel im Engadiner Tal bei Sankt Moritz und in anderen Gebieten des Kantons Graubünden. Ein Architekt, der diese Tradition aufgenommen und entscheidend modernisiert hat, ist der 1958 in Chur geborene Valerio Olgiati. Seine Familie ist jedoch in Flims ansässig, wo er auch sein Büro hat. Hier errichtete er 2007 ein neues Bürogebäude auf dem Gelände einer früheren Scheune (Seite 336). Der Bau aus dunklem Holz im Flimser Ortsteil Dado steht auf Betonpfeilern und wirkt von außen wie ein alte Scheuer. Bei diesem und anderen Projekten nutzt Olgiati alte Bauformen für neue Funktionen. Wenn die ursprünglichen Funktionen nicht mehr benötigt werden, ist dies eine Möglichkeit, den Dörfern ihr altes Erscheinungsbild zu erhalten und die Bauten einer modernen Nutzung zuzuführen. An anderen Orten hat Valerio Olgiati einen entschieden zeitgemäßen, wenn auch ungewöhnlichen Stil entwickelt, wobei er nur gelegentlich Holz bevorzugt.

VON EINER BAR ZU EINEM SONNENSCHIRM

Für einen völlig anderen Kontext hat Niall McLaughlin eine Café-Bar am Pier von Deal (Deal, Kent, United Kingdom, 2008, Seite 298) geplant. Der Ende der 1950er-Jahre aus Beton erbaute Pier ist leicht verwittert, daher suchte der Architekt nach einem Material, das „mit der

17
Murman Arkitekter, Tusen Restaurant,
Ramundberget, Sweden, 2007–08

17

Zeit verwittern und ansehnlicher werden" würde. Man entschied sich für Iroko-Schichtholz. Große Fenster bieten den Gästen Ausblick aufs Meer. Obwohl ganz früher hölzerne Piers die Regel waren, ist es interessant, dass man sich in diesem Fall für Holz entschied, eben weil es auch trotz Einwirkung der Elemente in Anmut altert. Man könnte annehmen, dass Beton besser altert als Holz, und doch war es genau die Verwitterung des Betons, die den Architekten zur Wahl von Holz veranlasste.

Obgleich für den Brückenbau lange Zeit andere Materialien, wie zum Beispiel Stahl, bevorzugt wurden, wählte der Architekt Enrique Browne Schichtholz für seine kleine, elegante Fußgängerbrücke (Zapallar, Chile, 2008, Seite 126). Zwar entschied er sich auch für ein Metallnetz und LED-Leuchten, doch schwebte ihm beim Entwerfen wohl das Bild eines Bootes vor. Holz kann eindeutig mit einfacheren Mitteln verarbeitet werden als entsprechende Mengen von Stahl oder anderer moderner Materialien. Auch wenn in diesem Band ein paar recht großmaßstäbliche Beispiele vorgestellt werden, ist es klar, dass Holz eher für relativ kleine Projekte geeignet ist, bei denen die Kosten einen wichtigen Faktor darstellen.

Gewissermaßen als Beweis für das Gegenteil umfasst ein anderes – wenn auch noch nicht ganz fertiggestelltes – Projekt 12 670 m² Fläche bei Baukosten von 51 Millionen Euro. Ein Werk des deutschen Architekten Jürgen Mayer H., der Metropol Parasol (Sevilla, Spanien, 2005–11, Seite 18), ist Teil der Umgestaltung der Plaza de la Encarnacion in Sevilla. Die als „neue Ikone" der Stadt bezeichnete Konstruktion soll Bars, Restaurants und andere öffentliche Bereiche überdecken und vor der Sonne schützen. Diese großen Schirme bestehen ganz aus Holz und sind mit einem Überzug aus Polyurethan versehen – ein weiterer Beweis dafür, dass sich aus Holz als Hauptmaterial sehr moderne Formen produzieren lassen, auch, wie in diesem Falle, in großem Maßstab.

HOLZ IN STRAHLENDEM NEUEN GEWAND

Eine Auswahl von etwa 60 Neubauten, die zum Teil oder ganz aus Holz bestehen, reicht nicht für eine wirkliche Übersicht dessen aus, was in der Welt passiert. Aber sie macht deutlich, dass Holz ein sehr zeitgemäßes Material ist, wenn es mithilfe neuester Technologie auf innovative Weise angewendet wird. Obgleich die Nutzung seltener Holzarten lange Zeit als Tabu galt, verbreiten sich rapide Zertifizierungen für Holz aus erneuerbaren Bezugsquellen und beweisen, dass es bei korrekter Anwendung bereits zu den besonders „grünen" Baumaterialien zählt. Wenn manche Planer auch so weit gehen, ein Holzskelett mit Corten-Stahl oder glänzendem Aluminium zu schützen, kann Holz doch Umwelteinwirkungen ebenso lange Widerstand leisten wie „modernere" Materialien; es nimmt eine Patina an, die sicherlich attraktiver ist als eine verwitterte Betonwand. Und auch mit Polyurethan überzogen, wie beim Projekt von Jürgen Mayer H. in Sevilla, kann Holz aus der gegenwärtigen Architekturszene hervorstechen in einem strahlenden neuen Gewand, das ihm gut zu Gesicht steht. Bei einigen der hier veröffentlichten Projekte wurde Holz aus Altbauten verwendet – was natürlich die Nachhaltigkeit eines Gebäudes erhöht, wenn auch nicht unbedingt seine Lebensdauer. Um es scherzhaft auszudrücken: Auf jeden Fall verursacht der Abriss eines Holzbaus wahrscheinlich weniger umweltschädliche Folgen als der eines üblichen, mit Asbest isolierten Stahlbaus. Aber ganz im Ernst: Wie dieses Buch klarmachen sollte, ist Holz ein

18
*Niall McLaughlin,
Café-Bar on Deal Pier,
Deal, Kent, UK, 2008*

18

durchaus geeignetes Produkt für eine wirtschaftlich ungewisse Zukunft und kann einen wichtigen Beitrag zum Schutz unserer Umwelt leisten, was von allen berücksichtigt werden sollte. Holz ist buchstäblich so „grün", wie Baumaterialien nur sein können, wenn es verantwortungsbewusst gewonnen und verarbeitet wird. Es altert, wenn es nicht geschützt wird, aber dasselbe gilt für andere Materialien. In der Hand eines entsprechenden Architekten kann es durch und durch modern gestaltet werden. Kurz gesagt: Holz ist etwas für unsere Zeit.

Philip Jodidio, Grimentz, Schweiz, 15. Mai 2010

[1] http://www.fsc.org/about-fsc.html, Stand 15.05.2010.

INTRODUCTION

DU BOIS, ICI ET MAINTENANT

Ordre et sainteté règnent dans ces plantations de Dieu, où se déroule une fête perpétuelle dont leur hôte ne pourrait se lasser en un millier d'années. Dans les bois, nous revenons à la raison et à la foi. Là, je sens que rien de mal ne peut m'arriver, ni malheur, ni calamité (si je ne perds pas la vue) que la nature ne puisse réparer. Debout sur le sol nu, ma tête baignée d'air pur et tendue vers l'espace infini, tout égotisme médiocre disparaît. Je deviens un globe oculaire transparent ; je ne suis rien, je vois tout ; les courants de l'Être universel circulent en moi ; je fais partie – ou suis une particule – de Dieu.
Ralph Waldo Emerson, *Nature*, 1836

Le bois, c'est avant tout la forêt, ces « plantations de Dieu » dont parle Emerson. C'est aussi là, sous la lune, que les personnages du *Songe d'une nuit d'été* de Shakespeare se livrent à la comédie de leurs transformations. C'est également de la forêt que l'architecte a tiré une bonne part de son inspiration, que ce soit pour dessiner une simple colonne, un temple ou une cathédrale. Sous forme de canopée de branchages ou d'empilement de troncs pour s'abriter de la tempête, le bois est un des éléments quintessentiels des premiers habitats de l'homme, lentement retournés à la terre. L'architecture en bois est souvent jugée éphémère, car des constructions soumises aux variations du climat et à un mauvais entretien ne peuvent subsister très longtemps. Néanmoins, pour ne prendre qu'un exemple, la pagode à cinq niveaux du temple de Daigoji, édifiée en 951, demeure le plus ancien bâtiment de Kyoto. Correctement mis en œuvre, le bois peut résister à tout un millénaire, aux tremblements de terre et au passage des générations humaines. Avant d'être coupés et détaillés, les arbres vivent, selon les espèces, plus longtemps que n'importe quel autre organisme sur terre. Un pin de Great Basin Bristlecone (*Pinus longaeva*), surnommé à juste titre Methusalem (White Mountains, Californie), serait âgé de plus de 4800 ans. Des colonies clonales d'arbres comme le Pando, un peuplier faux-tremble de l'Utah, produisent encore des pousses à partir de leur énorme système radiculaire qui serait vieux de 80 000 ans, beaucoup plus ancien donc que la civilisation des hommes. Nés de la terre, les arbres sont littéralement et figurativement à l'origine de l'abri, du bâti et de l'inspiration des architectes.

Le viol des forêts primitives, qui s'accomplit actuellement en Indonésie ou dans d'autres régions du globe, est sans aucun rapport avec l'approche écologique de la construction. Exploité selon les règles, le bois a retrouvé une vie nouvelle au XXIᵉ siècle pour devenir un des matériaux de prédilection de l'architecture. Parce qu'une forêt gérée se renouvelle naturellement, le bois, s'il n'est pas transporté sur de trop longues distances, est certainement l'un des matériaux de construction les plus écologiques. Des organismes, comme l'United States Green Building Council (USGBC, Conseil des États-Unis de la construction verte), ont mis au point des critères (LEED, Leadership en énergie et conception environnementale), qui certifient le bois dans ses utilisations en construction durable. L'USGBC collabore avec le Forest Stewardship Council (FSC, Conseil de la gestion des forêts). Ce dernier est un « organisme indépendant, non gouvernemental, à but non lucratif, fondé en 1993, pour répondre aux préoccupations de la déforestation globale. Le FSC est souvent considéré comme l'une des plus importantes initiatives de la décennie écoulée pour la promotion de la gestion responsable des forêts [1] ». En décembre 2008, 107 millions d'hectares de forêts dans 78 pays ont été certifiés conformes aux « principes et critères » du FSC.

19

Parce qu'il a été largement utilisé à travers l'histoire, et certainement pas dans le cadre de la seule architecture inventive, le bois possède une réelle image. Mais pourquoi se faire construire une maison en bois quand le béton et l'aluminium semblent tellement plus modernes et plus résistants ? *Wood Architecture Now!* traite d'une génération entièrement nouvelle de constructions, inspirées en partie par la tradition, mais aussi par les orientations écologiques récentes. Alors que le modernisme strict ou un minimalisme encore plus aride semblent passer de mode, de nombreux architectes et leurs clients recherchent la chaleur du bois et son aspect naturel. Matériau de construction « ancien », il peut néanmoins être travaillé selon les méthodes les plus avancées, dont les machines-outils à pilotage numérique, pour réaliser des formes complexes ou des pièces de coût accessible. Beaucoup d'architectes présentés dans cet ouvrage utilisent aussi le bois dans des buts spécifiques ou dans certaines parties seulement de leurs réalisations. Un bâtiment peut être habillé de bois, tout en étant construit en béton ou en acier. L'objectif de ce livre, comme le reste de la collection *Architecture Now!*, est d'offrir à son lecteur une vue d'ensemble de ce qui se réalise actuellement selon différents styles et techniques, et dans des lieux aussi variés que possible. Sans volonté d'exhaustivité, *Wood Architecture Now!* s'attache aux réalisations du XXIᵉ siècle et principalement aux chantiers de ces deux ou trois dernières années qui prouvent le grand retour du bois, un matériau de construction résolument contemporain.

L'APPEL DE LA NATURE

Les exemples d'églises, de chapelles ou de lieux de méditation édifiés en bois abondent tout au long de l'histoire de l'architecture. Il est donc naturel que cette tradition perdure. Bien qu'ils aient nommé leur agence BETON, Marta Rowińska et Lech Rowiński (tous deux nés en 1976) ont pris un plaisir évident à construire une petite église en bois de 60 mètres carrés à Tarnów, sur la rivière Vistule (Pologne, 2007–10, page 108). Posée sur une dalle de béton, cette petite structure a été en grande partie réalisée par des ouvriers non spécialisés, ce qui est certainement plus facile que pour des matériaux de construction plus modernes. Les architectes ont cherché à atteindre « une certaine qualité d'espace à travers une simplicité technique rudimentaire ». Pour un coût de 20 000 euros seulement, cette église d'une qualité stimulante, en particulier vue de l'intérieur, est aussi une belle métaphore de la spiritualité.

À l'autre bout du monde, dans le sud du Chili, les jeunes architectes Alejandro Dumay Claro, Nicolás Fones et Francisco Vergara Arthur, tous nés à Santiago en 1977, ont construit une chapelle de bois encore plus petite (21 mètres carrés) également à façade en pignon. La chapelle de Fuente Nueva (2006, page 184) donne directement sur le lac de Rupanco. L'ouverture toute hauteur aménagée derrière l'autel exprime le lien avec la nature. L'architecture est réduite au strict minimum et cependant cette construction maintient une modernité épurée qui accroît l'impact du cadre naturel sur les douze personnes qui peuvent s'y réunir. Bien que l'architecture religieuse se soit souvent lourdement appuyée sur l'ornementation ou les effets spatiaux complexes, ce type de petites structures dégagées de tout détail superflu témoigne d'un certain retour à des valeurs fondamentales, tant au niveau de la forme que de la fonction.

20
Appleton & Domingos,
Treehouse System, Azambuja,
Portugal, 2008–09

20

Beatriz Meyer, née à São Paulo en 1977, une collaboratrice de l'architecte Marcio Kogan, a conçu seule un certain nombre de projets, dont la chapelle en bois de Tatuí (São Paulo, 2006, page 310). Guère plus qu'un simple toit incliné posé sur trois murs de verre, elle n'a utilisé, en dehors du bois, que de la pierre pour le mur derrière l'autel, et quelques matériaux plus sophistiqués comme la membrane en Alwitra de la toiture. L'impression d'ensemble n'en reste pas moins d'une grande simplicité et élégance. Les arbres proches mettent en valeur une impression de chapelle perdue dans la forêt, dans une sorte d'allusion à l'origine des religions.

Bien qu'elle ne soit pas un édifice religieux, la plate-forme d'observation de Pinohuacho face au volcan de Villarica conçue par Rodrigo Sheward (Pinohuacho, Villarica, Chili, 2006, page 374) encourage certainement à la méditation. Située au milieu d'une ancienne exploitation forestière, elle relève d'une tentative de réflexion sur les dommages causés par des coupes claires. Construite en bois récupéré sur place, en partie par un ouvrier membre de l'équipe des bûcherons, cette plate-forme de 78 mètres carrés a été réalisée pour 3000 dollars seulement. Sheward, comme les autres architectes cités ici, a moins de 40 ans et semble avoir entendu l'appel de la forêt, passée ou présente, incarnée dans le bois, digne sujet de réflexion face aux nouveaux besoins de la construction.

COME RAIN OR COME SHINE [2]

La maison est certainement le plus fertile des champs d'investigation des architectes qui s'intéressent au bois de nos jours. Bien que des constructions de grandes dimensions puissent aussi être réalisées en bois, l'échelle généralement réduite de l'architecture résidentielle rend ce matériau attractif à de nombreux égards. On compte parmi ces derniers les bénéfices écologiques, si le bois est exploité et transporté selon les règles, sa relative facilité de travail par rapport aux processus mécaniques nécessaires pour le métal et autres matériaux récents et tout simplement la chaleur induite par ce matériau naturel, aussi bien en utilisation extérieure qu'intérieure.

Jular est une entreprise basée à Azambuja près de Lisbonne, qui s'est spécialisée dans les logements modulaires durables en bois. Si les maisons transportables ne semblent souvent guère compatibles avec l'élégance, le Treehouse System (Azambuja, Portugal, 2008–09, page 35), mis au point avec les architectes João Appleton et Isabel Domingos, est à la fois séduisant et pratique. Pour un coût de 900 euros le mètre carré, il est également très accessible. Doté d'ouvertures limitées pour s'adapter au climat local, le système fait entrer le bois dans le champ de l'architecture modulaire et transportable de manière très convaincante. Jular note d'ailleurs que des maisons de ce type ont pu exister dans le passé, mais qu'elles n'étaient pas conçues pour des climats comme celui du Portugal (climat atlantique influencé par le Gulf Stream) ou de pays méditerranéens, de l'Espagne à la Grèce.

Ni transportable ni modeste, la maison RW (Búzios, État de Rio de Janeiro, 2006–09, page 100) mesure 4900 mètres carrés de surface. De forme surbaissée en H, elle est suspendue à 50 centimètres au-dessus de la plage. Bien qu'elle soit d'un luxe évident, ses architectes Bernardes + Jacobsen ont utilisé un simple eucalyptus lamellé non traité tiré de zones reboisées. La ventilation naturelle, qui lie encore

21
Nic Lehoux and Jacqueline
Darjes, The Lilypad, Point Roberts,
Washington, USA, 2008–09

21

davantage la maison à son cadre, réduit la consommation d'énergie. Entre une chapelle de 21 mètres carrés et une maison de 4900 mètres carrés, il semble que le bois soit devenu un matériau de choix qui réconcilie la modernité avec sa présence chaleureuse, même quand il est posé de façon très rigoureuse. On peut dire ici que ces architectes, connus entre autres pour leurs vastes résidences de luxe, ont tiré le meilleur parti de ce qui n'est pas fondamentalement de l'architecture « verte ». Sans tenir compte du mode de vie de ces riches clients, il est néanmoins difficile d'imaginer qu'une maison aussi grande soit au final écologiquement responsable. Bois ou pas.

CE QUI ÉTAIT EN BOIS A OSCILLÉ, MAIS RÉSISTÉ

Marco Casagrande, né en 1971 à Turku en Finlande, écrit qu'une ruine se crée lorsque quelque chose « réalisé par l'homme vient à faire partie de la nature ». « Je cherche, dit-il, à concevoir des ruines. » Sa petite maison Chen de 62 mètres carrés (Sanjhih, Taipei, Taïwan, 2007–08, page 138) est en béton et acajou. Plus qu'une ruine, elle donne l'impression d'un lieu d'où l'on peut braver les éléments, quels qu'ils soient. Le site de la chaîne de montagnes de Datun est sujet aux tremblements de terre, aux typhons et aux inondations. Des lattes de bois laissent pénétrer à l'intérieur de la maison les brises rafraîchissantes, et le chauffage est assuré en hiver par une cheminée au bois. Ce n'est certainement pas un projet d'avant-garde, au sens habituel du terme, mais on y trouve une sorte de justesse rustique qui en fait presque un symbole pour ces temps difficiles, le bois restant un des principaux matériaux de survie. Casagrande cite un bref poème de Bertolt Brecht (1898–1956), intitulé « Fer «, qui pourrait s'appliquer à ce projet : « La nuit dernière, dans un rêve, j'ai vu une grande tempête. Elle a saisi l'échafaudage. Elle a arraché les croisillons, ceux qui étaient en fer. Et ce qui était en bois a oscillé, mais résisté. »

Nicolás del Río (né en 1975) et Max Núñez (né en 1976) à Santiago (dRN Architects) sont habitués à construire dans des conditions difficiles. Un certain nombre de leurs réalisations (Skibox, 2006 ; chalet refuge de montagne C6, 2006 ; et chalet refuge de montagne C7, 2008, tous à Portillo, Chili) sont situées à 2800 mètres d'altitude. La maison La Baronia (Quintero, Valparaíso, Chili, 2009, page 172) occupe le sommet d'une colline face à l'océan. En réponse à la corrosion marine et à la furie des éléments, les architectes ont choisi pour l'extérieur un acier Corten précorrodé et le verre. Mais à l'intérieur, l'ossature de la maison est en poutres de bois boulonnées. La maison La Baronia montre ainsi que le bois peut valablement tenir le rôle de matériau structurel même dans des conditions climatiques extrêmes. dRN est l'une des plus inventives jeunes agences chiliennes et cette maison confirme sa réputation. Le fait que l'acier Corten soit souvent utilisé dans des œuvres purement artistiques, comme celles de Richard Serra, accroît l'intérêt de la maison La Baronia, qui s'élève comme une sorte d'abri sculptural face aux éléments.

JOYEUX CAMPEURS

Le bois se rattache également à un esprit de praticité ou même d'économie qui attire un certain nombre de clients et d'architectes. C'est ainsi que Shin Ohori de l'agence General Design à Tokyo a reçu la visite d'un client qui voulait simplement un bon endroit pour planter une tente. Le résultat de cette collaboration inhabituelle est cette « résidence » appelée Recherche en montagne (Minamisaku, Nagano, Japon, 2007–08, page 208). Des plates-formes en mélèze et des cabines réservées à la cuisine, au rangement et à une salle de bains entourent une tente en forme de coupole de deux mètres de haut. Pour Shin Ohori : « J'espère que cette architecture sera un lieu où l'on pourra découvrir quelque chose de nouveau, et innover dans leur style de vie. » Ici, le bois était certainement le choix le plus approprié à l'environnement montagnard et au programme restreint de ce client, même si d'autres matériaux auraient pu être également utilisés pour cette construction de 97 mètres carrés. Ceci dit, n'y a-t-il pas une contradiction fondamentale entre le style de vie mobile suggéré par la tente et la nature fixe de ce projet ? Disons, qu'il s'agit d'une création intermédiaire, qui n'est ni vraiment une maison, ni vraiment un lieu de camping.

Le bois joue un rôle essentiel dans un certain nombre des tentatives les plus audacieuses pour rendre l'architecture écologiquement responsable. La maison Smart Air (2010, page 11) de l'agence d'architecture allemande Graft est un prototype de deux logements empilés à structure et planchers intérieurs en bois à stratification croisée. D'autres matériaux sont également utilisés, bien sûr, mais les concepts de base de cette maison sont issus des réflexions les plus récentes en matière de « technologies de construction intelligentes et efficaces agissant en symbiose avec la composition durable des matériaux, sans pour autant s'imposer techniquement aux habitudes des utilisateurs ». D'une certaine façon, l'architecture écologiquement responsable se trouve encore dans une phase constitutive, sans que des axes clairs n'aient encore été établis. Par exemple, beaucoup de matériaux dits durables le sont un peu moins si on examine en détail leur chaîne de production. Le bois est néanmoins une exception, quand il est exploité selon des techniques responsables.

La maison de Troie (Trojan House, Melbourne, Victoria, Australie, 2005, page 240) des architectes Jackson Clements Burrows met à mal l'idée que l'architecture en bois ne peut avoir l'air vraiment moderne. Faisant appel à « une peau de bois continue recouvrant le toit, les fenêtres et les murs » et à des volets de bois télécommandables, la maison de Troie est en fait l'extension d'une résidence existante qui se fait remarquer par ses façades aveugles lorsque les volets sont fermés. Ici encore, le bois, qui permet une transition sans heurt entre une construction ancienne et une construction nouvelle, se montre d'utilisation souple et pratique. Jackson Clements Burrows ne sont évidemment pas les seuls architectes à donner une forme actuelle à leurs réalisations en bois, mais leur maison illustre l'adaptabilité de ce matériau à une approche réellement contemporaine.

Une des maisons publiées dans cet ouvrage, la maison Lilypad (Point Roberts, Washington, 2008–09, page 286) surprend parce qu'elle n'est pas l'œuvre d'un architecte, mais celle d'un photographe, Nic Lehoux, réalisée avec la collaboration de Jacqueline Darjes. De 24 mètres carrés de surface seulement, et d'un coût de 4500 dollars, ce n'est certainement pas un projet ambitieux. Des terrasses en cèdre, des fenêtres en pin de Douglas récupéré et des poutres en lamellé-collé constituent les éléments de base de cette micromaison qui repose sur des pilotis en Sonotube (matériau servant habituellement au coffrage du béton). Dans le cadre d'un budget identique, il semble que des matériaux plus raffinés auraient rendu ce projet moins efficace. Le bois est un matériau récupérable que peuvent travailler des ouvriers sans équipement, ni formation élaborés. L'acier ou même le béton exigent des moyens et une expertise plus élevés quand il s'agit de construire une maison.

22

APPARTEMENTS EN CONTREPLAQUÉ ET REFUGES DE MONTAGNE

Le bois est communément utilisé dans les constructions individuelles, mais il est également souvent choisi pour des immeubles résidentiels plus importants, dont certains sont assez surprenants. Le premier publié ici est le Hameau de Plantoun (Bayonne, France, 2008–09, page 132) de l'architecte bordelais Bernard Bühler. Travaillant pour l'Office public des HLM de Bayonne, il a réalisé ce groupe de 39 maisons à ossature bois et bardage de contreplaqué, reposant sur des pilotis de bois et de fins piliers métalliques. On pourrait penser que le contreplaqué serait plutôt l'apanage des usages temporaires, comme les clôtures de chantiers, et que sa patine ne lui donne pas un aspect très séduisant. Si le Hameau de Plantoun surprend par son apparence et le choix de ses matériaux, son empreinte écologique est certainement plus faible que celle de constructions plus traditionnelles.

Si le bois est le matériau structurel d'évidence dans l'exemple précédent, sa présence passe inaperçue, au premier regard, dans le nouveau refuge du mont Rose (Zermatt, Suisse, 2008–09, page 196) entièrement paré d'aluminium. Et pourtant, ce projet (ETH Studio Monte Rosa / Bearth & Deplazes) réalisé pour célébrer le 150e anniversaire de l'ETH de Zurich a voulu limiter au maximum son impact environnemental. Implanté à 2883 mètres d'altitude, ce refuge a été pu être construit grâce à la livraison des matériaux par hélicoptère, ce qui n'est pas vraiment neutre sur le plan des émissions de CO_2, mais était inévitable étant donné la position du site. La plus grande partie de l'intérieur de ce bâtiment très moderne est en bois. Tous les matériaux sont récupérables, si le refuge devait être démoli, et, dans l'ensemble, il consomme beaucoup moins d'énergie que son prédécesseur. Comme le savent ceux qui fréquentent habituellement les refuges de haute montagne, le bois est très présent dans leurs aménagements, sans doute parce qu'il était plus facile à transporter jadis que la pierre par exemple. La peau d'aluminium est ici une réponse technologique à la dureté des conditions climatiques. Le bois utilisé à l'intérieur répond à une logique structurelle, mais aussi à la tradition de ce type de construction. L'ensemble est à la fois profondément moderne, pratique et efficace sur le plan de la consommation énergétique. Aucun matériau autre que le bois n'aurait pu être aussi indiqué à l'intérieur d'une construction de ce type.

ATOURS FINLANDAIS

Comme on pouvait s'y attendre, les pays scandinaves sont à l'avant-garde de l'architecture en bois contemporaine du fait de traditions locales qui incluent d'ailleurs l'œuvre de figures importantes de la modernité, dont Alvar Aalto. Emma Johansson (née en 1985 à Turku en Finlande) et Timo Leiviskä (né en 1981 à Ouli en Finlande) ont été appelés par l'hôtel Anttolanhovi de Mikkeli pour faire la démonstration que des maisons contemporaines en bois pouvaient figurer à l'avant-garde de l'architecture, du design et de l'art d'aujourd'hui. Leurs villas côté lac et côté colline (2007–08, Johansson ; 2006–08, Leiviskä, page 246) sont de luxueuses maisons en bois et en pierre. On peut se demander en les voyant pourquoi les architectes ont un jour négligé le bois. La jeunesse de ces deux praticiens et l'accent mis sur « l'art et le design » dans la promotion de l'hôtel Anttolanhovi replacent le bois au centre de la réflexion la plus contemporaine sur l'architecture des hôtels et des lieux de villégiature.

Deux architectes finlandais plus âgés, Kirsi Korhonen (né en 1958) et Mika Penttinen (né en 1951) ont conçu un alignement de maisons sur trois niveaux appelé Huvitus Terraced Housing (Helsinki, 2007–08, page 280). Cet ensemble de 1986 mètres carrés sur une colline sableuse boisée, est en poutres de bois lamifié (LVL) et bardage de façade peint en rouge et noir. La configuration de ces logements aux volumes répétitifs, mais individualisés, donne un sentiment de modernité qui ne renie pas pour autant les traditions locales. La réglementation sur l'incendie exigeait que le rez-de-chaussée soit en béton. Ceci dit, il a été vérifié en de nombreuses circonstances, que des matériaux comme l'acier pouvaient moins résister qu'un bois correctement traité. Néanmoins la présence de bois clairs pour les aménagements intérieurs, de l'habillage des murs au mobilier, montre que ce matériau est le composant essentiel de ces constructions, le béton sachant rester discret.

UN BLOB ET UNE MAISON DE THÉ

C'est peut-être parce qu'il est d'une utilisation très souple que le bois est souvent utilisé dans des petites structures non orthodoxes. Un certain nombre d'exemples en sont donnés dans ce livre. L'un des plus curieux est la maison en troncs d'arbres (Tree Trunk House, Hilversum, Pays-Bas, 2009, page 190) du célèbre designer Piet Hein Eek. Si celui-ci est connu pour ses meubles en bois de rebut qu'il a commencé à réaliser au début des années 1990, son agence s'est aussi lancée dans les projets architecturaux. C'est à la demande de l'acteur et chanteur allemand, Hans Liberg, qu'il a créé ce petit bureau de 9,3 mètres carrés évoquant une pile de bûches de bois, en particulier quand il est fermé. Des bûches de chêne forment les côtés de cette construction mobile et des planches de 5 centimètres d'épaisseur font office de bardage. C'est le type de trompe-l'œil utilisé à l'occasion par le camouflage militaire, mais réalisé ici avec un certain humour. L'importance du bois, ne serait-ce que visuelle, ne peut être déniée dans cet exemple.

Les architectes belges dmvA ont mis en œuvre une vision différente de la construction mobile en bois dans leur Blob VB3 (2008–09, page 164) conçu pour XfactorAgencies. Extension d'une maison et de bureaux existants, il a été pensé pour « échapper » à une réglementation locale particulièrement stricte. Contenant un lit, une cuisine, des rangements, une salle d'eau, cette petite structure peut s'adapter assez aisément à d'autres fonctions. Doté d'une ossature en bois recouverte d'une peau de polyester, le blob ne ressemble en rien aux constructions en bois du passé et la présence du matériau est même indétectable de l'extérieur. Si le terme de « blob » a pris certaines connotations négatives aux débuts de la CAO (Conception assistée par ordinateur), l'agence dmvA ne s'en est pas formalisée et l'applique apparemment à juste titre à cette petite construction en forme d'œuf.

Concrètement One Main (Cambridge, Massachusetts, 2009, page 158), conçu par Mark Goulthorpe (dECOi), n'est pas de l'architecture, mais de l'aménagement de bureaux. Sa coque de 1000 mètres carrés est constituée de morceaux de bois découpés par une machine à commande numérique. Les choix du matériau brut (épicéa), mais aussi de cette technique sophistiquée de fabrication, sont également justifiés par leurs faibles coûts énergétiques. Le prix du bois peut varier, mais les techniques de dessin et de découpe des composants architecturaux ont réalisé des gains d'efficacité indéniables, mesurables à la fois et entre autres en termes de coûts énergétiques.

23
Emma Johansson and Timo Leiviskä,
Anttolanhovi Art and Design Villas,
Mikkeli, Finland, 2007–08

La petite maison de thé (7 mètres carrés) édifiée par A1Architects à Prague (2008, page 56) est un exemple inattendu des possibilités du bois. Les architectes parlent « d'un lieu de rencontre minimaliste » qui évoque à l'évidence la tradition des maisons de thé japonaises, ce que confirme l'intérêt porté à ce projet par le célèbre architecte japonais et grand praticien du bois, Terunobu Fujimori. Posée sur quelques pierres trouvées dans un étang voisin, la construction est en chêne, mélèze, argile, plâtre et papier. Ses dimensions et son plan sont en harmonie avec les règles de la cérémonie du thé, tout en développant un esprit de modernité occidentale qui rend ce projet transculturel d'autant plus intéressant.

Terunobu Fujimori, professeur à l'Institut des sciences industrielles de Tokyo, a conçu plusieurs structures de ce type, largement publiées par la presse spécialisée internationale, dont la maison de cèdre carbonisé (Nagano City, Nagano, Japon, 2006–07). Il en compare l'intérieur à celui d'une caverne, le lieu de nos origines, le premier « foyer » abrité de l'homme, comme Lascaux en donne un exemple que cite d'ailleurs spécifiquement Fujimori. Connu pour ses maisons de thé étranges et minuscules, il a insufflé un peu d'air frais sur la scène architecturale japonaise en réinterprétant la tradition de façon essentiellement moderne, malgré l'aspect « rustique » de ses œuvres à de nombreux égards. Une maison de thé est perchée à une extrémité de la maison de cèdre carbonisé de façon sans doute humoristique, voire légèrement comique, même si elle fait allusion aux racines de l'architecture. Fujimori est sans doute emblématique d'un certain usage du bois qui renvoie aux origines de l'histoire de l'architecture, même s'il participe clairement d'une réflexion très contemporaine. La maison de thé de Prague par A1 peut sembler un peu hors contexte dans le cadre de la République tchèque, mais représente en même temps une approche qui prolonge, en la captant, l'influence essentiellement japonaise de Fujimori.

L'ESPRIT DE LA NATURE

Un certain nombre d'organismes officiels, convaincus des vertus de la construction en bois, ont entrepris d'en assurer la promotion par le biais d'aides techniques ou financières. Un exemple de ces efforts nous est donné par le petit Pavillon Piano (147 mètres carrés) édifié à Lahti (Finlande, 2007–08, page 406) par l'agence Wingårdhs pour la Wood in Culture Association (association le bois dans la culture), fondée en 1998 pour promouvoir l'industrie forestière. Elle remet par ailleurs le prix de l'Architecture en bois Esprit de la nature (Spirit of Nature Wood Architecture Award), décerné, au début de cette décennie, à des architectes comme Peter Zumthor (2006) ou Kengo Kuma (2002). La société Finnforest a offert les matériaux de construction, et la scierie UPM de Lahti le contreplaqué spécial pour l'habillage interne, ainsi que le matériau composite de bois et de plastique ProFi pour la terrasse. Des barreaux en peuplier ont été utilisés pour la façade et le mobilier du café est en frêne. Reposant sur une plate-forme en acier posée sur l'eau, ce pavillon est un hommage à l'œuvre de Renzo Piano qui a remporté le prix Esprit de la nature en 2000. Sa toiture fièrement cambrée rappelle certains gestes du maître italien.

Comme Terunobu Fujimori et d'autres grands architectes asiatiques l'ont démontré, le bois en architecture contemporaine est une pratique très vivante qui ne se cantonne pas à de petites résidences privées. Trois projets récents de *club-houses* de golf en Corée du Sud

24
Kirsi Korhonen and Mika Penttinen,
Huvitus Terraced Housing, Helsinki,
Finland, 2007–08

24

confirment l'affinité des architectes coréens ou japonais pour ce matériau, mais aussi ses possibilités dans le cadre de projets assez importants. Shigeru Ban est sans doute le plus célèbre d'entre eux, pour avoir beaucoup construit en tubes de carton – un sous-produit du bois – mais dans le cas du *club-house* du golf Haesley Nine Bringes (Yeoju, Corée du Sud, 2009, page 88, en collaboration avec Kyeong Sik Yoon, KACI International Inc.), ce sont les hautes colonnes en forme d'arbres qui attirent le plus l'attention dans ce bâtiment de 46 mètres de large par 72 de long. S'élevant sur trois niveaux, elles donnent une impression de forêt. Les architectes ont aussi été obligés d'utiliser un socle en pierre pour respecter la réglementation coréenne qui ne permet pas de construire un bâtiment de plus de 6000 mètres carrés entièrement en bois.

L'agence de Séoul SKM a construit deux autres *club-houses* dans lesquelles le bois joue un rôle significatif. Curieusement le club de golf et Spa de Kumgang Ananti (Gangwon-do, Corée du Nord, 2008, page 314) se trouve juste au nord de la frontière séparant les deux Corées, près des monts Kumgang, et le plan directeur de ces installations met l'accent sur la préservation de l'environnement naturel. Le projet fait appel à un système constructif à poteaux et poutres et à un système d'arcs en lamellé-collé pour l'auvent extérieur et le hall d'accueil, qui donne un certain style à ce bâtiment de 13 210 mètres carrés. Toujours de SKM, le *country club* des collines du lac de Suncheon (Suncheon, JeollaNam-do, Corée du Sud, 2008, page 320) utilise lui aussi un système de poteaux et poutres en lamellé-collé sur une base en béton. L'ensemble évoque également certains traits de l'architecture coréenne traditionnelle. Ce n'est cependant en rien un pastiche de formes anciennes, ne serait-ce que par le recours à des verrières, à des façades de verre et à un bardage métallique. La référence à l'architecture ancienne de ce complexe de 16 311 mètres carrés tient surtout aux courbes de ses toitures.

24 HEURES
Des bâtiments de dimensions plus importantes, allant de centres d'informations à des hôtels ou restaurants, font de plus en plus souvent appel au bois. L'une de ces réalisations les plus étonnantes est le Wisa Wooden Design Hotel (Helsinki, 2009, page 82) qui n'est d'ailleurs pas un hôtel au sens traditionnel du terme. Cette structure de 80 mètres carrés a remporté un concours organisé en 2009. Pieta-Linda Auttila a été choisie pour concevoir « une réalisation audacieuse et iconique en pin et épicéa finlandais ». Les participants à cette compétition organisée par UPM (entreprise d'énergie, de pulpe de papier et de matériaux) n'ont eu que 24 heures pour préparer leur projet. L'architecte a voulu « faire exploser un bloc de bois » en morceaux pour combiner des espaces ouverts et fermés composés de formes géométriques ou organiques. Étant donné la nature de ce projet, il ne traduit peut-être pas vraiment les tendances de l'architecture en bois, mais montre néanmoins que celui-ci permet d'obtenir des formes inattendues qui se prêtent à des interprétations très contemporaines.

Plus « solide » et moins expérimental, le Centre d'informations des visiteurs du Grand Teton (Moose Junction, Parc national du Grand Teton, Wyoming, 2007, page 114) des architectes Bohlin, Cywinski et Jackson, présente une ossature en bois et des poutres en bois lamifié. Quand ils n'ont pu se servir du bois pour des raisons climatiques, les architectes ont opté pour un béton en conservant le grain de son coffrage de bois. De grandes parois de verre font le lien avec un cadre naturel spectaculaire dominé par les montagnes et la forêt. L'agence a

P 42

25

25
Edouard François, Club Med-Aldiana,
near Nianing, Senegal, 2010–

l'habitude de construire dans les régions forestières de l'Ouest américain et son expérience se perçoit clairement dans ce centre qui combine une modernité réelle au respect de la fonction et de l'environnement.

L'architecte José Cruz Ovalle a eu la chance rarissime de concevoir un hôtel pour l'île de Pâques (Rapa Nui Explora Hotel, Miro O'one Sector, Chili, 2005–07, page 154). L'établissement est conçu comme un archipel d'îlots reliés entre eux par des terrasses en bois. Ce concept ne manque pas d'intérêt pour l'île de Pâques quand on sait que le déclin de la civilisation à l'origine des fameuses statues est dû à la déforestation. L'hôtel Rapa Nui Explora est soigneusement intégré dans le paysage et bénéficie de vues sur l'horizon grâce à ses immenses baies vitrées. Mis à part le socle de pierre brute, le bois est omniprésent dans cette construction. Un peu plus ancien, le chai Perez Cruz (Paine, Chili, 2001–02, page 146) réalisé par la même agence fait un usage spectaculaire du bois dans ce vaste bâtiment de 5433 mètres carrés. Il est intéressant de noter que le bois a été choisi, cette fois, pour offrir des conditions de température idéale à la vinification.

UN PARAPLUIE ET UN TRONC D'ARBRE
L'architecte français Édouard François est connu pour ses projets d'inspiration écologique. Son Club Med-Aldiana (Nianing, Sénégal, 2010–, page 202) est un audacieux complexe hôtelier de 100 000 mètres carrés qui regroupe 250 chambres et suites, des restaurants et des installations sportives. Édouard François fait largement référence aux traditions locales, comme les masques africains, et utilise abondamment le bois, y compris dans le restaurant en forme de « parapluie à l'envers ». Il se situe personnellement assez à l'écart des courants d'une conception architecturale qu'il considère comme « ordinaire », et n'hésite pas à secouer les idées reçues comme il le montre dans ce projet. Le bois, par sa souplesse d'utilisation, s'adapte bien aux projets écologiques et aux solutions surprenantes.

Le restaurant Tusen (Ramundberget, Suède, 2007–08, page 324) de Murman Arkitekter est une construction de 340 mètres carrés qui se veut en état permanent « d'harmonie avec la nature ». Les architectes ont utilisé des troncs de bouleau entier pour structurer et protéger à la fois la façade. Ces arbres sont les seuls à pousser à cette altitude et peuvent aisément être remplacés en cas de besoin. « En optant pour une construction en bois, expliquent les architectes, nous avons pu réduire le poids. Ce bâtiment préfabriqué à faible impact sur le sol a pu être monté en un temps minimum. » La légèreté est en effet souvent un facteur de choix important dans la préférence donnée au bois, comme on l'observe historiquement au cours des siècles dans les régions sismiques du Japon, par exemple. Le restaurant Tusen est une structure durable équipée de pompes à chaleur et de son propre système de traitement des eaux usées. Aujourd'hui, il est pratiquement acquis qu'une nouvelle construction en bois apporte des avantages écologiques qui vont plus loin que le simple choix du matériau.

ALLEMAND ET VERT
Le bois est utilisé dans pratiquement tous les types constructifs comme le montrent divers exemples publiés dans cet ouvrage. L'architecte allemand Jörg Aldinger s'en sert de façon très visible dans sa cafétéria et crèche de l'école Waldorf (Stuttgart, Allemagne, 2005–07,

26
*Auer+Weber+Assoziierte,
Central Facilities, Martinsried
Campus, Ludwig-Maximilians
University, Munich, Germany,
2004–09*

page 62), dont la structure à trois niveaux est en réalité en béton armé. Paré de mélèze, doté de châssis de fenêtres, de mobilier en bois et d'un toit végétalisé, ce projet illustre une autre tendance importante de l'architecture contemporaine : le bois en tant que matériau secondaire ou parement. Cette méthode se répand en particulier sur les façades pour lesquelles on a longtemps préféré jusqu'à récemment le béton ou le métal. Autres architectes allemands, Auer+Weber+Assoziierte ont conçu une façade en treillis de mélèze pour le bâtiment central du campus de Martinsried de l'université Ludwig-Maximilian (Munich, 2004–09, page 78). Comme pour l'école Waldorf, le bois n'est pas ici le matériau structurel principal, même si le mélèze joue un rôle essentiel dans ce projet. Le Centre de séminaires de Gut Siggen (Siggen, Allemagne, 2006–07, page 72) des mêmes architectes utilise des volets mobiles de mélèze, des plafonds en bois et des sols en chêne pour renforcer sa connexion avec la nature, très perceptible dans les photographies. S'appuyant sur ce qui pourrait bien être une tendance allemande, les architectes Kauffmann Theilig & Partner utilisent beaucoup le bois apparent dans leur restaurant d'entreprise de Boehringer Ingelheim (Biberach an der Riss, Allemagne, 2003–04, page 258). Ces installations de 3000 mètres carrés édifiées pour un laboratoire pharmaceutique possèdent une « structure spatiale en plaques pliées » habillée de bois. Ces éléments qui forment le plafond du restaurant se projettent vers l'extérieur comme d'énormes échardes de bois.

TRAVAILLER DANS LE BOIS

Deux réalisations récentes de l'architecte finlandais Seppo Häkli (né en 1951) offrent la démonstration de l'utilité et de la pertinence du bois dans le contexte d'un environnement de travail. Le bâtiment du Centre de conservation de Seurasaari (Helsinki, Finlande, 2007–09, page 16) construit pour l'Office national des antiquités fait partie du musée de plein air de Seurasaari. Cette construction à colonnes en bois contient un atelier de travail consacré à ce matériau. Les poutres en bois lamifié ou un bardage en lattes de pin goudronnées ont été mis en œuvre selon les principes de la construction en bois locale, même si le projet reste d'esprit moderne et par-dessus tout efficace. Le bâtiment de bureaux et de laboratoires du Metla (Haapastensyrjä, Finlande, 2007–08, page 216), du même architecte, est une construction de 550 mètres carrés inspirée de l'architecture des fermes finnoises. Il contient des laboratoires et des locaux techniques à murs en épicéa et bureaux en bois d'aulne. Au total douze bois différents ont été utilisés dans ce projet qui voulait également montrer le savoir-faire finlandais dans ce type de construction. Pour le Metla, SARC Architects a également conçu un centre de recherche sur le bois dans la construction et d'autres domaines le centre de l'Institut finlandais de recherche forestière (Joensuu, Finlande, 2004, page 368). D'une surface de 7400 mètres carrés, il est beaucoup plus important que les précédents. Le bois y est omniprésent, du système de poteaux et poutres au bardage extérieur, et des pins ont même été plantés dans la cour. La Finlande est peut-être le pays qui attache le plus de valeur aux traditions et à l'innovation de l'architecture en bois, ce qui ne manque pas de favoriser ses architectes à une période où ce matériau retrouve une faveur nouvelle partout dans le monde.

La Suisse possède également une longue tradition de la construction en bois, en particulier dans ses régions de montagne. Bien que des incendies aient fait disparaître des villes et des villages entièrement édifiés en bois, de nombreuses traces de cette tradition subsistent

27

dans des régions comme la vallée de l'Engadine près de Saint-Moritz et les Grisons. Un des architectes qui relève cette tradition, tout en la modernisant considérablement, est Valerio Olgiati, né à Chur, en 1958. Sa maison familiale se trouve dans la petite ville de Flims, où il a également installé son agence. En 2007, il a entrepris la construction d'un nouveau petit immeuble de bureaux à la place d'une ancienne grange (page 336) dans le quartier du Dado. Le bâtiment en bois sombre repose sur des piliers de béton et conserve les contours des granges locales. Dans ce projet comme dans d'autres, Olgiati utilise ainsi une forme constructive ancienne tout en modifiant sa fonction, ce qui permet aux villages dans lesquels il intervient de conserver leur style, tout en participant pleinement aux activités contemporaines. Ailleurs, Valerio Olgiati a opté pour un style entièrement contemporain, souvent surprenant, tout en ayant encore parfois recours au bois pour matériau principal.

DU BAR AU PARASOL

Dans un contexte entièrement différent, Niall McLaughlin a conçu le café-bar sur Deal Pier (Deal, Kent, G.-B., page 298). Construite à la fin des années 1950, la jetée de Deal est un peu décatie, et, pour son aménagement, l'architecte a cherché un matériau qui « se patine et s'améliore avec le temps ». Il a retenu l'iroko lamifié pour les châssis des vastes baies qui offrent une vue illimitée sur la mer. Si les jetées en bois ont longtemps existé, il est intéressant de noter que le bois a précisément été choisi pour sa capacité à se patiner avec style face aux éléments. Si l'on peut présumer que le béton vieillit mieux que le bois, c'est ici l'âge du béton qui a inspiré le choix de l'architecte.

Bien que les matériaux comme l'acier ont longtemps été préférés dans la construction des ponts, l'architecte Enrique Browne a choisi le bois lamifié pour son élégante petite passerelle piétonnière de Zapallar (Chili, 2008, page 126). L'image du bateau a servi ici de référence à l'architecte qui a opté par ailleurs pour des garde-corps métalliques et un éclairage par DEL. Le bois se prête à des traitements qui demandent des moyens moins élaborés que l'acier et d'autres matériaux modernes. Si les exemples publiés dans cet ouvrage atteignent à l'occasion des dimensions substantielles, il est clair que le bois reste peut-être mieux adapté à des projets de taille relativement réduite pour lesquels le coût joue un rôle important.

Mais, pour prouver que le contraire reste tout aussi possible, un autre projet, pas entièrement achevé, devrait atteindre une surface de 12 670 mètres carrés pour un budget de 51 millions d'euros. Cette œuvre de l'architecte allemand Jürgen Mayer H., le parasol métropolitain (Metropol Parasol, Séville, 2005–11, page 18), fait partie du projet de rénovation de la place de l'Incarnation. Qualifié de « nouveau monument iconique » de la ville, cette structure couvrante protégera du soleil des bars, des restaurants et divers espaces publics. Ces énormes parasols sont en bois recouvert d'un film de polyuréthane, une preuve supplémentaire que des formes très contemporaines peuvent être réalisées à partir du bois, y compris à très grande échelle.

LES NOUVEAUX ATOURS DU BOIS

La sélection d'une soixantaine de constructions récentes partiellement ou entièrement édifiées en bois ne suffit peut-être pas à donner une idée réelle de ce qui se passe exactement dans le monde, mais il est clair que le bois est devenu un matériau contemporain, y compris dans ses utilisations les plus novatrices et son appui sur les technologies les plus avancées. Si l'utilisation des bois rares reste un tabou, les systèmes de certification des bois tirés de forêts gérées selon les principes du développement durable se répandent rapidement et en ont fait l'un des matériaux de construction les plus « verts » qui soit, à condition d'être correctement employé. Si l'on observe parfois une ossature de bois protégée par de l'acier Corten ou de l'aluminium, le bois résiste à la plupart des environnements climatiques aussi longtemps que des matériaux plus « modernes », et prend avec l'âge une patine certainement plus séduisante que celle d'un mur en béton érodé. Revêtu d'une peau de polyuréthane comme dans le projet sévillan de Jürgen Mayer H., il sait trouver de nouveaux atours qui lui conviennent apparemment bien. Certains projets publiés ici font appel à des bois de récupération, ce qui accroît l'intérêt écologique de la structure, si ce n'est sa durée de vie. En tout état de cause, la démolition d'une construction en bois devrait entraîner moins de conséquences environnementales fâcheuses que, par exemple, celle d'immeubles en acier encore bardés d'amiante. Le bois semble vraiment être le matériau idéal pour un futur économiquement incertain, dans lequel la protection de l'environnement est devenue un facteur important que chacun doit prendre en considération. Le bois est aussi « vert » qu'un matériau de construction peut l'être dans la mesure où il est exploité et mis en œuvre de manière responsable. Il vieillit lorsqu'il n'est pas protégé, ce qui est, après tout, le cas de n'importe quel matériau. Il peut se révéler étonnamment moderne entre les mains d'un architecte quand celui-ci le désire. En bref, le bois est un matériau pour l'architecture d'aujourd'hui.

Philip Jodidio, Grimentz, Suisse, 15 mai 2010

[1] http://www.fsc.org/about-fsc.html, consulté le 15 mai 2010.
[2] Billie Holiday, chanson « Come rain or come shine », 1954.

70F

70F
Stamerbos 34
1358 EP Almere
The Netherlands

Tel: +31 36 540 29 00
Fax: +31 36 540 70 20
E-mail: info@70F.com
Web: www.70F.com

Bas ten Brinke was born in Amsterdam, the Netherlands, in 1972 and received his degree in Architecture at the Technical University in Eindhoven in 1995. Carina Nilsson was born in Lund, Sweden, in 1970 and received her degree in Architecture at Chalmers Technical University, Gothenburg, in 1998. Before that she studied sculpture, drawing, and jewelery making at Lawrence University in the United States. The pair worked in several different offices in the Netherlands before founding **70F** in 2000. Their current work includes several villas in the Netherlands; a group of 25 holiday homes in southern Sweden; a Sheep Stable (Almere, 2007, published here); a Petting Farm (Almere, 2008, also published here); the EBG Church in Amsterdam (2007–); and a luxury spa with five holiday homes, a villa, and a sheep stable in central Italy (Aquilonia, Avellino, 2010–).

Bas ten Brinke wurde 1972 in Amsterdam geboren und erhielt 1995 sein Diplom in Architektur an der Technischen Universität Eindhoven. Carina Nilson wurde 1970 in Lund, Schweden, geboren und machte 1998 ihr Diplom in Architektur an der Technischen Hochschule Chalmers in Göteborg. Davor hatte sie Bildhauerei, Zeichnen und Goldschmieden an der Lawrence University in den USA studiert. Bevor das Paar 2000 sein eigenes Büro **70F** gründete, arbeitete es bei verschiedenen Architekten in den Niederlanden. Zu den aktuellen Arbeiten von 70F zählen mehrere Villen in den Niederlanden, eine Gruppe von 25 Ferienhäusern in Südschweden, ein Schafstall (Almere, 2007, hier veröffentlicht), ein Kinderbauernhof (Almere, 2008, ebenfalls hier veröffentlicht), die Kirche der Herrnhuter Brüdergemeine in Amsterdam (2007–) und eine luxuriöse Wellnessanlage mit fünf Ferienhäusern, einer Villa und einem Schafstall in Mittelitalien (Aquilonia, Avellino, 2010–).

Bas ten Brinke, né à Amsterdam en 1972, est diplômé en architecture de l'Université polytechnique d'Eindhoven (1995). Carina Nilsson, née à Lund (Suède) en 1970, est diplômée en architecture de l'Université polytechnique de Göteborg (1998). Elle avait précédemment étudié la sculpture, le dessin et la joaillerie à la Lawrence University aux États-Unis. Le couple a travaillé dans différentes agences néerlandaises avant de fonder **70F** en 2000. Parmi leurs travaux récents : plusieurs villas aux Pays-Bas ; un ensemble de 25 résidences de vacances en Suède méridionale ; une bergerie (Almere, 2007, publiée ici) ; un mini-zoo (Almere, 2008, également publié ici) ; l'église EBG à Amsterdam (2007–) et un spa de luxe accompagné de cinq résidences de vacances, une villa et une bergerie dans le centre de l'Italie (Aquilonia, Avellino, 2010–).

SHEEP STABLE

Almere, The Netherlands, 2007

Address: Muiderweg, Almere, The Netherlands
Area: 400 m² (gross). Client: City of Almere. Cost: € 300 000

The Sheep Stable demonstrates clearly that neither the use of wood nor a farming function mean that a building cannot be thoroughly modern in appearance.

Der Schafstall ist ein Beweis dafür, dass auch bei Verwendung von Holz und landwirtschaftlicher Nutzung ein durchaus modernes Erscheinungsbild erreicht werden kann.

Cette bergerie montre que ni l'utilisation du bois, ni la fonction agricole n'empêchent un bâtiment d'avoir un aspect résolument moderne.

The city of Almere grazes approximately 80 sheep to keep weeds under control in forest areas and parks. A low area of the stable houses the animals, while a higher section allows for the storage of hay. This configuration was also designed to allow for natural airflow through the structure. Built in pine with western red cedar cladding, the **SHEEP STABLE** employs only some curved girders made of steel selected to "emphasize the tubelike shape of the building," which is open to the public. Three openings allow daylight to enter the building. Beech plywood cladding is used on vertical interior walls. A small office and a room for the shepherd are located at one end of the building on an upper floor. The stable also provides lambs as needed by the local Muslim community for ritual purposes.

Die Stadt Almere hält etwa 80 Schafe, die das Unkraut in Waldgebieten und Parks unter Kontrolle halten sollen. Im unteren Bereich des Stallgebäudes sind die Tiere untergebracht, im oberen wird das Heu gelagert. Diese Anordnung wurde auch vorgesehen, um eine natürliche Durchlüftung des Gebäudes zu gewährleisten. Für den aus Kiefernholz errichteten **SCHAFSTALL** mit einer Verkleidung aus amerikanischer Rotzeder wurden nur wenige gekrümmte Stahlträger verwendet, „um die röhren-förmige Gestalt des Gebäudes zu betonen", das der Öffentlichkeit zugänglich ist. Durch drei Öffnungen fällt Tageslicht ein. Die vertikalen Innenwände sind mit Birkenfur-nier verkleidet. Im Obergeschoss liegen an einem Ende des Gebäudes ein kleines Büro und ein Raum für den Schäfer. Der Stall liefert auch zu rituellen Anlässen Lämmer für die örtliche muslimische Gemeinde.

La ville d'Almere entretient un troupeau d'environ 80 brebis qui broutent les mauvaises herbes dans les parcs et les zones boisées. La partie basse de la **BERGERIE**, ouverte au public, est affectée aux animaux, tandis que la partie supérieure est réservée au foin. Cette configuration facilite la circulation de l'air naturel à travers le bâtiment. L'ossature en pin et à parement de cèdre rouge ne présente que quelques poutres d'acier cintrées qui « font ressortir l'aspect tubulaire du bâtiment. Trois ouvertures laissent pénétrer la lumière naturelle. Les parois intérieures sont doublées d'un bardage en contreplaqué de hêtre. Un petit bureau et une pièce pour le berger ont été aménagés en partie supérieure à une extrémité du bâtiment. La bergerie fournit également des agneaux attendus par la communauté musulmane pour ses rites religieux.

The smooth profile of the building with its rounded lines is unexpected in a farming context, but the operation of the structure does not suffer for aesthetic reasons.

Das glatte Profil des Gebäudes mit seinen runden Umrissen erstaunt im landwirtschaftlichen Kontext; seine Funktion wird jedoch durch die Ästhe-tik nicht beeinträchtigt.

Le profil de ce bâtiment aux lignes lisses et arrondies surprend dans ce contexte agricole, mais son fonction-nement ne souffre en rien de ce parti pris esthétique.

Below, a plan shows that the building is fully rectangular. Above, an interior view showing the wooden ribbing and relatively low, natural light levels.

Unten: Im Grundriss wird die absolut rechteckige Form des Gebäudes deutlich. Oben: Die Innenansicht zeigt die hölzernen Rippen und die relativ schwache natürliche Belichtung.

Ci-dessous, le plan rigoureusement rectangulaire du bâtiment. Au-dessus, une vue intérieure montre le nervurage en bois et le niveau relativement faible de l'éclairage naturel.

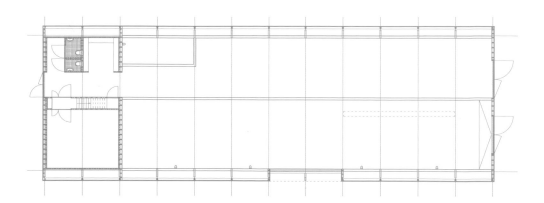

PETTING FARM

Almere, The Netherlands, 2008

Address: Den Uylpark, Almere, The Netherlands
Area: 114 m². Client: Municipality of Almere. Cost: € 180 000

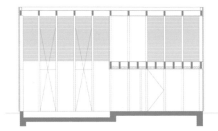 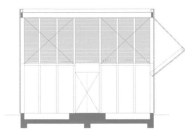 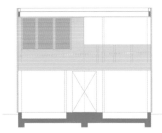

Like the Sheep Stable, the Petting Farm gives an impression of having almost blank, wooden façades, but in this case, large doors fold up, revealing the interior.

Ebenso wie der Schafstall zeigt auch der Kinderbauernhof fast geschlossene Holzfassaden. In diesem Fall können jedoch große Türen aufgeklappt werden, um den Blick ins Innere freizugeben.

Comme la bergerie, le mini-zoo donne l'impression de se cacher derrière des façades de bois presque aveugles, mais ici de grandes portes se soulèvent pour donner accès à l'intérieur.

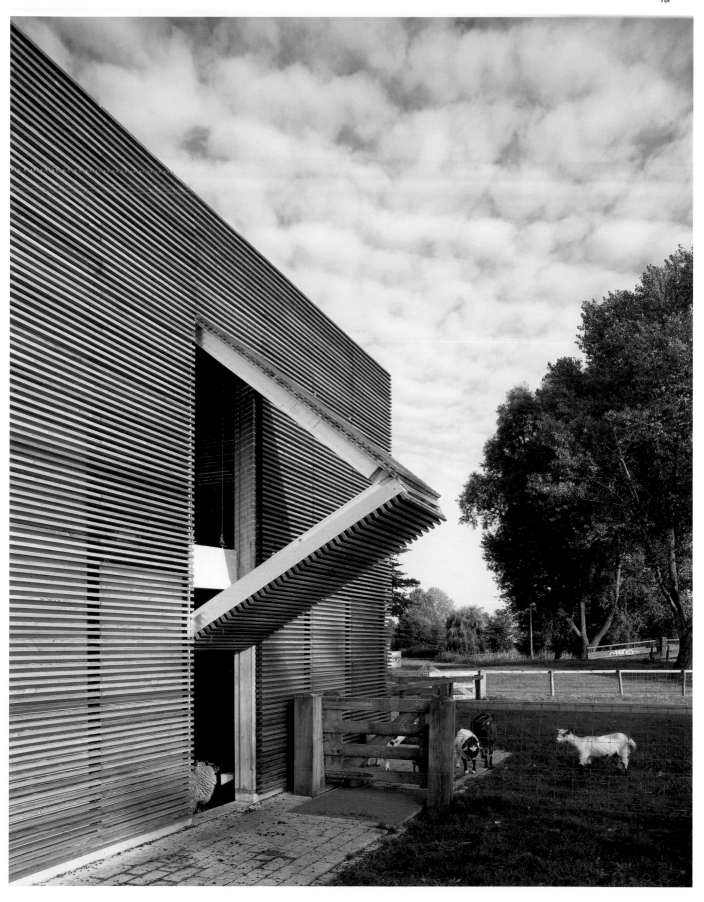

The architects were approached in 2005 to design a **PETTING FARM** structure on the site of an earlier building that had been destroyed by fire in the early 1980s. Built entirely using money from sponsors, the building makes use of the preexisting foundations. The architects state: "We designed a wooden box with an open façade system for the upper half of the building, allowing the wind to ventilate the whole farm continuously." The stable occupies half the building, with offices, storage space, and toilets making up the rest of the project. With no doors but six shutters, two for the public and four for the animals, the shutters can be opened automatically or manually in the morning and are closed at night. The animals are visible on both sides as the public passes through the middle of the building. With its slat structure, the Petting Farm glows from within at night. The architects conclude: "One could say that the box, a building extensively reduced in aesthetic violence, wakes up and goes to sleep every day."

Die Architekten wurden 2005 beauftragt, ein Gebäude für den **KINDERBAUERNHOF** auf dem Gelände eines Anfang der 1980er-Jahre abgebrannten Altbaus zu planen. Für das ausschließlich mit Spendengeldern errichtete Bauwerk wurden die vorhandenen Fundamente genutzt. Die Architekten erklären: „Wir planten eine hölzerne Kiste mit einem offenen Fassadensystem für die obere Hälfte des Gebäudes, damit der Wind ständig den ganzen Bauernhof durchlüften kann." Der Stall nimmt die Hälfte des Bauwerks ein, in dem anderen Teil befinden sich Büros, Lagerraum und Toiletten. Der Bau hat keine Türen, sondern nur sechs Klappläden, zwei für Besucher und vier für die Tiere. Sie können morgens automatisch oder manuell geöffnet und nachts geschlossen werden. Besucher werden mittig durch das Gebäude geführt, die Tiere sind an beiden Seiten untergebracht. Bei Nacht dringt das Licht durch die Lattenkonstruktion nach außen und lässt das Gebäude leuchten. Abschließend erklären die Architekten: „Man kann sagen, dass diese in ihrer ästhetischen Wirkung extrem reduzierte Kiste jeden Tag aufwacht und schlafen geht."

C'est en 2005 que les architectes avaient été consultés pour la création de ce **MINI-ZOO** pour animaux domestiques sur le site d'un bâtiment détruit par un incendie au début des années 1980. Entièrement financée par des sponsors, la construction repose sur les fondations préexistantes. « Nous avons conçu cette boîte en bois à système de façade ouvrante en partie supérieure, ce qui permet au vent de le ventiler en permanence, » expliquent les architectes. L'étable proprement dite occupe la moitié de l'installation, des bureaux, un espace de stockage et des toilettes se partagent le reste. Pas de portes mais six volets, deux pour le public et quatre pour les animaux, qui s'ouvrent automatiquement ou manuellement le matin et sont refermés le soir. Les animaux sont visibles des deux côtés d'un passage central emprunté par le public. Habillée de lattes de bois, la ferme semble illuminée de l'intérieur pendant la nuit. « On pourrait dire que cette boîte, bâtiment largement dénué de toute agressivité esthétique, se réveille le matin et s'endort le soir, chaque jour », concluent les architectes.

Night views with light coming through the wooden slats show that the building is more open than it appears during the day.

Die Nachtansichten, bei denen das Licht durch die Holzlatten scheint, zeigen, dass das Gebäude offener ist, als es am Tage wirkt.

Vue nocturne. L'éclairage qui diffuse à travers les lattes de bois rend ce bâtiment plus ouvert que pendant le jour.

Simple hanging lamps and a generous
disposition of openings between the
slats allow air and light to circulate
through the structure.

Einfache Hängeleuchten und großzügig angeordnete Öffnungen zwischen
den Latten lassen Licht und Luft in
das Gebäude ein.

De simples suspensions et la généreuse implantation des ouvertures
protégées par les lattis permettent à
l'air et à la lumière de circuler dans
tout le bâtiment.

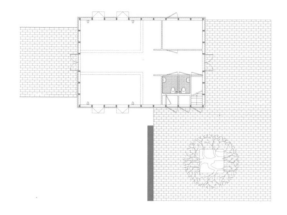

The building glows brightly from
the inside at night when seen from
certain angles.

Bei Nacht strahlt das Gebäude,
wenn man es von der richtigen
Seite betrachtet.

La nuit, vu sous certains angles,
le bâtiment semble illuminé de
l'intérieur.

A1ARCHITECTS

A1Architects
Dobrovského 8
Prague 7
Czech Republic

Tel: +420 775 90 32 77
E-mail: info@a1architects.cz
Web: www.a1architects.cz

David Maštálka was born in 1978 in Hradec Králové, in former Czechoslovakia. He studied at the Faculty of Architecture (CTU, Prague, 1996–2000), as well as in the architecture studio AAAD (Academy of Arts, Architecture and Design, Prague, 2001–08). He cofounded **A1ARCHITECTS** in 2005 with Lenka Křemenová (born in 1982), a partner and classmate from the AAAD. The graphic designer Marta Maštálková (born in 1984) joined the firm in 2006. David Maštálka also cofounded Versus Architekt in 2007. Current and recent work of A1 includes the House on the Marsh, a timber weekend house (in design); the Teahouse (2008, published here); interiors for the Botas Concept Store (2009); D. Vision Dental Clinic (2009); the Plum Orchard House, a timber structure (2010–); and the Garden Hat Teahouse (2010–), all in the Czech Republic.

David Maštálka wurde 1978 in Hradec Králové in der früheren Tschechoslowakei geboren. Er studierte an der Architekturfakultät der Tschechischen Technischen Universität Prag (CTU, 1996–2000) sowie an der Architekturabteilung der Akademie für Kunst, Architektur und Design in Prag (VŠUP, 2001–08). Mit Lenka Křemenová, seiner Partnerin und Studienkollegin von der VŠUP (geboren 1982), gründete er 2005 das Büro **A1ARCHITECTS**. 2006 trat die Grafikerin Marta Maštálková (geboren 1984) in die Firma ein. David Maštálka war 2007 auch Mitbegründer des Büros Versus Architekt. Zu den aktuellen und neueren Arbeiten von A1 gehören das Haus auf der Marsch, ein hölzernes Wochenendhaus (in Planung), das Teehaus (2008, hier veröffentlicht), die Innenräume des Botas Concept Store (2009), die Zahnklinik D. Vision (2009), das Pflaumengartenhaus, eine Holzkonstruktion (2010–), und das Gartenhut-Teehaus (2010–), alle in der Tschechischen Republik.

David Maštálka, né en 1978 à Hradec Králové (ex-Tchécoslovaquie) a étudié à la faculté d'architecture de la CTU à Prague (1996–2000) et à l'atelier d'architecture AAAD (Académie d'art, d'architecture et de design, Prague, 2001–08). Il a fondé **A1ARCHITECTS** en 2005 avec Lenka Křemenová (née en 1982), sa condisciple à l'AAAD. La graphiste Marta Maštálková (née en 1984) a rejoint l'agence en 2006. David Maštálka a également fondé Versus Architekt en 2007. Parmi les travaux récents et actuels d'A1, tous en République tchèque : la maison du marais, résidence de week-end en bois (en cours de conception) ; la maison de thé (2008, publiée ici) ; l'aménagement intérieur du magasin-concept Botas (2009) ; la clinique dentaire D. Vision (2009) ; la maison des pruniers (maison en bois, 2010–) et la maison de thé-chapeau (2010–).

TEAHOUSE

Prague, Czech Republic, 2008

Address: not disclosed
Area: 7 m². Client: not disclosed. Cost: not disclosed. Collaboration: Vojtech Bilisic (Carpenter)

Despite its decidedly Japanese interior appearance, the teahouse has a structure that also links it to a more Western, contemporary architecture.

Trotz seines zweifellos japanischen Erscheinungsbilds ist das Teehaus ein Bauwerk, das eher der westlichen, zeitgenössischen Architektur zuzuordnen ist.

Malgré son aspect résolument japonais, la maison de thé possède une structure qui la relie conceptuellement à une architecture contemporaine plus occidentale.

P 60

Built in 35 days in April and May 2008, this structure is called "a minimal place to gather" by its architect. It is made of oak and charred larch, clay, plaster, and paper and contains a black, welded, steel hearth. David Maštálka specifically acknowledges the influence of the noted Japanese architect and professor, Terunobu Fujimori, who visited the project during construction. "When first reasoning about such a place," says Maštálka, "I thought of the places that had made an impression upon me and came to the decision of building it on a circular platform enclosed by a translucent dome breathing the inner peace of small sacred buildings." Beyond the Japanese tradition of the tea ceremony, the architect thinks of this structure as a place for people to gather in unexpected circumstances. The wooden structure sits on stones gathered from a nearby pond.

Dieses im April/Mai 2008 in 35 Tagen errichtete Gebäude wird von seinem Architekten als „kleiner Ort zum Zusammenkommen" bezeichnet. Es wurde aus Eiche und gebrannter Lärche, Lehm, Putz und Papier erbaut und enthält einen geschmiedeten, schwarzen Herd aus Stahl. David Maštálka betont ausdrücklich den Einfluss des bekannten japanischen Architekten und Hochschullehrers Terunobu Fujimori, der das Projekt während der Bauphase besichtigte. „Bei meinen ersten Überlegungen über einen solchen Ort", sagt Maštálka, „fielen mir andere Bauten ein, die mich beeindruckt hatten, und ich beschloss, das Haus auf einer kreisförmigen Plattform zu errichten und mit einer lichtdurchlässigen Kuppel zu versehen, die den inneren Frieden kleiner Sakralbauten vermittelt." Der Architekt dachte bei diesem Gebäude wohl an die japanische Teezeremonie, wollte aber auch einen Ort schaffen, an dem Menschen unter besonderen Umständen zusammenkommen können. Die Holzkonstruktion steht auf Steinen, die aus einem nahe gelegenen Teich stammen.

Construite en 35 jours entre avril et mai 2008, cette petite construction en bois qui repose sur un socle de pierres trouvées dans un étang voisin est qualifiée de « lieu de rencontre minimaliste » par son architecte. Elle est en chêne et mélèze carbonisé, argile, plâtre et papier sans oublier un âtre en acier soudé noirci. David Maštálka reconnaît l'influence spécifique du célèbre architecte et professeur japonais Terunobu Fujimori qui a d'ailleurs visité le chantier en cours. « Lorsque j'ai commencé à réfléchir à un lieu de ce type, explique l'architecte, j'ai pensé à différents endroits qui m'avaient impressionné et je suis arrivé à la décision de construire une plate-forme circulaire protégée par une coupole translucide qui respire la paix des petits bâtiments religieux. » Au-delà de la tradition japonaise de la cérémonie du thé, Maštálka pense que cette petite structure pourrait servir de lieu de réunion dans des circonstances particulières.

Lifted off the ground on wooden pillars, the building seems to be a curious hybrid, linked to old traditions of the East and still modern.

Das auf Holzstützen vom Boden abgehobene Gebäude wirkt seltsam hybrid, östlichen Traditionen verbunden und dennoch modern.

Surélevée sur des piliers de bois, la construction fait penser à un curieux hybride, lié à d'anciennes traditions orientales mais néanmoins moderne.

Teahouses in Japan are rarely of circular form, nor are translucent domes a likely feature, thus the architects are renewing the genre in some sense.

Teehäuser in Japan sind selten rund und haben normalerweise auch keine durchsichtigen Kuppeln; so haben die Architekten diesen Bautyp in gewisser Weise erneuert.

Les maisons de thé japonaises sont rarement circulaires et ne possèdent pas de coupoles translucides, mais les architectes ont en quelque sorte renouvelé le genre.

*Cafeteria and Day Care Center,
Waldorf School ►*

ALDINGER ARCHITEKTEN

*aldingerarchitekten
Große Falterstr. 23a
70597 Stuttgart
Germany*

*Tel: +49 711 97 67 80
Fax: +49 711 97 678 33
E-mail: info@aldingerarchitekten.de
Web: www.aldingerarchitekten.de*

JÖRG ALDINGER was born in Stuttgart, Germany, in 1955. He completed his architectural studies at the University of Stuttgart (1975–80) and worked as a free-lance architect, creating Aldinger & Aldinger in 1983, as a professor of Building Physics and Design at the Biberach University of Applied Sciences (1994), and as a visiting professor at California State Polytechnic University (Los Angeles, 1999) before founding Aldinger Architekten in 2009. **DIRK HERKER** was born in 1964 in Bremen, Germany. He studied architecture at the University of Stuttgart (1984–87), and then at Arizona State University (Phoenix, 1987–88). He returned to the University of Stuttgart (1988–91) for further studies and became a partner at Aldinger Architekten in 2009. **THOMAS STRÄHLE** was born in 1966 in Nellingen, Germany, and studied at the Biberach University of Applied Sciences (since 1994). Like Dirk Herker he worked with the earlier firm Aldinger & Aldinger before becoming a partner of Aldinger Architekten in 2009. In addition to the Cafeteria and Day Care Center, Waldorf School (Stuttgart, 2005–07, published here), current work of the firm includes the reconstruction and creation of an annex for an administrative and retail building in Bietigheim-Bissingen (2009–11); the restoration of castles in Meersburg (2010–11) and Schwetzingen (2009–12); and a school in Bad Aibling (2009–13), all in Germany.

JÖRG ALDINGER wurde 1955 in Stuttgart geboren. Nach Beendigung seines Architekturstudiums an der Universität Stuttgart (1975–80) arbeitete er als frei-schaffender Architekt und gründete 1983 das Büro Aldinger & Aldinger; er war Professor für Bauphysik und Entwerfen an der Hochschule Biberach (1994) und Gastprofessor an der California State Polytechnic University (Los Angeles, 1999). 2009 gründete er die Firma Aldinger Architekten. **DIRK HERKER** wurde 1964 in Bremen geboren. Er studierte Architektur an der Universität Stuttgart (1984–87) und danach an der Arizona State University (Phoenix, 1987–88). Dann kehrte er zu weiterem Studium an die Universität Stuttgart zurück (1988–91) und wurde 2009 Partner bei Aldinger Architekten. **THOMAS STRÄHLE** wurde 1966 in Nellingen geboren und studierte (ab 1994) an der Hochschule Biberach. Ebenso wie Dirk Herker arbeitete er im früheren Büro Aldinger & Aldinger, bevor er 2009 Partner bei Aldinger Architekten wurde. Außer der Cafeteria und der Tagesstätte der Waldorfschule (Stuttgart, 2005–07, hier veröffentlicht) umfasst das aktuelle Werk des Büros u. a. den Umbau und die Erweiterung eines Verwaltungs- und Geschäftshauses in Bietigheim-Bissingen (2009–11), die Restaurierung von Schlössern in Meersburg (2010–11) und Schwetzingen (2009–12) sowie eine Schule in Bad Aibling (2009–13), alle in Deutschland.

JÖRG ALDINGER, né à Stuttgart (Allemagne) en 1955, a étudié l'architecture à l'université de Stuttgart (1975–80) et travaillé en free-lance avant de créer l'agence Aldinger & Aldinger en 1983. Il a été professeur de conception et de physique de la construction à l'Université des sciences appliquées de Biberach (1994), professeur invité à la California State Polytechnic University (Los Angeles, 1999) et a fondé Aldinger Architekten en 2009. **DIRK HERKER**, né en 1964 à Brême (Allemagne), a étudié l'architecture à l'université de Stuttgart (1984–87) et à l'Arizona State University (Phoenix, 1987–88). Il est revenu compléter ses études à l'université de Stuttgart (1988–91) avant de devenir partenaire d'Aldinger Architekten en 2009. **THOMAS STRÄHLE**, né en 1966 à Nellingen (Allemagne), a commencé ses études à l'Université des sciences appliquées de Biberach en 1994. Comme Dirk Herker, il a travaillé pour Aldinger & Aldinger avant de devenir partenaire d'Aldinger Architekten en 2009. En dehors de la cafétéria et de la garderie de l'école Waldorf (Stuttgart, 2005–07, publiée ici), l'agence a réalisé le projet de reconstruction-création d'une annexe pour un immeuble de bureaux et de commerces à Bietigheim-Bissingen (2009–11) ; la restauration de châteaux à Meersburg (2010–11) et Schwetzingen (2009–12) ainsi que la construction d'une école à Bad Aibling (2009–13), tous en Allemagne.

CAFETERIA AND DAY CARE CENTER, WALDORF SCHOOL

Stuttgart, Germany, 2005–07

Address: Haussmannstr. 44, 70188 Stuttgart, Germany, +49 711 21 00 20, www.uhlandshoehe.de
Area: 1200 m². Client: Waldorf School Uhlandshoehe Association. Cost: €3.4 million
Collaboration: Maren Pettenpohl

The architects have used a "villa-typology" to better integrate this **ADDITION TO THE CAMPUS OF THE WALDORF SCHOOL** "Uhlandshöhe" into its neighborhood. An existing playground has been redefined to provide the main access to the structure that provides after-school care and houses a cafeteria, kitchen, high-school library, and a multipurpose room. A central staircase and an elevator also lead up to the top floor which includes a meeting area and access to a roof terrace. Although this is a three-story, reinforced-concrete building, it is clad in larch, has wood window frames, and a green roof. Inside built-in wooden furniture and colored, glazed concrete surfaces create a warm atmosphere.

Die Architekten verwendeten eine „Villentypologie", um diese **ERWEITERUNG DER WALDORFSCHULE** auf der Stuttgarter Uhlandshöhe besser in ihre Umgebung zu integrieren. Ein vorhandener Spielplatz wurde umgeplant zur Haupterschließung des Gebäudes, das zur Betreuung der Schüler nach dem Unterricht dient und eine Cafeteria, eine Küche, die Schulbibliothek und einen Mehrzweckraum enthält. Eine zentral angeordnete Treppe und ein Fahrstuhl führen bis ins oberste Geschoss, auf dem sich ein Versammlungssaal befindet und der Zugang zu einer Dachterrasse. Obgleich es sich hier um einen dreigeschossigen Betonbau handelt, wurde er mit Lärchenholz verkleidet und hat Fensterrahmen aus Holz sowie ein begrüntes Dach. Innen sorgen das hölzerne Mobiliar und die farbigen, lasierten Betonwände für eine warme Atmosphäre.

Les architectes ont opté pour une « typologie de villa » afin de mieux intégrer cette **NOUVELLE CONSTRUCTION** à l'environnement du **CAMPUS DE L'ÉCOLE WALDORF**. Un terrain de jeux existant a été redessiné pour dégager l'accès principal au bâtiment qui regroupe une garderie, une cafétéria, une cuisine, la librairie du collège et une salle polyvalente. Un escalier central et un ascenseur conduisent au niveau supérieur qui comprend une salle de réunion et un accès à une terrasse en toiture. Réalisé en béton armé, ce petit immeuble de trois niveaux est habillé de mélèze, équipé d'huisseries en bois et d'une toiture végétalisée. À l'intérieur, un mobilier en bois intégré et des plans de couleur vernis créent une atmosphère chaleureuse.

As seen from most exterior angles, the school does, indeed, resemble a large private house or small apartment building. Here, larch is used as a cladding material, while the structure is in concrete and steel.

Aus fast allen Richtungen gesehen, gleicht die Schule eher einem großen Privathaus oder einem kleinen Mehrfamilienhaus. Hier wurde Lärchenholz als Verkleidung gewählt, das Tragwerk ist aus Beton und Stahl.

Vue sous la plupart des angles, cette école fait penser à une grande résidence privée ou à un petit immeuble d'appartements. La structure est en acier et béton, le parement en mélèze.

ATELIER MASUDA

Atelier Masuda
1409–38 Yoshioka, Angyo
Kawaguchi
Saitama 334–0072
Japan

Tel/Fax: +81 48 285 2856
E-mail: izc04225@nifty.com
Web: http://homepage2.nifty.com/04225

KEISUKE MASUDA was born in 1973 in Saitama, Japan. He graduated from the Department of Architecture, Faculty of Fine Arts, Tokyo National University of Fine Arts and Music (1997) and has been a lecturer at the ICS College of Arts since 2003. **RYOKO MASUDA** was born in 1974 in Chiba, Japan, and graduated from the Department of Architecture, Faculty of Fine Arts, Tokyo National University of Fine Arts and Music (1998). They jointly established Atelier Masuda in 2000. Their recent work includes House in Angyohara (Saitama, 2004); House in Rokusyomaki (Saitama, 2005–06, published here); House in Kitamoto (Saitama, 2007); and the House in Azami (Gunma, 2009).

KEISUKE MASUDA wurde 1973 in Saitama, Japan, geboren. 1977 beendete er sein Studium an der Architekturabteilung der Tokyo National University of Fine Arts and Music und lehrt seit 2003 am ICS College of Arts. **RYOKO MASUDA** wurde 1974 in Chiba, Japan, geboren und schloss 1998 ihr Studium an der Architekturabteilung der Tokyo National University of Fine Arts and Music ab. Gemeinsam gründeten beide im Jahr 2000 das Atelier Masuda. Zu ihren aktuellen Werken gehören ein Wohnhaus in Angyohara (Saitama, 2004), ein Wohnhaus in Rokusyomaki (Saitama, 2005–06, hier veröffentlicht), ein Wohnhaus in Kitamoto (Saitama, 2007) sowie ein Wohnhaus in Azami (Gunma, 2009).

KEISUKE MASUDA, né en 1973 à Saitama au Japon est diplômé du département d'Architecture de la faculté des beaux-arts de l'Université nationale des beaux-arts et de la musique de Tokyo (1997). Il est assistant à l'ICS College of Arts depuis 2003. **RYOKO MASUDA**, née en 1974 à Chiba (Japon) est diplômée du département d'Architecture de la faculté des beaux-arts de l'Université nationale des beaux-arts et de la musique de Tokyo (1998). Ils ont fondé ensemble l'Atelier Masuda en 2000. Parmi leurs travaux récents : une maison à Angyohara (Saitama, 2004) ; une maison à Rokusyomaki (Saitama, 2005–06, publiée ici) ; une maison à Kitamoto (Saitama, 2007) et une maison à Azami (Gunma, 2009).

HOUSE IN ROKUSYOMAKI

Kawaguchi, Saitama, Japan, 2005–06

Address: not disclosed
Area: 39 m². Client: not disclosed. Cost: not disclosed

This small house is intended for a retired mother and her son. A 6.9-meter-diameter, eight-meter-high cylinder that is set 40 centimeters above the ground forms the main body of the house. The architects write, inside the house "stairs and niches are built as if they were carved out of a wooden block." The first level contains a toilet and bed, while a dining room, Buddhist altar, kitchen, and another toilet are on the second level. The sky is visible through an opening in the northern part of the ceiling above the dining area. The third level, in a "half-moon" configuration, houses a balcony and bathroom. "In the summer days," say the architects, "the bath tub can be turned into a tiny swimming pool by opening the window."

Dieses kleine Wohnhaus ist für eine pensionierte Mutter und ihren Sohn bestimmt. Es hat die Form eines 8 m hohen Zylinders mit 6,9 m Durchmesser, der 40 cm über Bodenniveau steht. Zur Innenausstattung des Hauses schreibt der Architekt: „Treppen und Nischen wurden so gestaltet, als wären sie aus einem Holzblock ausgeschnitten." Die erste Ebene enthält eine Toilette und einen Schlafraum, die zweite das Esszimmer, einen buddhistischen Altar, die Küche und eine weitere Toilette. Durch eine Öffnung im nördlichen Bereich des Dachs über dem Esszimmer ist der Himmel sichtbar. Auf der dritten Ebene, die in Halbmondform gestaltet ist, befinden sich ein Balkon und das Badezimmer. „An Sommertagen", erklären die Architekten, „kann die Badewanne durch das Öffnen des Fensters in einen kleinen Swimmingpool verwandelt werden."

Cette petite maison a été réalisée pour une mère et son fils. Le corps principal se présente sous la forme d'un cylindre de 8 m de haut et 6,9 m de diamètre surélevé de 40 cm par rapport au sol. À l'intérieur, écrit l'architecte : « Les escaliers et diverses niches semblent creusés dans un bloc de bois. » Le rez-de-chaussée contient un lit et des toilettes, l'étage une salle à manger, une cuisine, des autres toilettes et un autel bouddhiste. On aperçoit le ciel par une ouverture percée dans le plafond au-dessus du coin des repas. Le second étage en forme de demi-lune est occupé par une salle de bains et un balcon. « L'été, précise l'architecte, la baignoire peut se transformer en petite piscine en ouvrant la fenêtre. »

The cylindrical house has a curving stairway, a wooden floor, and white-painted wood walls.

Das zylinderförmige Haus hat eine gewundene Treppe, einen Holzboden und weiß gestrichene Holzwände.

Cylindrique, la maison possède un escalier en courbe, des sols en bois et des murs en bois peint en blanc.

A view up through the space gives
an impression of much more complex
geometry than the basic cylinder
would imply.

Ein Blick hinauf in den Raum zeigt
eine weit komplexere Geometrie,
als die Grundform des Zylinders
vermuten ließe.

Une vue en contre-plongée donne
l'impression d'une composition
géométrique beaucoup plus complexe
que ne paraissait l'impliquer la
simplicité du cylindre.

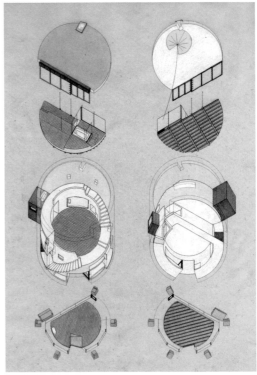

Axonometric drawings of the house
show how the cylinder is employed by
the architects, with the stairway following the curve of the house itself.

Die Axonometrien des Hauses zeigen,
wie die Architekten die zylindrische
Form ausgenutzt haben; die Treppe
folgt der Krümmung des Hauses.

Les vues axonométriques de la
maison montrent comment les architectes ont mis à profit la forme cylindrique. L'escalier suit la courbure
de la maison.

A wood-beam ceiling gives a
spatial richness to the sparsely
furnished interior.

Eine hölzerne Balkendecke verleiht
dem sparsam möblierten Inneren
räumliche Vielfalt.

Le plafond à poutres de bois apporte
une richesse spatiale supplémentaire
à l'intérieur peu meublé.

AUER+WEBER+ASSOZIIERTE

Auer+Weber+Assoziierte
Haussmannstr. 103a
70188 Stuttgart
Germany

Tel: +49 711 268 40 40
Fax: +49 711 268 40 488
E-mail: stuttgart@auer-weber.de
Web: www.auer-weber.de/

FRITZ AUER, born in Tübingen, Germany, in 1933, became a partner in the firm of Behnisch & Partner in 1966 and created the office Auer+Weber in 1980. **CARLO WEBER** was born in Saarbrücken, Germany, in 1934 and attended the Technische Hochschule in Stuttgart before going to the Beaux-Arts in Paris. Like Auer, he became a partner at Behnisch & Partner in 1966. They have worked extensively on urban renewal in Bonn, Stuttgart, and other cities. The firm, with offices in Munich and Stuttgart, currently employs 90 to 100 people and includes managing partners Moritz Auer, Philipp Auer, Jörn Scholz, Achim Söding, and Stephan Suxdorf. They completed the University Library of Magdeburg (2003); the Welle department store in Bielefeld (2003); Gut Siggen Seminar Building (Siggen, 2006–07, published here); ECE Stadtgalerie, Façade (Passau, 2005–08); an office building (Altstadt-Palais, Munich, 2008); additions and alterations to the Olympic Halls (Munich, 2008); the Central Bus Terminal in Munich (2009); Chenshan Botanical Garden (Shanghai, China, 2009); and the Martinsried Campus (2009) and the Central Facilities on the Campus (Ludwig-Maximilians University, Munich, 2004–09, also published here). Current work includes a Youth Center and Hostel (Stuttgart–Bad Cannstatt, 2010); the Archeological Museum in Chemnitz (2011); General Archive of Baden-Württemberg (Karlsruhe, 2012); and the extension for the 2nd Base of Operation of the Federal Ministry of Defense (Berlin, 2012), all in Germany unless stated otherwise.

FRITZ AUER, geboren 1933 in Tübingen, wurde 1966 Partner im Büro Behnisch & Partner und gründete 1980 das Büro Auer+Weber. **CARLO WEBER** wurde 1934 in Saarbrücken geboren und studierte an der Technischen Hochschule Stuttgart und danach an der École des Beaux-Arts in Paris. Ebenso wie Auer wurde er 1966 Partner bei Behnisch & Partner. Beide haben große Stadterneuerungsprojekte in Bonn, Stuttgart und anderen Städten durchgeführt. Das Büro mit Niederlassungen in München und Stuttgart beschäftigt zurzeit 90 bis 100 Personen einschließlich der verantwortlichen Partner Moritz Auer, Philipp Auer, Jörn Scholz, Achim Söding und Stephan Suxdorf. Zu ihren neueren Werken zählen die Universitätsbibliothek Magdeburg (2003), das Kaufhaus Welle in Bielefeld (2003), das Seminargebäude Gut Siggen (Ostholstein, 2006–07, hier veröffentlicht), die Fassade der ECE-Stadtgalerie (Passau, 2005–08), ein Bürogebäude (Altstadt-Palais, München, 2008), Erweiterung und Umbau der Olympiabauten (München, 2008), der Zentrale Omnibusbahnhof in München (2009), der Botanische Garten Chenshan (Shanghai, China, 2009) und der Campus Martinsried (2009) sowie die zentralen Einrichtungen auf dem Campus der Ludwig-Maximilians-Universität (München, 2004–09, ebenfalls hier veröffentlicht). Aktuelle Projekte sind ein Jugendhaus mit Jugendherberge (Stuttgart-Bad Cannstatt, 2010), das Archäologische Museum in Chemnitz (2011), das Generallandesarchiv Baden-Württemberg (Karlsruhe, 2012) und die 2. Erweiterung des Bundesministeriums für Verteidigung (Berlin, 2012).

FRITZ AUER, né à Tübingen (Allemagne) en 1933, a créé l'agence Auer+Weber en 1980 après savoir été partenaire de Behnisch & Partner à partir de 1966. **CARLO WEBER**, né à Saarebruck (Allemagne) en 1934 a étudié à la Technische Hochschule de Stuttgart puis à l'École des beaux-arts à Paris. Comme Auer, il est devenu partenaire de Behnisch & Partner en 1966. Ils ont réalisé des grands projets de rénovation urbaine à Bonn, Stuttgart et ailleurs. Leur agence, installée à Munich et Stuttgart, emploie actuellement de 90 à 100 personnes dont les partenaires Moritz Auer, Philipp Auer, Jörn Scholz, Achim Söding et Stephan Suxdorf. Ils ont réalisé la bibliothèque universitaire de Magdebourg (2003) ; le grand magasin Welle à Bielefeld (2003) ; le centre de séminaires de Gut Siggen (Siggen, 2006–07, publié ici) ; la façade de la ECE Stadtgalerie (Passau, 2005–08) ; un immeuble de bureaux (Altstadt-Palais, Munich, 2008) ; des extensions et des modifications des halls olympiques (Munich, 2008) ; le terminal central des bus de Munich (2009) ; le jardin botanique de Chenshan (Shanghaï, 2009) ; le campus de Martinsried (2009) et l'immeuble central du campus de l'université Ludwig-Maximilian (Munich, 2004–09, également publié ici). Actuellement, l'agence travaille sur les projets d'un centre et d'une auberge pour la jeunesse (Stuttgart-Bad Cannstatt, 2010) ; le musée d'archéologie de Chemnitz (2011) ; les archives du Bade-Wurtemberg (Karlsruhe, 2012) et l'extension de la deuxième base d'opérations du ministère fédéral de la Défense (Berlin, 2012).

GUT SIGGEN SEMINAR BUILDING

Siggen, Germany, 2006–07

Address: auf Gut Siggen, Siggen, Ostholstein, Germany, +49 40 33 402 14, http://toepfer-fvs.de/siggen.html
Area: 715 m². Client: Alfred Toepfer Stiftung F.V.S. Hamburg
Cost: € 1.5 million. Collaboration: Thorsten Ruppe (Project Architect)
Torsten Cattau (construction management/loose furnishing)

The Seminar Building appears to float in its setting, with the impression of lightness highlighted by the approach bridge and the use of wood cladding.

Das Seminargebäude scheint in seinem Umfeld zu schweben; die scheinbare Leichtigkeit wird durch die Erschließungsbrücke und die Holzverkleidung zusätzlich betont.

Le bâtiment de séminaires semble presque suspendu. L'impression de légèreté est soulignée par sa passerelle d'accès et son parement de bois.

Built on the site of old horse stables, the new structure reuses part of the stable's layout as is appropriate given the environment of old buildings. The architects clearly aim for a classical modernist simplicity that is well integrated into the green site. Moveable larch shades, wood ceilings, and oak floors further emphasize the connection to nature seen in views from the building. The architects explain that the rooms determine the character of the building: seminar area and lobby are oriented to the more public side of the building and reveal their purpose depending on their use, the time of day, and lighting. This area opens to an open space, with its old trees, and can be extended to the forecourt on days when the weather is good. Guest rooms are oriented to the quieter side of the building, looking out to a pond, and can be used independently from the seminar area.

Der Neubau auf dem Gelände der früheren Pferdeställe folgt teilweise deren Anordnung – durchaus angemessen in diesem Umfeld von Altbauten. Die Architekten planten bewusst im schlichten Stil der klassischen Moderne, der sich gut in das begrünte Gelände einfügt. Verstellbare Sonnenschutzelemente aus Lärchenholz sowie hölzerne Decken und Eichenböden betonen darüber hinaus die Verbindung zur Natur, die aus dem Gebäude sichtbar ist. Die Architekten erklären, dass die Funktion der Räume den Charakter des Bauwerks bestimmt: Der Seminarbereich und die Lobby sind zur öffentlichen Seite des Gebäudes orientiert und zeigen ihre Nutzung, abhängig von der Tageszeit und der Lichtverhältnisse. Dieser Bereich ist zu einem Freiraum mit altem Baumbestand geöffnet, der bei gutem Wetter zum Vorhof erweitert werden kann. Die Gästezimmer liegen auf der ruhigeren Seite des Gebäudes; sie sind zum Teich ausgerichtet und können unabhängig vom Seminarbereich genutzt werden.

Édifié sur le terrain d'anciennes écuries, la nouvelle construction réutilise en partie leur plan, pour s'adapter à son cadre marqué par la présence de bâtiments anciens. Les architectes ont à l'évidence cherché à jouer d'une simplicité moderniste classique qui puisse s'intégrer à ce site verdoyant. Comme le montrent les photographies, les volets mobiles en mélèze, les plafonds en bois et les sols en chêne renforcent la connexion avec la nature. Les architectes expliquent que la fonction des diverses salles a déterminé l'esprit de ce bâtiment : la partie séminaires et le hall d'accueil sont orientés vers la façade la plus publique du centre et dévoilent leur fonction selon leur utilisation, l'heure du jour ou l'éclairage. Cette zone donne sur un espace ouvert planté d'arbres anciens et peut s'étendre vers l'avant-cour lorsque le temps le permet. Les chambres d'hôtes qui regardent vers un étang sont implantées sur une façade plus abritée des regards. Elles sont utilisables indépendamment de la partie réservée aux séminaires.

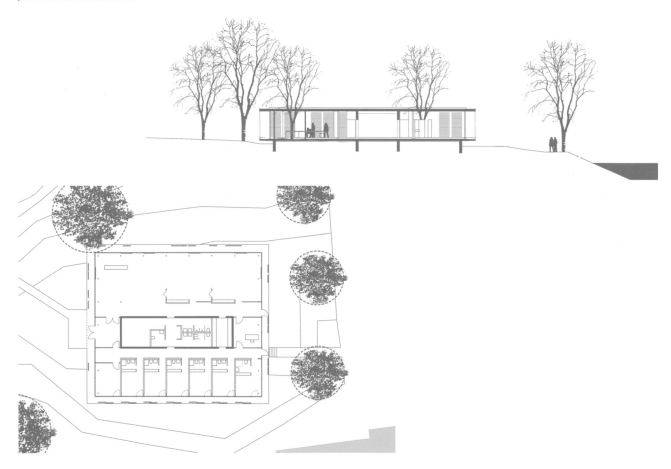

A site plan and an elevation confirm the impression of strict modernist lines in this building, as does the slight elevation above the ground plane, a bit in the spirit of the Farnsworth House by Mies van der Rohe.

Lageplan und Ansicht bestätigen ebenso wie die leichte Anhebung über Bodenniveau den strengen, modernen Eindruck dieses Gebäudes – ein wenig im Geiste des Farnsworth House von Mies van der Rohe.

Le plan au sol et une élévation confirment l'impression de stricte modernité du bâtiment, de même que sa légère suspension au-dessus du sol, un peu dans l'esprit de la Farnsworth House de Mies van der Rohe.

It is the use of wood that differentiates this building from its early modernist predecessors. The column-like disposition of external wooden screens affirms classical intentions, albeit expressed in a new way.

Es ist die Verwendung von Holz, die dieses Gebäude von seinen Vorgängern der Moderne abhebt. Die Anordnung von hölzernen Gitterwänden als außenstehende Stützen bestätigt den Bezug zur klassischen Moderne, wenngleich auf neuartige Weise.

Le recours au bois différencie ce projet de ces prédécesseurs modernistes. La disposition en pilastres des écrans extérieurs en bois affiche des intentions classiques, mais exprimées de façon nouvelle.

CENTRAL FACILITIES, MARTINSRIED CAMPUS, LUDWIG-MAXIMILIANS UNIVERSITY

Munich, Germany, 2004–09

Address: Großhaderner Straße 6, Martinsried, Munich, Germany
Area: 2060 m². Client: Freistaat Bayern v.d. Bayer. Staatsministerium der Wissenschaft, Forschung und Kunst v.d. staatl. Bauamt Munich
Cost: € 12.25 million. Collaboration: Peter Hofmann (Project Architect), Sonja Mutterer (Project Architect),
Stefan Busch, Sascha Dehnst, Anna-Maria Meister, Jakob Plötz, Matthias Wunderlich

This building contains a **CAFETERIA, CHILD CARE CENTERS, AND ADMINISTRATIVE SPACE FOR THE MARTINSRIED CAMPUS OF THE LUDWIG-MAXI-MILIANS UNIVERSITY**. The architects explain that the building "presents itself as less of a freestanding structure than as an integral element of the open space concept. Like a gazebo, the low building, with a trellis-like timber external façade, blends into the landscaped garden." The trellis structure is made of larch and is set 60 centimeters from the actual charcoal-colored building façade. Large openings emphasize the relationship of the building to surrounding open spaces, while three roof terraces allow for outdoor seating. Monochrome cladding chosen for interior walls, floors, and ceilings are contrasted with intense colors in the red-pink-orange range used for the lobby staircase, the atrium of the children's day care area, and the furnishings.

Dieser Bau enthält eine **CAFETERIA, EINE KINDERTAGESSTÄTTE SOWIE VERWALTUNGSRÄUME FÜR DEN CAMPUS MARTINSRIED DER LUDWIG-MAXI-MILIANS-UNIVERSITÄT**. Die Architekten erklären, dass er „sich weniger als frei stehendes Gebäude, sondern vielmehr als ein in das Freiraumkonzept integriertes Element darstellt. Wie ein Pavillon fügt sich der Flachbau mit seiner gitterartigen Holzfassade in den Landschaftsgarten ein." Das Gitter besteht aus Lärchenholz und ist 60 cm von der eigentlichen grauen Gebäudewand abgesetzt. Große Öffnungen betonen die Verbindung des Gebäudes mit den umgebenden Freiräumen; drei Dachterrassen bieten sich zum Aufenthalt im Freien an. Für die Innenwände, Böden und Decken wurden einfarbige Verkleidungen gewählt, die im Kontrast zu den intensiven Rot-, Rosa- und Orangetönen des Treppenhauses, des Atriums in der Kindertagesstätte und der Möblierung stehen.

Ce bâtiment du campus de Martinsried contient une **CAFÉTÉRIA, UNE GARDERIE POUR ENFANT ET DES LOCAUX ADMINISTRATIFS DE L'UNIVERSITÉ LUDWIG-MAXIMILIAN**. Selon les architectes, il se présente « moins comme une structure indépendante qu'un élément relevant du concept d'espace ouvert. Comme une gloriette, le bâtiment bas à façade habillée d'un treillis en bois, se fond dans les jardins paysagés ». Le treillis de couleur charbonneuse est en mélèze, posé à 60 cm de la façade. De vastes ouvertures amplifient la relation du bâtiment avec les espaces verts qui l'entourent. On peut aller s'asseoir sur les trois terrasses en toiture. L'habillage monochrome retenu pour les murs internes, les sols et les plafonds contraste avec l'intensité de la gamme de rouges, roses et orangés utilisée pour l'escalier du hall d'entrée, l'atrium de la garderie d'enfant et le mobilier.

As elevation drawings (below) show, the building is quite a "normal" rectangular volume, made different from other structures by the use of the distinctive, diagonal trellis.

Wie die Ansichten (unten) zeigen, ist das Gebäude ein ganz „normales" quaderförmiges Volumen, das sich vor allem durch die diagonale Gitterwand von anderen Bauten unterscheidet.

Comme le montrent les coupes ci-dessous, le bâtiment est un volume parallélépipédique « normal » dont l'originalité tient à la forte présence du treillis posé en diagonale.

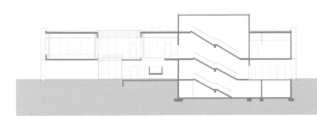

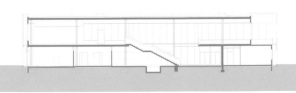

Despite its rectilinear design,
the building is both original and
unexpected, factors that are directly
related to the use of wood on such
a large scale.

Trotz seiner rechtwinkligen Form
wirkt das Gebäude originell und über-
raschend zugleich – was unmittelbar
auf die Verwendung von Holz in einem
derart großen Maßstab zurückzuführen ist.

Malgré la simplicité de ses lignes,
ce bâtiment original surprend, ce qui
doit beaucoup à l'utilisation du bois
à une telle échelle.

Held in place by metal frames, the
outside trellis layer defines not only
the exterior appearance of the
building, but also views from the
interior looking out.

Das in Metallrahmen gefasste Außen-
gitter bestimmt nicht nur das äußere
Erscheinungsbild des Gebäudes,
sondern auch den Ausblick von innen
nach draußen.

Maintenus par des cadres
métalliques, les treillis extérieurs
définissent non seulement l'aspect
externe du bâtiment, mais jouent
également sur les vues que l'on
a de l'intérieur.

Plans (below) reveal a strict square, while the trellis façade, seen above in its garden context, gives a much more "natural" feeling to the building than its geometric rigor would imply.

Die Grundrisse (unten) zeigen ein strenges Quadrat, während die Gitterfassade (oben) im Umfeld des Gartens eine viel „natürlichere" Wirkung hat, als ihre geometrische Strenge vermuten ließe.

Les plans (ci-dessous) sont de forme strictement carrée. La façade en treillis (ci-dessus dans le cadre du jardin), apporte un aspect beaucoup plus « naturel » que la rigueur géométrique du bâtiment ne pourrait le laisser penser.

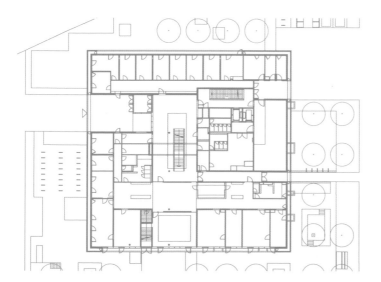
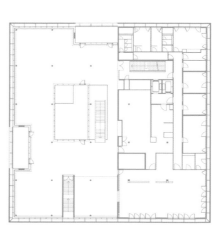

PIETA-LINDA AUTTILA

Pieta-Linda Auttila
NoMad Productions

Tel: +358 503 622 465
E-mail: pietalinda@hotmail.com

PIETA-LINDA AUTTILA was born in 1974 in Tampere, Finland. She received a master's degree as a spatial designer and interior architect from the University of Art and Design (Helsinki, 2009). She was the coordinator of an "artistically rich and multicultural workshop" (Studio, Helsinki, 2005–07). She worked for Arkkitehtiruutu Oy (Lahti, 2007) and Stratakissaravuo Architects (Rethymno, Crete, 2008), before designing the Wisa Wooden Design Hotel (Helsinki, 2009, published here).

PIETA-LINDA AUTTILA wurde 1974 in Tampere, Finnland, geboren. Sie erhielt ihren Master als Raumgestalterin und Innenarchitektin an der Kunst- und Designschule der Aalto-Universität in Helsinki (2009). Sie war die Koordinatorin einer „künstlerisch reichen, multikulturellen Werkstatt" (Studio, Helsinki, 2005–07). Auttila arbeitete für die Büros Arkkitehtiruutu Oy (Lahti, 2007) und Stratakissaravuo Architects (Rethymnon, Kreta, 2008), bevor sie das Wisa Wooden Design Hotel (Helsinki, 2009, hier veröffentlicht) plante.

PIETA-LINDA AUTTILA, née en 1974 à Tampere (Finlande) obtenue son M. A. en design d'espace et architecture d'intérieur de l'Université d'art et de design d'Helsinki (2009). Elle a été coordinatrice d'un « atelier polyculturel d'une grande richesse artistique », le Studio (Helsinki, 2005–07), et a travaillé pour les agences Arkkitehtiruutu Oy (Lahti, 2007) et Stratakissaravuo Architects (Rethymno, Crète, 2008), avant de concevoir le Wisa Wooden Design Hotel (Helsinki, 2009, publié ici).

WISA WOODEN DESIGN HOTEL

Helsinki, Finland, 2009

Address: Valkosaari, Helsinki, Finland, +358 20 414 7021, www.wisa24.com
Area: 80 m². Client: UPM Kymmene. Cost: not disclosed

Pieta-Linda Auttila was chosen to design the **WISA WOODEN DESIGN HOTEL** through a 2009 competition organized by UPM, an energy, pulp, paper, and engineered materials company that employs 23 000 people worldwide. Participants in the competition were given just 24 hours to design "a bold and iconic work from Finnish pine and spruce." The Wisa Wooden Design Hotel is set at the northern point of Valkosaari Island in Helsinki's Southern Harbor. According to the firm: "Despite its name, the Wisa Wooden Design Hotel wasn't designed for public use, yet the building will offer facilities for a sleepover. The Wisa Wooden Design Hotel is meant to be noticed and admired." The designer states: "I wanted to blow the wooden block in pieces from the middle. By bending the block, I forced the slats to a new form that offers a contrast to the original shape, the block. Thus the solid shape becomes partly transparent, and the strictly geometrical shape becomes organic. The interior space is secondary as the partly sheltered patio takes the leading role."

Pieta-Linda Auttila erhielt den Auftrag zur Planung des **WISA WOODEN DESIGN HOTELS** aufgrund eines Wettbewerbs, der 2009 von UPM ausgeschrieben wurde, einer Energie, Zellstoff, Papier und Baumaterialien produzierenden Firma, die weltweit 23 000 Mitarbeiter hat. Den Teilnehmern des Wettbewerbs wurden nur 24 Stunden gewährt, um „ein gewagtes und einprägsames Bauwerk aus finnischer Kiefer und Fichte" zu entwerfen. Das Wisa Wooden Design Hotel steht an der Nordspitze der Insel Valkosaari im Südhafen von Helsinki. Laut Aussage der Firma ist „das Wisa Wooden Design Hotel, seiner Bezeichnung zum Trotz, nicht zur öffentlichen Nutzung bestimmt; dennoch bietet das Gebäude auch Übernachtungsmöglichkeiten an. Das Wisa Wooden Design Hotel soll beachtet und bewundert werden." Die Architektin erklärt: „Ich wollte den hölzernen Block, von der Mitte ausgehend, in Stücke zerlegen. Durch Biegen des Blocks zwang ich die Latten in eine neue Form, die einen Gegensatz zum Original darstellt. Dadurch wird die geschlossene Form teilweise transparent und die streng geometrische Form organisch. Der Innenraum wird sekundär, weil der teilüberdachte Patio die führende Rolle übernimmt."

Pieta-Linda Auttila a été sélectionnée pour concevoir le **WISA WOODEN DESIGN HOTEL** à l'issue d'un concours organisé par UPM, entreprise de production d'énergie, de pulpe de papier, de papier et de matériaux de transformation qui emploie 23 000 personnes dans le monde. Les participants n'avaient disposé que de 24 heures pour concevoir « une réalisation audacieuse et iconique en pin et épicéa de Finlande ». L'hôtel est situé à la pointe nord de l'île de Valkosaari dans le port sud d'Helsinki. Selon l'entreprise : « Malgré son nom, cet hôtel n'a pas été conçu pour un usage public, mais pourra néanmoins accueillir des personnes pour la nuit. Il a été conçu pour être vu et admiré. » Pour le designer : « Je voulais faire exploser un bloc de bois à partir de son centre. En le cintrant, j'ai forcé les lattes à prendre une forme contrastant avec le volume d'origine. Ainsi un solide est devenu en partie transparent et une forme strictement géométrique est devenue organique. L'espace intérieur est secondaire, le patio en partie protégé joue le premier rôle. »

The Wisa Wooden Design Hotel is a very small, experimental structure intended to show the kind of things that can be done in such circumstances with wood. Elevations (below) show the adaptation of the structure to the terrain.

Das Wisa Wooden Design Hotel ist ein sehr kleines, experimentelles Gebäude, das beweisen soll, was sich unter derartigen Umständen aus Holz machen lässt. Die Ansichten (unten) zeigen die Einfügung des Bauwerks in das Gelände.

Le Wisa Wooden Design Hotel est une très petite construction expérimentale destinée à montrer ce que l'on peut faire avec du bois dans des circonstances particulières. Les élévations (ci-dessous) illustrent l'adaptation de la structure au terrain.

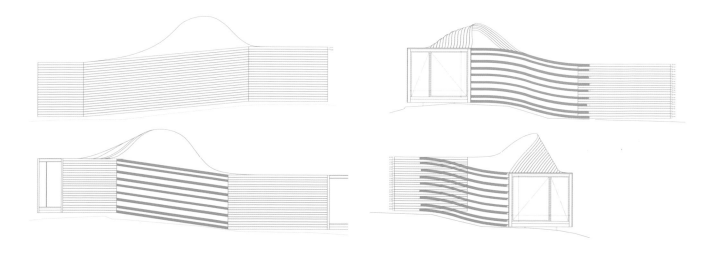

The central, freely curving form of the hotel makes use of open slats in a sculptural pattern that reveal views of the water.

Die zentrale, frei gekrümmte Form des Hotels entsteht durch Latten in plastischer Anordnung, durch die Ausblicke zum Wasser geboten werden.

La forme centrale libre organise en une mise en scène sculpturale le déploiement des lattes de bois qui, par moments, permettent de découvrir des vues du fleuve.

SHIGERU BAN

Shigeru Ban Architects
5–2–4 Matsubara
Setagaya-ku
Tokyo 156–0043
Japan

Tel: +81 3 3324 6760 / Fax: +81 3 3324 6789
E-mail: tokyo@shigerubanarchitects.com
Web: www.shigerubanarchitects.com

Born in 1957 in Tokyo, **SHIGERU BAN** studied at SCI-Arc from 1977 to 1980. He then attended the Cooper Union School of Architecture, where he studied under John Hejduk (1980–84). He worked in the office of Arata Isozaki (1982–83), before founding his own firm in Tokyo in 1985. His work includes numerous exhibition designs (such as the Alvar Aalto show at the Axis Gallery, Tokyo, 1986). His buildings include the Odawara Pavilion (Kanagawa, 1990); the Paper Gallery (Tokyo, 1994); the Paper House (Lake Yamanaka, 1995); and the Paper Church (Takatori, Hyogo, 1995), all in Japan. He has also designed ephemeral structures such as his Paper Refugee Shelter made with plastic sheets and paper tubes for the United Nations High Commissioner for Refugees (UNHCR). He designed the Japanese Pavilion at Expo 2000 in Hanover. Recent work includes the Hanegi Forest Annex (Setagaya, Tokyo, 2004); Mul(ti)houses (Mulhouse, France, 2001–05); the Takatori Church (Kobe, Hyogo, 2005); the disaster relief Post-Tsunami Rehabilitation Houses (Kirinda, Hambantota, Sri Lanka, 2005); the Papertainer Museum (Seoul Olympic Park, Songpa-Gu, South Korea, 2006); the Nicolas G. Hayek Center (Tokyo, 2007); Haesley Nine Bridges Golf Clubhouse (Yeoju, South Korea, 2009, published here); and the Metal Shutter Houses on West 19th Street in New York (New York, USA, 2010). He installed his Paper Temporary Studio on top of the Centre Pompidou in Paris to work on the new Centre Pompidou-Metz (Metz, France, 2010).

Der 1957 in Tokio geborene **SHIGERU BAN** war von 1977 bis 1980 Student am SCI-Arc, Los Angeles. Danach besuchte er die Cooper Union School of Architecture in New York, wo er bei John Hejduk studierte (1980–84). Er arbeitete im Büro von Arata Isozaki (1982–83), bevor er 1985 seine eigene Firma in Tokio gründete. Zu seinen Arbeiten zählen viele Ausstellungsarchitekturen (etwa die Alvar-Aalto-Ausstellung in der Axis Gallery, Tokio, 1986), zu seinen ausgeführten Bauten der Odawara-Pavillon (Kanagawa, 1990), die Paper Gallery (Tokio, 1994), das Paper House (Yamanaka-See, 1995) und die Paper Church (Takatori, Hyogo, 1995), alle in Japan. Er hat auch temporäre Bauten geplant, u. a. Flüchtlingsquartiere aus Plastikfolie und Pappröhren für den Hohen Flüchtlingskommissar der Vereinten Nationen (UNHCR). Für die Expo 2000 in Hannover plante Shigeru Ban den japanischen Pavillon. Zu seinen neueren Bauten zählen der Anbau im Hanegi-Wald (Setagaya, Tokio, 2004), die Mul(ti) houses (Mülhausen, Frankreich, 2001–05), die Takatori-Kirche (Kobe, Hyogo, 2005), das Katastrophenhilfeprojekt nach dem großen Tsunami (Kirinda, Hambantota, Sri Lanka, 2005), das Papertainer Museum (Olympiapark Seoul, Songpa-Gu, Südkorea, 2006), das Nicolas G. Hayek Center (Tokio, 2007), das Golfklubhaus Haesley Nine Bridges (Yeoju, Südkorea, 2009, hier veröffentlicht) und die Metal Shutter Houses an der West 19th Street in New York (New York, USA, 2010). Auf dem Dach des Centre Pompidou in Paris installierte er ein temporäres Studio aus Papier, um dort am neuen Centre Pompidou-Metz zu arbeiten (Metz, Frankreich, 2010).

Né en 1957 à Tokyo, **SHIGERU BAN** a étudié à la SCI-Arc (Los Angeles) de 1977 à 1980 et à la Cooper Union School of Architecture (New York) auprès de John Hejduk (1980–84). Il a travaillé chez Arata Isozaki (1982–83) avant de fonder son agence à Tokyo en 1985. Son œuvre comprend de nombreuses installations d'expositions (Alvar Aalto Show à la gallerie Axis, Tokyo, 1986) et des bâtiments comme le Odawara Pavilion (Kanagawa, 1990) ; la Paper Gallery (Tokyo, 1994) ; la Paper House (Lake Yamanaka, 1995) et la Paper Church (Takatori, Hyogo, 1995), tous au Japon. Il a également conçu des structures éphémères comme son abri en papier pour réfugiés en film plastique et tubes de carton pour le Haut Commissariat des Nations Unies pour les réfugiés (HCR). Il est aussi l'auteur du pavillon japonais pour Expo 2000 à Hanovre. Parmi ses autres réalisations récentes : l'annexe de la forêt d'Hanegi (Setagaya, Tokyo, 2004) ; les Mul(ti)houses (Mulhouse, France, 2001–05) ; l'église de Takatori (Kobé, Hyogo, 2005) ; les maisons de la reconstruction après le tsunami (Kirinda, Hambantota, Sri Lanka, 2005) ; le Papertainer Museum (Parc olympique de Séoul, Songpa-Gu, Corée du Sud, 2006) ; le Nicolas G. Hayek Center (Tokyo, 2007) ; le *club-house* du golf Haesley Nine Bridges (Yeoju, Corée du Sud, 2009, publié ici) ; les maisons à volets de métal (Metal Shutter Houses, West 19th Street, New York, 2010). Par ailleurs, il avait installé au sommet du Centre Pompidou à Paris un atelier temporaire en carton pendant la durée du chantier du Centre Pompidou-Metz (2010).

HAESLEY NINE BRIDGES GOLF CLUBHOUSE

Yeoju, South Korea, 2009

Address: Nine Bridges Golf Course, Kwangpyong-ri, Anduk-myon, South Jeju-gun, Jeju Island, South Korea,
+82 64 793 9999, www.ninebridges.co.kr
Area: 20 977 m². Client: not disclosed. Cost: not disclosed
Collaboration: Kyeong Sik Yoon, KACI International Inc.

The **HAESLEY NINE BRIDGES GOLF CLUBHOUSE** is a 16 000-square-meter facility that serves a golf course. It has an underground and three floors above grade. There is a main building, a VIP lobby building, and a structure with private suites. The atrium and the upper portion of the main building include timber columns and a glass curtain wall, while the base is made of stone (random rubble masonry typical of Korea). The timber area includes the reception zone, a member's lounge, and a party room. The stone podium houses locker rooms, bathrooms, and service areas. The roof over the main building measures 36 x 72 meters in length. The unusual tree-like timber columns in the atrium reach to a height of three stories. The partially-timber structure was used to conform to Korean regulations that do not allow timber buildings to exceed 6000 square meters in size. The first floor of the atrium has 4.5-meter-wide glass shutters that open fully.

Das **GOLFKLUBHAUS HAESLEY NINE BRIDGES** ist ein ca. 16 000 m² großer Komplex mit drei Geschossen und einem Untergeschoss. Er besteht aus einem Hauptbau, einem VIP-Lobby-Trakt und einem Gebäude mit privaten Suiten. Das Atrium und der obere Teil des Hauptgebäudes sind mit Holzstützen und einer gläsernen Vorhangfassade ausgestattet, die Basis ist aus Naturstein (dem für Korea typischen unregelmäßigen Bruchsteinmauerwerk). Im hölzernen Teil liegen der Empfangsbereich, ein Aufenthaltsraum für die Mitglieder und ein Partyraum, im Steinsockel Umkleiden, Nassräume und Versorgungsbereiche. Das Dach des Hauptgebäudes hat eine Größe von 36 x 72 m. Die ungewöhnlichen, baumartigen Holzstützen im Atrium erreichen eine Höhe von drei Geschossen. Das nur teilweise aus Holz bestehende Tragwerk wurde gewählt, um den koreanischen Bauvorschriften gerecht zu werden, die keine über 6000 m² großen Holzbauten zulassen. Die 4,5 m breiten, gläsernen Wandelemente im Obergeschoss des Atriums lassen sich vollständig öffnen.

Le **CLUB-HOUSE DU GOLF HAESLEY NINE BRIDGES** développe ses 16 000 m² sur quatre niveaux dont un en sous-sol. Il se compose d'un bâtiment principal, d'un hall pour VIP et d'une partie réservée à des suites privées. L'atrium et la partie supérieure du bâtiment principal se composent d'un mur-rideau de verre, de colonnes de bois et d'un socle en pierre (maçonnerie rustiquée typique de la Corée). Entre les colonnes se trouvent l'accueil, un salon pour les membres et une salle pour réceptions. Dans le socle de pierre ont été implantés des vestiaires, des salles de bains et des équipements techniques de service. La toiture du bâtiment principal mesure 72 m de long par 32 m de large. Dans l'atrium, des curieuses colonnes de bois en forme d'arbres s'élèvent sur les trois niveaux. La construction n'est qu'en partie en bois car la réglementation coréenne n'autorise pas des réalisations de plus de 6000 m² dans ce matériau. Le premier niveau de l'atrium est fermé par des volets en verre de 4,5 m de large qui peuvent intégralement s'ouvrir.

The clubhouse is located in an
idyllic setting, which makes the use
of wood for the architecture all the
more appropriate.

Das Klubhaus liegt in einer idyllischen
Landschaft, was die Verwendung
von Holz für die Architektur umso
angemessener erscheinen lässt.

Le club-house est implanté dans un
cadre idyllique, qui justifie d'autant
plus l'utilisation du bois dans son
architecture.

The wooden, lattice work structure devised by the architects brings to mind the pattern employed by Shigeru Ban for the Centre Pompidou-Metz.

Das von den Architekten entworfene hölzerne Gitterfachwerk erinnert an das von Shigeru Ban für das Centre Pompidou-Metz vorgesehene System.

La structure en lattis de bois mise au point par l'architecte rappelle les formes qu'il avait utilisées pour le Centre Pompidou-Metz.

The spaces inside are generous and open, in part because the wooden support columns open freely into the roof, something like trees.

Die Innenräume sind offen und großzügig, auch weil die hölzernen Stützen sich wie Bäume frei bis in den Dachraum erheben.

Les espaces intérieurs sont ouverts et de dimensions généreuses, en partie parce que les importantes colonnes de bois s'évasent vers la toiture, un peu à la manière des arbres.

BEALS-LYON ARQUITECTOS / CHRISTIAN BEALS

Beals-Lyon Arquitectos / Christian Beals
119 Sinclair Road
London W14 0NP
UK

Teniers 4919
Santiago
Chile

Tel: +44 20 76 10 46 38 / +56 27 16 13 65
E-mail: bealsarquitectos@gmail.com
Web: www.beals-lyon.cl

ALEJANDRO BEALS was born in Santiago, Chile, in 1976. He graduated from the Pontificia Universidad Católica de Chile (2001), and since 2002 he has taught at the same university. Between 2001 and 2006 he worked in the office of Mathias Klotz. In 2006 he founded Beals-Lyon Architects with the architect **LORETO LYON** (born in Santiago, Chile, 1976). Since 2006, they have collaborated frequently with the architect Smiljan Radic. **CHRISTIAN BEALS**, born in Santiago, Chile, in 1974, studied architecture at Finis Terrae University (Chile, 2000). He has worked with Gonzalo Mardones (2000) and with Felipe Assadi (2001–03). Recent work of the office includes the House on Lake Rupanco (Lake District, with Christian Beals, 2006, published here); House in Tunquen (Valparaiso, 2007); Capri Restaurant (Santiago, 2007); Gran Via House (Santiago, 2008); House for Two Golf Players (Maitencillo, 2008); the Costa Cachagua House (Valparaiso, 2009); and the Las Palmeras Winery (Colchagua, 2009), all in Chile.

ALEJANDRO BEALS wurde 1976 in Santiago de Chile geboren. 2001 beendete er sein Studium an der Pontificia Universidad Católica de Chile und lehrt dort seit 2002. Von 2001 bis 2006 arbeitete er im Büro von Mathias Klotz. 2006 gründete er die Firma Beals-Lyon Arquitectos gemeinsam mit dem Architekten **LORETO LYON** (geboren 1976 in Santiago de Chile). Seit 2006 arbeiten sie auch häufig mit dem Architekten Smiljan Radic zusammen. **CHRISTIAN BEALS**, geboren 1974 in Santiago de Chile, studierte Architektur an der Universität Finis Terrae (Chile, 2000). Er arbeitete bei Gonzalo Mardones (2000) und bei Felipe Assadi (2001–03). Zu den neueren Werken des Büros zählen das Haus am Lago Rupanco (Seen-Distrikt, mit Christian Beals, 2006, hier veröffentlicht), ein Wohnhaus in Tunquen (Valparaiso, 2007), das Restaurant Capri (Santiago, 2007), das Haus Gran Via (Santiago, 2008), ein Wohnhaus für zwei Golfspieler (Maitencillo, 2008), das Haus Costa Cachagua (Valparaiso, 2009) und die Weinkellerei Las Palmeras (Colchagua, 2009), alle in Chile.

ALEJANDRO BEALS, né à Santiago du Chili en 1976, est diplômé de l'Université catholique du Chili (2001) où il enseigne depuis 2002. De 2001 à 2006 il a travaillé dans l'agence de Mathias Klotz. En 2006, il a fondé Beals-Lyon Architects avec **LORETO LYON** (né à Santiago du Chili en 1976). Depuis 2006, ils collaborent fréquemment avec l'architecte Smiljan Radic. **CHRISTIAN BEALS**, né à Santiago du Chili en 1974, a étudié l'architecture à l'université Finis Terrae (Chili, 2000). Il a travaillé avec Gonzalo Mardones (2000) et Felipe Assadi (2001–03). Parmi les récents travaux de l'agence, tous au Chili : la maison sur le lac Rupanco (Région des lacs, avec Christian Beals, 2006, publiée ici) ; la maison à Tunquen (Valparaiso, 2007) ; le restaurant Capri (Santiago, 2007) ; la maison Gran Via (Santiago, 2008) ; la maison pour deux golfeurs (Maitencillo, 2008) ; la maison de la Costa Cachagua (Valparaiso, 2009) et le chai, de Las Palmeras (Colchagua, 2009).

HOUSE ON LAKE RUPANCO

Lake District, Chile, 2006

Address: not disclosed
Area: 206 m². Client: not disclosed. Cost: not disclosed

Built on a sloped, 5000-square-meter site on the edge of Lake Rupanco in southern Chile, this house is made up of two parallel volumes oriented to optimize the relationship of the structure to the landscape, according to the architects. A dining room, kitchen, and terrace form a basically continuous space, while bedrooms are set on the upper floor at the extremities of the main volumes. The pine building was built using local materials and handcrafting techniques, due to its isolated location. Its appearance, including the façades coated in black sealer to protect against the rain, is inspired by buildings in the area. Interior surfaces are clad in local mañío and ulmo wood.

Dieses Wohnhaus auf einem 5000 m² großen Hanggrundstück am Ufer des Rupanco-Sees im Süden Chiles besteht aus zwei parallel angeordneten Trakten, wodurch der Bezug des Hauses zur Landschaft optimiert werden soll, so die Architekten. Esszimmer, Küche und Terrasse bilden einen zusammenhängenden Bereich; die Schlafräume sind im Obergeschoss jeweils am Ende der Haupttrakte angeordnet. Das Gebäude aus Kiefernholz wurde – aufgrund seiner abgelegenen Lage – aus vor Ort verfügbaren Materialien und mit handwerklichen Methoden errichtet. Sein Erscheinungsbild mit schwarz beschichteten Fassaden zum Schutz vor dem Regen entspricht den Bauten in dieser Region. Im Innern sind die Wände mit örtlichem Mañío- und Ulmo-Holz verkleidet.

Édifiée sur un terrain de 5000 m² qui descend jusqu'à la rive du lac Rupanco (sud du Chili), cette maison se compose de deux volumes parallèles orientés de façon à optimiser leur relation avec le paysage. Une salle à manger, une cuisine et une terrasse forment un espace pratiquement continu. Les chambres sont implantées en étage aux extrémités des deux volumes principaux. Réalisée en pin, la construction a fait appel à des matériaux et des techniques manuelles locales, en partie pour des raisons dues à l'isolement du site. Son aspect, y compris les façades recouvertes d'un enduit noir pour les protéger de la pluie, s'inspire des constructions de la région. L'intérieur est habillé de bois locaux (mañío et ulmo).

Elevation drawings show how the house fits into the hillside. Generous openings offer spectacular views of Lake Rupanco (left page).

Die Ansichten zeigen, wie das Haus sich dem Hanggelände anpasst. Großzügige Öffnungen bieten spektakuläre Ausblicke auf den Rupanco-See (linke Seite).

Les dessins d'élévation montrent la manière dont la maison s'intègre dans le flanc de la colline. De généreuses ouvertures offrent des vues spectaculaires sur le lac Rupanco (page de gauche).

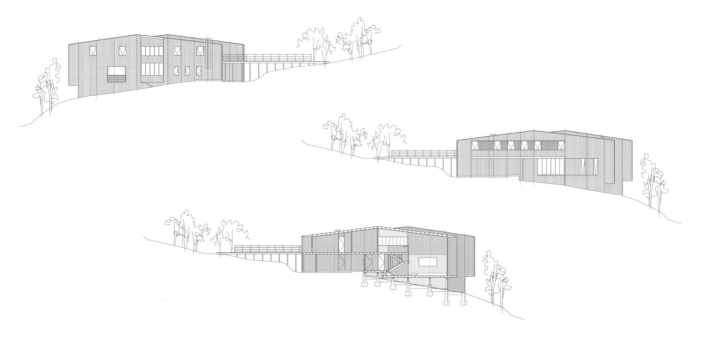

Plans show the two staggered, rectangular volumes that form the house. Wood is omnipresent inside. The high, warm spaces are punctuated by large glazed surfaces.

Die Grundrisse zeigen die beiden gestaffelten, rechtwinkligen Volumen, aus denen das Haus besteht. Im Innern ist Holz allgegenwärtig. Die hohen, behaglichen Räume sind von großen Glasflächen durchsetzt.

Les plans montrent les deux volumes rectangulaires décalés qui constituent la maison. À l'intérieur, le bois est omniprésent. Les volumes chaleureux et de bonne hauteur sont ponctués de grands plans vitrés.

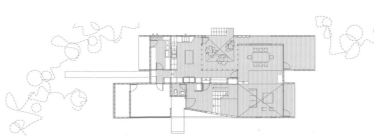

BERNARDES + JACOBSEN

Bernardes + Jacobsen Arquitetura
Rua Corcovado 250
Jardim Botânico
22460–500 Rio de Janeiro, RJ
Brazil

Tel/Fax: +55 21 2512 7743
E-mail: bjrj@bja.com.br
Web: www.bja.com.br

Thiago Bernardes was born in Rio de Janeiro in 1974. The office of **BERNARDES + JACOBSEN** was created in 1980 by his father, Claudio Bernardes, and Paulo Jacobsen, pioneers of a new type of residential architecture based on an effort to combine contemporary design and Brazilian culture. Thiago Bernardes worked in his father's office from 1991 to 1996, when he left to create his own firm, working on more than 30 residential projects between that date and 2001. With the death of his father, Thiago Bernardes reintegrated the firm and began to work with Paulo Jacobsen, who was born in 1954 in Rio. He studied photography in London before graduating from the Bennett Methodist Institute in 1979. The office of Bernardes + Jacobsen currently employs approximately 50 people in Rio de Janeiro and São Paulo and they work on roughly 40 projects per year. Some of their significant projects include the Gerdau Headquarters (Santa Catarina, 2005); FW House (Guaruja, 2005); and the MPM Agency Main Office (São Paulo, 2006). Recent work includes the JH House (São Paulo, 2008); the JZ House (Bahia, 2008); RW House (Búzios, Rio de Janeiro, 2006–09, published here); and the FN and DB Houses (both in São Paulo, 2009), all in Brazil.

Thiago Bernardes wurde 1974 in Rio de Janeiro geboren. Das Büro **BERNARDES + JACOBSEN** war 1980 von seinem Vater Claudio Bernardes und Paulo Jacobsen gegründet worden, zwei Vorreitern für einen neuen Typ der Wohnhausarchitektur, die versucht hatten, moderne Gestaltung mit brasilianischer Kultur zu verbinden. Thiago Bernardes arbeitete von 1991 bis 1996 im Büro seines Vaters und gründete dann seine eigene Firma, die bis 2001 mehr als 30 Wohnbauten ausgeführt hat. Nach dem Tod seines Vaters übernahm er dessen Büro und begann die Zusammenarbeit mit dem 1954 in Rio geborenen Paulo Jacobsen. Dieser hatte Fotografie in London studiert, bevor er 1979 seine Studien am Bennett Methodist Institute abschloss. Gegenwärtig beschäftigt das Büro Bernardes + Jacobsen etwa 50 Personen in Rio de Janeiro sowie São Paulo und arbeitet an ca. 40 Projekten pro Jahr. Zu seinen wichtigsten Bauten zählen die Hauptverwaltung der Firma Gerdau (Santa Catarina, 2005), das Haus FW (Guaruja, 2005) und das Hauptbüro der MPM Agency (São Paulo, 2006). Neuere Projekte sind das Haus JH (São Paulo, 2008), das Haus JZ (Bahia, 2008), das Haus RW (Búzios, Rio de Janeiro, 2006–09, hier veröffentlicht) sowie die Häuser FN und DB (beide in São Paulo, 2009), alle in Brasilien.

Thiago Bernardes est né à Rio de Janeiro en 1974. L'agence **BERNARDES + JACOBSEN** a été fondée en 1980 par son père, Claudio Bernardes, et Paulo Jacobsen, pionniers d'un nouveau type d'architecture résidentielle voulant associer un type de conception contemporaine à la culture brésilienne. Thiago Bernardes a travaillé dans l'agence paternelle de 1991 à 1996, puis a créé sa propre structure, réalisant plus de 30 projets résidentiels jusqu'en 2001. Après le décès de son père, il a réintégré l'agence paternelle et commencé à collaborer avec Paulo Jacobsen, né en 1954 à Rio de Janeiro. Jacobsen avait également étudié la photographie à Londres, avant d'être diplômé du Bennett Methodist Institute en 1979. L'agence Bernardes + Jacobsen emploie actuellement près de 50 personnes à Rio et São Paulo et intervient sur une quarantaine de projets chaque année. Parmi leurs réalisations les plus significatives : le siège de Gerdau (Santa Catarina, 2005) ; la maison FW (Guaruja, 2005) ; la maison CF (Angra dos Reis, Rio de Janeiro, 2001-06) et le siège de l'agence MPM (São Paulo, 2006). Parmi leurs travaux actuels : les maisons JH (São Paulo, 2008), JZ (Bahia, 2008), RW (Búzios, Rio de Janeiro, 2006–09, publiée ici) ainsi que FN et DB (São Paulo, 2009), tous au Brésil.

RW HOUSE

Búzios, Rio de Janeiro, Brazil, 2006–09

Address: not disclosed
Area: 4900 m². Client: not disclosed. Cost: not disclosed

Despite its very large size, this house is barely visible from the beach, given its horizontal H-shaped layout containing just the two master suites on the upper level. Lifted 50 centimeters above the ground, the residence appears to be lighter than its volume would imply. H-shaped, the house is logically divided into three axes. One of these wings contains the bedrooms, while the central volume connects the private areas to the six-meter-high living-room area looking to the garden and beach. The third axis is dedicated to leisure with a swimming pool and relaxation areas. Laminated, untreated eucalyptus wood from reforested areas is used for the structure. Natural ventilation is privileged via the internal gardens planted with native plants. The architects explain: "The wood panel concept was created to work as a protection from the sun and was adopted as the aesthetical concept of the house. It also works very well with the tropical weather of the region. These panels differentiate the external circulation areas, but also the private ones, since they protect the private area accesses."

Dieses Haus ist, trotz seiner beachtlichen Größe, aufgrund der horizontalen H-Form vom Strand her kaum sichtbar, weil das Obergeschoss nur die beiden Schlafsuiten der Besitzer enthält. Das Gebäude ist 50 cm aufgeständert und wirkt leichter, als die Baumasse es vermuten lässt. Die H-Form teilt das Haus in drei Trakte auf. Einer dieser Flügel enthält die Schlafzimmer, das zentrale Volumen verbindet die privaten Räume mit dem 6 m hohen Wohnbereich, der zum Garten und zum Strand orientiert ist. Die dritte Achse mit Swimmingpool und Erholungsbereichen ist der Freizeit gewidmet. Für die Konstruktion wurde verleimtes, unbehandeltes Eukalyptusholz aus aufgeforsteten Gebieten verwendet. Natürlicher Belüftung durch innenliegende Gärten mit einheimischer Bepflanzung wurde der Vorzug gegeben. Die Architekten erklären: „Das Konzept mit den Holzpaneelen entstand zum Schutz vor der Sonne und wurde auch als ästhetisches Konzept des Hauses übernommen. Es funktioniert sehr gut im tropischen Klima dieser Region. Die Tafeln begrenzen die außen liegenden Freibereiche ebenso wie die privaten, indem sie die Zugänge zu den Privaträumen schützen."

Malgré ses très grandes dimensions, cette maison reste à peine visible de la plage du fait de sa forme en H surbaissé sur laquelle viennent se greffer les deux suites principales en étage. Suspendue de 50 cm au-dessus du sol, elle semble plus légère que son volume ne pourrait le laisser penser. Elle est divisée en trois zones. L'une des ailes contient les chambres tandis que le volume central fait le lien entre les parties privées et le séjour de 6 m de haut qui donne à la fois sur le jardin et la plage. Le troisième axe est consacré à des espaces de détente et une piscine. L'ensemble est en eucalyptus laminé non traité, issu de forêts replantées. Des jardins intérieurs plantés de végétaux locaux assurent une ventilation naturelle. Selon les architectes : « Le concept de panneaux de bois a été mis au point pour protéger du soleil mais est également devenu le principe esthétique général de la maison. Il est parfaitement adapté au climat tropical de la région. Ces panneaux différencient les circulations externes, mais aussi les zones privées puisqu'ils protègent leurs accès. »

The long, low lines of the RW House are visible in the photo above, but even more clearly in the elevation drawings on the right page.

Die langen, niedrigen Umrisse des Hauses RW sind im oberen Foto erkennbar, aber noch deutlicher in den Ansichten auf der rechten Seite.

La photo ci-dessus, encore davantage les élévations de la page de droite, mettent en valeur les lignes allongées et surbaissées de la maison RW.

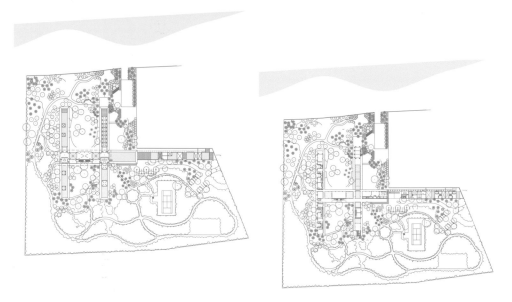

The H-shape of the house is seen in the site plans, above. The house has vast protected spaces where outdoors and interior meet in a seamless way.

Die H-Form des Gebäudes ist in den Lageplänen (oben) abzulesen. Das Haus hat große, geschützte Freibereiche, in denen Innen- und Außenräume nahtlos ineinander übergehen.

La forme en H de la maison se discerne sur les plans ci-dessus. Elle possède de vastes espaces protégés à la limite desquels l'extérieur et l'intérieur se fondent avec délicatesse.

A long swimming pool that can be covered echoes the narrow, rectangular forms of the volume of the house.

Ein langer Swimmingpool, der abgedeckt werden kann, folgt den schmalen, rechteckigen Gebäudeformen.

La piscine couvrable de forme allongée vient en écho aux volumes rectangulaires étroits de la maison.

Wood is present in ceilings and many other surfaces of the house, emphasizing its close connection to the natural setting.

Holz ist an den Decken und vielen anderen Flächen des Hauses präsent, was seine enge Verbindung zur natürlichen Umgebung betont.

Présent dans les plafonds et de nombreux autres surfaces, le bois renforce la connexion étroite de la résidence avec son cadre naturel.

The Brazilian climate allows for many spaces of the house to be open to the outside while still being enclosed within the volume of the house.

Das brasilianische Klima macht es möglich, viele Bereiche des Hauses nach außen zu öffnen, auch wenn sie im Gesamtvolumen des Gebäudes eingeschlossen sind.

Le climat brésilien permet de maintenir de nombreux espaces ouverts sur l'extérieur, bien qu'ils fassent partie du volume de la maison proprement dite.

BETON

BETON
Tarchominska 6 lok. 10
03–746 Warsaw
Poland

Tel: +48 22 403 89 96
E-mail: kle@betonon.com
Web: www.betonon.com

MARTA ROWINSKA was born in 1976 in Warsaw, Poland. She completed her studies at the University of Detroit Mercy (UDM, Detroit) and at the Warsaw University of Technology, Faculty of Architecture. **LECH ROWINSKI** was also born in 1976 in Warsaw, and attended the Warsaw University of Technology, Faculty of Architecture. They created their firm BETON in 2007 in their native city. They have dealt with industrial and graphic design projects as well as architecture, and they have created costumes and set designs for theater. As it does in French, BETON means concrete in Polish. The architects state: "And this is what we would like to be. As concrete as possible. And solid. And really hard to demolish!" Their recent work includes the Wooden Church in Tarnów (Tarnów on the Vistula, 2007–10, published here); "Dion.is.us", a set design for contemporary dance (Bretoncaffe Theatre, Warsaw, 2009); a typological study for semidetached wooden houses (Warsaw, 2010); and a series of objects for daily use inspired by Polish folk tradition, Etnodesign Festival (Kraków, 2010).

MARTA ROWINSKA wurde 1976 in Warschau geboren und studierte an der University of Detroit Mercy (UDM) sowie an der Architekturabteilung der Technischen Universität in Warschau. Auch **LECH ROWINSKI** wurde 1976 in Warschau geboren und studierte an der Warschauer Technischen Universität Architektur. 2007 gründeten sie in ihrer Heimatstadt die Firma BETON. Sie befassen sich mit Industrie- und Grafikdesign wie auch mit Architektur und haben sogar Kostüme und Kulissen für das Theater entworfen. BETON hat auf Polnisch die gleiche Bedeutung wie im Deutschen. Die Architekten erklären: „Und so wollen wir sein: so konkret wie möglich. Und solide. Und wirklich schwer zu zerstören!" Zu ihren aktuellen Arbeiten zählen die Holzkirche in Tarnów (Tarnów an der Vistula, 2007–10, hier veröffentlicht), „Dion.is.us", ein Szenenbild für modernen Tanz (Theater Bretoncaffe, Warschau, 2009), ein Typenentwurf für Doppelhäuser aus Holz (Warschau, 2010) sowie eine Reihe von Objekten für den täglichen Gebrauch, inspiriert von traditioneller polnischer Volkskunst, für das Festival Etnodesign (Krakau, 2010).

MARTA ROWINSKA, née en 1976 à Varsovie, a effectué ses études à l'université de Detroit Mercy (UDM, Detroit) et à la faculté d'architecture de l'Université de technologie de Varsovie. **LECH ROWINSKI**, également né en 1976 à Varsovie, a aussi étudié à la faculté d'architecture de l'Université de technologie de cette ville. Ils ont fondé l'agence BETON dans leur ville natale en 2007. Ils ont réalisé des projets aussi bien de design industriel et graphique que d'architecture et ont créé des décors et des costumes pour le théâtre. BETON a le même sens en français qu'en polonais. « C'est ce que nous aimerions faire. Aussi concret que possible. Et solide. Et très difficile à démolir », déclarent les architectes. Parmi leurs réalisations récentes : l'église en bois de Tarnów (Tarnów sur la Vistule, 2007–10, publiée ici) ; « Dion.is.us », décor pour un ballet de danse contemporaine (théâtre Bretoncaffe, Varsovie, 2009) ; une étude typologique pour des maisons jumelles en bois (Varsovie, 2010) et divers objets d'usage quotidien inspirés des traditions populaires polonaises (Festival Etnodesign, Cracovie, 2010).

CHURCH IN TARNÓW

Tarnów on the Vistula, Poland, 2007–10

Address: not disclosed
Area: 60 m². Cost: € 20 000. Client: not disclosed

Built for a well-known Polish writer, this small wooden church is intended as a place of meditation and prayer for the local community and is located on the bank of the Vistula River. It has only one glass wall that is the backdrop for the altar. The architects write: "Inside, you can find your peace by looking through the wall at the river and the distant horizon." Built largely by unskilled workers, the entirely wooden structure has a concrete slab foundation. According to the architects: "There is almost no detail, no fancy elements. This is also a kind of experiment—how to create a certain quality of space with the use of rudimentary technical simplicity." The arrangement, which consists in a private client financing an essentially public facility, is rare in Poland, especially in a religious context. But, as its designers say, "a church is something people still respect, so presenting it to them in such an unexpected scenery draws their minds to new, unexpected thoughts…"

Diese für einen bekannten polnischen Schriftsteller erbaute kleine Holzkirche soll der örtlichen Gemeinde als Ort der Meditation und des Gebets dienen. Der Bau steht am Ufer des Flusses Vistula und hat nur eine Glaswand, die den Hintergrund für den Altar bildet. Die Architekten schreiben: „Im Inneren kann man Frieden finden, wenn man durch die Wand auf den Fluss und zum weiten Horizont blickt." Das von überwiegend ungelernten Arbeitern errichtete, ganz aus Holz bestehende Gebäude hat ein Fundament aus Betonplatten. Laut Aussage der Architekten „gibt es fast keine Details, keine Dekorationselemente. Dies ist auch eine Art Experiment – wie sich eine gewisse Raumqualität mit elementarer technischer Einfachheit erzielen lässt." Dass ein privater Bauherr eine vorwiegend öffentliche Einrichtung finanziert, ist in Polen selten, besonders in einem religiösen Kontext. Aber, wie die Planer es ausdrücken, „eine Kirche wird von den Menschen immer noch respektiert. Wenn man sie ihnen in einer derart unerwarteten Umgebung anbietet, werden sie zu neuartigen, unerwarteten Gedanken angeregt."

Construite pour un célèbre écrivain polonais, cette petite église en bois est un lieu de méditation et de prière destiné à la communauté locale. Elle se dresse au bord de la Vistule. Un mur de verre s'élève derrière l'autel. Selon les architectes : « À l'intérieur, vous pouvez trouver la paix intérieure en regardant à travers ce mur vers le fleuve et l'horizon lointain. » Construite en grande partie par des ouvriers non spécialisés, cette structure entièrement en bois repose sur une dalle en béton. Selon les architectes : « On ne trouve presque aucun détail, aucun élément de fantaisie. C'est aussi une sorte d'expérience : comment créer une certaine qualité d'espace au moyen d'une simplicité technique rudimentaire. » Ce type de projet – un financement par un client privé d'une installation essentiellement publique – est rare en Pologne, surtout dans le contexte religieux, mais, comme l'expliquent ses concepteurs : « Une église est quelque chose que les gens respectent encore. Leur présenter celle-ci dans un cadre aussi inattendu peut orienter leur esprits vers des pensées nouvelles, inattendues … »

The strictly aligned shingles that
cover the church give a decidedly
modern impression despite the use
of an old cladding technique.

*Die gerade ausgerichteten Schindeln,
mit denen die Kirche überzogen ist,
verleihen ihr eine entschieden
moderne Wirkung, trotz Anwendung
der alten Verkleidungstechnik.*

*Les shingles soigneusement
alignés qui recouvrent l'extérieur de
l'église créent un effet de modernité,
même s'il s'agit d'une très ancienne
technique d'habillage.*

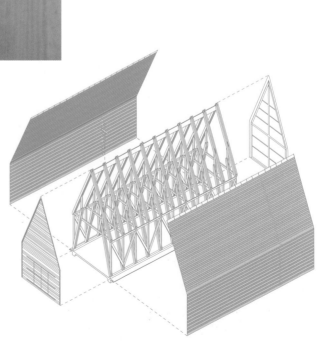

As the exploded axonometric drawing to the right shows, the church is built with a wooden frame and exterior surfaces that bend slightly, transforming the outer walls into the roof. Right page, the glazed interior.

Wie die Explosionszeichnung rechts zeigt, wurde die Kirche mit einem Holzskelett und leicht geneigten Außenwänden errichtet, die in das Dach übergehen. Rechte Seite: der verglaste Innenraum.

Comme le montre la vue axonométrique éclatée (à droite), l'église est contenue dans un cadre de bois dont les parois latérales se rabattent pour se transformer en toiture. À droite, le mur de l'autel entièrement vitré.

BOHLIN CYWINSKI JACKSON

Bohlin Cywinski Jackson
8 West Market Street, Suite 1200, Wilkes-Barre, PA 18701, USA
Tel: +1 570 825 8756 / Fax: +1 570 825 3744
E-mail: info_request@bcj.com / Web: www.bcj.com

BOHLIN CYWINSKI JACKSON was founded in 1965 by Peter Bohlin and Richard Powell in Wilkes-Barre, Pennsylvania. Peter Bohlin received a B.Arch from Rensselaer Polytechnic Institute (1959), and an M.Arch from Cranbrook Academy of Art (1961). Today the principals are Peter Bohlin, Bernard Cywinski, Jon Jackson, Dan Haden, Frank Grauman, William Loose, Randy Reid, Karl Backus, Gregory Mottola, Roxanne Sherbeck, and Robert Miller. The firm has additional offices in Pittsburgh, Philadelphia, Seattle, and San Francisco. In 1994, the practice received the Architecture Firm Award from the American Institute of Architects. Significant work includes the Pacific Rim Estate (Medina, Washington, 1997, joint venture with Cutler Anderson Architects); Headquarters for Pixar Animation Studios (Emeryville, California, 2001); and the Liberty Bell Center Independence National Historical Park (Philadelphia, Pennsylvania, 2003). In 2005, they completed the Ballard Library and Neighborhood Service Center (Seattle, Washington), listed by the AIA as one of the "Top Ten Green Buildings" for that year, and a couple of years later the two projects published here: Grand Teton Discovery and Visitor Center, Moose Junction (Grand Teton National Park, Wyoming, 2007) and Combs Point Residence (Finger Lakes Region, New York, 2007). Current work includes the Trinity College Master Plan (Hartford, Connecticut, 2008); Williams College Faculty Buildings and Library (Williamstown, Massachusetts, 2008 and 2012); California Institute of Technology Chemistry Building (Pasadena, California, 2010); Peace Arch US Port of Entry (Blaine, Washington, 2012), all in the USA, and retail stores for Apple Inc. in various locations worldwide.

Das Büro **BOHLIN CYWINSKI JACKSON** wurde 1965 von Peter Bohlin und Richard Powell in Wilkes-Barre, Pennsylvania, gegründet. Peter Bohlin machte seinen B.Arch in Architektur am Rensselaer Polytechnic Institute (1959) und den M.Arch an der Cranbrook Academy of Art (1961). Die gegenwärtigen Chefs sind Peter Bohlin, Bernard Cywinski, Jon Jackson, Dan Haden, Frank Grauman, William Loose, Randy Reid, Karl Backus, Gregory Mottola, Roxanne Sherbeck und Robert Miller. Die Firma hat weitere Büros in Pittsburgh, Philadelphia, Seattle und San Francisco. 1994 erhielt das Büro den Architecture Firm Award vom American Institute of Architects (AIA). Zu seinen bedeutenden Bauwerken gehören Pacific Rim Estate (Medina, Washington, 1997, als Joint Venture mit Cutler Anderson Architects), die Hauptverwaltung der Pixar Animation Studios (Emeryville, Kalifornien, 2001) sowie das Liberty Bell Center im Independence National Historical Park (Philadelphia, Pennsylvania, 2003). 2005 wurden die Ballard Library und das Neighborhood Service Center (Seattle, Washington) fertiggestellt, die das AIA in die Liste der Top Ten Green Buildings des Jahres aufnahm, und zwei Jahre später die beiden hier veröffentlichten Projekte: das Grand Teton Discovery and Visitor Center, Moose Junction (Grand Teton National Park, Wyoming, 2007) und das Wohnhaus Combs Point (Finger Lakes Region, New York, 2007). Zu den aktuellen Arbeiten des Büros gehören der Masterplan für das Trinity College (Hartford, Connecticut, 2008), Fakultätsbauten und Bibliothek des Williams College (Williamstown, Massachusetts, 2008 und 2012), das Chemistry Building am California Institute of Technology (Pasadena, Kalifornien, 2010), das Monument Peace Arch am US Port of Entry (Blaine, Washington, 2012), alle in den USA, sowie Ladengeschäfte für Apple Computer an verschiedenen Orten weltweit.

L'agence **BOHLIN CYWINSKI JACKSON** a été fondée en 1965 par Peter Bohlin et Richard Powell à Wilkes-Barre (Pennsylvanie). Peter Bohlin est diplômé B. Arch. du Rensselaer Polytechnic Institute (1959) et M. Arch. de la Cranbrook Academy of Art (1961). Les associés actuels sont Peter Bohlin, Bernard Cywinski, Jon Jackson, Dan Haden, Frank Grauman, William Loose, Randy Reid, Karl Backus, Gregory Mottola, Roxanne Sherbeck et Robert Miller. L'agence possède des bureaux à Pittsburgh, Philadelphie, Seattle et San Francisco. En 1994, elle a reçu le prix de l'Agence d'architecture de l'American Institute of Architects. Parmi ses réalisations les plus significatives : le Pacific Rim Estate (Medina, Washington, 1997, avec Cutler Anderson Architects) ; le siège des Pixar Animation Studios (Emeryville, Californie, 2001) et le Liberty Bell Center dans l'Independence National Historical Park (Philadelphie, Pennsylvanie, 2003). En 2005, ils ont achevé la bibliothèque Ballard et un centre de services de quartier (Seattle, Washington) désigné par l'AIA comme une « des dix grandes constructions vertes » de l'année, et deux ans plus tard deux projets publiés ici : centre d'informations des visiteurs de Grand Teton (Moose Junction, Parc national de Grand Teton, Wyoming, 2007) et la résidence Combs Point (Finger Lakes Region, New York, 2007). Plus récemment ils ont réalisé le plan directeur de Trinity College (Hartford, Connecticut, 2008) ; les bâtiments de la faculté et la bibliothèque du Williams College (Williamstown, Massachusetts, 2008 et 2012) ; le bâtiment de la chimie du California Institute of Technology (Pasadena, Californie, 2010) ; l'Arche de la Paix, port d'entrée américain (Blaine, Washington, 2012) et plusieurs magasins Apple dans le monde.

GRAND TETON DISCOVERY AND VISITOR CENTER

Moose Junction, Grand Teton National Park, Wyoming, USA, 2007

*Address: about 800 meters west of Moose Junction, Moose, Grand Teton National Park, Wyoming,
+1 307 739 3300, www.grand.teton.national-park.com
Area: 1812 m². Client: National Park Service, Grand Teton National Park Foundation, Grand Teton Association
Cost: not disclosed*

This building was made with log timber frames and laminated wood beams harvested from sustainably grown forests. The architects state: "The logs tell us of themselves, they remind us of great northern forests; the sounds, the smells, the soft touch of the earth. The milled timbers tell us of the nature of wood, its grain, how it is cut and planed." Board-formed concrete walls used for exterior walls, because of the presence of deep snowfalls, also show the trace of wood, although cedar siding is also used. An exposed concrete floor honed to reveal its aggregate and an upward looking window wall add more modern touches, but the presence of nature is so overwhelming on this site that visitors need not look far to see and sense it.

Dieses Gebäude wurde mit einer Rahmenkonstruktion aus Baumstämmen und verleimten Holzbalken errichtet, die aus nachhaltig bewirtschafteten Wäldern stammen. Die Architekten erklären: „Die Baumstämme erzählen uns ihre Geschichte, sie erinnern uns an die großen Wälder des Nordens, deren Rauschen, deren Gerüche, das Berühren ihres weichen Bodens. Die gefrästen Balken sprechen von der Natur des Holzes, seiner Maserung, wie es geschnitten und gehobelt wird." Wegen der heftigen Schneefälle bestehen die Außenwände aus Beton, der die Spuren der Schalbretter zeigt, wenngleich auch Verkleidung aus Zedernholz verwendet wurde. Der geschliffene Boden aus Sichtbeton, der seinen Zuschlag zeigt, und die schräg stehende Fensterwand setzen einige moderne Akzente, aber die Präsenz der Natur auf diesem Gelände ist so überwältgend, dass jeder Besucher sie sehen und spüren kann.

Ce bâtiment repose entièrement sur une ossature en grumes et poutres de bois lamellé issu de forêts d'exploitation durable. Pour les architectes : « Ces grumes nous parlent d'elles-mêmes, elles nous rappellent les grandes forêts nordiques, les sons, les odeurs, la douceur de la terre au toucher. Les bois travaillés nous parlent de la nature du bois, de son grain, de la façon dont il a été coupé et débité. » Les murs en béton nécessaires pour protéger le centre des importantes chutes de neige ont également conservé la trace de leur coffrage de bois. Ailleurs, on trouve aussi des bardages en cèdre. Un sol en béton brut sablé pour montrer sa composition et un mur de fenêtres regardant vers le ciel font partie des quelques touches plus modernes, mais la présence de la nature reste si forte que les visiteurs n'ont pas à se rendre plus loin pour la voir et la sentir.

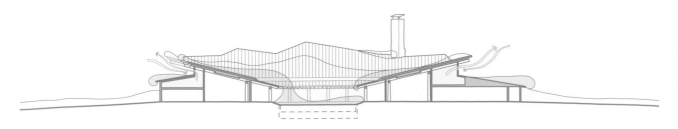

The low, but spectacular forms of the Center seem to respond to the natural setting, as seen in the images on these pages and in the site drawing.

Die niedrigen, aber eindrucksvollen Formen des Zentrums scheinen auf die natürliche Umgebung Bezug zu nehmen, wie aus den Bildern auf dieser Seite und dem Lageplan abzulesen ist.

Les formes surbaissées mais spectaculaires du centre semblent répondre à son cadre naturel, comme le montrent les images de ces pages et un dessin du site.

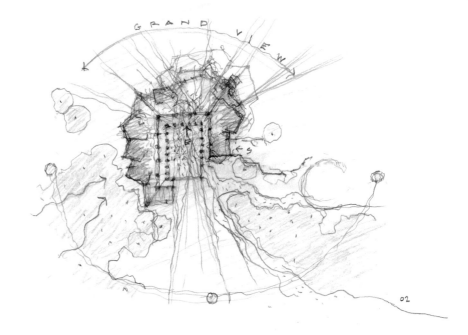

The interiors of the Center continue the overall use of wood, though the floors are made of concrete. Full-height glazing allows visitors to see the surrounding mountains.

Auch im Inneren des Zentrums wurde überall Holz verwendet; die Böden sind allerdings aus Beton. Die geschosshohe Verglasung bietet den Besuchern Aussicht auf die Berge der Umgebung.

Le bois est tout aussi présent à l'intérieur, mais les sols sont en béton. De grands murs de verre permettent de voir les montagnes environnantes.

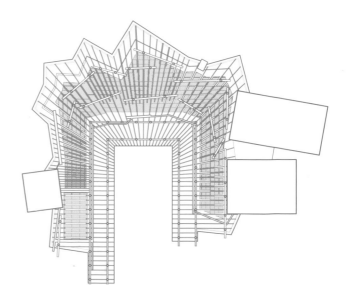

COMBS POINT RESIDENCE

Finger Lakes Region, New York, USA, 2007

Address: not disclosed
Area: 502 m² (main house); 130 m² (guesthouse). Client: Wendell and Kim Weeks
Cost: not disclosed

This residence was conceived as a "string of structures" formed essentially by the main house, office, and guesthouse. This string is drawn out between a lakefront and a valley waterfall. Circulation is organized along the southern glass wall, while an elevated exterior walkway also brings together the elements of the complex. Douglas fir glulam post and beams were used as structural elements. The woods used are Forest Stewardship Council (FSC) certified, with such choices as formaldehyde-free plywood figuring in the choice of the architects for environmental reasons. Gently lifted off the ground, with their broad glazing and generous wood surfaces, the elements of the **COMBS POINT RESIDENCE** take full advantage of the natural setting while disturbing the environment as little as possible.

Dieses Wohnhaus wurde als „Gebäudekette" konzipiert, die sich aus Haupthaus, Bürobau und Gästetrakt zusammensetzt. Diese Kette erstreckt sich zwischen dem Seeufer und einem Tal mit Wasserfall. Die Erschließung erfolgt entlang der südlichen Glaswand; ein erhöht angebrachter Außengang verbindet ebenfalls die einzelnen Elemente des Komplexes. Ein Ständerbau aus verleimter Douglastanne bildet die Konstruktion. Die verwendeten Hölzer sind vom Forest Stewardship Council (FSC) zertifiziert; die Architekten entschieden sich aus Rücksicht auf die Umwelt für formaldehydfreies Sperrholz. Die leicht vom Boden abgehobenen Bauten der **WOHNANLAGE COMBS POINT** fügen sich mit ihren großen Glas- und Holzflächen bestens in ihr natürliches Umfeld ein und belasten ihre Umgebung so wenig wie nur möglich.

Cette résidence est un « chapelet de structures » constitué par la maison principale, un bureau et une maison d'amis. Il s'étire entre le lac et une cascade dans une vallée. La circulation s'organise au sud le long d'un mur de verre. Une passerelle en bois suspendue réunit les divers composants de l'ensemble. L'ossature est à poteaux et poutres en lamellé-collé de pin de Douglas. Pour des raisons environnementales, les bois retenus sont certifiés par le FSC (Forest Stewardship Council), en particulier des contreplaqués sans formaldéhyde. Légèrement surélevés du sol, bénéficiant de généreux vitrages et d'importantes parois de bois, les différents composants de la **RÉSIDENCE COMBS POINT** profitent pleinement de leur cadre naturel et exercent un impact environnemental minimum.

The site drawing to the right shows
the insertion of the stringlike form of
the residence in its natural setting.

*Der Lageplan rechts zeigt die
Einfügung des kettenförmigen Wohnhauses in seine natürliche Umgebung.*

*Un dessin du site, à droite, montre
l'insertion du plan en chapelet de la
résidence dans son cadre naturel.*

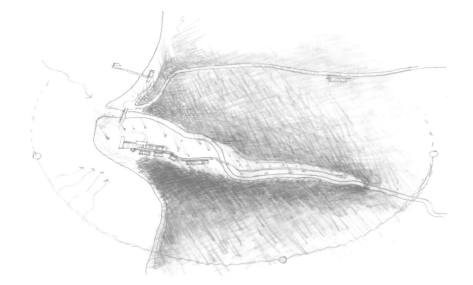

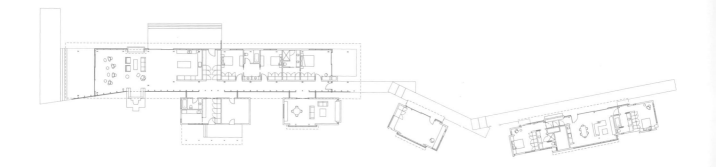

The long, low succession of volumes is inserted into a forest environment, with generous glazing emphasizing the connection with nature.

Die lange, niedrige Folge der Baumassen ist in eine bewaldete Umgebung gesetzt; durch großzügige Verglasung wird die Verbindung zur Natur betont.

La longue succession des petites constructions basses s'insère dans un environnement boisé. Le généreux vitrage met en valeur la connexion avec la nature.

A wooden walkway links the different parts of the residence, while such elements as the angled roof seen above break the sensation of strict rectangular volumes.

Ein hölzerner Steg verbindet die verschiedenen Teile des Wohnhauses, während bestimmte Elemente, wie das oben sichtbare, abgewinkelte Dach, die Wirkung der streng rechteckigen Volumen aufbrechen.

Une allée en bois relie les différentes parties de la résidence. Des éléments comme le toit à contre-pente, ci-dessus, rompt le sentiment de volumes strictement rectangulaires.

Full-height glazing offers astonishing views of the nearby lake. Sparse furnishing fits well into the architectural environment.

Die geschosshohe Verglasung bietet erstaunliche Ausblicke auf den nahe gelegenen See. Die sparsame Möblierung passt sich gut in das architektonische Umfeld ein.

Le vitrage toute hauteur offre des vues étonnantes sur le lac proche. Peu abondant, le mobilier est bien adapté à son environnement architectural.

As the drawing below shows, the upward angle of the roof is calculated in places to allow sunlight to penetrate into the interiors.

Aus der Zeichnung unten lässt sich ablesen, dass das abgewinkelte Dach so ausgebildet wurde, um mehr Sonnenlicht in die Innenräume einzulassen.

Comme le montre le dessin ci-dessous, la pente du toit est calculée pour permettre aux rayons du soleil de pénétrer jusqu'à l'intérieur des maisons.

ENRIQUE BROWNE

Enrique Browne y Asociados Arquitectos
Los Conquistadores 2461, Providencia
Santiago 6650046
Chile

Tel: +56 2 234 2027
Fax: +56 2 231 5630
E-mail: ebrowne@entelchile.net
Web: www.ebrowne.cl

ENRIQUE BROWNE was born in Santiago, Chile, in 1942. He received an architecture degree (1965) and a master of urban planning degree (1968) both from the Universidad Católica de Chile. He was finalist for the first Mies van der Rohe Prize for Latin America (Barcelona, 1998) and has lectured widely and participated in numerous international competitions. His most significant projects (all in Santiago unless otherwise indicated) include Houses on Charles Hamilton Street (1974); House on Paul Harris Street (1980); Caracola House (1985); "El Agora" Convention Center and Youth Accommodation (1986); Consorcio-Santiago Building (1990); Chapel of Villa Maria School (1992); Pioneer Offices (Paine, 1995); Los Conquistadores Office (1995); a Pedestrian Bridge (Zapallar, 2008, published here); Sonda Building (1996); and Luksic Mining Center (2009–).

ENRIQUE BROWNE wurde 1942 in Santiago de Chile geboren. Er machte sowohl seinen Abschluss in Architektur (1965) als auch einen Master in Stadtplanung (1968) an der Universidad Católica de Chile. Browne war Finalist beim ersten Mies-van-der-Rohe-Preis für Lateinamerika (Barcelona, 1998); er hat vielerorts gelehrt und an zahlreichen internationalen Wettbewerben teilgenommen. Zu seinen bedeutendsten Projekten (alle in Santiago, sofern nicht anders angegeben) zählen Wohnhäuser in der Avenida Charles Hamilton (1974), ein Wohnhaus in der Avenida Paul Harris (1980), das Haus Caracola (1985), das Kongresszentrum und Jugendherberge El Agora (1986), das Edificio Consorcio-Santiago (1990), die Kapelle der Schule Villa Maria (1992), die Pioneer-Büros (Paine, 1995), das Bürogebäude Los Conquistadores (1995), eine Fußgängerbrücke (Zapallar, 2008, hier veröffentlicht), das Edificio Sonda (1996) und das Luksic Centro de Minería (2009–).

ENRIQUE BROWNE, né à Santiago du Chili en 1942, est diplômé en architecture (1965) et en urbanisme (1968) de l'Université catholique du Chili. Il a été finaliste du premier prix Mies van der Rohe pour l'Amérique latine (Barcelone, 1998), a donné de nombreuses conférences et a participé à de multiples concours internationaux. Parmi ses projets les plus significatifs, tous à Santiago sauf exceptions mentionnées : des maison rue Charles Hamilton (1974) ; une maison rue Paul Harris (1980) ; la maison Caracola (1985) ; le centre de congrès et auberge de jeunesse El Agora (1986) ; l'immeuble Consorcio-Santiago (1990) ; la chapelle de l'école Villa Maria (1992) ; les bureaux de la société Pioneer (Paine, 1995) ; les bureaux Los Conquistadores (1995 ; une passerelle piétonnière (Zapallar, 2008, publiée ici) ; l'immeuble Sonda Building (1996) et le Luksic Mining Center (2009–).

PEDESTRIAN BRIDGE
Zapallar, Valparaíso, Chile, 2008

Address: Route F-30-E, Zapallar, Valparaíso, Chile
Area: 40 m². Client: City of Zapallar. Cost: not disclosed

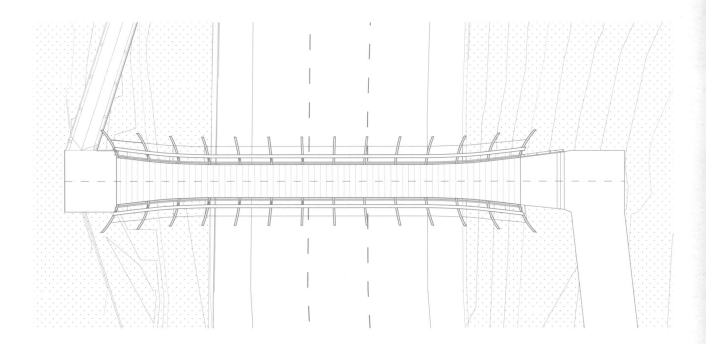

This **PEDESTRIAN BRIDGE** links the resort town of Zapallar to social housing on the opposite side of Route F30-E. Built of laminated wood that was partially assembled in a factory, the structure rests on simple concrete bases. The architect states: "Although it has the cross-form of a rowboat, it also corresponds to an inverted arch... It can be seen as an inverted boat from the bay, a beauty queen's tiara, an arch of access to the town, or a fish backbone." The bridge, which also carries drain pipes across the road, has metallic netting to deter stones being thrown on passing vehicles below, and LED illumination. Enrique Browne explains that for reasons against his will the location of the bridge was moved some 50 meters from the high point of the road where he planned it, and ramps and pedestrian access paths were not carried out according to his plans.

Diese **FUSSGÄNGERBRÜCKE** verbindet den Kurort Zapallar mit dem sozialen Wohnungsbau auf der anderen Seite der Ruta F30-E. Die Konstruktion besteht aus Schichtholz, das zum Teil in der Fabrik montiert wurde; sie steht auf einer einfachen Betonbasis. Der Architekt erklärt: „Obgleich die Brücke im Querschnitt einem Ruderboot ähnelt, entspricht sie auch einem umgekehrten Bogen ... Von der Bucht aus wirkt sie wie ein umgekehrtes Boot, das Diadem einer Schönheitskönigin, ein Eingangsbogen zur Stadt oder das Rückgrat eines Fisches." Die Fußgängerbrücke, die auch die über die Straße führenden Entwässerungsrohre aufnimmt, ist mit einem Metallnetz versehen, damit keine Steine auf die darunter verkehrenden Fahrzeuge geworfen werden können, und hat eine LED-Beleuchtung. Enrique Browne erklärt, dass die Brücke gegen seinen Willen um etwa 50 m vom Hochpunkt der Straße versetzt wurde und dass man die Rampen und die Fußgängererschließung nicht nach seinen Plänen ausgeführt habe.

Cette **PASSERELLE** relie la ville de villégiature de Zapallar à des logements sociaux situés de l'autre côté de la route F30-E. Construite en bois lamellé-collé et partiellement assemblée en usine, elle s'appuie sur de simples culées en béton. Comme l'explique l'architecte : « Si elle ressemble en coupe à une coque de skiff, cette passerelle peut aussi évoquer un arc inversé... Vue de la baie, on peut penser à un bateau renversé, une tiare de reine de beauté, un arc triomphal ou une arrête de poisson. » La passerelle, à laquelle sont fixés des tuyaux de drainage, est équipée de filets métalliques pour éviter le lancer de cailloux sur les véhicules passant en contrebas et est éclairée par des DEL. Enrique Browne explique aussi que, pour des raisons indépendantes de sa volonté, l'implantation a été décalée de 50 m par rapport au point supérieur de la voie prévu au départ, et que les accès piétonniers comme les rampes n'ont pas été exécutés selon ses plans.

Although the drawing above reveals an essentially regular form, the Pedestrian Bridge arcs over the roadway, with its spine-like superstructure evoking a nave-like wooden form.

Obgleich die Zeichnung oben eine ziemlich gleichmäßige Form der Fußgängerbrücke zeigt, ist sie über der Straße gewölbt; ihr axialer hölzerner Oberbau hat eine schiffsähnliche Form.

De forme régulière, comme le montre le dessin ci-dessus, la passerelle piétonnière forme un arc au-dessus de la route, l'habillage du tablier est en coque de bateau et le garde-corps évoque les côtes d'un squelette.

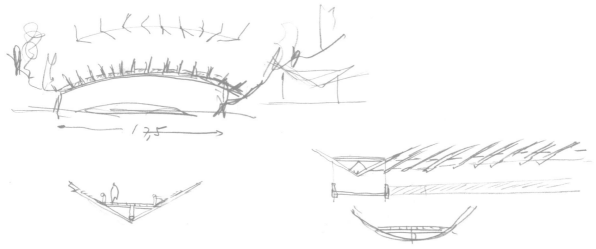

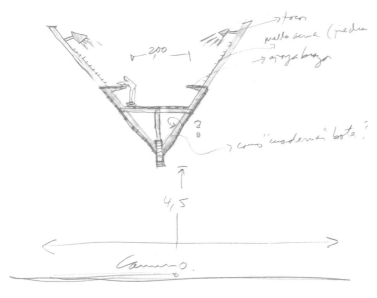

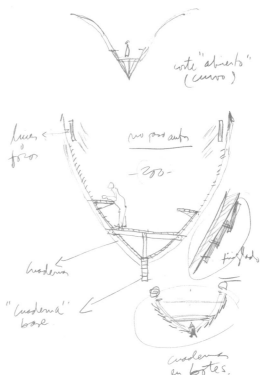

The V-form of the bridge is seen in these drawings. Metal is used in the handrails and protective netting on either side of the platform.

Die V-Form der Brücke ist auf diesen Zeichnungen zu erkennen. Für die Geländer und das schützende Netz auf beiden Seiten des Gehwegs wurde Metall verwendet.

La forme en V du pont apparaît nettement sur ces dessins. La rampe des garde-corps et le treillis de protection sont en métal.

Though it was built with a low budget and not completed according to the wishes of the architect, the bridge gives pedestrians an unexpected and rather thrilling way to cross the road.

Obgleich die Brücke mit einem geringen Budget und nicht nach den Wünschen des Architekten ausgeführt wurde, bietet sie Fußgängern eine unerwartete und aufregende Möglichkeit zur Überquerung der Straße.

Bien que construite avec un faible budget et non achevée selon les désirs de l'architecte, la passerelle offre aux piétons un mode de traversée inattendu de cette artère.

BERNARD BÜHLER

Agence Bernard Bühler
5 quai de Bacalan
33300 Bordeaux
France

Tel: +33 5 56 39 27 33
Fax: +33 5 56 69 15 62
E-mail: bernard-buhler@wanadoo.fr
Web: www.bernard-buhler.com

BERNARD BÜHLER was born in 1954 in Laparade, France. He grew up in Bordeaux where his practice is based. He received a BEP (a high-school level qualification, 1972) in civil engineering. He worked in a Bordeaux office (Sallier) until 1985 at which time he succeeded in being certified as an architect based on his personal work. He opened his own office the following year and created his present firm in 2000. His work is essentially based on social housing in the area of Bordeaux. As he says, he attempts to offer the residents of low-cost housing "an optimal quality of life," interpreting sustainable development in a way that affords sustainable living conditions. His work includes Arc en Ciel Housing (Bordeaux, 2010); the Hameau de Plantoun (Bayonne, 2008–09, carried out with his daughter Marie Bühler, published here); Les Chais housing (Bordeaux, 2009); Cité Prost housing (Paris, 2007); and the Clos des Sablières housing (Bordeaux, 2009), all in France. He has numerous other similar projects underway.

BERNARD BÜHLER wurde 1954 in Laparade, Frankreich, geboren. Er wuchs in Bordeaux auf, wo sich auch sein Büro befindet. 1972 machte er ein Diplom in Ingenieurbau. Er arbeitete in einem Büro in Bordeaux (Salier), bis es ihm 1985 gelang, aufgrund seiner eigenen Arbeiten als Architekt anerkannt zu werden. Im darauffolgenden Jahr eröffnete er sein eigenes Büro, 2000 seine gegenwärtige Firma. Er beschäftigt sich vorwiegend mit sozialem Wohnungsbau in der Umgegend von Bordeaux. Nach eigener Aussage versucht er, den Bewohnern von preiswerten Wohnungen „eine optimale Lebensqualität" zu bieten, und interpretiert nachhaltige Bebauung in einer Weise, die auch nachhaltige Lebensbedingungen garantiert. Zu seinen Projekten zählen die Wohnanlage Arc en Ciel (Bordeaux, 2010), Hameau de Plantoun (Bayonne, 2008–09, ausgeführt zusammen mit seiner Tochter Marie Bühler, hier veröffentlicht), der Wohnungsbau Les Chais (Bordeaux, 2009), die Wohnanlage Cité Prost (Paris, 2007) sowie die Wohnbauten Clos des Sablières (Bordeaux, 2009), alle in Frankreich. Zahlreiche weitere ähnliche Projekte sind in Arbeit.

BERNARD BÜHLER, né en 1954 à Laparade (France), a grandi à Bordeaux où se trouve aujourd'hui son agence. Il a passé un BEP en ingénierie civile en 1972 puis a travaillé dans une agence bordelaise (Sallier) jusqu'en 1985, date à laquelle il est devenu architecte certifié grâce à ses réalisations personnelles. Il a ouvert une agence l'année suivante, puis son agence actuelle en 2000. Il intervient essentiellement dans le secteur du logement social en région bordelaise. Il s'efforce d'offrir aux habitants de ces logements « une qualité de vie optimale » et de mettre la règlementation du développement durable au service de conditions de vie écologiques. Parmi ses réalisations : les logements collectifs Arc en Ciel (Bordeaux, 2010) ; le Hameau de Plantoun (Bayonne, 2008–09, en collaboration avec sa fille Marie Bühler, publié ici) ; les logements collectifs Les Chais (Bordeaux, 2009), ceux de la Cité Prost (Paris, 2007), du Clos des Sablières (Bordeaux, 2009) et de nombreux projets de ce type en cours.

HAMEAU DE PLANTOUN

Bayonne, France, 2008–09

Address: Avenue Marcel Breuer, Bayonne, France
Area: 3327 m². Client: OPHLM Bayonne. Cost: € 3.804 million. Collaboration: Marie Bühler

This complex is located on Avenue Marcel Breuer, near the Hauts de Sainte-Croix housing (1963–74) designed by Breuer that is currently being renovated. The **HAMEAU DE PLANTOUN** contains 39 residences located in a staggered pattern on either side of a curving path. The architect explains that his choice of wood is related both to cost considerations and to environmental concerns. The light design of the housing, which is set up on wood pilotis and thin metal posts allowed the site to be left relatively intact, while permitting residents parking below the houses. Essentially geometric, the volumes of the houses are variable according to their type, and the overall impression they give is one of unity that emerges from an accumulation of similar forms. The extensive use of plywood is certainly unexpected, as is the resulting overall appearance of the complex. There is a suggestion of temporary housing in the way the Hameau de Plantoun looks, even a certain industrial feeling, and yet the houses themselves are both comfortable and coherent.

Dieser Wohnkomplex liegt an der Avenue Marcel Breuer, nahe der von Breuer geplanten Wohnanlage Hauts de Sainte-Croix (1963–74), die gegenwärtig saniert wird. **HAMEAU DE PLANTOUN** besteht aus 39 Wohnungen in gestaffelter Anordnung zu beiden Seiten eines geschwungenen Wegs. Der Architekt erklärt, dass er sich sowohl aus Kosten- als auch aus Umweltschutzgründen für Holz entschieden habe. Die leichte Gestaltung der Häuser, die auf hölzernen Pilotis und dünnen Metallstützen stehen, machte es möglich, das Grundstück relativ unberührt zu belassen, und bietet den Bewohnern Parkmöglichkeiten unter den Gebäuden. Die im Wesentlichen geometrischen Volumen der Häuser variieren entsprechend ihrem Typ und erscheinen in ihrer Gesamtwirkung als einheitliche Zusammenstellung ähnlicher Formen. Die Verwendung von so viel Sperrholz ist zweifellos ungewöhnlich, ebenso das daraus resultierende Erscheinungsbild des gesamten Komplexes. Hameau de Plantoun wirkt ein wenig wie temporäre oder sogar industrielle Bauten; trotzdem sind die Häuser selbst wohnlich und stimmig.

Cet ensemble est situé avenue Marcel Breuer, non loin des logements des Hauts de Sainte-Croix (1963-74) conçus par Breuer et en cours de rénovation. Le **HAMEAU DE PLANTOUN** regroupe 39 résidences selon un plan en zigzag de chaque côté d'une allée en courbes. L'architecte explique que le choix du bois tient à la fois à des considérations de coût et à des préoccupations environnementales. La conception légère de ces logements qui reposent sur des pilotis de bois ou de fins poteaux de métal laisse le site relativement intact tout en permettant aux résidants de garer leurs voitures sous les maisons. Les volumes de géométrie simple sont de dimensions variables, selon leur type. L'impression d'unité naît de l'accumulation de formes similaires. Le recours massif au contreplaqué est assez inattendu et détermine l'aspect général de l'ensemble. Si l'on ressent une impression de logements temporaires ou même de constructions industrielles, ces maisons semblent néanmoins à la fois confortable et de conception cohérente.

Seen from a distance, the Hameau de Plantoun looks something like a temporary encampment. The natural aging of the wood will make it blend into its wooded background.

Aus der Entfernung sieht Hameau de Plantoun aus wie ein provisorisches Feldlager. Wenn das Holz altert, wird es mit dem bewaldeten Hintergrund verschmelzen.

Vu de loin, le Hameau de Pantoun fait un peu penser à un campement temporaire. La patine progressive du bois favorisera son intégration dans son cadre forestier.

An overall site plan (below) shows the irregular placement of the housing units along the wooded site. Above, the buildings seem very much in harmony with the trees.

Der Gesamtlageplan (unten) zeigt die unregelmäßige Anordnung der Wohneinheiten auf dem bewaldeten Gelände. Oben: Die Bauten wirken inmitten der Bäume sehr harmonisch.

Le plan d'ensemble du site (ci-dessous) montre l'implantation irrégulière des petits immeubles en lisière de la forêt. Ci-dessus, les immeubles semblent très en harmonie avec les arbres.

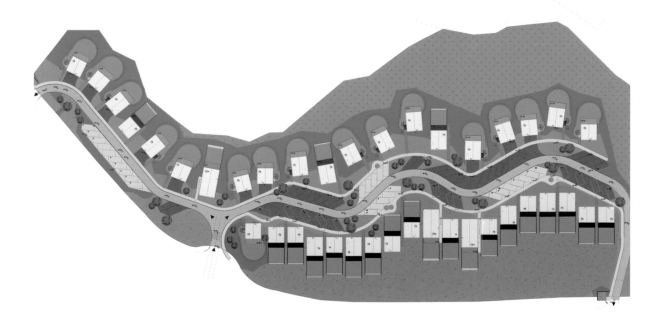

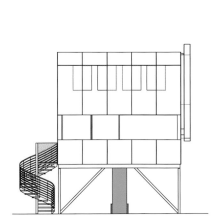
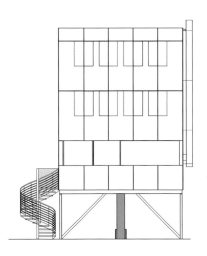
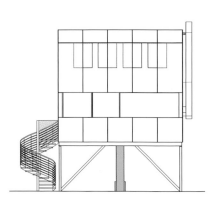

Plans show the flexibility of the architectural system and the basic, geometric simplicity of the design.

Die Grundrisse bezeugen die Flexibilität des architektonischen Systems und die zugrunde liegende einfache Geometrie des Entwurfs.

Les plans montrent la souplesse du système constructif et la simplicité géométrique du projet.

Lifted up off the ground on metal pilotis, the structures have an even more "temporary" appearance, yet they are designed as permanent residences.

Die auf Metallstützen aufgeständerten Gebäude wirken noch „temporärer"; sie sind jedoch als dauerhafte Wohnbauten geplant.

Décrochés du sol par des pilotis métalliques, les immeubles prennent une apparence encore plus « temporaire » bien qu'ils soient conçus pour une résidence permanente.

Chen House ▶

MARCO CASAGRANDE

Casagrande Laboratory
Linnankatu 16
20100 Turku
Finland

Tel: +358 50 308 91 66
E-mail: info@clab.fi
Web: www.clab.fi

Born in 1971 in Turku, Finland, **MARCO CASAGRANDE** attended the Helsinki University of Technology, Department of Architecture. He worked in the office of Casagrande & Rintala (1998–2003) and has been the principal of the Casagrande Laboratory since 2003. His work includes Floating Sauna (Rosendal, Norway, 2002); Treasure Hill (Taipei, Taiwan, 2003); Post-Industrial Fleet (Venice Biennale, Italy, 2004); 7-Eleven Sauna (Taipei, Taiwan, 2007); Chen House (Sanjhih, Taiwan, 2007–08, published here); Guandu River City (Taipei, Taiwan, 2009), and the Bug Dome (Shenzhen and Hong Kong Bi-City Biennale of Architecture/Urbanism, Shenzhen, China, 2009). He is currently working on a new university of architecture and urbanism in Taipei. Marco Casagrande says that a ruin emerges when something "man-made has become part of nature. I am looking forward," he says, "to designing ruins."

Der 1971 in Turku, Finnland, geborene **MARCO CASAGRANDE** studierte Architektur an der Technischen Universität Helsinki. Er arbeitete im Büro Casagrande & Rintala (1998–2003) und leitet seit 2003 die Firma Casagrande Laboratory. Zu seinen Arbeiten zählen die Floating Sauna (Rosendal, Norwegen, 2002), Treasure Hill (Taipeh, Taiwan, 2003), Post-Industrial Fleet (Biennale von Venedig, 2004), die 7-Eleven Sauna (Taipeh, Taiwan, 2007), das Haus Chen (Sanjhih, Taiwan, 2007–08, hier veröffentlicht), die Guandu River City (Taipeh, Taiwan, 2009) und der Bug Dome (Shenzhen and Hong Kong Bi-City Biennale of Architecture/Urbanism, Shenzhen, China, 2009). Gegenwärtig plant er eine neue Universität für Architektur und Städtebau in Taipeh. Marco Casagrande sagt, dass eine Ruine entstehe, wenn etwas „von Menschen Gemachtes Teil der Natur wird. Ich freue mich darauf", sagt er, „Ruinen zu entwerfen."

Né en 1971 à Turku (Finlande), **MARCO CASAGRANDE** a fait ses études au département d'Architecture de l'Université de technologie d'Helsinki. Après avoir créé l'agence Casagrande & Rintala (1998–2003), il dirige depuis 2003 Casagrande Laboratory. Parmi ses réalisations : un sauna flottant (Rosendal, Norvège, 2002) ; la restauration de Treasure Hill (Taipei, Taïwan, 2003) ; le projet de Flotte postindustrielle (Biennale de Venise, 2004) ; le sauna 7-Eleven (Taipei, Taïwan, 2007) ; la maison Chen (Sanjhih, Taïwan, 2007–08, publiée ici) ; la Guandu River City (Taipei, Taïwan, 2009) et le Bug Dome (Biennale d'architecture/urbanisme Bi-City de Shenzhen et Hong Kong, Shenzhen, Chine, 2009). Il travaille actuellement à un projet de nouvelle université d'architecture et d'urbanisme pour Taipei. Marco Casagrande explique qu'une ruine apparaît lorsque « quelque chose réalisé par l'homme vient à faire partie de la nature … Je cherche, dit-il, à concevoir des ruines ».

CHEN HOUSE
Sanjhih, Taipei, Taiwan, 2007–08

Address: not disclosed
Area: 62 m². Client: Chen family. Cost: not disclosed

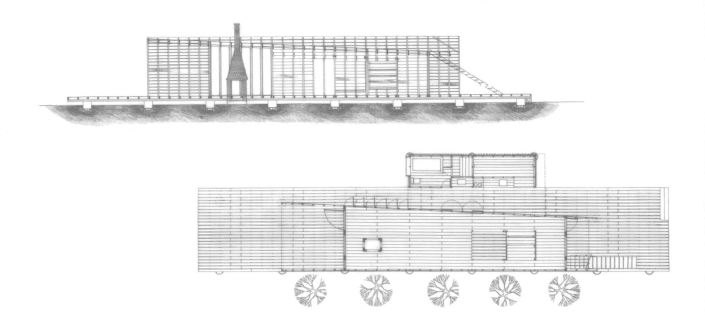

This house, made of mahogany and concrete, is set on 3890 square meters of farmland in the Datun Mountains. It is set up off the ground to allow for occasional flooding conditions and has a total footprint of 138 square meters. The site is also subject to typhoon or even earthquake conditions. The slatted design is intended to capture cooling breezes in warm months, while a fireplace is used for winter heating. With its extended wooden deck, the house offers an easy transition between interior and exterior. Marco Casagrande states: "The house is not strong or heavy—it is weak and flexible. It is also not closing the environment out, but designed to give farmers a needed shelter." He quotes a short poem called "Iron" by Bertolt Brecht (1898–1956) that can readily be applied to this design: "In a dream last night, I saw a great storm. It seized the scaffolding. It tore the cross-clasps, the iron ones, down. But what was made of wood, swayed and remained."

Dieses Wohnhaus aus Mahagoni und Beton steht auf einem 3890 m² großen landwirtschaftlichen Gelände in den Datun-Bergen. Es ist aufgeständert, um es vor gelegentlich vorkommenden Überschwemmungen zu sichern, und hat eine Gesamtgrundfläche von 138 m². Das Gebiet ist auch durch Taifune und sogar durch Erdbeben gefährdet. Die Gestaltung mit Holzlatten dient dazu, im Sommer kühlende Winde einzulassen; ein Kamin sorgt für Wärme im Winter. Die große Holzterrasse bietet fließende Übergänge zwischen Innen- und Außenbereichen. Marco Casagrande erklärt: „Das Haus ist nicht fest oder schwer – es ist schwach und flexibel. Es schließt auch seine Umgebung auch nicht aus, sondern dient dazu, Bauern den notwendigen Schutz zu gewähren." Er zitiert ein kurzes Gedicht von Bertolt Brecht (1898–1956) mit dem Titel „Eisen", das auf diesen Entwurf zutreffen könnte: „Im Traum heute Nacht/ Sah ich einen großen Sturm./ Ins Baugerüst griff er/ Den Bauschragen riss er/ Den eisernen, abwärts./ Doch was da aus Holz war/ Bog sich und blieb."

Cette maison en béton et acajou a été construite sur un terrain agricole de 3890 mètres carrés dans les montagnes Datun. D'une emprise au sol de 138 mètres carrés, elle est surélevée par rapport au sol pour la protéger des inondations éventuelles. La région est également soumise à des typhons ou des tremblements de terre. La façade en lattis permet de capter les brises rafraîchissantes pendant la saison chaude. Une cheminée est prévue pour l'hiver. Tout autour de la maison, une terrasse en bois assure la transition entre l'intérieur et l'extérieur. Selon Marco Casagrande : « Cette maison n'est ni massive ni lourde, elle est légère et flexible. Elle ne se ferme pas par rapport à son environnement mais est conçue pour offrir aux fermiers un abri nécessaire. » Il cite un bref poème de Bertolt Brecht (1898–1956) intitulé « Fer » qui pourrait s'appliquer à ce projet : « La nuit dernière, dans un rêve, j'ai vu une grande tempête. Elle s'en est prise à l'échafaudage. Elle a arraché les croisillons, qui étaient en fer. Mais ce qui était en bois a oscillé, mais résisté. »

The house has a decidedly temporary feeling to it, perhaps inspired as much by shipping containers as by more traditional wooden structures.

Das Haus macht einen eindeutig temporären Eindruck; der Entwurf wurde wohl von Transportcontainern ebenso wie von traditionellen Holzkonstruktionen beeinflusst.

L'aspect de la maison semble décidément temporaire, effet peut-être dû à son inspiration qui vient davantage des conteneurs d'expédition que des constructions en bois traditionnelles.

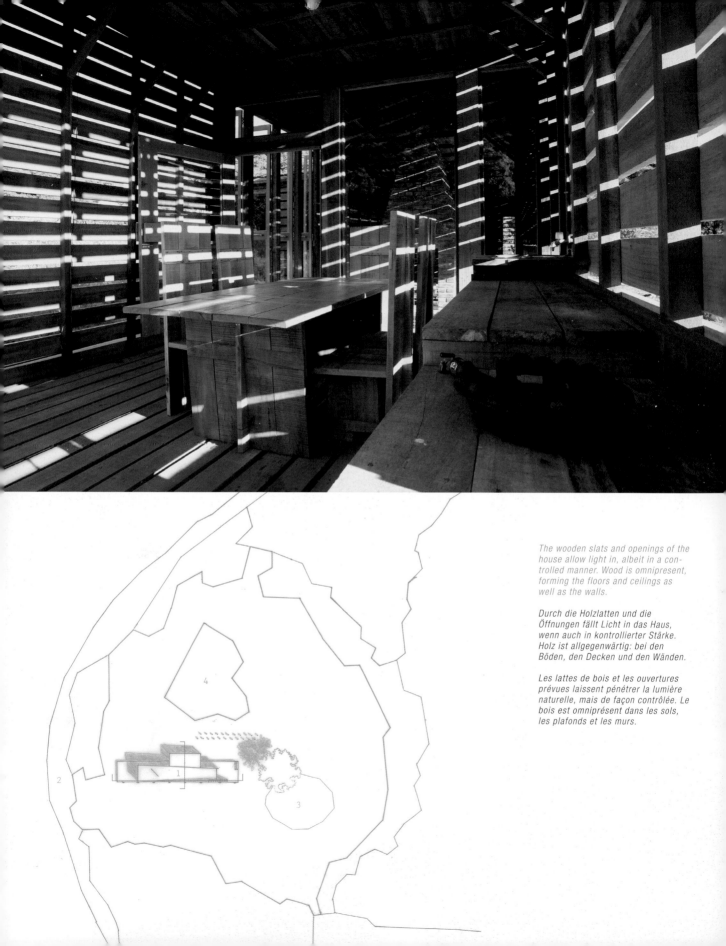

The wooden slats and openings of the
house allow light in, albeit in a controlled manner. Wood is omnipresent,
forming the floors and ceilings as
well as the walls.

Durch die Holzlatten und die
Öffnungen fällt Licht in das Haus,
wenn auch in kontrollierter Stärke.
Holz ist allgegenwärtig: bei den
Böden, den Decken und den Wänden.

Les lattes de bois et les ouvertures
prévues laissent pénétrer la lumière
naturelle, mais de façon contrôlée. Le
bois est omniprésent dans les sols,
les plafonds et les murs.

The interior is as sparsely furnished
as might be expected. Although
electrical light is provided for, it too
is minimal.

Innen ist das Haus erwartungsgemäß
sparsam möbliert. Elektrisches Licht
ist zwar vorhanden, wird aber auch
sparsam eingesetzt.

L'intérieur est aussi peu abondamment meublé que l'on pouvait s'y
attendre. L'éclairage électrique est lui
aussi minimal.

JOSÉ CRUZ OVALLE

Estudio de Arquitectura José Cruz Ovalle
Espoz 2902
Vitacura, Santiago
Chile

Tel: +56 2 206 6145
Fax: +56 2 206 0857
E-mail: cruzarquitectura@mi.cl

JOSÉ CRUZ OVALLE was born in Santiago, Chile, in 1948, and began studying architecture at the Catholic University of Chile in 1968, and continued, beginning in 1970, at the School of Architecture of the Polytechnic University of Barcelona, from which he graduated in 1973. He worked as an independent architect in Barcelona between 1974 and 1987, the year when he moved back to Chile, where he associated himself with his partners ANA TURELL in 1988, JUAN PURCELL in 1995, and HERNÁN CRUZ in 2000. His most significant works include the Pavilion of Chile at the Universal Exposition (Seville, Spain, 1992); Hotel Explora Patagonia (1995); and the Campus of the Universidad Adolfo Ibáñez in Penalolen (Santiago), which was awarded first prize for the best work of architecture at the IV Bienal Iberoamericana de Arquitectura, 2004. Juan Purcell Mena was born in Viña del Mar, Chile, in 1963. He studied architecture at the Catholic University of Chile. He graduated as an architect in 1991 and in 1995 he joined José Cruz Ovalle as a partner and later as an associated architect. Together they completed the Perez Cruz Winery (Paine, 2001–02, published here); the Rapa Nui Explora Hotel, Miro O'one Sector (Easter Island, 2005–07, also published here); and the Valle Escondido House (Lo Barnechea, Santiago, 2007), all in Chile.

JOSÉ CRUZ OVALLE wurde 1948 in Santiago de Chile geboren und begann 1968 das Studium der Architektur an der Universidad Católica de Chile, das er ab 1970 an der Architekturabteilung der Universitat Polytècnica in Barcelona fortsetzte und 1973 dort abschloss. Er arbeitete von 1974 bis 1987 freiberuflich in Barcelona und ging dann wieder zurück nach Chile, wo er 1988 mit ANA TURELL ein Büro gründete, in dem 1995 JUAN PURCELL und 2000 HERNÁN CRUZ Partner wurden. Zu seinen wichtigsten Bauten gehören der chilenische Pavillon auf der Weltausstellung in Sevilla (1992), das Hotel Explora Patagonia (1995) und der Campus der Universidad Adolfo Ibáñez in Penalolen (Santiago de Chile), der 2004 auf der IV. Bienal Iberoamericana de Arquitectura mit dem ersten Preis für die beste Architektur ausgezeichnet wurde. Juan Purcell Mena wurde 1963 in Viña del Mar, Chile, geboren und studierte Architektur an der Universidad Católica de Chile. Er machte dort 1991 seinen Abschluss und trat 1995 als Partner in das Büro von José Cruz Ovalle ein, später als assoziierter Architekt. Gemeinsam realisierten sie die Weinkellerei Perez Cruz (Paine, 2001–02, hier veröffentlicht), das Hotel Rapa Nui Explora, Miro O'one Sector (Osterinsel, 2005–07, ebenfalls hier veröffentlicht) und das Haus Valle Escondido (Lo Barnechea, Santiago, 2007), alle in Chile.

Né à Santiago en 1948, JOSÉ CRUZ OVALLE a commencé ses études d'architecture à l'Université catholique du Chili en 1968 et les a poursuivies à partir de 1970 à l'École d'architecture de l'Université polytechnique de Barcelone dont il est sorti diplômé en 1973. Il a travaillé comme architecte indépendant à Barcelone de 1974 à 1987, puis est revenu au Chili où il s'est associé à ANA TURELL en 1988, JUAN PURCELL en 1995 et HERNÁN CRUZ en 2000. Parmi ses réalisations les plus notables : le pavillon du Chili à l'Exposition universelle de Séville (1992) ; l'hôtel Explora Patagonia (1995) et le campus de l'université Adolfo Ibáñez de Penalolen (Santiago du Chili), qui a reçu le premier prix de la Meilleure œuvre d'architecture à la IVᵉ Biennale ibéro-américaine d'architecture (2004). Juan Purcell Mena, né à Viña del Mar (Chili) en 1963, a étudié l'architecture à l'Université catholique du Chili dont il est architecte diplômé (1991). Il a rejoint José Cruz Ovalle en 1995 comme partenaire puis architecte associé. Ensemble, ils ont réalisé au Chili le chai Perez Cruz (Paine, 2001–02, publié ici) ; l'hôtel Rapa Nui Explora, Miro O'one Sector (Île de Pâques, 2005–07, également publié ici) et la maison de Valle Escondido (Lo Barnechea, Santiago, 2007).

PEREZ CRUZ WINERY

Paine, Santiago, Chile, 2001–02

Address: Fundo Ligual de Helquén s/n, Paine, Maipo Alto, Santiago, Chile, +56 2 82 42 405, www.perezcruz.com
Area: 5433 m². Client: Perez Cruz Winery. Cost: not disclosed

Located 50 kilometers south of Santiago, this **WINERY** is located in the midst of 530 hectares of vineyards. The architect set out to avoid the usual "front" and "back" hierarchy in the structure, making all sides of the structure equivalent. The building also seeks to express the simultaneity of the processes that lead to the production of wine. The choice of wood was made in part in order to provide proper temperature conditions on the inside of the facility. The architect contrasts the slanted, planar roofs with the arched naves of the six parts of the complex that are connected by a 140-meter-long walkway. With its curving supports, the winery establishes what the architect describes as a boundary between outdoor light and the indoor shadows needed to produce and store the wine.

Diese 50 km südlich von Santiago gelegene **WEINKELLEREI** steht inmitten von 530 ha Weingärten. Der Architekt wollte die übliche Hierarchie von „vorne" und „hinten" vermeiden und gab allen Seiten des Gebäudes ein gleichwertiges Erscheinungsbild. Er hat auch versucht, die Gleichzeitigkeit der Prozesse auszudrücken, die der Produktion von Wein zugrunde liegen. Die Entscheidung für Holz fiel u. a., um geeignete Temperaturbedingungen im Innern der Anlage zu gewährleisten. Der Architekt setzt die geneigten, ebenen Dächer in Kontrast zu den gewölbten Hallen der sechs Teile der Anlage, die durch einen 140 m langen Gang miteinander verbunden sind. Die gekrümmten Stützen bilden in der Kellerei – nach den Worten des Architekten – eine Grenze zwischen dem Außenlicht und dem im Innern für die Produktion und Lagerung von Wein erforderlichen gedämpften Licht.

Situé à 50 km au sud de Santiago, ce **CHAI** a été édifié au cœur d'un vignoble de 530 ha. L'architecte a évité la hiérarchie habituelle « avant/arrière » et a traité chaque côté de la construction de façon similaire. Le bâtiment cherche à exprimer la simultanéité des processus de la production de vin. Le choix du bois se justifie en partie par la volonté d'offrir des conditions de température particulières à l'intérieur des installations. L'architecture fait contraster les toits inclinés avec des nefs à plafond en berceau des six parties de l'ensemble, réunies par une passerelle de 140 m de long. Par ses piliers incurvés, le chai organise ce que l'architecte présente comme une frontière entre la lumière extérieure et l'ombre de l'intérieur propice à la production et au vieillissement du vin.

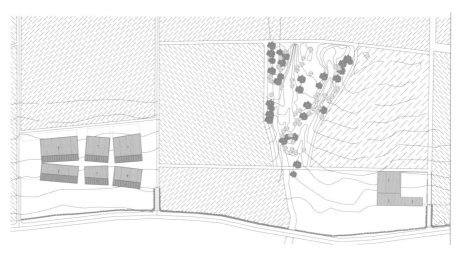

The slight irregularity of the
positioning of the structures, as
seen in the plan, is related to the
topography of the site.

Wie am Plan abzulesen, sind
die Bauten leicht unregelmäßig
angeordnet, was auf die Topografie
des Grundstücks zurückzuführen ist.

Comme le montre le plan, la
légère irrégularité de l'alignement
des constructions est dictée par
la topographie.

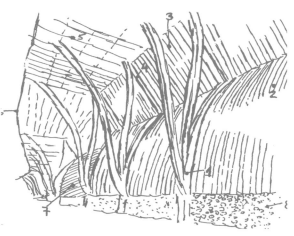

The unusual curved wood columns of the structure can be seen in the drawing above, and in the photos on this page.

Die ungewöhnlich gekrümmten Holz-stützen des Gebäudes sind in der Zeichnung oben sowie auf den Fotos dieser Seite zu erkennen.

Le dessins ci-dessus et les photos de ce page montrent la curieuse incurvation des colonnes de soutien.

The structure blends harmoniously with its vineyard setting. As the section drawings to the right demonstrate, careful attention has been paid to the industrial nature of the winery.

Das Gebäude fügt sich harmonisch in die Weingärten ein. Wie die Schnitte rechts zeigen, wurde die industrielle Produktionsweise der Kellerei ausreichend berücksichtigt.

La construction se fond harmonieusement dans son cadre viticole. Comme le montrent les coupes de droite, un soin particulier a été apporté au caractère industriel des installations du chai.

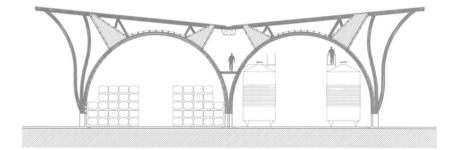

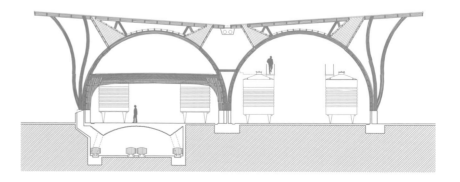

The six main volumes of the winery are grouped into two areas. Interior views show the required low-light conditions as well as the generous spaces fashioned from wood.

Die sechs Haupttrakte der Kellerei sind in zwei Gruppen angeordnet. Die Innenansichten zeigen das notwendige gedämpfte Licht sowie die großzügigen, mit Holz gestalteten Räume.

Les six bâtiments principaux sont regroupés en deux zones. Les vues intérieures montrent à la fois les généreux volumes intégralement en bois et le faible éclairage nécessaire au processus de vieillissement du vin.

RAPA NUI EXPLORA HOTEL

Miro O'one Sector, Easter Island, Chile, 2005–07

*Address: Miro O'one Sector, Easter Island, Chile, +1 866 750 6699, www.explora.com
Area: 4600 m². Client: Explora SA. Cost: not disclosed
Collaboration: Juan Purcell, Ana Turell, Hernán Cruz*

The low, curving design is intended to offer guests an agreeable stay, but also to respect the unusual site of the hotel on Easter Island.

Die niedrige, gekrümmte Form des Hotels soll den Gästen einen angenehmen Aufenthalt bieten, aber auch der ungewöhnlichen Situation auf der Osterinsel gerecht werden.

Le profil tout en courbe des bâtiments répond à la volonté d'offrir aux clients un séjour plaisant tout en respectant le cadre de l'île de Pâques.

Seen in elevation, the drawings below show how the hotel is nestled into its site. The building stands out in the evening view above.

Die Aufrisse des Hotels zeigen, wie es in das Gelände eingefügt wurde. Das Foto demonstriert die Wirkung des Gebäudes nachts.

Les dessins de coupe ci-dessous montrent comment l'hôtel se niche dans le terrain, ce qui ne l'empêche pas de se détacher dans le panorama nocturne.

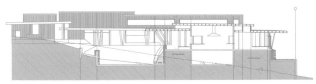
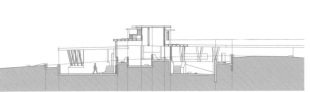

Given its isolated location in the Pacific, the architect notes that the horizon is an ever-present element of any Easter Island landscape. Walls built with local stones "sink or rise slightly from the ground to raise or lower the horizon and vibrate the relationship between earth and sky, the sea and earth, the sky and sea, offering a new relationship between proximity and remoteness," according to José Cruz Ovalle. The walls are the key to the architecture, essentially widening to create the hotel, to which wooden decks are added, between interior and exterior. The concept of the architecture is related to that of an archipelago with islands and inland seas. José Cruz Ovalle also refers (inevitably) to the enigmatic stone figures that make Easter Island a place to visit despite its distant location. Plans show how the structure is drawn out along the topographic lines of the site, almost as though it, too, were a remnant of some lost civilization, brought into modern time by the architect.

Angesichts der isolierten Lage im Pazifik meint der Architekt, dass der Horizont ein allgegenwärtiges Element in der Landschaft der Osterinsel darstelle. Mauern aus örtlichem Naturstein „versinken im Boden oder steigen an und heben oder senken den Horizont und lassen das Verhältnis von Erde zu Himmel, Meer zu Erde, Himmel zu Meer vibrieren, sodass eine neue Beziehung zwischen Nähe und Entfernung entsteht", laut Aussage von José Cruz. Die Mauern bilden das zentrale Element der Architektur, erweitern sich zum Hotel, bei dem hölzerne Terrassen zwischen Innen- und Außenraum vermitteln. Das architektonische Konzept ähnelt dem eines Archipels mit Inseln und Binnenseen. José Cruz Ovalle nimmt auch (unweigerlich) Bezug auf die rätselhaften Statuen, die viele Besucher trotz der entfernten Lage auf die Osterinsel ziehen. Die Pläne zeigen, wie das Gebäude dem topografischen Verlauf des Geländes folgt, als wäre es ebenfalls ein Überbleibsel einer vergangenen Kultur, das der Architekt in die Moderne übertragen hat.

Dans cette île perdue du Pacifique, l'horizon est un élément omniprésent dans le paysage, fait remarquer Ovalle : les murs dressés en pierre locale « s'enfoncent ou s'élèvent légèrement par rapport au sol pour relever ou abaisser la ligne d'horizon et faire vibrer la relation entre la terre et le ciel, la mer et la terre, le ciel et la terre, pour proposer un nouvelle relation, entre proximité et éloignement ». Les murs sont la clé de cette architecture, s'écartant pour former l'hôtel auquel viennent s'arrimer des terrasses de bois qui font lien entre intérieur et extérieur. Le concept du projet est celui d'un archipel composé d'îles et de lagons. José Cruz Ovalle se réfère également (et inévitablement) aux énigmatiques figures de pierre qui font de l'Île de Pâques un haut lieu touristique en dépit de son éloignement. Les plans montrent comment le bâtiment s'étire le long des lignes de niveau du terrain, comme si elles étaient les vestiges d'une civilisation perdue ramenés vers la modernité par l'architecte.

Located near the oceanfront, the hotel appears as a two-armed structure articulated around a central core in the site plan to the right. Wood is used in the interiors as well as the outside of the building.

Im Lageplan rechts erscheint das am Ufer des Ozeans gelegene Hotel als zweigliedriger Bau, der um einen zentralen Kern angeordnet ist. Holz wurde am Gebäude außen wie auch für die Innenräume verwendet.

Situé en bordure du front de mer, l'hôtel est une construction à deux ailes qui s'articulent autour d'un noyau central (plan à droite). Le bois est aussi présent à l'extérieur qu'à l'intérieur.

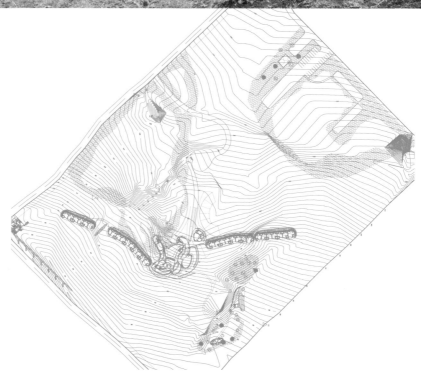

DECOI ARCHITECTS

Mark Goulthorpe
Associate Professor, MIT, 77 Massachusetts Avenue, Cambridge, MA 02143, USA
Tel: +1 617 852 3527, E-mail: mg_decoi@mit.edu, Web: www.hyposurface.org
http://web.mit.edu/mg_decoi/www/miran

DECOI is a small architectural/design practice that looks to opening the boundaries of conventional practice by a fresh and exploratory approach to design. Mark Goulthorpe, born in Kent, UK, and educated in Liverpool and in Oregon, established dECOi in 1991 after having worked for four years in the office of Richard Meier in New York. dECOi was awarded the prestigious international FEIDAD Digital Design Award in 2002 and again in 2004, and was invited to the *Architecture of the Non-Standard Manifesto* exhibition at the Centre Pompidou in Paris in 2003. Mark Goulthorpe was a unit master intermediate, unit 2, at the Architectural Association (London, 1995–96), and is currently teaching advanced digital design at MIT. dECOi's work ranges from pure design and artwork through interior design to architecture and urbanism. Projects include the Chan (Origin) House (Kuala Lumpur, 1995); Missoni Showroom (Paris, France, 1996); Swiss Re Headquarters (technical/design studies for Foster & Partners, London, UK, 1998); Dietrich House (London, UK, 2000); Glapyros House (Paris, France, 2001); Bankside ECOmorph, addition of a penthouse to the top of a tower (South Bank, London, UK, 2004/2007–); and One Main (Cambridge, Massachusetts, USA, 2009, published here). Art and research works include Aegis HypoSurface, dynamically reconfigurable, interactive architectural surface (Birmingham, UK, 2000); Excideuil Folly, parametric 3D glyphting (Excideuil, France, 2001); IMTS HypoSurface, the frontispiece for the International Manufacturers Technology Show (Chicago, USA; 2006); and "Enchanted," a choreographed event in which HypoSurface was used to take further the protocols of the interactive systems with a multi-disciplinary team (Chicago, USA, 2008).

DECOI ist ein kleines Architektur- und Designbüro, das die Grenzen der konventionellen Praxis durch neuartiges Vorgehen und Forschungsarbeit überwinden will. Der im britischen Kent geborene Mark Goulthorpe studierte in Liverpool und Oregon und gründete dECOi 1991, nachdem er vier Jahre im Büro von Richard Meier in New York gearbeitet hatte. dECOi erhielt 2002 und 2004 den renommierten internationalen FEIDAD Digital Design Award und war 2003 zur Ausstellung *Architecture of the Non-Standard Manifesto* im Centre Pompidou in Paris eingeladen. Mark Goulthorpe war Unit Master Intermediate, Unit 2, an der Architectural Association (London, 1995–96); gegenwärtig lehrt er Advanced Digital Design am Massachusetts Institute of Technology (MIT). Die Tätigkeit von dECOi reicht von reinem Design und künstlerischer Gestaltung über Innenausstattung bis zu Architektur und Städtebau. Zu den Projekten zählen das Haus Chan (Origin) in Kuala Lumpur (1995), der Showroom von Missoni in Paris (1996), die Hauptverwaltung Swiss Re (technische und Entwurfsstudien für Foster & Partners, London, 1998), das Haus Dietrich (London, 2000), das Haus Glapyros (Paris, 2001), Bankside ECOmorph, Erweiterung eines Hochhauses durch ein Penthouse (South Bank, London, 2004/2007–) und One Main (Cambridge, Massachusetts, 2009, hier veröffentlicht). Zu den künstlerischen und Forschungsarbeiten gehören Aegis HypoSurface, eine dynamisch veränderbare, interaktive Architekturfläche (Birmingham, 2000), Excideuil Folly, ein parametrischer 3D-Entwurf (Excideuil, Frankreich, 2001), IMTS HypoSurface, das Eingangsportal für die International Manufacturers Technology Show (Chicago, 2006), sowie „Enchanted", ein choreografiertes Event, bei dem HypoSurface dazu verwendet wurde, um die Anwendungsmöglichkeiten der interaktiven Systeme mit einem interdisziplinären Team weiterzuentwickeln (Chicago, 2008).

DECOI est une petite agence d'architecture et de design qui cherche à dépasser les limites de la pratique conventionnelle par une approche fraîche et exploratoire du processus de conception. Mark Goulthorpe, né dans le Kent (G.-B.) et élevé à Liverpool et dans l'Oregon, a fondé dECOi en 1991 après avoir travaillé quatre ans pour Richard Meier à New York. dECOi a reçu le prestigieux Prix international de la conception numérique FEIDAD en 2002 et 2004 et a été invité à l'exposition *Architectures non-standard* organisée par le Centre Pompidou à Paris en 2003. Mark Goulthorpe a été Unit Master Intermediate, pour l'Unité 2 à l'Architectural Association (Londres, 1995–96) et enseigne actuellement la conception numérique avancée au Massachusetts Institute of Technology (MIT). Les interventions de dECOi vont de la pure conception et du travail artistique à l'aménagement intérieur, l'architecture et l'urbanisme. Parmi ses projets et réalisations figurent : la maison Chan (Origin) (Kuala Lumpur, 1995) ; le showroom Missoni (Paris, 1996) ; le siège de Swiss Re (études de conception et études techniques pour Foster & Partners, Londres, 1998) ; la maison Dietrich (Londres, 2000) ; la maison Glapyros (Paris, 2001) ; Bankside ECOmorph, adjonction d'une penthouse au sommet d'une tour (South Bank, Londres, 2004/2007–) et One Main (Cambridge, Massachusetts, USA, 2009, publié ici). Parmi les réalisations artistiques et de recherche de l'agence figurent : Aegis HypoSurface, une surface architecturale interactive reconfigurable dynamiquement (Birmingham, G.-B., 2000) ; le projet Excideuil Folly, parametric 3D glyphting (Excideuil, France, 2001) ; IMTS HypoSurface, frontispice pour l'International Manufacturers Technology Show (Chicago, 2006), et « Enchanted », une manifestation chorégraphiée au cours de laquelle une HypoSurface servait de base au développement de protocoles de systèmes interactifs par une équipe multidisciplinaire (Chicago, 2008).

ONE MAIN

Cambridge, Massachusetts, USA, 2009

Address: One Main Street, Cambridge, Massachusetts, USA
Area: 1000 m². Client: not disclosed. Cost: not disclosed
Collaboration: Raphael Crespin (Project Architect)

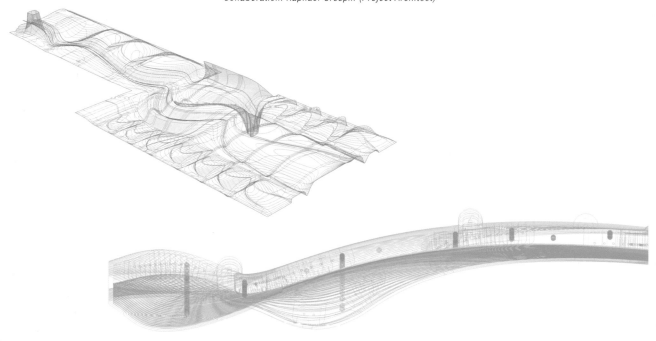

Located at One Main Street in Cambridge, this is an office refurbishment project that "relentlessly deploys numeric command machining of sustainable plywood to evidence the versatility and efficiency available via CAD-CAM design-build processes." Mark Goulthorpe has long defended the qualities of computer-driven design and manufacturing and in this instance he gives form to his concept of a "seamless and non-standard protocol of customized fabrication." His point is that these tools can be used to create a unique environment that is not dependent on "old-fashioned" industrial manufacturing procedures. And in this instance wood is the main element. Goulthorpe concludes: "In a material sense, the project assumes a radical environmental agenda, using a sustainable and carbon-absorbing raw material (forested spruce), translated efficiently into refined and functional elements via dexterous, low-energy digital tooling."

Bei diesem Projekt handelt es sich um die Modernisierung eines in der Main Street in Cambridge gelegenen Bürogebäudes, bei der „durch ausschließlich computergesteuerte Bearbeitung von nachhaltig gewonnenem Sperrholz die mit den Planungs- und Ausführungsverfahren CAD-CAM erzielbare vielseitige Anwendbarkeit und Effizienz bewiesen werden sollen". Mark Goulthorpe setzt sich schon seit langer Zeit für computergesteuertes Entwerfen und Produzieren ein, und in diesem Fall verleiht er seinem Konzept des „durchgehenden und nicht standardisierten Verfahrens individueller Fabrikation" eine sichtbare Gestalt. Seiner Meinung nach können diese Instrumente dazu genutzt werden, eine einzigartige Umwelt zu gestalten, die nicht auf „altmodischen" industriellen Produktionsverfahren beruht. Und im vorliegenden Fall ist Holz das Hauptelement dafür. Goulthorpe erklärt abschließend: „In materieller Hinsicht ist dieses Projekt radikal umweltfreundlich, weil es ein nachhaltiges und Kohlenstoff absorbierendes Rohmaterial (Fichte aus bewirtschafteten Wäldern) mittels geeigneter digitaler Low-Energy-Instrumente effizient in veredelte funktionale Elemente verwandelt."

Cette rénovation de bureaux situés 1, Main Street à Cambridge « déploie implacablement des processus d'usinage à commande numérique de contreplaqués de qualité durable pour faire apparaître la versatilité et les qualités offertes par les processus de conception et de réalisation par CAO-FAO ». Mark Goulthorpe a longtemps défendu cette orientation et donne ici forme à un concept de « protocole continu de fabrication sur mesure non-standard ». Son argument est que ces outils peuvent servir à créer des environnements uniques, qui ne dépendent pas des processus de fabrication industrielle « démodés ». « Le bois est ici l'élément principal. Au sens matériel, le projet s'est fixé un objectif environnemental radical, par l'utilisation d'un matériau brut durable et absorbeur de CO_2 (épicéa d'exploitation rationnelle), transformé avec efficacité en éléments fonctionnels raffinés par des outils numériques habiles à faible consommation d'énergie », conclut Goulthorpe.

As is usually the case in his work, Mark Goulthorpe of dECOi has used sophisticated computer modeling and manufacturing to conceive this space.

Wie üblich hat sich Mark Goulthorpe von dECOi ausgefeilter Computermodelle und Produktionsmethoden für die Gestaltung dieser Räume bedient.

Comme la plupart du temps, Mark Goulthorpe de l'agence dECOi a utilisé des techniques de modélisation et de fabrication sophistiquées pour concevoir cet espace.

Interior perspectives show that
the overall design has also been
applied to the furnishings. Within the
relatively straightforward space, the
architect adds unexpected elements.

Die Innenansichten zeigen, dass in
die Gesamtplanung auch die Möblierung einbezogen war. In den relativ
klaren Raum hat der Architekt unerwartete Elemente eingefügt.

Ces vues intérieures montrent que la
conception de l'ensemble a également été appliquée au mobilier. Dans
cet espace relativement classique,
l'architecte a inséré des éléments
inattendus.

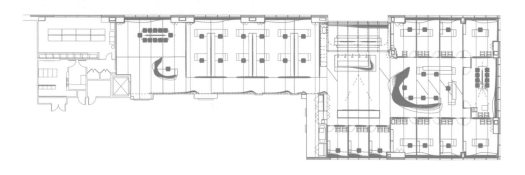

*The detailing and furniture design
are a product of the fully computer-
oriented work of Mark Goulthorpe,
allying wood with the most
contemporary techniques.*

*Detailgestaltung und Möblierung
sind das Produkt der vollständig
computerorientierten Arbeit von
Mark Goulthorpe, der Holz mit den
modernsten Techniken verbindet.*

*Les finitions et le mobilier sont
des productions caractéristiques
du travail de Mark Goulthorpe,
entièrement orienté vers les techniques numériques les plus modernes
auxquelles il associe le bois.*

DMVA

dmvA Architects
Schuttersvest 26
2800 Mechelen
Belgium

Tel: +32 15 33 09 86
E-mail: info@dmva-architecten.be
Web: www.dmva-architecten.be

TOM VERSCHUEREN was born in Hoogstraten, Belgium, in 1970 and studied architecture at the Henry van de Velde College in Antwerp (1993). He created dmvA with **DAVID DRIESEN** in 1997. dmvA is the Dutch abbreviation for "by means of Architecture." David Driesen was born in 1968 in Duffel, Belgium. In 1992, he graduated in architecture, with town planning as his specialty, from Sint Lucas, Brussels. The architects explain that they "act like screenwriters, turn the program into a screenplay, spaces into sequences and allow the building to tell another story each time." Their work includes Blob VB3 (various locations, 2008–09, published here); the Beele-Vyvey Pharmacy (Mechelen, 2009); B Seat, a seat in the form of a pill designed for the same pharmacy (2009); the B&B Red Spot (Mechelen, 2009); and offices for Mahla Solicitors (Mechelen, 2010), all in Belgium.

TOM VERSCHUEREN wurde 1970 in Hoogstraten, Belgien, geboren und studierte Architektur am Henry van de Velde College in Antwerpen (1993). Er gründete das Büro dmvA 1997 zusammen mit **DAVID DRIESEN**. dmvA ist die niederländische Abkürzung für „mittels Architektur". David Driesen wurde 1968 in Duffel, Belgien, geboren und beendete 1992 sein Architekturstudium mit Schwerpunkt Stadtplanung an der Hochschule Sint Lucas in Brüssel. Die Architekten erklären, dass sie „wie Drehbuchautoren arbeiten, die das Programm in ein Bühnenstück, Räume in Szenen umwandeln und das Gebäude jedesmal eine andere Geschichte erzählen lassen". Zu ihren Projekten zählen Blob VB3 (verschiedene Standorte, 2008–09, hier veröffentlicht), die Beele-Vyvey Apotheke (Mechelen, 2009), B Seat, ein Sitz in Form einer Pille für dieselbe Apotheke (2009), das B&B Red Spot (Mechelen, 2009) sowie Büros für die Rechtsanwälte Mahla (Mechelen, 2010), alle in Belgien.

TOM VERSCHUEREN, né à Hoogstraten (Belgique) en 1970, a étudié l'architecture au collège Henry van de Velde à Anvers (1993). Il a créé dmvA avec **DAVID DRIESEN** en 1997. dmvA est un sigle signifiant en néerlandais « au moyen de l'architecture ». David Driesen, né en 1968 à Duffel (Belgique), est diplômé en architecture (spécialisation en urbanisme) de l'École supérieure Saint-Luc à Bruxelles (1992). Tous deux se présentent comme des « scénaristes, qui transforment le programme en scénario, l'espace en séquences et font raconter à chaque projet une histoire différente ». Parmi leurs réalisations, toutes en Belgique : le Blob VB3 (divers lieux, 2008–09, publié ici) ; la pharmacie Beele-Vyvey (Mechelen, 2009) ; le B Seat, siège en forme de pilule dessiné pour la même pharmacie (2009) ; les chambres d'hôtes Red Spot (Mechelen, 2009) et des bureaux pour le cabinet d'avocats Mahla (Mechelen, 2010).

BLOB VB3
various locations, Belgium, 2008–09

Address: various locations
Area: 20 m². Client: XfactorAgencies. Cost: not disclosed
Collaboration: AD&S Thomas Denturck

Intended as an extension to a house and an office for XfactorAgencies, this structure was considered contrary to local building regulations, until the architects decided to make it moveable. "As a mobile construction," say the architects, "with a high dose of art, it skirted around the strict building codes." The egglike form, built by AD&S, the Blob contains a bathroom, kitchen, bed, and storage spaces. The nose opens to form a porch. The designers suggest that the structure could be used as an office, reception space, garden house, "or whatever you want." Exhibited at the Kemzeke Art Foundation (Verbeke), made of wood covered in polyester, the Blob is the size of a mobile home and "can be moved anyplace you like."

Dieses als Erweiterung eines Wohnhauses und Büros für die XfactorAgencies geplante Gebäude wurde abgelehnt, weil es nicht mit den örtlichen Bauvorschriften vereinbar war, bis die Architekten beschlossen, es transportabel zu machen. „Als mobiles, eher als Kunstwerk zu betrachtendes Bauwerk", sagen die Architekten, „umging es die strengen Bauvorschriften". Der eiförmige, von AD&S ausgeführte Blob enthält Bad, Küche, Schlaf- und Abstellräume. Die Spitze öffnet sich zu einem überdachten Eingang. Die Planer schlagen vor, den Bau als Büro, Empfangsbereich, Gartenhaus oder „für jeden beliebigen Zweck" zu nutzen. Der von der Kunststiftung Kemzeke (Verbeke) ausgestellte hölzerne, mit Polyester verkleidete Blob in der Größe eines Wohnwagens „kann an jeden beliebigen Ort transportiert werden".

Extension d'une maison et bureau pour XfactorAgencies, cette petite construction a été jugée contraire à la réglementation locale de la construction jusqu'à ce que les architectes aient décidé de la rendre mobile. « Présentée comme une construction mobile, expliquent les architectes, avec beaucoup d'habileté, elle a pu contourner les rigueurs de la réglementation ». Cette forme en œuf (réalisée en bois recouvert de polyester par AD&S) contient une cuisine, une salle de bains, un lit et des espaces de rangement. Le nez ouvrant forme un auvent. Ses concepteurs suggèrent que ce Blob pourrait servir de bureau, de lieu de réception, de maison de jardin « ou de tout ce que vous voulez ». Exposé à la Fondation artistique Kemzeke (Verbeke), le Blob est de la taille d'une petite caravane et « peut être transporté où vous le souhaitez ».

The white, egglike form of the Blob
does not immediately reveal that
wood is a basic material in the construction, but the photos on the left
page show its inner workings.

Die weiße, eiförmige Gestalt des
Blobs lässt nicht unmittelbar erkennen, dass Holz das entscheidende
Baumaterial darstellt. Aber die Fotos
auf der linken Seite zeigen seine Verwendung im Inneren.

La forme d'œuf du Blob ne laisse pas
immédiatement deviner que le bois
est son matériau de construction de
base. Les photos de la page de gauche montrent sa construction.

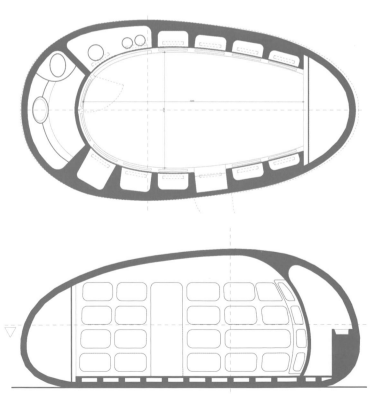

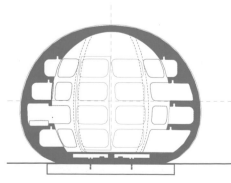

The squat, ovoid shape surely justifies the name of the project. Ample
storage spaces and working areas
are shown in these drawings.

Die gedrungene, eiförmige Gestalt
rechtfertigt sicherlich den Namen des
Projekts. Die Zeichnungen zeigen,
dass reichlich Stauraum und Arbeits-
flächen vorhanden sind.

La forme ovoïde et compacte du
Blob justifie certainement son nom.
L'importance des rangements et
des plans de travail se note dans
ces dessins.

Shelves are built into the
structure around its walls, making
the otherwise difficult to use space
quite practical.

In die Wände sind rundum Regale
eingebaut; sonst wäre eine praktische
Nutzung des Raums kaum möglich.

Les étagères sont intégrées aux
parois, ce qui rend assez pratique
un volume qui ne l'était pas à
première vue.

DRN ARCHITECTS

dRN Architects
Isidora Goyenechea 3200
Santiago
Chile

Tel: +56 2 231 4114
E-mail: contacto@drn.cl
Web: www.drn.cl

dRN Architects was established in 2005 by **NICOLÁS DEL RÍO** and **MAX NÚÑEZ** in Santiago, Chile. Born in Santiago in 1975, Nicolás del Río studied at the Universidad Católica de Chile, obtaining his degree in 2001. He also studied at the Politecnico di Milano (Italy, 1998–99) and obtained a master in sustainable design from Oxford Brookes University, UK, in 2010. Since 2005 he has taught a first year design studio at the Universidad Andrés Bello (Santiago). Born in Santiago in 1976, Max Núñez received his M.Arch degree from the Universidad Católica de Chile in 2004 and an M.Arch degree from Columbia University, New York, in 2010. He also studied prior to that at the Politecnico di Milano (1998–99). Since 2005 he has taught a second year design studio at the Universidad Andrés Bello, in Santiago. Their work includes the Skibox (Portillo, 2006); Mountain Refuge Chalet C6 (Portillo, 2006); Mountain Refuge Chalet C7 (Portillo, 2008); Beach House (Cerro Tacna, 2008); Los Canteros Mountain Refuge (Farellones, 2008); Beach House (Cachagua, 2009); La Baronia House (Quintero, V Region, 2009, published here); and the House at Punta Chilen (Chiloé Island, X Region, 2009, also published here), all in Chile.

Das Büro dRN Architects wurde 2005 von **NICOLÁS DEL RÍO** und **MAX NÚÑEZ** in Santiago de Chile gegründet. Der 1975 in Santiago geborene Nicolás del Río studierte an der Universidad Católica de Chile, wo er 2001 seinen Abschluss machte, außerdem am Politecnico di Milano (Italien, 1998–99); den Master in nachhaltigem Entwerfen erwarb er 2010 an der Brookes University im britischen Oxford. Seit 2005 unterrichtet er den Anfängerkurs in Entwerfen an der Universidad Andrés Bello (Santiago). Max Núñez, 1976 in Santiago geboren, machte 2004 seinen M.Arch an der Universidad Católica de Chile sowie 2010 einen M.Arch an der Columbia University, New York. Davor studierte er auch am Politecnico di Milano (1998–99). Seit 2005 unterrichtet er den zweiten Kurs im Entwerfen an der Universidad Andrés Bello in Santiago. Zu den Bauten des Büros zählen die Skibox (Portillo, 2006), die Berghütte Chalet C6 (Portillo, 2006), die Berghütte Chalet C7 (Portillo, 2008), ein Ferienhaus in Cerro Tacna (2008), die Berghütte Los Canteros (Farellones, 2008), ein Ferienhaus in Cachagua (2009), das Wohnhaus La Baronia (Quintero, V. Region, 2009, hier veröffentlicht) und ein Wohnhaus in Punta Chilen (Insel Chiloé, X. Region, 2009, ebenfalls hier veröffentlicht), alle in Chile.

L'agence dRN Architects a été fondée en 2005 par **NICOLÁS DEL RÍO** et **MAX NÚÑEZ** à Santiago du Chili. Né à Santiago en 1975, Nicolás del Río a étudié à l'Université catholique du Chili, dont il est diplômé (2001), au Politecnico de Milan (1998–99), et a obtenu un mastère en conception durable de la Brookes University à Oxford (G.-B.) en 2010. Depuis 2005, il enseigne en première année d'atelier de conception à l'université Andrés Bello (Santiago). Né à Santiago en 1976, Max Núñez a passé son diplôme d'architecture à l'Université catholique du Chili en 2004 et avait étudié précédemment au Politecnico de Milan (1998–99). Depuis 2005, il enseigne en seconde année d'atelier de conception à l'université Andrés Bello de Santiago. Parmi leurs réalisations, toutes au Chili : la Skibox (Portillo, 2006) ; le refuge de montagne C6 (Portillo, 2006) ; le refuge de montagne C7 (Portillo, 2008) ; une maison de plage (Cerro Tacna, 2008) ; le refuge de montagne de Los Canteros (Farellones, 2008) ; une maison de plage (Cachagua, 2009) ; la maison La Baronia (Quintero, Vᵉ Région, 2009, publiée ici) et la maison de Punta Chilen (île de Chiloé, Xᵉ Région, 2009, également publiée ici).

LA BARONIA HOUSE

Quintero, Valparaíso, Chile, 2009

Address: not disclosed
Area: 150 m². Client: not disclosed. Cost: not disclosed

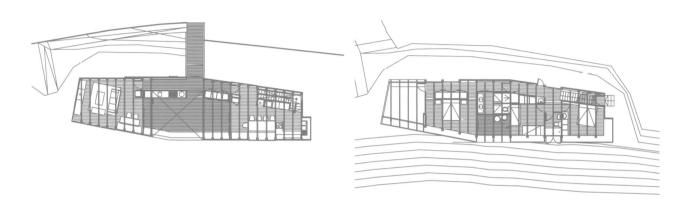

Dominating the coastline, the house has ample glazed surfaces. The light bridge that leads to the entrance affirms the maritime vocabulary employed.

Das die Küste dominierende Haus hat reichlich verglaste Flächen. Die leichte Erschließungsbrücke unterstreicht die Anwendung eines maritimen Vokabulars.

Dominant le littoral, la maison possède de généreuses surfaces vitrées. La passerelle légère qui conduit à l'entrée confirme lo vocabulaire maritime utilisé par l'architecte.

Set up above the shore, the house has something of the appearance of a beached ship in the image to the left. Drawings show the slightly angled forms.

Das Foto links zeigt, dass das hoch über dem Ufer stehende Haus einem gestrandeten Schiff ähnelt. An den Zeichnungen sind seine etwas eckigen Formen ablesbar.

Implantée au-dessus de la côte, la maison fait un peu penser à un bateau échoué (image de gauche). Les plans donnent le détail de sa forme légèrement inclinée.

This unusual residence sits on a hill above the ocean in an exposed position. The architects took this location as the theme for their design in some sense, noting that the "corroding power of the salty breeze coming from the Pacific Ocean can wear out an unprotected structure in a short period of time. Here the braking waves are not a romantic vision of nature but a very crude reality of the temporal condition of architecture." Their solution was to cover a good part of the house in pre-weathered Cor-ten steel while allowing views to the ocean through generous glazed surfaces. The interior of the structure is made of bolted wooden frames, and is intended to be flexible enough to be converted to different uses over time. Thus the surface of this house is harder and stronger than its interior, an inversion of the usual relation between skin and structure.

Dieses ungewöhnliche Wohnhaus steht exponiert auf einem Berg hoch über dem Ozean. Die Architekten wählten diesen Standort in gewisser Weise als Thema für ihren Entwurf und erwähnen, dass die „starke Korrosion durch die salzhaltigen Winde vom Pazifischen Ozean ein ungeschütztes Bauwerk in kurzer Zeit zerstören kann. Hier ist die Brandung keine romantische Naturerscheinung, sondern harte Realität im Hinblick auf die Lebensdauer eines Gebäudes." Ihre Lösung bestand darin, einen Großteil des Hauses mit Corten-Stahl zu verkleiden, aber den Ausblick zum Ozean durch großzügige Verglasung freizugeben. Die innenliegende, verschraubte Holzkonstruktion soll flexibel genug sein, um sich später veränderter Nutzung anpassen zu lassen. So ist die Außenfläche des Hauses härter und widerstandsfähiger als sein innenliegendes Tragwerk – eine Umkehr des üblichen Verhältnisses zwischen Außenhaut und Konstruktion.

Cette curieuse maison implantée sur la crête d'une falaise au-dessus de l'océan occupe une position très exposée. En un sens, les architectes ont pris ce lieu pour thème, notant que « le pouvoir de corrosion de la brise de mer salée venant de l'océan Pacifique peut venir à bout d'une construction non protégée en une brève période de temps ». La solution choisie a été d'habiller une bonne partie de la maison d'acier Corten prépatiné, ce qui permet par ailleurs d'ouvrir de grandes baies vitrées vers l'océan. L'ossature est en poutres de bois boulonnées, système assez flexible pour prévoir des évolutions de la maison dans le futur. La « surface » est donc plus dure et plus solide que l'intérieur, inversion de la relation habituelle entre peau et structure.

Broad windows wrap around a bedroom, providing dramatic views of the ocean in the wood-framed structure.

Große Fenster umgeben einen Schlafraum und bieten aus der Holzrahmenkonstruktion dramatische Ausblicke auf den Ozean.

Un bandeau de fenêtres devant l'ossature en bois entoure une des chambres qui bénéficie ainsi de vues spectaculaires sur l'océan.

Bathroom and dining areas are also open to waterside views. Two drawings show the slightly cantilevered form of the house and its insertion into the sharply sloped site.

Auch das Bad und der Essbereich öffnen sich zu Ausblicken auf das Wasser. Die beiden Zeichnungen zeigen die leicht auskragende Form des Hauses und seine Einfügung in das steile Hanggrundstück.

Comme les coins-repas, la salle de bains ouvre également sur l'océan. Deux dessins montrent le léger porte-à-faux de la maison et son insertion dans la pente marquée.

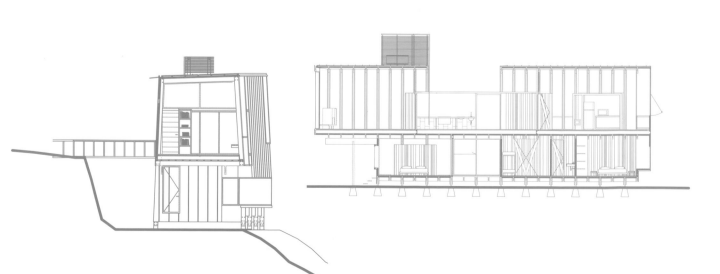

HOUSE AT PUNTA CHILEN

Chiloé Island, Lake District, Chile, 2009

Address: not disclosed
Area: 276 m². Client: not disclosed. Cost: not disclosed

Chiloé is a large island located off the coast of Chile. This house is set at the tip of a peninsula on a site that offers residents a 360° view. The Andes and no less than eight volcanoes can be seen in the distance. The architects state: "A rhythmic repetition of columns on the first floor carries the structure to the perimeter and generates changing shadows on the interiors. The oblique shape of the Cor-ten steel roof on the second floor defines an irregular perimeter opposed to the flat line of the horizon." Within its protective shell of steel and glass, the interior of the house is entirely clad in wood, again generating a contrast between the skin or shell of the architecture and its gentler interior.

Chiloé ist eine große, der Küste von Chile vorgelagerte Insel. Dieses Haus steht dort an der Spitze einer Halbinsel auf einem Grundstück, das den Bewohnern einen Rundblick von 360 Grad bietet. In der Ferne sind die Anden und nicht weniger als acht Vulkane zu sehen. Die Architekten erklären: „Eine rhythmische Wiederholung der Stützen im Erdgeschoss führt um das ganze Gebäude und erzeugt wechselnde Schatten im Innern. Die schräge Form des Dachs aus Corten-Stahl auf dem Obergeschoss erzeugt einen unregelmäßigen Umriss im Gegensatz zur flachen Linie des Horizonts." Innerhalb seiner schützenden Hülle aus Stahl und Glas ist das Haus vollkommen mit Holz verkleidet, wodurch wiederum ein Gegensatz zwischen Haut oder Hülle des Gebäudes und seinem freundlicheren Innern entsteht.

Chiloé est une grande île qui fait face à la côte du Chili. La maison s'élève à l'extrémité d'une péninsule et offre une vue panoramique à 360°. On peut apercevoir dans le lointain les Andes et pas moins de huit volcans. « La répétition rythmique des colonnes au rez-de-chaussée, qui soutiennent la construction dans son périmètre génère un jeu d'ombres mouvantes à l'intérieur. La forme en oblique du toit en acier Corten dessine un tracé irrégulier qui s'oppose à la ligne de l'horizon », expliquent les architectes. Protégé par cette coque de verre et d'acier, l'intérieur entièrement habillé de bois provoque un contraste entre la rigueur vigoureuse de l'extérieur et l'aspect plus chaleureux de l'intérieur.

Both generously glazed, the two levels of the house as seen from this angle form a base with a lighter, perched element placed above.

In diesem Blickwinkel bilden die beiden großzügig verglasten Ebenen des Hauses eine Basis mit einem darauf gesetzten, leichteren Element.

Tous deux généreusement vitrés, les deux niveaux de la maison vus sous cet angle semblent former le socle d'un élément perché plus léger.

The upper-level deck and the sloped roof take on unexpected forms and the entire house offers a broad view of the water.

Die Terrasse auf der oberen Ebene und das geneigte Dach zeigen ungewöhnliche Formen; das ganze Haus ist zum Wasser hin weit geöffnet.

La terrasse du niveau supérieur et les versants de la toiture prennent des formes inattendues. La maison toute entière offre de vastes panoramas de l'océan.

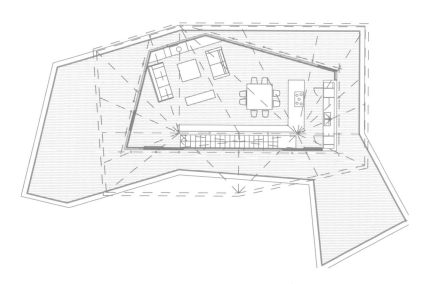

With its full-height glazing contrasting with the wooden ceiling and floor,
the house appears to be entirely open
to its natural surroundings.

Mit seiner geschosshohen Verglasung
im Gegensatz zu den hölzernen
Decken und Böden erscheint das
Haus vollkommen zu seiner natürlichen Umgebung geöffnet.

À travers ses murs entièrement
vitrés, qui contrastent avec les sols
et les plafonds en bois, la maison
semble s'ouvrir entièrement vers
son cadre naturel.

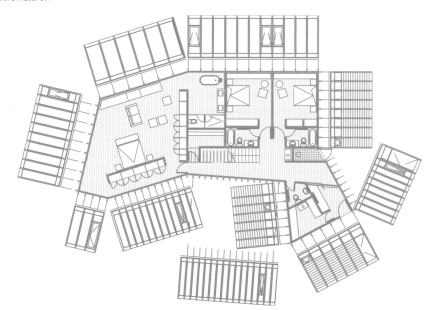

Even the bathroom and bathtub have fully glazed windows with views to the water.

Sogar aus dem Badezimmer und der Wanne hat man durch die großen Glasfenster Ausblicke auf das Wasser.

Même la salle de bains possède un mur entièrement vitré qui donne sur l'océan.

Abgesehen von den Metallstützen und -geländern, wurde im Haus überwiegend Holz verwendet, von den Böden bis zur Dachunterseite.

Aside from the metallic supports and railings, the house makes a broad use of wood, from the floors to the underside of the roof.

Mis à part les piliers métalliques et les rampes, la maison utilise essentiellement le bois pour les sols ou les sous-faces de la toiture.

DUMAY + FONES + VERGARA

Dumay + Fones + Vergara Architects
Ernesto Pinto Lagarrigue 156 Of. F
Barrio Bellavista
8420492 Santiago
Chile

Tel: +56 2 735 0417
Fax: +56 2 735 0417
E-mail: contacto@ftres.cl
Web: www.ftres.cl

ALEJANDRO DUMAY CLARO was born in Santiago, Chile, in 1977. **NICOLÁS FONES CLARO** was also born in Santiago in 1977, as was **FRANCISCO VERGARA ARTHUR**. They all graduated from the Faculty of Architecture of Mayor University (Santiago, 2002). In 2005, they created their own firm, F3, recently renamed to Dumay + Fones + Vergara. Their work, either collective or individual, includes the Lake Rupanco House (2005); the moveable Minga House (2005); the Hotel Equidomos (Pisco Elqui, 2005); the María Pinto House (María Pinto, 2006); the Fuente Nueva Chapel (Lake Rupanco, 2006, published here); and the Emilia Tellez Building (Santiago, 2006), all in Chile.

ALEJANDRO DUMAY CLARO wurde ebenso wie **NICOLÁS FONES CLARO** und **FRANCISCO VERGARA ARTHUR** 1977 in Santiago de Chile geboren. Alle drei beendeten 2002 ihr Studium an der Architekturfakultät der Universidad Mayor in Santiago. 2005 gründeten sie ihr eigenes Büro, F3, das kürzlich in Dumay + Fones + Vergara umbenannt wurde. Zu ihren individuellen oder gemeinsamen Arbeiten zählen das Haus am Rupanco-See (2005), das mobile Haus Minga (2005), das Hotel Equidomos (Pisco Elqui, 2005), ein Haus in María Pinto (2006), die Kapelle Fuente Nueva (Rupanco-See, 2006, hier veröffentlicht) und das Edificio Emilia Tellez (Santiago, 2006), alle in Chile.

ALEJANDRO DUMAY CLARO est né à Santiago du Chili en 1977, comme **NICOLÁS FONES CLARO** et **FRANCISCO VERGARA ARTHUR**. Tous trois sont diplômés de la faculté d'architecture de l'université Mayor (Santiago, 2002). En 2005, ils ont créé leur agence, F3, qui a récemment pris le nom de Dumay + Fones + Vergara. Toutes au Chili, leurs réalisations, collectives ou individuelles, comprennent : la maison du lac Rupanco (2005) ; la maison mobile Minga (2005) ; l'hôtel Equidomos (Pisco Elqui, 2005) ; la maison à María Pinto (María Pinto, 2006) ; la chapelle de Fuente Nueva (Lac Rupanco, 2006, publiée ici) et l'immeuble Emilia Tellez (Santiago, 2006).

FUENTE NUEVA CHAPEL

Lake Rupanco, Lake District, Chile, 2006

Area: 21 m². Client: not disclosed. Cost: not disclosed

Located in southern Chile, this project is set on a three-hectare site near Lake Rupanco. The austere chapel with a capacity for twelve people was built with simple materials at a low cost. The architects conceived of it "as a totality without differentiation of structural elements (walls, ceilings, windows)." Impregnated pine paneling is used on the exteriors, while, according to the architects, "inside, the image of the altar is provided by the landscape itself, the lake and the mountains; this defines the orientation of the volume and its direction." A shrine and two niches for sculptures designed by the owner are set in the north façade. A terrace forms the entrance to the chapel and somewhat expands its presence within the natural setting.

Dieser Bau steht auf einem 3 ha großen Gelände am Rupanco-See im Süden Chiles. Die in nüchterner Form gestaltete Kapelle, die zwölf Personen fasst, wurde zu geringen Kosten aus einfachen Materialien errichtet. Die Architekten konzipierten sie „als Gesamtform ohne Differenzierung der Konstruktionselemente (Wände, Decken, Fenster)". Für die Außenwände wurden Paneele aus imprägniertem Kiefernholz verwendet, während, laut Aussage der Architekten, „innen die Ansicht des Altars von der Landschaft, dem See und den Bergen gebildet wird. Diese bestimmen auch die Orientierung des Gebäudes und seine Stellung." Ein Schrein und zwei Nischen für vom Besitzer gestaltete Skulpturen befinden sich an der Nordseite. Eine Terrasse bildet den Eingang zur Kapelle und erweitert ein wenig ihre Präsenz im natürlichen Umfeld.

Cette chapelle est érigée sur un terrain de trois hectares près du lac Rupanco situé dans le sud du Chili. Cette petite construction austère d'une capacité de douze personnes a été réalisée avec un budget modeste et des matériaux simples. Les architectes l'ont conçue comme « une totalité, sans différenciation entre les éléments structurels (murs, plafonds, fenêtres) ». L'extérieur est en panneaux de pin imprégné tandis que, « à l'intérieur, l'image du mur de l'autel est fournie par le paysage même, le lac et les montagnes, ce qui définit l'orientation du volume ». Un petit autel et deux niches pour des sculptures dessinées par le propriétaire ont été prévus dans la façade nord. L'entrée est signalée par une terrasse qui renforce encore la présence de l'édifice dans son cadre naturel.

The use of solid wood in this exceptional setting makes the chapel quite unusual, despite the use of a form that is apparently quite "ordinary."

Die Anwendung von Massivholz an diesem besonderen Standort macht die Kapelle außergewöhnlich, trotz ihrer scheinbar „gewöhnlichen" Form.

Le recours au bois massif dans ce cadre exceptionnel fait l'originalité de cette chapelle malgré sa forme apparemment classique.

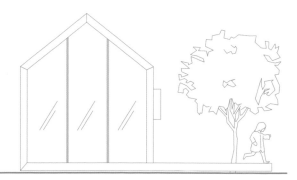

Drawings of the structure and the photo to the left show its scale and simple design.

Die Zeichnungen vom Gebäude und das Foto links lassen Maßstab und die schlichte Gestaltung erkennen.

Les dessins et la photo de gauche montrent l'échelle et la simplicité de ce projet.

The notched entrance to the chapel, with the simple bell, emphasizes the austerity of the structure and signals its function.

Der zurückgesetzte Eingang zur Kapelle und die schlichte Glocke betonen die Strenge des Gebäudes und verweisen auf seine Funktion.

La découpe de l'entrée de la chapelle et sa petite cloche font ressortir l'austérité de la construction tout en signalant sa fonction.

Closer views show that the planks used in the platform continue right over the walls and roof of the chapel, leaving room for protruding windows.

Bei näherer Betrachtung zeigt sich, dass die für die Plattform verwendeten Bretter sich über die Wände und das Dach der Kapelle fortsetzen und Platz für vorkragende Fenster lassen.

Des vues rapprochées montrent que les planches de la terrasse sont dans l'alignement précis de celles des murs et de la toiture de la chapelle, ne s'interrompant que pour les avancées des fenêtres.

PIET HEIN EEK

Eek & Ruijgrok BV
Halvemaanstraat 30
5651BP Eindhoven
The Netherlands

Tel: +31 40 285 66 10
Fax: +31 40 285 94 60
E-mail: info@pietheineek.nl
Web: www.pietheineek.nl

PIET HEIN EEK was born Purmerend, the Netherlands, in 1967 and graduated from the Design Academy in Eindhoven in 1990. He is known mainly as a designer of furniture, made of such materials as reclaimed wood, but Piet Hein Eek has also carried out architectural work including home renovations, and a three-story structure for a flower show in the Netherlands. Piet Hein Eek states that his scrap-wood cupboard (1990) "was my reaction against the prevalent craving for flawlessness. I wanted to show that products that aren't perfect can still appeal to our sense of aesthetics and functionality. I also wanted to design a product that could be made with limited means, material that was abundant." He completed the Tree Trunk House (Hilversum, The Netherlands, published here) in 2009.

PIET HEIN EEK wurde 1967 in Purmerend, Niederlande, geboren und beendete 1990 sein Studium an der Design Academy in Eindhoven. Er ist vorwiegend als Designer von Möbeln, etwa aus wiederverwendetem Holz, bekannt geworden, hat aber auch Architekturarbeiten ausgeführt, z. B. Hauserneuerungen sowie ein dreige-schossiges Gebäude für eine Blumenausstellung in den Niederlanden. Piet Hein Eek erklärt, dass sein Schrank aus Abfallholz (1990) seine „Reaktion auf das allgemeine Streben nach Makellosigkeit" gewesen sei. „Ich wollte zeigen, dass auch nicht perfekte Produkte unser Gefühl für Ästhetik und Funktionalität ansprechen können. Zudem wollte ich ein Produkt gestalten, das mit beschränkten Mitteln und einem im Überfluss vorhandenen Material hergestellt werden kann." 2009 hat er das Baumstammhaus (Hilversum, Niederlande, hier veröffentlicht) ausgeführt.

PIET HEIN EEK, né à Purmerend (Pays-Bas) en 1967, est diplômé de la Design Academy d'Eindhoven (1990). Il est principalement connu pour concevoir des meubles fabriqués dans des matériaux comme du bois de récupération mais a aussi à son actif des réalisations architecturales dont quelques rénovations de maisons et un bâtiment de trois niveaux pour une exposition florale aux Pays-Bas. Sur son célèbre bahut en rebuts de bois (1990), il a déclaré : « C'était ma réaction contre la mode dominante de l'absence de défauts. Je voulais montrer que des produits qui ne sont pas parfaits peuvent encore séduire notre sens de l'esthétique et du fonctionnalisme. Je souhaitais aussi concevoir un produit réalisable à partir de moyens limités, et un matériau abondant. » Il a achevé la maison en troncs d'arbres en 2009 (Hilversum, Pays-Bas, publiée ici).

TREE TRUNK HOUSE

Hilversum, The Netherlands, 2009

Address: not disclosed
Area: 9.3 m². Client: Hans Liberg. Cost: €110 000

The use of real logs in the cladding gives a very "real" impression to the exterior of the house, as though it might indeed be just a neat pile of logs.

Die Verwendung echter Baumstämme für die Verkleidung verleiht dem äußeren Erscheinungsbild des Hauses eine sehr „echte" Wirkung, als wäre es tatsächlich nur ein ordentlicher Stapel von Baumstämmen.

L'utilisation de vraies grumes pour le bardage donne l'impression très « réaliste » qu'elle ne serait en fait qu'une pile de bûches.

With its windows open (above) the Tree Trunk House reveals its trompe l'oeil design.

Bei geöffneten Fenstern (oben) offenbart sich die „Trompe-l'oeil"-Gestaltung des Baumstammhauses.

C'est fenêtres ouvertes (ci-dessus) que la maison en troncs d'arbres révèle sa conception en trompe-l'œil.

According to Piet Hein Eek: "A customer called and asked if we could build a log shack in his field, one that would be large enough to sit and write inside. I loved the idea from the start." The resulting structure closely resembles a stack of logs, but sliding windows, camouflaged with thin slices of wood, can open to reveal the true nature of the small building. The client was the Dutch musical and comedy performer Hans Liberg, who had previously commissioned Piet Hein Eek to create several pieces of furniture for his house. "It is difficult to feel close to nature in the city," says the designer. "We created a fairy tale." Actual oak logs line the sides and top of the structure, while five-centimeter-thick trunk sections are fixed to the 4.6-meter-long main elevations, continuing the illusion of an actual stack of logs. The **TREE TRUNK HOUSE** is built on wheels to allow the structure to comply with local building regulations, but it is provided with heating and electricity.

Piet Hein Eek berichtet: „Ein Kunde kam und fragte, ob wir eine Blockhütte auf seinem Grundstück errichten könnten, die groß genug wäre, um darin sitzen und schreiben zu können. Mir gefiel diese Idee sofort." Das Ergebnis sieht genau so aus wie ein Stapel Baumstämme, hat jedoch Schiebefenster, die hinter dünnen Holzscheiben verborgen, aber zu öffnen sind, um die wahre Natur des kleinen Gebäudes zu zeigen. Bauherr war der niederländische Musical- und Komödienproduzent Hans Liberg, der zuvor Piet Hein Eek beauftragt hatte, mehrere Möbelstücke für sein Wohnhaus zu entwerfen. „Es ist schwierig, sich in der Stadt der Natur nahe zu fühlen", sagt der Architekt, „wir schufen eine Märchenwelt." Eichenstämme bilden tatsächlich die Querwände und das Dach des Bauwerks, während 5 cm starke Baumscheiben an den 4,6 m langen Hauptfassaden angebracht sind und die Illusion eines Holzstapels vermitteln. Das **BAUMSTAMMHAUS** wurde auf Räder gestellt, um den örtlichen Bauvorschriften zu entsprechen, ist aber mit Heizung und Elektrizität ausgestattet.

Comme l'explique Piet Hein Eek : « Un client nous a appelé et nous a demandé si nous pouvions construire une cabane en rondins dans un champ … quelque chose de suffisamment grand pour pouvoir s'y asseoir et écrire. J'ai immédiatement aimé cette idée. » La structure réalisée ressemble beaucoup à une pile de rondins, mais les fenêtres coulissantes, dissimulées par de fines tranches de bois, qui peuvent s'ouvrir révèlent la vraie nature de cette petite construction. Le client, un acteur de comédies musicales et de théâtre néerlandais appelé Hans Liberg, avait préalablement demandé à Piet Hein Eek de lui dessiner plusieurs meubles pour sa maison. « Il est difficile de se sentir près de la nature dans une ville, explique le designer. Nous avons créé un conte de fée. » Des rondins de chêne habillent les façades et la toiture de la cabane. Des sections de tronc d'arbre de 5 cm d'épaisseur sont fixées sur les élévations de 4,6 m de long pour donner l'illusion d'une pile de rondins. La **MAISON EN TRONCS D'ARBRES** est sur roulettes pour des raisons de réglementations locale de la construction. Elle est équipée d'un chauffage et de l'électricité.

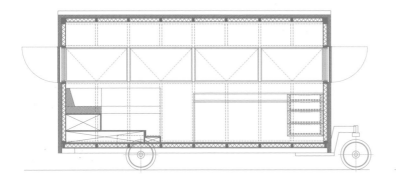
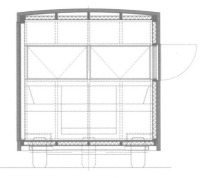
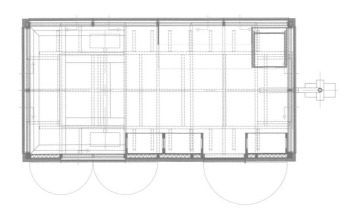

Die Zeichnungen und die Innenansichten zeigen, dass die Gesamtplanung des Hauses und der Möblierung eher konventionell ist – ganz im Gegensatz zum Eindruck, den es von außen vermittelt.

Drawings and interior views show that the house is almost conventional in its overall design and furnishing, quite the contrary of what one might expect from the exterior.

Les dessins et les vues intérieures montrent une maison presque conventionnelle dans son plan d'ensemble et son mobilier, au contraire de ce que l'on pouvait attendre d'après son aspect extérieur.

ETH-STUDIO MONTE ROSA / BEARTH & DEPLAZES

ETH-Studio Monte Rosa, Faculty of Architecture, ETH Zurich
Wolfgang-Pauli-Str. 15
8093 Zurich
Switzerland

Tel: +41 44 633 36 10
Fax: +41 44 633 11 49
E-mail: baumgartner@arch.ethz.ch
Web: www.deplazes.arch.ethz.ch

Born in 1960 in Chur, Switzerland, **ANDREA DEPLAZES** graduated from the ETH Zurich, in 1988. He cofounded the office Bearth & Deplazes in 1995 with Valentin Bearth. He has been a professor of architecture and construction at the ETH Zurich since 1997. The Faculty of Architecture at the ETH Zurich is one of the largest and most highly reputed architecture schools in the world. In the summer of 2003 Andrea Deplazes was asked by Meinrad Eberle, the project manager for the 150th Anniversary Jubilee of the ETH Zurich to work on the development of a new hut for the Monte Rosa, near Zermatt (2008–09, published here). Over a period of four semesters, students in the **ETH-STUDIO MONTE ROSA** worked on several designs for the structure, settling on a "rock crystal" form. The project was developed as an interdisciplinary collaboration between the ETH Zurich, the Swiss Alpine Club (SAC), industry, and experts in construction in extreme environments.

ANDREA DEPLAZES, geboren 1960 in Chur, Schweiz, beendete 1988 sein Studium an der ETH Zürich. Mit Valentin Bearth gründete er 1995 das Büro Bearth & Deplazes. Seit 1997 ist er Professor für Architektur und Konstruktion an der ETH Zürich. Die Architekturfakultät der ETH Zürich ist eine der größten und renommiertesten Architekturschulen der Welt. Im Sommer 2003 wurde Andrea Deplazes von Meinrad Eberle, dem Manager der 150-Jahr-Feier der ETH Zürich, aufgefordert, an der Planung einer neuen Berghütte für den Monte Rosa bei Zermatt (2008–09, hier veröffentlicht) mitzuarbeiten. Über einen Zeitraum von vier Semestern arbeiteten Studenten im **ETH-STUDIO MONTE ROSA** an mehreren Entwürfen für das Gebäude und entschieden sich für die Form eines „Bergkristalls". Das Projekt wurde in interdisziplinärer Zusammenarbeit von der ETH Zürich, dem Schweizer Alpen-Club (SAC), der Industrie und Experten für das Bauen an extremen Standorten entwickelt.

Né en 1960 à Chur, en Suisse, **ANDREA DEPLAZES** est diplômé de l'ETH (Zurich, 1988). En 1995, il fonde avec Valentin Bearth l'agence Bearth & Deplazes, et enseigne l'architecture et la construction à l'ETH à Zurich depuis 1997. La faculté d'architecture de l'ETH est un des plus grands et plus réputés centres d'enseignement de l'architecture dans le monde. À l'occasion du 150ᵉ anniversaire de l'école en 2003, Meinrad Eberle, responsable de ce jubilé, a demandé à Andrea Deplazes de réfléchir à un nouveau refuge sur le mont Rose près de Zermatt (2008–09, publié ici). Pendant quatre semestres, les étudiants du **ETH-STUDIO MONTE ROSA** ont travaillé sur plusieurs projets et se sont arrêtés sur une forme en « cristal de roche ». La mise au point du projet a été l'objet d'une collaboration interdisciplinaire entre l'ETH Zurich, le Club alpin suisse, des entreprises et des experts spécialisés dans la construction en environnements extrêmes.

NEW MONTE ROSA HUT SAC

Zermatt, Switzerland, 2008–09

Address: "Untere Plattje" between the Monte Rosa and the Grenz Glacier
(coordinates 629.146 / 089.553), 2883.50 m a.s.l., Zermatt, Valais, Switzerland, +41 27 967 21 15,
www.neuemonterosahuette.ch
Area: 1154 m². Client: Swiss Alpine Club SAC. Cost: € 4.3 million
Collaboration: Andrea Deplazes, Marcel Baumgartner (Project Manager), Kai Hellat, Daniel Ladner

The **MONTE ROSA HUT**, owned by the Swiss Alpine Club, is a mountain hut located at the base of the Monte Rosa at an altitude of 2883 meters. It is the starting point for climbers trying to reach the Monte Rosa and other nearby peaks. The first hut was built on this site in 1895. The participants in the project analyzed the energy consumption of the original hut to see how they could improve the environmental impact of the new building. CO_2 emissions of the new structure are three times lower than those of the previous building, and 90 percent of its energy needs are provided by sunlight. Lead-acid accumulators provide power even during low sunlight periods. Construction materials brought up to the site by no less than 3000 helicopter lifts were selected for minimum environmental impact, and they can all be recovered from the site at the moment of demolition. Numerically controlled manufacturing methods were used to allow the creation of unique structural and cladding elements. The basic internal structure of the hut, which is set on a stainless-steel foundation, is made of wood, while the external shell is in aluminum.

Die **MONTE-ROSA-HÜTTE** des Schweizer Alpen-Club ist eine Berghütte in 2883 m Höhe am Fuß des Monte Rosa. Sie ist der Ausgangspunkt für Bergsteiger auf den Monte Rosa und die Gipfel der benachbarten Berge. Die erste Hütte wurde 1895 auf diesem Gelände errichtet. Die an diesem Projekt Beteiligten untersuchten den Energiebedarf der alten Hütte, um festzustellen, wie die Auswirkungen des Neubaus auf die Umwelt verringert werden könnten. Die CO_2-Emissionen der neuen Hütte sind dreimal niedriger als die des Altbaus, und 90 % ihres Energiebedarfs werden durch Sonnenlicht gedeckt. Bleisäure-Akkumulatoren liefern Strom auch in Perioden geringer Sonneneinstrahlung. Die mit nicht weniger als 3000 Helikopterflügen angelieferten Baumaterialien wurden nach dem Grad ihrer Umwelteinwirkung ausgewählt und können alle bei Abriss des Gebäudes wiederverwendet werden. Computergesteuerte Produktionsmethoden ermöglichten die Herstellung besonderer Konstruktions- und Verkleidungselemente. Das innenliegende Tragwerk der Hütte, die auf einem Edelstahlfundament steht, ist aus Holz, die Außenhülle aus Aluminium.

Le **REFUGE DU MONT ROSE**, propriété du Club alpin suisse, est situé à la base du mont, à 2883 m d'altitude. C'est le point de départ pour les alpinistes vers le mont Rose et d'autres sommets. Un premier refuge avait été construit en 1895. Les participants au projet ont analysé la consommation d'énergie de cette première construction pour voir comment ils pourraient améliorer l'impact environnemental de la nouvelle. Les émissions de CO_2 sont maintenant trois fois inférieures à celle du précédent refuge et 90 % de ses besoins énergétiques sont remplis par la lumière solaire. Des accumulateurs plomb-acide fournissent l'énergie pendant les périodes de faible intensité lumineuse. Les matériaux de construction livrés sur le site par pas moins de 3000 rotations d'hélicoptère, ont été sélectionnés pour leur impact environnemental minimal. Ils pourront tous être récupérés en cas de démolition. Des processus d'usinage à commande numérique ont été utilisés pour les éléments d'habillage de dimensions uniques. La structure interne de ce refuge est en bois, recouvert d'aluminium à l'extérieur, le tout reposant sur des fondations en acier inoxydable.

Set in the range of mountains near the Matterhorn, the Monte Rosa Hut is just barely visible in the image to the left.

Auf dem Foto links ist die Monte-Rosa-Hütte in der Bergkette am Matterhorn kaum zu erkennen.

Le refuge du mont Rose est à peine visible dans le majestueux panorama de la chaîne de montagnes du mont Cervin.

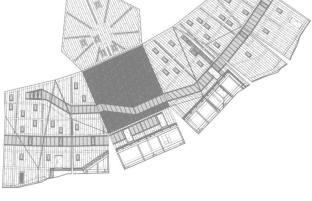

A topographical site plan, an "unfolded" drawing of the structure and detail images above show how the use of wood is integrated into an extremely modern structure.

Ein topografischer Lageplan, eine „entfaltete" Zeichnung des Gebäudes und Detailfotos (oben) zeigen, wie das Material Holz in ein extrem modernes Bauwerk integriert wurde.

Le plan de la topographie du terrain, une représentation « dépliée » de la construction et les images de détails ci-dessus montrent comment le bois a été intégré dans cette construction extrêmement moderne.

The structure of the cabin is in wood, as are the interiors. Drawings show the floor plan and demonstrate how the building is anchored into its site.

Das Tragwerk der Hütte ist aus Holz, ebenso die Innenausstattung. Die Zeichnungen zeigen den Grundriss und die Einfügung des Bauwerks in das Gelände.

L'ossature est en bois, de même que les aménagements intérieurs. Les dessins montrent le plan au sol et l'ancrage du bâtiment dans son terrain.

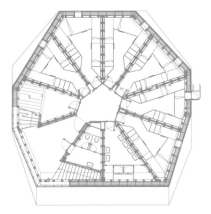

EDOUARD FRANÇOIS

Edouard François
136, rue Falguière
75015 Paris
France

Tel: +33 1 45 67 88 87
Fax: +33 1 45 67 51 45
E-mail: agence@edouardfrancois.com
Web: www.edouardfrancois.com

EDOUARD FRANÇOIS was born in Paris in 1957 and educated as an architect and urban designer. He attended the Beaux-Arts in Paris and the École Nationale des Ponts et Chaussées, becoming an architect in 1983. He has taught at the École Nationale Supérieure du Paysage in Versailles (1998–99), the Architectural Association in London (1997–98), and the École Spéciale d'Architecture in Paris the same year. The work of Edouard François emphasizes sustainable design and direct relations with nature. He completed the extension and renovation of the Buffon Primary School in Thiais (1996); an apartment building called L'Immeuble qui Pousse (the Building that Grows—a structure covered in a mesh of steel cages containing loosely compacted stones in which plants can grow, Montpellier, 2000); Flower Tower (Paris, 2001–03); the covering for a ventilation tower in La Défense (Paris, 2004); Fouquet's Barrière Hotel (Paris, 2006); the renovation and extension of the Ternes Parking facility (Paris, 2007); and Eden Bio (Paris, 2008), all in France. Current projects include 114 housing units in Champigny-sur-Marne (Opac de Paris); a further 70 housing units in Grenoble for the local rent-controlled housing office (Opac, 2008–); a school in Chartres (2010); and Club Med-Aldiana (near Nianing, Senegal, 2010–, published here).

EDOUARD FRANÇOIS wurde 1957 in Paris geboren und studierte bis 1983 Architektur und Städtebau an der École des Beaux-Arts in Paris und der École Nationale des Ponts et Chaussées. Er hat an der École Nationale Supérieure du Paysage in Versailles (1998–99), der Architectural Association in London (1997–98) und im gleichen Jahr an der École Spéciale d'Architecture in Paris gelehrt. Edouard François legt den Schwerpunkt seiner Arbeit auf nachhaltige Planung und direkte Bezüge zur Natur. Er realisierte die Erweiterung und Modernisierung der Primarschule Buffon in Thiais (1996), ein Apartmenthaus namens L'Immeuble qui pousse („das wachsende Gebäude" – es ist mit Kästen aus Stahlgeflecht überzogen, die locker zusammengefügte Steine enthalten, zwischen denen Pflanzen wachsen können; Montpellier, 2000), den Flower Tower (Paris, 2001–03), die Verkleidung eines Belüftungskamins in La Défense (Paris, 2004), das Hotel Fouquet's Barrière (Paris, 2006), die Erneuerung und Erweiterung des Parkhauses Ternes (Paris, 2007) und Eden Bio (Paris, 2008), alle in Frankreich. Zu seinen aktuellen Projekten zählen 114 Wohneinheiten in Champigny-sur-Marne (Opac de Paris), weitere 70 Wohneinheiten in Grenoble für den städtischen sozialen Wohnungsbau (Opac, 2008–), eine Schule in Chartres (2010) sowie der Club Med-Aldiana (bei Nianing, Senegal, 2010–, hier veröffentlicht).

EDOUARD FRANÇOIS, né à Paris en 1957, est architecte et urbaniste depuis 1983, après avoir étudié à l'École des beaux-arts et à l'École des ponts et chaussées à Paris. Il a enseigné à l'École nationale supérieure du Paysage à Versailles (1998–99), à l'Architectural Association à Londres (1997–98) et à l'École spéciale d'architecture à Paris la même année. Son travail est axé sur un développement durable en relation directe avec la nature. Il a réalisé l'extension et la rénovation de l'école primaire Buffon à Thiais (1996) ; un immeuble d'appartements, « L'Immeuble qui pousse », à la structure habillée de gabions à travers lesquels poussent des plantes (Montpellier, 2000) ; la tour Fleur (Paris, 2001–03) ; la couverture d'une tour de ventilation à La Défense (Paris, 2004) ; l'hôtel Fouquet's Barrière (Paris, 2006) ; la rénovation et l'extension du parking des Ternes (Paris, 2007) et l'Eden Bio (Paris, 2008). Ses projets actuels comprennent 114 logements à Champigny-sur-Marne (Opac de Paris) ; 70 logements à Grenoble pour l'office des HLM local (Opac, 2008–) ; une école à Chartres (2010) et le Club Med Aldiana (à proximité de Nianing, Sénégal, 2010–, publié ici).

CLUB MED-ALDIANA
near Nianing, Senegal, 2010–

*Address: Club Med-Aldiana, near Nianing, Senegal, www.clubmed.com
Area: 100 000 m². Client: Vacap. Cost: €40 million*

Perspective renderings give a clear idea of the integration of the architecture of Edouard François into this site in Senegal.

Die Perspektivdarstellungen geben eine Vorstellung davon, wie die Architektur von Edouard François in dieses Gelände im Senegal integriert wurde.

Les perspectives illustrent bien l'intégration de l'architecture d'Édouard François dans ce site au Sénégal.

P 206

This large facility for the French-based resort community group includes 250 rooms and suites, reception area, boutiques, bars, lounge, restaurants, swimming pools, sports facilities, a riding school and golf course, and its own water treatment facility. Located one and a half hours from Dakar, between the lagoon and the ocean, the complex offers three different types of stays: in the middle of the forest, in "original" huts; suspended between the trees in wood houses on stilts; or on the lagoon, facing a nature reserve. The architect states: "The entrance hall is a hut made out of traditional clay. The scenography uses African masks, traditional motifs, pendulum clocks, recycled bottle tops… The main building takes the shape of a snake and links the entrance hall, the restaurants, the lounge the swimming pool, and the beach area. It is a wood structure covered by straw tiles. The restaurant is a 100 percent wood structure in the shape of 'reversed umbrellas,' covered with straw, wood, and fabric."

Dieser große Komplex der in Frankreich ansässigen Firmengruppe für Freizeitanlagen enthält 250 Räume und Suiten, Empfangsbereich, Boutiquen, Bars, Lounge, Restaurants, Swimmingpool, Sporteinrichtungen, eine Reitschule und einen Golfplatz sowie eine eigene Wasseraufbereitungsanlage. Der anderthalb Stunden von Dakar entfernt, zwischen der Lagune und dem Ozean gelegene Komplex bietet drei verschiedene Unterbringungsmöglichkeiten: in „Original"-Hütten mitten im Wald, in zwischen den Bäumen aufgehängten oder aufgeständerten Holzhäusern oder in der Lagune vor einem Naturschutzgebiet. Der Architekt erklärt: „Die Eingangshalle ist ein Hütte in traditionellem Lehmbau. Die Ausstattung besteht aus afrikanischen Masken, überlieferten Motiven, Pendeluhren, recycelten Flaschenverschlüssen … Das Hauptgebäude hat die Form einer Schlange und verbindet die Eingangshalle, die Restaurants, die Lounge und den Swimmingpool mit dem Strand. Es handelt sich um eine mit Strohplatten gedeckte Holzkonstruktion. Das Restaurant ist eine zu 100 % aus Holz bestehende Konstruktion in Form ‚umgekehrter Schirme', die mit Stroh, Holz und Gewebe gedeckt sind."

Ces importantes installations réalisées pour le grand club de vacances français comprennent 250 chambres et suites, une réception, des boutiques, des bars, des salons, des restaurants, des piscines, des équipements sportifs, une école d'équitation, un club de golf, ainsi qu'une installation de traitement de l'eau. À une heure et demie de Dakar, entre le lagon et l'océan, ce complexe propose trois types de séjours : au milieu de la forêt dans des huttes « originelles », dans des maisons de bois suspendues entre les arbres sur pilotis ou sur le lagon face à une réserve naturelle. Selon l'architecte : « Le hall d'entrée est une hutte en terre de construction traditionnelle. La scénographie fait appel à des masques africains, des motifs traditionnels, des horloges à pendules, des capsules de bouteille recyclées … Le bâtiment principal en forme de serpent relie le hall d'entrée, les restaurants, le salon, la plage et la piscine. L'ensemble est une construction en bois couverte de tuiles de paille. Le restaurant est un bâtiment 100 % en bois en forme de 'parapluies inversés' recouverts de paille, de bois et de tissu. »

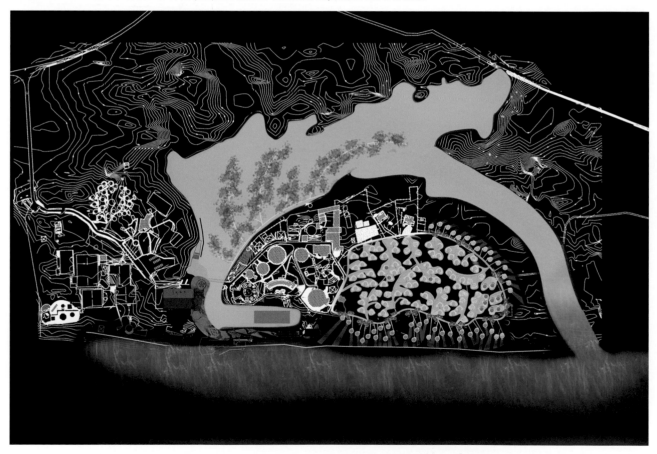

An overall site plan shows the use of both structures on the water and on the water's edge, creating different environments for guests.

Der Gesamtlageplan zeigt die Anlage der Bauten auf dem Wasser und am Ufer, wodurch unterschiedliche Umgebungen für die Gäste geboten werden.

Le plan d'ensemble du site montre l'implantation des constructions tantôt sur l'eau, tantôt en bordure de l'eau, afin de proposer des environnements différents à la clientèle.

Edouard François has been consistently interested in "green" architecture—here making use of an enveloping wood cladding.

Edouard François engagiert sich konsequent für „grüne" Architektur hier in Form einer umhüllenden Holzverkleidung.

Édouard François s'intéresse de longue date à l'architecture « verte », ici exprimée dans un bardage en bois enveloppant.

Although the architect has the country's culture as one source of ideas, some of his forms (left) appear to be decidedly contemporary despite their use of local materials.

Obgleich der Architekt die Kultur des Landes als Inspiration nutzte, wirken einige seiner Formen (links) ausgesprochen modern, trotz der Verwendung lokaler Materialien.

Si l'architecte s'est inspiré de la culture du pays, certaines formes (à gauche) paraissent résolument contemporaines malgré l'utilisation de matériaux locaux.

GENERAL DESIGN

General Design Co., Ltd.
3–13–3 Jingumae
Shibuya, Tokyo 150–0001
Japan

Tel: +81 3 5775 1298
Fax: +81 3 5775 1299
E-mail: email@general-design.net
Web: www.general-design.net

SHIN OHORI was born in Gifu, Japan, in 1967 and graduated from Musashino Art University (Tokyo) in 1990. He completed his M.Arch at the same institution in 1992. He cofounded Intentionallies in Tokyo in 1995 and General Design in 1999. His work includes a Photographer's Weekend House (Kujyukuri, Chiba, 2007); Mountain Research, Minamisaku (Nagano, 2007–08, published here); House In Sakurajyosui (Suginami, Tokyo, 2008); Zucca Aoyama (Minato, Tokyo, 2008); Zucca Paris (Rue Cambon, Paris, France, 2008); Edition Marunouchi (Chiyoda, Tokyo, 2008); T2 Project (Shibuya, Tokyo, 2009); and a House in Sendagaya (Shibuya, Tokyo, 2009), all in Japan, unless stated otherwise.

SHIN OHORI wurde 1967 in Gifu, Japan, geboren und studierte bis 1990 an der Musashino Art University (Tokio). 1992 machte er an der gleichen Hochschule den Master in Architektur. Er war 1995 Mitbegründer des Büros Intentionallies in Tokio und 1999 von General Design. Zu seinen Bauten zählen ein Wochenendhaus für einen Fotografen (Kujyukuri, Chiba, 2007), Mountain Research, Minamisaku (Nagano, 2007–08, hier veröffentlicht), ein Wohnhaus in Sakurajyosui (Suginami, Tokio, 2008), Zucca Aoyama (Minato, Tokio, 2008), Zucca Paris (Rue Cambon, Paris, 2008), Edition Marunouchi (Chiyoda, Tokio, 2008), das Projekt T2 (Shibuya, Tokio, 2009) sowie ein Wohnhaus in Sendagaya (Shibuya, Tokio, 2009), alle in Japan, sofern nicht anders angegeben.

SHIN OHORI, né à Gifu (Japon) en 1967, est diplômé de l'Université artistique Musashino (Tokyo, 1990) et a obtenu M. Arch de la même institution (1992). Il est l'un des fondateurs de l'agence Intentionallies à Tokyo (1995) et de General Design en 1999. Parmi ses réalisations : une maison de week-end pour un photographe (Kujyukuri, Chiba, 2007) ; une petite structure appelée Mountain Research (Minamisaku, Nagano, 2007–08, publiée ici) ; une maison à Sakurajyosui (Suginami, Tokyo, 2008) ; Zucca Aoyama (Minato, Tokyo, 2008) ; le magasin Zucca Paris (rue Cambon, Paris, 2008) ; Edition Marunouchi (Chiyoda, Tokyo, 2008) ; le T2 Project (Shibuya, Tokyo, 2009) et une maison à Sendagaya (Shibuya, Tokyo, 2009).

MOUNTAIN RESEARCH

Minamisaku, Nagano, Japan, 2007–08

Address: not disclosed
Area: 97 m². Client: not disclosed. Cost: not disclosed

A drawing and a photo of the structure on this page show how tents are supported on the exposed platforms.

Die Zeichnung und das Foto des Gebäudes auf dieser Seite zeigen, wie die Zelte auf den offenen Plattformen stehen.

Le dessin et la photo de cette page montrent comment les tentes sont dressées sur des plates-formes.

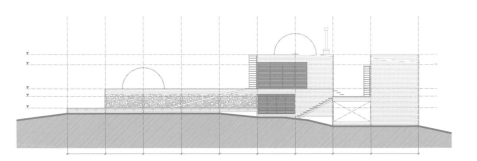

The densely wooded site is visible on the drawing below and in the photos published here. The yellow tents sit on top of the wooden structure.

Das dicht bewaldete Grundstück ist auf der Zeichnung unten und den Fotos zu erkennen. Die gelben Zelte stehen auf der hölzernen Konstruktion.

Le terrain très boisé est visible sur le dessin ci-dessous et dans les photographies. Les tentes jaunes sont posées sur la couverture de la construction en bois.

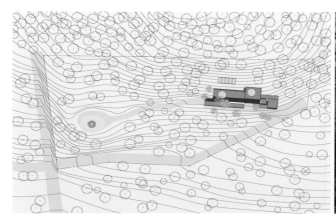

Shin Ohori explains that the client just wanted a place in the woods to set up a tent. The site concerned is a 5300-square-meter area in the mountains of Nagano Prefecture. The architect provided a rough larch deck, kitchen, storage space, bathroom, toilet, shelves for firewood, and a solar panel system, and the client was able to put up his two-meter dome tent. The deck serves as a "living room" while the clients sleep in the tent. "I did not intend to design a regular weekend house," says the architect, "and didn't want comfortable and protected rooms with beautiful views. I was determined to support his clear and powerful vision of nature, so I eliminated anything that would interfere with his thoughts." It seems in this instance that the desires of the architect met closely with those of his client. "I don't want architecture to be a convenient 'tool' that guarantees safe and ordinary lives," says Shin Ohori. "I hope that architecture will be a place where people discover something new, and make innovations in their lifestyles."

Shin Ohori erklärt, dass der Bauherr nur einen Ort im Wald suchte, um ein Zelt aufzustellen. Das entsprechende Gelände in den Bergen der Präfektur Nagano ist 5300 m² groß. Der Architekt lieferte ein grobes Deck aus Lärchenholz, eine Küche, Abstellraum, Bad, Toilette, Regale für Feuerholz sowie ein System von Solarzellenpaneelen, sodass der Kunde sein 2 m hohes Kuppelzelt aufstellen konnte. Das Deck dient als „Wohnraum", während die Auftraggeber im Zelt schlafen. „Ich hatte nicht die Absicht, ein richtiges Wochenendhaus zu planen", sagt der Architekt, „und auch keine bequemen und geschützten Räume mit schöner Aussicht. Ich war entschlossen, seine klare und kraftvolle Sicht der Natur zu unterstützen, daher ließ ich alles weg, was seiner Auffassung im Weg gestanden hätte." In diesem Fall scheinen die Absichten des Architekten mit denen des Bauherrn übereingestimmt zu haben. „Ich will nicht, dass Architektur ein bequemes ‚Instrument' ist, das ein sicheres und normales Leben garantiert", sagt Shin Ohori. „Ich hoffe, dass die Architektur einen Ort erzeugt, wo Menschen otwas Neues entdecken und ihre Lebensweise erneuern können."

Shin Ohori explique que son client voulait juste pouvoir disposer d'un endroit dans les bois pour planter sa tente. Le terrain de 5300 m² est situé dans les montagnes de la préfecture de Nagano. L'architecte a créé une vaste terrasse de mélèze, une cuisine, un espace de rangement, une salle de bains, des toilettes, des rayonnages pour le bois à brûler et un système de panneaux solaires. Le client a pu y installer ses tentes en forme de dôme de deux mètres de diamètre qui font office de chambres. La terrasse sert de « séjour ». « Je ne souhaitais pas dessiner une maison de week-end classique, précise l'architecte, et je ne voulais pas de belles chambres bien protégées ouvrant sur des vues superbes. J'étais déterminé à donner une vision claire et puissante de la nature et j'ai éliminé tout ce qui pouvait s'y opposer. » Il semble qu'ici le désir de l'architecte ait été en phase profonde avec celui de son client. « Je ne veux pas d'une architecture qui devienne un outil pratique au service d'une vie sûre et ordinaire », explique Shin Ohori : « J'espère que cette architecture sera un lieu d'où l'on pourra découvrir quelque chose de nouveau et qui favorisera des changements de style de vie. »

A bathroom opens out onto the main
platform area, while chairs are placed
in front of a low table, opposite the
view.

Das Badezimmer öffnet sich zur
großen Plattform; gegenüber sind
Stühle vor einem niedrigen Tisch
zu sehen.

Une salle de bains grande ouverte
sur la terrasse principale. En face,
des chaises longues disposées autour
d'une table basse.

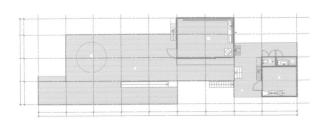
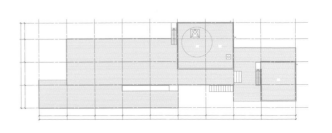

The fairly closed interior spaces are entirely made of wood and provide for some of the basic storage space, and some comforts that are not usually available in tents.

Die geschlosseneren Innenräume sind ganz aus Holz und bieten den notwendigen Stauraum oder sonstige Annehmlichkeiten, die Zelte normalerweise nicht aufweisen.

Les espaces intérieurs assez fermés sont entièrement doublés de bois. Ils offrent divers rangements et un confort que l'on aurait du mal à trouver dans une tente.

SEPPO HÄKLI

Häkli Ky Architects
Kuortaneenkatu 5
00520 Helsinki
Finland

Tel: +358 9 753 22 53
Fax: +358 9 753 22 56
E-mail: hakli@arkhakli.fi
Web: www.arkhakli.fi

SEPPO HÄKLI was born in Kuusjärvi, Finland, in 1951. He graduated as an architect from the Tampere University of Technology in 1978. He worked in various architectural offices from 1974 to 1986, and with Hyvämäki-Karhunen-Parkkinen Architects from 1986 to 1989. Seppo Häkli worked in the Built Heritage Department of the Finnish National Board of Antiquities in 1980 and created Häkli & Karhunen Architects (1989–93), before creating his current firm, Häkli Ky Architects, in 1993. From 1994 to 1997 and again, since 2003, he has taught a wood studio at the Helsinki University of Technology, Department of Architecture. His recent work includes the Metla Office and Laboratory Building, Haapastensyrjä, 2007–08, published here) and the Seurasaari Building Conservation Center (Helsinki, 2007–09), both in Finland.

SEPPO HÄKLI wurde 1951 in Kuusjärvi, Finnland, geboren und beendete 1978 sein Architekturstudium an der Technischen Universität in Tampere. Von 1974 bis 1986 arbeitete er in verschiedenen Architekturbüros und von 1986 bis 1989 bei Hyvämäki-Karhunen-Parkkinen Architects. Er arbeitete 1980 auch für die finnische Denkmalpflege und gründete das Büro Häkli & Karhunen Architects (1989–93), bevor er 1993 die gegenwärtige Firma Häkli Ky Architects etablierte. Von 1994 bis 1997 und dann wieder seit 2003 lehrt er Holzbau an der Technischen Universität Helsinki. Zu seinen aktuellen Werken zählen das Büro- und Laborgebäude Metla (Haapastensyrjä, 2007–08, hier veröffentlicht) und das Seurasaari Building Conservation Center (Helsinki, 2007–09), beide in Finnland.

SEPPO HÄKLI, né à Kuusjärvi (Finlande) en 1951, est architecte diplômé de l'Université de technologie de Tampere (1978). Il a travaillé dans plusieurs agences de 1974 à 1986 et chez Hyvämäki-Karhunen-Parkkinen Architects de 1986 à 1989. Il a aussi collaboré avec le Département du patrimoine architectural du Conseil national finlandais des antiquités en 1980, et a fondé Häkli & Karhunen Architects (1989–93) avant de créer son agence actuelle, Häkli Ky Architects, en 1993. De 1994 à 1997 et depuis 2003, il a enseigné dans un atelier du bois au département d'Architecture de l'Université de technologie d'Helsinki. Parmi ses récentes réalisations : le bâtiment de bureaux et de laboratoires du Metla (Haapastensyrjä, 2007–08, publié ici) et l'immeuble du Centre de conservation de Seurasaari (Helsinki, 2007–09), tous deux en Finlande.

METLA OFFICE AND LABORATORY BUILDING
Haapastensyrjä, Finland, 2007–08

Address: Haapastensyrjäntie 34, 12600 Läyliäinen, Finland, +358 10 21 11, www.metla.fi
Area: 550 m². Client: Finnish Forest Research Institute. Cost: € 1.7 million

Narrow and rectangular, this project is related in its appearance to traditional Finnish farmhouses. The central area contains an entrance hall, library, and café. Offices in an open-plan configuration looking out onto greenery are located on either side of the foyer. Laboratory and technical areas are set in spruce-walled blocks located to the north of the two office areas. Small blocks of offices clad in alder wood are located at the far end of each open-plan office area. The architect states: "A dozen different species of timber were used in the building, mainly spruce, pine, birch, and alder. Inside the building, the wooden surfaces are either waxed or left untreated, while externally the surfaces are treated with a translucent finish."

Dieses schmale, rechteckige Gebäude ähnelt in seiner Gestalt traditionellen finnischen Bauernhäusern. Der zentrale Bereich enthält die Eingangshalle, eine Bibliothek und ein Café. Die offen angelegten Büros haben Ausblick ins Grüne und sind zu beiden Seiten des Foyers angeordnet. Laboratorien und technische Bereiche liegen in mit Fichtenholz verkleideten Blocks nördlich der beiden Bürozonen. Kleine Gruppen mit Erlenholz verkleideter Büroräume sind am Ende der beiden Großraum-Bürobereiche angeordnet. Der Architekt erklärt: „Ein Dutzend unterschiedlicher Holzarten wurde im Gebäude verwendet, vorwiegend Fichte, Kiefer, Birke und Erle. Die Holzflächen im Inneren wurden entweder gewachst oder unbehandelt belassen, die Außenflächen mit einem farblosen Anstrich versehen."

De plan rectangulaire étroit, ce bâtiment se rattache par son apparence aux fermes traditionnelles finlandaises. La partie centrale regroupe le hall d'entrée, une bibliothèque et un café. Situés de chaque côté de l'accueil, les bureaux de plan ouvert donnent sur la nature. Le laboratoire et les pièces techniques sont répartis dans des blocs à murs à parement en épicéa implantés au nord des deux zones de bureaux. Des petits blocs de bureaux habillés d'aulne occupent les extrémités des zones en plan ouvert. « Une douzaine d'espèces de bois différentes ont été utilisées, essentiellement l'épicéa, le pin, le bouleau et l'aulne. À l'intérieur les panneaux de bois sont cirés ou non traités tandis qu'à l'extérieur, l'habillage de bois est recouvert d'une finition translucide », précise l'architecte.

This building for the Finnish Forest Research Institute is logically located in a densely wooded area.

Dieses Gebäude für das Finnische Waldforschungsinstitut steht logischerweise in einem dicht bewaldeten Gebiet.

Très logiquement, ce bâtiment construit pour l'Institut finlandais de recherche forestière se dresse dans une zone densément boisée.

A site plan (right) shows the narrow building, while the photo above emphasizes the very modern use of wood in the design.

Der Lageplan (rechts) zeigt das schmale Gebäude, während das Foto oben die sehr moderne Verwendung von Holz in der Gestaltung wiedergibt.

Le plan du site (à droite) montre le bâtiment de forme assez étroite. La photo ci-dessus fait ressortir l'utilisation très contemporaine du bois dans le projet.

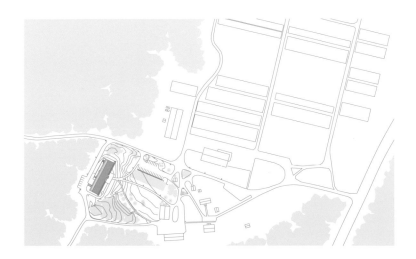

The relation to farmhouse typology is more apparent in the elevation drawings on the right page than in the photos published here. Generous interior spaces are logically clad in wood.

Der Bezug zur Typologie des Bauernhauses ist in den Ansichtszeichnungen auf der rechten Seite besser erkennbar als auf diesen Fotos. Die großzügigen Innenräume sind selbstredend auch mit Holz verkleidet.

Le lien avec la typologie des fermes locales est plus apparent dans les élévations de la page de droite que dans les photos. Les généreux volumes intérieurs sont également habillés de bois.

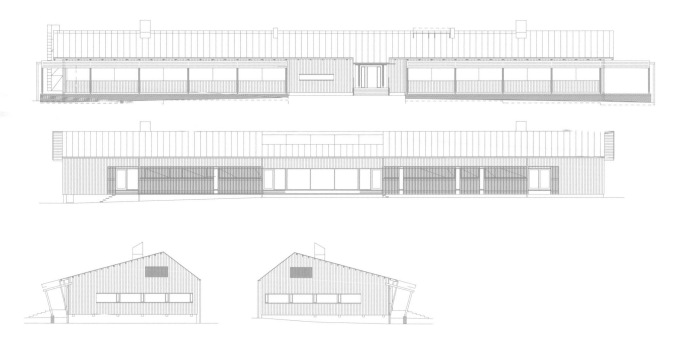

YOSUKE INOUE

Yosuke Inoue Architect & Associates
201, 4–16–7 Ekoda
Nakano-ku
Tokyo 165–0022
Japan

Tel: +81 3 5913 3525
Fax: +81 3 5913 3526
E-mail: usun@gol.com
Web: www.yosukeinoue.com

YOSUKE INOUE was born in Tokyo, Japan, in 1966. He graduated from the Department of Architecture of Kyoto University in 1991. He worked in the office of Sakakura Associates from 1991 to 2000, when he established his own office, Yosuke Inoue Architect & Associates, in Tokyo. His work includes House in Fuji (Fuji, Shizuoka, 2002); House in Nakanobu (Shinagawa, Tokyo, 2004); House in Setagaya-Sakura (Setagaya, Tokyo, 2004); House in Azamino (Yokohama, Kanagawa, 2005); House in Ichikawa (Ichikawa, Chiba, 2006); Villa in Hayama (Hayama, Kanagawa, 2006–07, published here); House in Den-en-chofu (Ohta, Tokyo, 2007); House in Tsujido (Fujisawa, Kanagawa, 2008); and House in Yotsuya (Shinjuku, Tokyo, 2008). He completed the House in Yoga (Tokyo) and the House in Daita (Tokyo) in 2010, all in Japan.

YOSUKE INOUE wurde 1966 in Tokio geboren und beendete 1991 sein Architekturstudium an der Universität von Kioto. Von 1991 bis 2000 arbeitete er im Büro Sakakura Associates. 2000 gründete er seine eigene Firma, Yosuke Inoue Architect & Associates, in Tokio. Zu seinen ausgeführten Bauten zählen ein Wohnhaus in Fuji (Fuji, Shizuoka, 2002), ein Wohnhaus in Nakanobu (Shinagawa, Tokio, 2004), ein Wohnhaus in Setagaya-Sakura (Setagaya, Tokio, 2004), ein Wohnhaus in Azamino (Yokohama, Kanagawa, 2005), ein Wohnhaus in Ichikawa (Ichikawa, Chiba, 2006), eine Villa in Hayama (Hayama, Kanagawa, 2006–07, hier veröffentlicht), ein Wohnhaus in Den-en-chofu (Ohta, Tokio, 2007), ein Wohnhaus in Tsujido (Fujisawa, Kanagawa, 2008) sowie ein Wohnhaus in Yotsuya (Shinjuku, Tokio, 2008). 2010 fertiggestellt wurden ein Wohnhaus in Yoga (Tokio) und ein Wohnhaus in Daita (Tokio), alle in Japan.

YOSUKE INOUE, né à Tokyo en 1966, est diplômé du département d'Architecture de l'Université de Kyoto (1991). Il a travaillé dans l'agence Sakakura Associates de 1991 à 2000 avant de fonder sa propre structure, Yosuke Inoue Architect & Associates, à Tokyo. Parmi ses réalisations figurent de nombreuses maisons : à Fuji (Shizuoka, 2002) ; Nakanobu (Shinagawa, Tokyo, 2004) ; Setagaya-Sakura (Setagaya, Tokyo, 2004) ; Azamino (Yokohama, Kanagawa, 2005) ; Ichikawa (Ichikawa, Chiba, 2006) ; Hayama (Kanagawa, 2006–07 publiée ici) ; Den-en-chofu (Ohta, Tokyo, 2007) ; Tsujido (Fujisawa, Kanagawa, 2008) et à Yotsuya (Shinjuku, Tokyo, 2008, publiée ici). Il vient d'achever une maison à Yoga (Tokyo, 2010) et une maison à Faita (Tokyo, 2010).

VILLA IN HAYAMA

Hayama, Kanagawa, Japan, 2006–07

Address: not disclosed
Area: 157 m². Client: not disclosed. Cost: not disclosed
Collaboration: Keiichi Amano

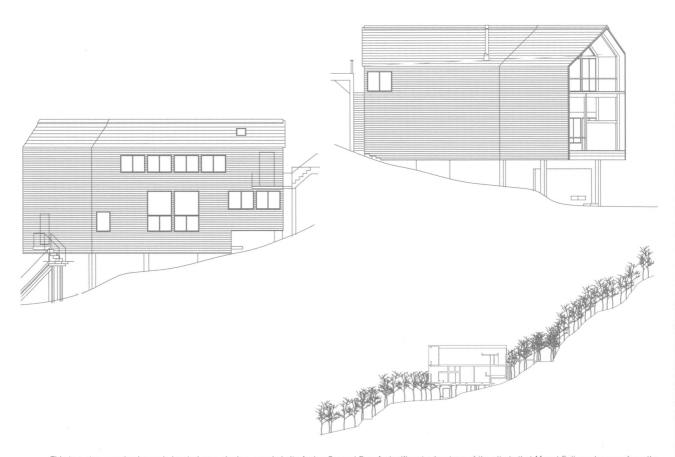

This two-story wooden house is located on a sloping, wooded site facing Sagami Bay. A significant advantage of the site is that Mount Fuji can be seen from the house on a clear day. The residence is set on concrete pilotis that increase in height as the ground slopes down. The entrance to the building, kitchen, and double-height living and dining areas are located on the upper level. The inflected shape of the plan is related to the form of the site and of course to the direction of the views of the ocean and Mount Fuji. Wood is visible everywhere, both in the dark exterior cladding and in the sometimes lighter wood used within the residence.

Dieses zweigeschossige Holzhaus steht auf einem bewaldeten Hanggrundstück mit Blick auf die Bucht von Sagami. Ein beachtlicher Vorzug dieses Geländes ist an klaren Tagen die Sicht auf den Berg Fuji. Das Gebäude steht auf Betonstützen, die es auf dem abfallenden Gelände anheben. Der Eingang, die Küche und der doppelgeschosshohe Wohn- und Essbereich liegen auf der oberen Ebene. Die gebogene Form des Grundrisses folgt dem Verlauf des Grundstücks und natürlich den Blickrichtungen zum Ozean und zum Berg Fuji. Holz tritt überall in Erscheinung, an der dunklen Außenverkleidung sowie teilweise etwas heller innerhalb des Hauses.

Cette villa entièrement en bois de deux niveaux est située sur un terrain en forte pente, face à la baie de Sagami. Une des caractéristiques de ce site est de permettre d'apercevoir le mont Fuji par beau temps. La construction s'appuie sur des pilotis de béton qui compensent la pente du terrain. On accède à la cuisine, le séjour double hauteur et la zone des repas par le niveau supérieur. La forme d'ensemble est déterminée par la déclivité du terrain et l'orientation vers les vues sur l'océan et le mont Fuji. Le bois est omniprésent, aussi bien dans le bardage extérieur de couleur sombre que dans les essences un peu plus claires retenues pour les aménagements intérieurs.

Backed against a steep hillside, as the site drawing above shows, the house has an asymmetric form that is lifted off the ground on the downhill side.

Wie die Zeichnungen oben zeigen, hat das an einen steilen Hang gelehnte Haus eine asymmetrische Form und ist auf der Talseite vom Boden angehoben.

Appuyée contre le flanc d'une colline abrupte, comme le montre le dessin ci-dessus, cette maison de plan asymétrique est suspendue du côté de la pente.

The full glazing under the gables of the house allows for a spectacular view of the water and the mountains beyond.

Aus den voll verglasten Giebeln bieten sich spektakuläre Ausblicke zum Wasser und auf die dahinter liegenden Berge.

Le pignon entièrement vitré offre une vue spectaculaire sur l'océan et les montagnes dans le lointain.

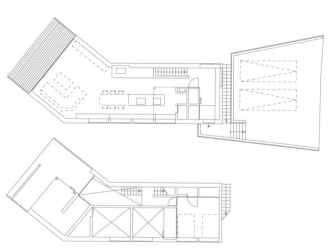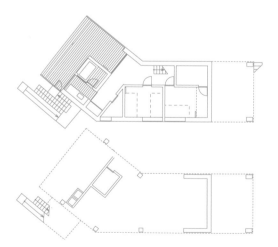

Floor plans show the angled shape of the house, culminating in the framed view seen in the image above.

Die Grundrisse zeigen die eckige Form des Hauses, die in dem gerahmten Ausblick gipfelt, der auf dem oberen Foto zu sehen ist.

Les plans au sol des différents niveaux illustrent la forme en angle de la maison qui aboutit à la vue cadrée ci-dessus.

Wood is present everywhere, including the steeply angled ceilings seen in the page to the right.

Holz ist überall präsent, auch an den steil ansteigenden Decken, wie am Foto rechts abzulesen.

Le bois est omniprésent, y compris dans les plafonds dont la forte Inclinaison suit la toiture (page de droite).

The same wooden floor continues from the inside of the house to the balcony, as seen in the image above.

Der gleiche hölzerne Boden im Innern des Hauses wird auf den Balkon weitergeführt, wie das Foto oben zeigt.

Le sol en bois de l'intérieur se prolonge vers le balcon (photo ci-dessus).

Lim Geo Dang ▶

IROJE KHM ARCHITECTS

IROJE KHM Architects
1805 Gardentower Building
98–78 Unni-dong, Jongro-gu
Seoul 110–795
South Korea

Tel: +82 2 766 1928
Fax: +82 2 766 1929
E-mail: iroman@unitel.co.kr
Web: www.irojekhm.com

HYOMAN KIM is the principal of IROJE KHM Architects. He graduated from the Department of Architecture of DanKook University (Seoul, 1978). Since 2004 he has been a professor at the Graduate School of Architecture, KyongGi University (Seoul) and at the Department of Architecture of DanKook University (now located in Yongin). His work includes Lim Geo Dang (Go Yang, 2001, published here); Hye Ro Hun (Gwangju, 2005, also published here); Purple Whale (Paju Book City, Gyeounggi-do, 2008); Island House (Gapyung-gun, Gyeounggi-do, 2007–09); Purple Hill House (Youngin, Gyeounggi-do, 2009); and BuYeonDang House (SungNam, Gyeounggi-do, 2009). Ongoing work includes the PyeongChang Institute for Buddhism (PyeongChangGun, GangWonDo, 2009–), and Green Hill Village (Seoul, 2009–), all in South Korea. "Concept is an ideal and abstract thought," says HyoMan Kim. "The concept does not hold value until the concept is embodied into a concrete building in reality."

HYOMAN KIM ist Chef der Firma IROJE KHM Architects. Er studierte Architektur an der DanKook University (Seoul, 1978). Seit 2004 hat er eine Professur an der Graduate School of Architecture, KyongGi University (Seoul), sowie an der Architekturabteilung der DanKook University (jetzt in Yongin). Zu seinen Bauwerken zählen das Haus Lim Geo Dang (Go Yang, 2001, hier veröffentlicht), das Haus Hye Ro Hun (Gwangju, 2005, ebenfalls hier veröffentlicht), Purple Whale (Paju Book City, Gyeounggi-do, 2008), Island House (Gapyung-gun, Gyeounggi-do, 2007–09), das Haus Purple Hill (Youngin, Gyeounggi-do, 2009) und das Haus BuYeonDang (SungNam, Gyeounggi-do, 2009). Zu seinen aktuellen Arbeiten gehören das PyeongChang Institute for Buddhism (PyeongChangGun, GangWonDo, 2009–) und das Green Hill Village (Seoul, seit 2009–), alle in Südkorea. „Das Konzept ist ein idealer und abstrakter Gedanke", sagt HyoMan Kim. „Das Konzept hat keinerlei Bedeutung, bevor es in einem konkreten Gebäude realisiert wurde."

HYOMAN KIM, diplômé du département d'Architecture de l'Université Dankook (Séoul, 1978), dirige l'agence IROJE KHM. Depuis 2004, il est également professeur à l'École supérieure d'architecture de l'université KyongGi (Séoul) et au département d'Architecture de l'université Dankook (aujourd'hui relocalisée à Yongin). Parmi ses réalisations, toutes en Corée du Sud, figurent la maison Lim Geo Dang (Go Yang, 2001, publiée ici) ; la maison Hye Ro Hun (Gwangju, 2005, également publiée ici) ; le bâtiment industriel de la Baleine pourpre (Purple Whale, Paju Book, Gyeounggi-do, 2008) ; la Maison-île (Island House, Gapyung-gun, Gyeounggi-do, 2007–09) ; la maison de la Colline pourpre (Purple Hill House, Youngin, Gyeounggi-do, 2009) et la maison BuYeonDang (SungNam, Gyeounggi-do, 2009). Il travaille actuellement sur les projets de l'Institut du bouddhisme de PyeongChang (PyeongChangGun, GangWonDo, 2009–) et le village de la Colline verte (Green Hill Village, Séoul, 2009–). « Le concept est un idéal, une pensée abstraite », écrit HyoMan Kim : « Le concept n'a pas de valeur tant qu'il ne s'incarne pas dans une construction concrète, réelle. »

LIM GEO DANG

Go Yang, South Korea, 2001

Address: JangHangDong, IlSan, Go Yang, South Korea
Area: 108 m². Client: Jong Gi Lim. Cost: $176 000

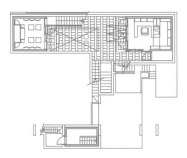 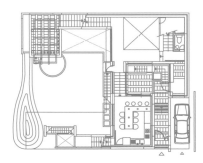 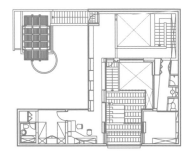

The basic square form of the plan is notched to create a partially enclosed courtyard, as seen in the drawings above and the photo below.

Die Grundform des Quadrats ist aufgebrochen, um einen teilumschlossenen Innenhof zu bilden, wie die Pläne oben und das Foto unten zeigen.

Le plan essentiellement carré est entaillé pour créer une cour en partie fermée, comme le montrent les dessins ci-dessus et la photo ci-dessous.

The architect makes a powerful and unexpected combination of a concrete base and a wooden upper volume.

Dem Architekten ist eine eindrucksvolle und ungewöhnliche Kombination aus einem Betonfundament und dem darauf gesetzten Volumen aus Holz gelungen.

L'architecte a réussi la combinaison inattendue et frappante d'un socle en béton et d'un volume supérieur en bois.

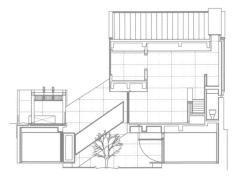

The clients for this small house were authors and publishers who asked for a building that was "traditional but modern." The site of the residence measures just 231 square meters. The architect responded to this request, stating: "The spatial design concept set for this small house was based on its dramatic circulation, which was characteristic of traditional architecture in Korea. The circulation of ancient Korea continues infinitely in space, overlapping and penetrating asymmetrically, and, finally, producing several picturesque frames relating nature and building." A "madang" or traditional inner courtyard is included in the design. Only the living and dining spaces are located at ground level to allow for the largest possible courtyard. The bedroom area above is a pilotis structure, with space beneath that is also a type of courtyard. Using sublimated ideas about traditional wooden architecture in particular, the architect has sought to "read this inheritance in modern language."

Die Auftraggeber dieses kleinen Hauses waren Autoren und Verleger, die sich ein „traditionelles, aber modernes" Gebäude wünschten. Das Grundstück des Wohnhauses misst nur 231 m². Der Architekt erklärt zu diesem Wunsch: „Das Raumkonzept für dieses kleine Wohnhaus basiert auf seinen ungewöhnlichen Verbindungswegen, die für die traditionelle Architektur in Korea charakteristisch sind. Die Verbindungswege im antiken Korea führten in die Unendlichkeit des Raums, überschnitten und durchdrangen sich asymmetrisch und bildeten schließlich mehrere pittoreske Rahmen, die Natur und Gebäude in Beziehung zueinander setzten." Ein „Madang" oder traditioneller Innenhof ist auch in diesem Haus enthalten. Im Erdgeschoss liegen nur der Wohn- und Essbereich, um Raum für den größtmöglichen Innenhof zu gewinnen. Die Schlafräume darüber befinden sich in einer Piloti-Konstruktion; darunter entsteht ebenfalls eine Art Innenhof. Der Architekt hat versucht, „dieses Erbe in eine moderne Sprache zu übersetzen", indem er traditionelle Vorstellungen vor allem über Holzarchitektur übernahm.

Les clients – auteurs et éditeurs – avaient demandé à l'architecte de leur concevoir une maison « traditionnelle mais moderne » sur un petit terrain de 231 mètres carrés. HyoMan, qui a répondu à leur demande, explique que « le concept spatial mis au point pour cette petite maison s'appuie sur un spectaculaire système de circulation, caractéristique de l'architecture traditionnelle coréenne. Dans l'ancienne Corée, la circulation se poursuit à l'infini dans l'espace. Elle s'entrecroise, pénètre l'espace asymétriquement pour, finalement, produire plusieurs modes de relations pittoresques entre la nature et le bâti ». Le projet a intégré un *madang* ou cour intérieure traditionnelle. Seuls le séjour et la zone des repas occupent le rez-de-chaussée pour laisser à la cour le maximum de surface. Le niveau des chambres, sous lequel un autre espace sert également de cour, est monté sur pilotis. Par l'utilisation des principes subliminaux de l'architecture traditionnelle, en particulier en bois, l'architecte a recherché « une lecture de cet héritage à travers un langage moderne ».

The relatively cold concrete surfaces are contrasted with the warmer wood. Both materials are present inside and outside the house.

Die relativ kalt wirkenden Betonflächen stehen in Kontrast zum wärmeren Holz. Beide Materialien sind im Hause innen und außen präsent.

Contraste entre les plans en béton relativement froids et la chaleur du bois. Les deux matériaux se retrouvent à l'intérieur et à l'extérieur de la maison.

HYE RO HUN

Gwangju, South Korea, 2005

Address: Ilgok-dong, Bukgu, Gwangju, South Korea
Area: 169 m². Client: Hyung Sub Sim. Cost: $351 000. Collaboration: SuMi Jung

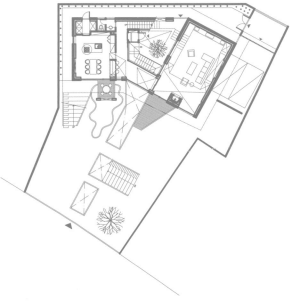

The architect uses rectilinear volumes but makes them "collide" in unexpected ways, generating relatively complex spaces.

Der Architekt verwendet rechtwinklige Formen, die er auf ungewöhnliche Weise „kollidieren" lässt und dadurch relativ komplexe Räume erzeugt.

L'architecte utilise des volumes simples qu'il fait entrer en « collision » de manière inattendue pour créer des espaces relativement complexes.

Wood covers the nearly symmetrical towers that stand above the concrete and glass base.

Holz überzieht die fast symmetrischen Türme, die auf einer Basis aus Beton und Glas stehen.

Les tours presque symétriques qui s'élèvent d'une base en béton et verre sont bardées de bois.

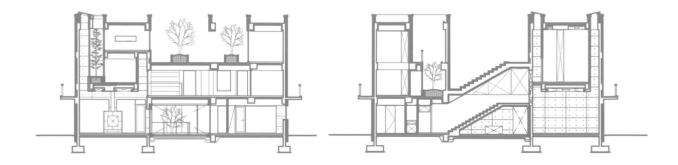

This house is set at the limit between an urban environment and that of the mountains. Both landscapes are taken into account by the design. The designer describes the entrance walkway as an "architectural canyon." Two wooden boxes contain duplex rooms that are laid on a landscaped architectural mass that contains the nine-meter-high living room with an overhead natural light source and dining room. One box contains the double-height master bed and study room and another box contains two bedrooms and study rooms for two children. The exterior finish of the house is in exposed concrete and red cedar, while exposed concrete, lacquer, and plywood are employed in the interior. The architect states that he has willfully made the continuity of space, both vertical and horizontal, the theme of his work here.

Dieses Haus steht an der Grenze zwischen städtischer Bebauung und gebirgiger Umgebung. Der Entwurf bezieht beide Landschaften ein. Der Architekt beschreibt den Erschließungsweg als „architektonischen Canyon". Zwei Holzkisten enthalten Räume auf verschiedenen Ebenen in einer Architekturlandschaft, die auch den 9 m hohen Wohnraum mit einem Oberlicht als natürliche Lichtquelle sowie den Essraum enthält. In einer der Kisten befinden sich der doppelgeschosshohe Schlafraum und das Arbeitszimmer der Bauherren, in der anderen zwei Schlaf- und Arbeitszimmer für die beiden Kinder. Die Außenwände des Hauses bestehen aus Sichtbeton und Rotzeder, wobei im Innenraum Sichtbeton, Lack und Sperrholz zur Anwendung kamen. Der Architekt erklärt, dass er dabei bewusst den vertikalen und horizontalen Raumfluss zum Thema seines Entwurfs gemacht habe.

Cette maison est implantée entre une zone urbaine et une région de montagnes, deux types de paysages qui ont été pris en compte dans le projet. L'architecte compare l'allée d'entrée à un « canyon architectural ». Les deux boîtes habillées de bois contenant les pièces en duplex reposent sur une base paysagée occupée par un séjour de 9 m de haut à éclairage zénithal et par la salle à manger. Une des boîtes accueille la chambre principale double hauteur et un bureau, et l'autre deux chambres et des bureaux pour les deux enfants. Les façades sont en béton brut et cèdre rouge tandis qu'à l'intérieur règnent le béton brut, le contreplaqué et la laque. L'architecte précise que le thème de ce projet est la continuité de l'espace, à la fois verticale et horizontale.

Throughout the composition, wood and concrete clash and blend, attracting attention to the similarities of the materials as well as their overt differences.

Im gesamten Entwurf treffen Holz und Beton aufeinander und verbinden sich; sie machen auf die Verwandtschaft dieser Materialien wie auch ihre Unterschiede aufmerksam.

Le bois et le béton se fondent ou se heurtent dans l'ensemble de la composition en attirant l'attention sur les similarités et les contrastes des matériaux.

A potted tree between the two wooden "towers" contrasts with the rather strict and austere lines of the architecture.

Ein Baum zwischen den beiden hölzernen „Türmen" bildet einen Gegensatz zu den ansonsten recht strengen Umrissen der Architektur.

Un arbre en pot placé entre les deux « tours » de bois apporte une note contrastée par rapport aux lignes assez strictes, voire austères, de l'architecture.

Trojan House ▶

JACKSON CLEMENTS BURROWS

Jackson Clements Burrows Pty Ltd. Architects
One Harwood Place
Melbourne, Victoria 3000
Australia

Tel: +61 3 9654 6227
Fax: +61 3 9654 6195
E-mail: jacksonclementsburrows@jcba.com.au
Web: www.jcba.com.au

TIM JACKSON was born in San Francisco, USA, in 1964. He worked in the office of Denton Corker Marshall before joining his father's practice (Daryl Jackson Architects), and then running his own firm between 1993 and 1998. In Australia he was the project director for the Abito Apartments (Fitzroy, Victoria) that won the 2007 Royal Australian Institute of Architects Architecture Award for Multi-Residential Housing. He also worked on the Kew House (Kew, Victoria, 2004; RAIA Award for Residential Architecture). **JONATHAN CLEMENTS** was born in 1971 in Melbourne, Australia. He received his B.Arch degree from Deakin University and worked prior to the formation of Jackson Clements Burrows in 1998 with Daryl Jackson. Projects he has been involved with at Jackson Clements Burrows include Cape Schanck House (Cape Schanck, Victoria, 2006) and Pier Point Apartments (Geelong, Victoria, 2006–). **GRAHAM BURROWS** was born in 1971 in Johannesburg, South Africa. He studied at the University of Melbourne and was employed prior to 1998 in the office of Daryl Jackson. Projects he has run for Jackson Clements Burrows include the Separation Creek Residence (Separation Creek, Victoria, 2007) and the Saint Kilda Foreshore Promenade Development in Melbourne (2008). Other recent work by Jackson Clements Burrows includes the Trojan House (Melbourne, Victoria, 2005, published here) and the Hue Apartments, a multi-residential project with 29 apartments (Richmond, Melbourne, 2007), all in Australia.

TIM JACKSON wurde 1964 in San Francisco geboren. Er arbeitete bei Denton Corker Marshall und trat danach in das Büro seines Vaters (Daryl Jackson Architects) ein. Von 1993 bis 1998 leitete er ein eigenes Büro. In Australien war er Projektleiter für die Abito Apartments (Fitzroy, Victoria), die 2007 vom Royal Australian Institute of Architects (RAIA) mit dem Architekturpreis für Mehrfamilienhäuser ausgezeichnet wurden. Er war auch am Wohnhaus in Kew (Kew, Victoria, 2004, RAIA Award for Residential Architecture) beteiligt. **JONATHAN CLEMENTS** wurde 1971 in Melbourne, Australien, geboren. Er erwarb seinen B.Arch an der Deakin University und arbeitete vor der Gründung von Jackson Clements Burrows im Jahr 1998 bei Daryl Jackson. Bei Jackson Clements Burrows war er an folgenden Projekten beteiligt: einem Wohnhaus in Cape Schanck (Cape Schanck, Victoria, 2006) und den Pier Point Apartments (Geelong, Victoria, 2006–). **GRAHAM BURROWS** wurde 1971 in Johannesburg, Südafrika, geboren und studierte an der University of Melbourne. Bis 1998 war er im Büro Daryl Jackson angestellt. Zu seinen Projekten für Jackson Clements Burrows gehören ein Wohnhaus in Separation Creek (Separation Creek, Victoria, 2007) und die Uferbebauung Saint Kilda in Melbourne (2008). Weitere aktuelle Arbeiten von Jackson Clements Burrows sind das Trojan House (Melbourne, Victoria, 2005, hier veröffentlicht) und der Mehrfamilienkomplex Hue mit 29 Wohnungen (Richmond, Melbourne, 2007), alle in Australien.

TIM JACKSON, né à San Francisco en 1964, a travaillé pour Denton Corker Marshall avant de rejoindre l'agence de son père (Daryl Jackson Architects) puis de fonder et diriger la sienne (1993–98). Il a été en charge du projet des Abito Apartments (Fitzroy, Victoria) qui a remporté le prix d'Architecture du logement collectif 2007 du Royal Australian Institute of Architects. Il a également travaillé sur le projet de la maison Kew (Kew, Victoria, 2004; prix d'Architecture résidentielle du RAIA). **JONATHAN CLEMENTS**, né en 1971 à Melbourne, a obtenu son B. Arch. de la Deakin University et a travaillé avec Daryl Jackson avant la création de Jackson Clements Burrows en 1998. Parmi les projets auxquels il a participé chez Jackson Clements Burrows figurent la maison du cap Schanck (Victoria, 2006) et l'immeuble de logements de Pier Point (Geelong, Victoria, 2006–). **GRAHAM BURROWS**, né en 1971 à Johannesburg (Afrique du Sud), a étudié à l'Université de Melbourne et travaillé chez Daryl Jackson avant 1998. Pour Jackson Clements Burrows, il a dirigé les projets de la résidence à Separation Creek (Victoria, 2007) et la promenade de front de mer de Saint Kilda à Melbourne (2008). Parmi les récentes réalisations de Jackson Clements Burrows figurent la maison de Troie (Trojan House, Melbourne, Victoria, 2005, publiée ici) et les Hue Apartments, projet multirésidentiel de 29 appartements (Richmond, Melbourne, 2007).

TROJAN HOUSE

Melbourne, Victoria, Australia, 2005

Address: not disclosed
Area: 250 m². Client: not disclosed. Cost: not disclosed
Collaboration: Joachim Quino Holland

This project involved the addition of space for three small children to an existing house. Seeking to avoid reducing the garden at the back of the house, the architects cantilevered the new space above the garden on two large steel trusses embedded in the walls, leaving living space below. A "seamless timber skin, covering roof, windows, and walls," was used as cladding. Operable timber shutters are provided for all openings, emphasizing the impression that the internal function of the volume cannot be determined from the outside. Visual communication and openings between the levels assure that the children do not feel isolated in their new space. Passive thermal shading and on-site water collection is used for the pool and garden. The master bedroom area in the existing house was reworked by the architects as well. The architects state: "In summary this project is about a house that engages with childhood in a playful way, that reconciles the programmatic requirements of a growing family with an unexpected sculptural response: a **TROJAN HOUSE**."

Dieses Projekt beinhaltete die Erweiterung eines bestehenden Hauses, um Raum für drei kleine Kinder zu gewinnen. Anstatt den Garten an der Rückseite des Hauses zu verkleinern, ließen die Architekten die neuen Räume auf zwei großen, in die Wände eingelassenen Stahlträgern über den Garten auskragen, sodass die Grünfläche darunter erhalten blieb. Eine „Holzhaut, die Dach, Fenster und Wände nahtlos überzieht", dient als Verkleidung. Alle Öffnungen sind mit verstellbaren Holzläden versehen, was den Eindruck verstärkt, dass die innere Funktion der Räume nicht von außen beeinflusst werden kann. Sichtbeziehungen und der offene Zugang zu allen Ebenen sorgen dafür, dass sich die Kinder in ihrem neuen Bereich nicht verlassen fühlen. Passiver thermaler Sonnenschutz und auf dem Grundstück aufgefangenes Wasser werden für den Swimmingpool und den Garten genutzt. Der Bereich des Elternschlafzimmers im Altbau wurde von den Architekten ebenfalls erneuert. Sie erklären dazu: „Kurz gesagt ist dies ein Projekt, das auf spielerische Weise für Kinder engagiert, und das die programmatischen Bedürfnisse einer wachsenden Familie in ungewöhnlicher skulpturaler Form erfüllt: ein **TROJANISCHES HAUS**."

Ce projet consistait à réaliser l'extension d'une maison existante afin de loger trois enfants. Les architectes ont placé le nouveau volume en porte-à-faux au-dessus du petit jardin arrière dont on ne souhaitait pas réduire la surface. L'extension est soutenue par deux importantes poutres d'acier prises dans les murs. Une « peau de bois continue recouvre le toit, les fenêtres et les murs ». Des volets de bois masquent toutes les ouvertures et renforcent l'impression d'indétermination de la fonction de ce nouveau volume vu de l'extérieur. Des ouvertures aménagées entre les niveaux permettent aux enfants de ne pas se sentir isolés dans leur nouvel espace. Le bassin et le jardin bénéficient d'un ombrage thermique passif et de la collecte des eaux de pluie. La partie réservée à la chambre principale de la maison existante a été également retravaillée. « En résumé, ce projet porte sur une maison qui entretient un dialogue ludique avec l'enfance et réconcilie les attentes programmatiques d'une famille qui s'agrandit par une réponse sculpturale inattendue : **UNE MAISON DE TROIE** en quelque sorte, » explique l'architecte.

As the name of the house implies, the form of the house might well bring to mind a toy wooden horse, with its dramatically cantilevered section corresponding to the "head." Elevations show the new and old volumes.

Wie der Name des Hauses andeutet, erinnert seine Form an ein hölzernes Spielzeugpferd, wobei der dramatisch auskragende Teil dem „Kopf" entspricht. Die Ansichten zeigen die alten und neuen Teile.

Comme son nom l'implique, la forme de la maison peut évoquer un cheval de bois d'enfant, le spectaculaire porte-à-faux correspondant à la tête. Les élévations précisent les rapports entre l'ancien volume et le nouveau.

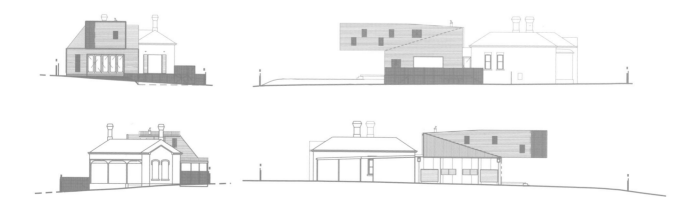

Wood is used in interior spaces for the floors, but otherwise a rather sharply delineated modernity holds in these spaces.

Holz wurde für die Böden verwendet; ansonsten wurden die Innenräume durchgehend modern gestaltet.

Les sols sont en bois, mais les espaces intérieurs sont néanmoins d'une modernité fortement affirmée.

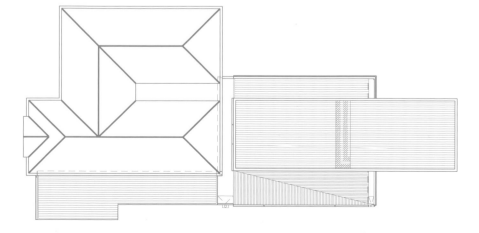

The roof plan on this page makes clear the relation of the new volume to the existing house. Above, a large opening in the wood façade looks directly out onto a swimming pool.

Die Dachaufsicht auf dieser Seite macht die Beziehung des neuen Volumens zum Altbau deutlich. Oben: Eine große Öffnung in der hölzernen Fassade gibt den Blick zum Swimmingpool frei.

Le plan des toitures (ci-contre) montre clairement la relation entre la nouvelle construction et l'ancienne. Ci-dessus, une grande ouverture découpée dans la façade habillée de bois donne directement sur la piscine.

EMMA JOHANSSON AND TIMO LEIVISKÄ

Arkkitehtitoimisto Emma Johansson
Kaikukuja 1 h 100
00530 Helsinki
Finland

Tel: +358 50 372 27 13
E-mail: emma.johansson@oulu.fi
Web: www.emmajohansson.fi

Arkkitehtitoimisto Timo Leiviskä
Kajaanintie 36, 5 C 44
90130 Oulu
Finland

Tel: +358 50 530 35 48
E-mail: timo.leiviska@gmail.com
Web: www.timoleiviska.webs.com

EMMA JOHANSSON was born in 1985 in Turku, Finland. She is studying architecture at the University of Oulu in architecture (2004–). She created her own office, Arkkitehtitoimisto Emma Johansson Oy, in 2007. Her work includes the Anttolanhovi Lakeside Villas (Mikkeli, 2007–08, published here); a mobile dwelling consisting of small units destined to the Finnish archipelago area (2009–11); and a Sustainable Wooden Village (Pudasjärvi, in collaboration with Kristian Järvi, 2009–12), all in Finland. **TIMO LEIVISKÄ** was born in 1981 in Oulu, Finland. He studied architecture at the University of Oulu (2000–ongoing) and at the Faculty of Architecture of the University of Porto, Portugal (2005–06). His office, Arkkitehtitoimisto Timo Leiviskä Oy, was founded in 2007. His work includes the Anttolanhovi Hillside Villas (Mikkeli, 2007–08, published here); a Villa (Pulolanka, 2009–10); and another Villa (Kuhmo, 2010–12), all in Finland.

EMMA JOHANSSON wurde 1985 in Turku, Finnland, geboren. Sie studiert seit 2004 Architektur an der Universität von Oulu. 2007 eröffnete sie ihr eigenes Büro, Arkkitehtitoimisto Emma Johansson Oy. Zu ihren Arbeiten zählen die Anttolanhovi-Seevillen (Mikkeli, 2007–08, hier veröffentlicht), eine mobile, aus kleinen Elementen bestehende Wohneinheit, gedacht für die finnische Seenlandschaft (2009–11), sowie ein nachhaltig gebautes Dorf aus Holz (Pudasjärvi, in Zusammenarbeit mit Kristian Järvi, 2009–12), alle in Finnland. **TIMO LEIVISKÄ** wurde 1981 im finnischen Oulu geboren. Er studiert seit 2000 Architektur an der Universität von Oulu und war 2005 bis 2006 Student der Architekturfakultät der Universität Porto (Portugal). Sein Büro, Arkkitehtitoimisto Timo Leiviskä Oy, gründete er 2007. Zu seinen Arbeiten gehören die Anttolanhovi-Bergvillen (Mikkeli, 2007–08, hier veröffentlicht), eine Villa (Pulolanka, 2009–10) sowie eine weitere Villa (Kuhmo, 2010–12), alle in Finnland.

EMMA JOHANSSON, née en 1985 à Turku (Finlande), étudie l'architecture à l'université d'Oulu (Finlande, 2004–). Elle a créé son agence, Arkkitehtitoimisto Emma Johansson Oy, en 2007. Parmi ses réalisations : les villas Anttolanhovi côté lac (Mikkeli, 2007–08, publiées ici) ; un logement mobile composé de petites unités pour l'archipel de Finlande (2009–11) et un village durable en bois (Pudasjärvi, en collaboration avec Kristian Järvi, 2009–12). **TIMO LEIVISKÄ**, né en 1981 à Oulu, a étudié l'architecture à l'université d'Oulu (2000–en cours) et à la Faculté d'architecture de l'université de Porto (Portugal, 2005–06). Son agence, Arkkitehtitoimisto Timo Leiviskä Oy, a été fondée en 2007. Parmi ses réalisations, toutes en Finlande, les villas Anttolanhovi côté colline (Mikkeli, 2007–08, publiées ici) ; une villa à Pulolanka (2009–10) et une villa à Kuhmo (2010–12).

ANTTOLANHOVI ART AND DESIGN VILLAS

Mikkeli, Finland, 2007–08

Address: Hovintie 224, Mikkeli, Finland, +358 207 57 52 38, www.anttolanhovi.fi
Area: 132 m² (Lakeside Villas); 180 m² (Hillside Villas)
Client: Anttolanhovi Hotel. Cost: not disclosed

Designed by Emma Johansson (Lakeside Villas) and Timo Leiviskä (Hillside Villas), the **ANTTOLANHOVI ART AND DESIGN VILLAS** have their own saunas, open fireplaces, and hotel services. Each villa is associated with an artist who has contributed to the house. The artists for the Art and Design Villas are Kari Cavén, Kaarina Kaikkonen, Marika Mäkelä, Teemu Saukkonen, Hanna Vahvaselkä, Rauha Mäkilä, Antti Keitilä, Johanna Ilvessalo, and Jussi Tiainen (the photographer who took the photos for this entry). They are designed to have as small an "ecological footprint" as possible. They are built with natural materials, principally timber. The wall cladding is either Finnish birch or Finnish spruce, while the floors are made of natural stone. Linen, cotton, and wool have been used for all indoor textiles. The Lakeside Villas, situated about 25 meters from the Saimaa lakeshore, have a lounge, kitchen, and three bedrooms. The Hillside Villas are semidetached structures measuring 103 square meters on one side and 77 square meters on the other, with a total of five bedrooms for each pair of structures. They are 70 meters from the lakeshore.

Die von Emma Johansson (Seevillen) und Timo Leiviskä (Bergvillen) geplanten **ANTTOLANHOVI ART AND DESIGN VILLEN** haben eigene Saunen, offene Kamine und erhalten Dienstleistungen vom Hotel. Jede Villa ist mit einem Künstler verbunden, der zu ihrer Ausstattung beigetragen hat. Beteiligt waren die Künstler Kari Cavén, Kaarina Kaikkonen, Marika Mäkelä, Teemu Saukkonen, Hanna Vahvaselkä, Rauha Mäkilä, Antti Keitilä, Johanna Ilvessalo und Jussi Tiainen (der Fotograf, der die Bilder für dieses Buch aufgenommen hat). Die Häuser haben die bestmögliche Ökobilanz; sie wurden aus natürlichen Materialien, vorwiegend aus Holz, errichtet. Die Wandverkleidung besteht aus einheimischer Birke bzw. Fichte, während die Böden aus Naturstein sind. Im Innern sind alle Textilien aus Leinen, Baumwolle oder Wolle. Die Seevillen stehen etwa 25 m vom Ufer des Saimaa-Sees entfernt; sie enthalten jeweils einen Aufenthaltsraum, eine Küche und drei Schlafräume. Die Bergvillen sind Doppelhäuser mit je 103 m² respektive 77 m² Grundfläche und zusammen fünf Schlafräumen. Sie stehen 70 m vom Seeufer entfernt.

Conçues par Emma Johansson (villas côté lac) et Timo Leiviskä (villas côté colline), les **VILLAS D'ART ET DE DESIGN D'ANTTOLANHOVI** possèdent des saunas, des cheminées ouvertes et bénéficient de services hôteliers. Chacune est associée au nom d'un artiste qui a contribué à son aménagement : Kari Cavén, Kaarina Kaikkonen, Marika Mäkelä, Teemu Saukkonen, Hanna Vahvaselkä, Rauha Mäkilä, Antti Keitilä, Johanna Ilvessalo et Jussi Tiainen (le photographe auteur des photos reproduites ici). Elles ont été conçues de façon à exercer la plus faible empreinte écologique possible et sont construites en matériaux naturels, principalement du bois. L'habillage des murs est soit en bouleau de Finlande soit en épicéa de Finlande et les sols sont en pierre naturelle. À l'intérieur, les tissus retenus sont en lin, coton ou laine. Les villas côté lac, situé à 25 mètres environ de la rive du lac de Saimaa possèdent un salon, une cuisine et trois chambres. Celles côté colline, à 70 mètres du lac sont des villas doubles de 103 et 77 mètres carrés comptant 5 chambres par paire.

The site plan on the left page shows the Lakeside and Hillside Villas in their respective locations. Above, the Hillside Villas.

Der Lageplan auf der linken Seite zeigt die See- und die Bergvillen an ihren jeweiligen Standorten. Oben: die Bergvillen.

Le plan du terrain (page de gauche) montre les deux ensembles de villas – côté lac et côté collines – dans leur situation respective. En haut les villas côté collines.

Below, two images of the Lakeside Villas designed by Emma Johansson, with their partially covered terraces and generous use of wood.

Zwei Fotos der von Emma Johansson entworfenen Seevillen mit ihren teilüberdachten Terrassen und der großzügigen Verwendung von Holz.

Ci-dessous, deux images des villas côté lac, en grande partie en bois et conçues par Emma Johansson. Leurs terrasses sont en partie couvertes.

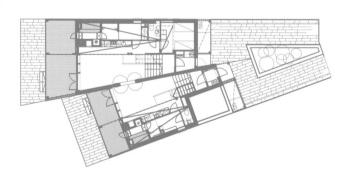

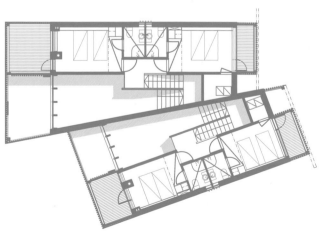

Plans of the Hillside Villas and an interior view of one of the Lakeside Villas.

Grundrisse der Bergvillen und eine Innenaufnahme einer Seevilla.

Des plans des villas côté colline et la vue intérieure d'une des villas côté lac.

Drawings of the Lakeside Villas showing their low, open V-form and insertion into the wooded setting.

Die Zeichnungen der Seevillen zeigen deren flache, offene V-Form sowie ihre Einfügung in die bewaldete Umgebung.

Représentations de villas côté lac montrant leur forme surbaissée et leur toit à pente asymétrique, et de leur insertion dans leur environnement boisé.

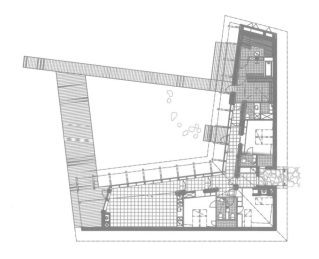

Two interior views of these houses are seen above.

Zwei Innenansichten der oben dargestellten Häuser.

Deux vues intérieures des maisons.

KAUFFMANN THEILIG & PARTNER

Kauffmann Theilig & Partner / Freie Architekten BDA
Zeppelinstr. 10 / 73760 Ostfildern / Germany

Tel: +49 711 45 12 20 / Fax: +49 711 45 12 240
E-mail: info@ktp-architekten.de / Web: www.ktp-architekten.de

KAUFFMANN THEILIG was founded in 1988 by Andreas Theilig and Dieter Ben Kauffmann. Rainer Lenz (1995) and Manfred Ehrle (1999–2005) became partners and the office was renamed Kauffmann Theilig & Partner in 1995. Andreas Theilig was born in 1951 in Stuttgart, Germany, and received his diploma from the Technical University of Darmstadt (1978). He worked as a project manager and partner at Behnisch & Partner Architects (Stuttgart, 1979–88). Dieter Ben Kauffmann was born in Sindelfingen, Germany, in 1954 and graduated from the University of Applied Science in Augsburg (1978). He was a project architect at Behnisch & Partner (Stuttgart, 1980–84) and at Heinle Wischer and Partner (Stuttgart, 1984–88), before creating Kauffmann Theilig with Andreas Theilig in 1988. He was chairman of the German Federation of Architects for Baden-Württemberg (2002–08). Rainer Lenz was born in Rohrdorf (1960), graduated from the University of Applied Sciences (Biberach an der Riss, 1989), and then joined Kauffmann Theilig in 1989. Recent projects of the firm include the CSC Business Center (Wiesbaden, 2002); refurbishment of the State Theatre in Mainz (2002); the Boehringer Ingelheim Employee Restaurant (Biberach an der Riss, 2003–04, published here), the Nagold Residence (Rohrdorf, 2003–04, also published here); the House of Economy of the Chamber of Industry and Commerce of Kiel (Schleswig-Holstein, 2004); the ADVA Office, Research and Manufacturing Buildings (Meiningen, 2006); the Fildorado Sports and Leisure Facility (Filderstadt, 2006); Mercedes-Benz Galleries (Munich and Berlin, 2009); and the Open-Air Swimming Pool (Eichstätt, 2010), all in Germany.

Das Büro **KAUFFMANN THEILIG** wurde 1988 von Andreas Theilig und Dieter Ben Kauffmann gegründet. Partner wurden 1995 Rainer Lenz und 1999 bis 2005 Manfred Ehrle; 1995 wurde die Firma in Kauffmann Theilig & Partner umbenannt. Andreas Theilig wurde 1951 in Stuttgart geboren und machte 1978 sein Diplom an der Technischen Universität Darmstadt. Er arbeitete als Projektmanager im Büro Behnisch & Partner (Stuttgart, 1979–88). Dieter Ben Kauffmann wurde 1954 in Sindelfingen geboren und studierte bis 1978 an der Hochschule Augsburg – University of Applied Sciences. Er arbeitete als Projektarchitekt bei Behnisch & Partner (Stuttgart, 1980–84) und bei Heinle Wischer und Partner (Stuttgart, 1984–88), bevor er 1988 mit Andreas Theilig das Büro Kauffmann Theilig gründete. Von 2002 bis 2008 war er Vorsitzender des Landesverbands Baden-Württemberg des Bundes Deutscher Architekten. Rainer Lenz wurde 1960 in Rohrdorf geboren, absolvierte 1989 die Hochschule Biberach an der Riss und trat im gleichen Jahr in das Büro Kauffmann Theilig ein. Zu dessen neueren Projekten zählen das CSC Business Center (Wiesbaden, 2002), die Modernisierung des Staatstheaters in Mainz (2002), das Mitarbeiterrestaurant der Firma Boehringer Ingelheim (Biberach an der Riss, 2003–04, hier veröffentlicht), ein Wohnhaus über der Nagold (Rohrdorf, 2003–04, ebenfalls hier veröffentlicht), das Haus der Wirtschaft der Industrie- und Handelskammer (Kiel, 2004), Büro-, Forschungs- und Produktionsgebäude der Firma ADVA (Meiningen, 2006), die Freizeitanlage Fildorado (Filderstadt, 2006), Ausstellungsräume für Mercedes-Benz (München und Berlin, 2009) sowie ein Freibad (Eichstätt, 2010), alle in Deutschland.

L'agence **KAUFFMANN THEILIG** a été fondée en 1988 par Andreas Theilig et Dieter Ben Kauffmann. Rainer Lenz (1995) et Manfred Ehrle (1999–2005) en sont devenus partenaires par la suite et l'agence a pris le nom de Kauffmann Theilig & Partner en 1995. Andreas Theilig, né en 1951 à Stuttgart, est diplômé de l'Université polytechnique de Darmstadt (1978). Il a été directeur de projet et partenaire chez Behnisch & Partner (Stuttgart, 1979–88). Dieter Ben Kauffmann, né à Sindelfingen (Allemagne) en 1954, est diplômé de l'Université des sciences appliquées d'Augsburg (1978). Il a été directeur de projet chez Behnisch & Partner (Stuttgart, 1980–84) et Heinle Wischer und Partner (Stuttgart, 1984–88) avant de fonder Kauffmann Theilig avec Andreas Theilig en 1988. Il a été président de la Fédération des architectes du Bade-Wurttemberg (2002–08). Rainer Lenz, né à Rohrdorf (Allemagne) en 1960, est diplômé de l'Université des sciences appliquées de Biberach an der Riss (1989). Il a rejoint Kauffmann Theilig en 1989. Parmi les projets récents de l'agence figurent le centre d'affaires CSC (Wiesbaden, 2002) ; la rénovation du théâtre d'État (Mayence, 2002) ; le restaurant du personnel de Boehringer Ingelheim (Biberach an der Riss, 2003–04, publié ici) ; la résidence Nagold (Rohrdorf, 2003–04, également publiée ici) ; la Maison de l'économie de la Chambre de commerce et d'industrie de Kiel (Schleswig-Holstein, 2004) ; des bureaux, centre de recherche et usine de fabrication pour ADVA (Meiningen, 2006) ; les installations de sports et de loisirs Fildorado (Filderstadt, 2006) ; les galeries Mercedes-Benz (Munich et Berlin, 2009) et une piscine de plein air (Eichstätt, 2010).

NAGOLD RESIDENCE

Rohrdorf, Germany, 2003–04

Address: Friedhofstr. 32, 72229 Rohrdorf, Germany
Area: 250 m². Client: not disclosed. Cost: € 380 000
Collaboration: IG Lagger-Renz, Rohrdorf (Structural Planning), Horstmann + Berger, Altensteig (Construction Physics)

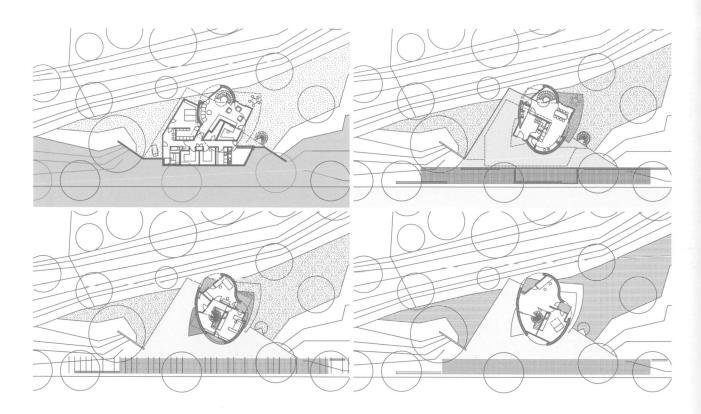

The lower floor of this structure is inserted into the sloped site. A bedroom, bath, sauna, and living space for the parents of this family are located on that floor. The children's space is on the upper level which is described by the architects as resembling a "tree house." A spiral staircase leads to a studio and guest space above. The prefabricated larch façade "swings out like a curtain" around the structure. The architects state: "The materials used inside create a friendly and warm atmosphere. The unclad concrete ceilings are painted in a sunny, light-yellow tone. Vibrant floors of larch as well as the largely wooden interior compensate for the harsh concrete surface." Self-confident but also self-evident the unusual house rises up the slope.

Das untere Geschoss dieses Gebäudes ist in das Hanggrundstück gesetzt. Auf dieser Ebene liegen ein Schlafraum, Bad, Sauna und der Wohnbereich für die Eltern. Die Räume der Kinder befinden sich auf der oberen Ebene, die die Architekten mit einem „Baumhaus" vergleichen. Eine Wendeltreppe führt zu einem darüber liegenden Atelier und Gästezimmer. Die vorgefertigte Lärchenholzfassade „schwingt wie ein Vorhang" um das Gebäude. Die Architekten erklären: „Die im Innern verwendeten Materialien erzeugen eine freundliche und warme Atmosphäre. Die unverkleideten Betondecken sind in einem hellgelben, sonnigen Farbton gestrichen. Die schwingenden Lärchenböden sowie die überwiegend aus Holz bestehende Innenausstattung kompensieren die rauen Außenflächen aus Beton." Selbstbewusst, aber auch wie selbstverständlich erhebt sich dieses ungewöhnliche Haus auf dem Hang.

Le niveau inférieur de cette maison – chambre, salle de bains, sauna et séjour des parents – est en partie creusé dans le sol. La partie réservée aux enfants se trouve à l'étage supérieur, décrit par les architectes comme ressemblant à une « maison dans les arbres ». Un escalier en colimaçon conduit à un studio et une chambre d'amis. La façade préfabriquée en mélèze « se déploie comme un rideau » autour de la structure. « Les matériaux utilisés à l'intérieur créent une atmosphère chaleureuse et conviviale, précisent les architectes : Les plafonds en béton brut sont peints dans un jaune léger et lumineux. Des sols de mélèze vernis et la présence importante du bois à l'intérieur compensent la rudesse des plans en béton. » Sûre d'elle-même, mais aussi très expressive, cette curieuse maison prolonge vers le ciel la pente du terrain.

The prefabricated larch façade of the main section of the building wraps around it revealing terraces and large glazed surfaces.

Die den Haupttrakt dieses Hauses umhüllende, vorgefertigte Lärchenholzfassade gibt Terrassen und große, verglaste Flächen frei.

La façade préfabriquée en mélèze enveloppe la partie principale tout en laissant place aux balcons et à de grands plans vitrés.

The elegant spiraling staircase that gives access to the upper part of the house is seen in the living space (above).

Die elegante, gewundene Treppe, die den oberen Teil des Hauses erschließt, ist im Wohnbereich (oben) zu sehen.

L'élégant escalier en spirale qui donne accès à la partie supérieure de la maison, vu du séjour (ci-dessus).

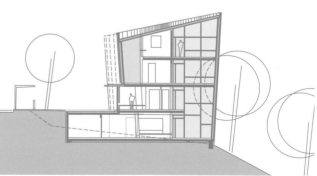

Sections of the house (above) and two images on the right page give an impression of the generous living spaces—with full-height glazing in a bedroom (above, right).

Die Schnitte des Hauses (oben) und zwei Fotos auf der rechten Seite bieten einen Eindruck vom groß-zügigen Wohnbereich sowie einem geschosshoch verglasten Schlafraum (oben, rechts).

Deux coupes de la maison (ci-dessus) et deux photographies de la page de droite confirment l'impression d'ampleur donnée par les pièces à vivre. En haut à droite, une chambre entièrement vitrée.

BOEHRINGER INGELHEIM EMPLOYEE RESTAURANT

Biberach an der Riss, Germany, 2003–04

Address: Birkendorfer Str. 65, 88397 Biberach an der Riss, Germany, +49 7351 54 0, www.boehringer-ingelheim.de
Area: 3000 m². Client: Boehringer Ingelheim Pharma GmbH & Co. KG. Cost: €16 million
Collaboration: Pfefferkorn Ingenieure, Stuttgart (Structural Engineers), Schreiber Ingenieure, Ulm (HVAC),
Ernst F. Ambrosius & Söhne, Frankfurt (Construction Firm Roof), Transsolar Energietechnik, Stuttgart (Climate Concept),
Flashaar Ingenieure, Bingen a. R. (Light Planning)

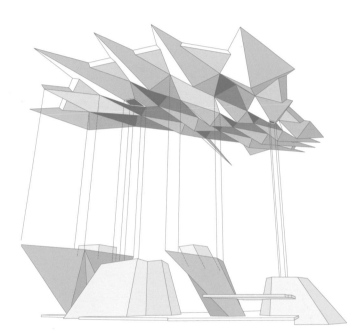
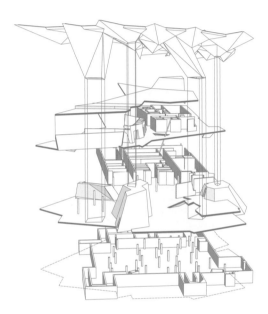

This **CORPORATE RESTAURANT FOR THE PHARMACEUTICAL FIRM BOEHRINGER INGELHEIM** makes the transition from the company site to the neighboring residential area. The two-story seating space is marked by the "spatial folded-plate structure" of the underside of the roof. Clad in wood, these forms are echoed by fractured exterior protrusions. Open kitchen stations are set in the central food court, fully visible to the patrons. A store and café located next to the seating area, meeting, conference, and social rooms, all served by the kitchen as required, are on an upper level and are oriented toward a large roof terrace.

Dieses **MITARBEITERRESTAURANT FÜR DIE PHARMAFIRMA BOEHRINGER INGELHEIM** bildet den Übergang vom Firmengelände zum benachbarten Wohnviertel. Den zweigeschossigen Speisebereich kennzeichnet ein „gefaltetes Raumfachwerk" an der Unterseite des Dachs. Dessen Formen werden außen von holzverkleideten, gebrochenen Auskragungen aufgenommen. Offene Küchenbereiche sind in den zentralen Speisesaal gesetzt und für alle Besucher sichtbar. Ein Laden und ein Café neben dem Speisesaal, Versammlungs-, Konferenz- und Sozialräume, die bei Bedarf ebenfalls von der Küche versorgt werden können, liegen im Obergeschoss und bieten Zugang zu einer großen Dachterrasse.

Ce **RESTAURANT D'ENTREPRISE DES LABORATOIRES PHARMACEUTIQUES BOERHINGER INGELHEIM** fait transition entre le site de la société et le quartier résidentiel voisin. Le bâtiment de deux niveaux est marqué par la sous-face de sa toiture, « structure spatiale en plaques pliées ». Habillées de bois, ces formes se retrouvent en écho à l'intérieur dans des projections fracturées. Des postes de cuisine ouverts, visibles des clients, ont été aménagés dans la partie en self-service. Une boutique et un café, des salles à manger, de conférence et de réunions, sont desservies par la cuisine si nécessaire. Installées à l'étage, elles sont orientées vers une grande terrasse en toiture.

The pointed, wood-clad protrusions of the restaurant, one of its most surprising features, are visible in the drawings above, and in the photos on the right page.

Die spitzen, holzverkleideten Auskragungen des Restaurants – eines seiner erstaunlichsten Merkmale – sind in den Zeichnungen oben und auf den Fotos rechts erkennbar.

Dans les dessins ci-dessus et les photos de la page de droite : les projections habillées de bois du plafond du restaurant, une de ses caractéristiques les plus étonnantes.

A section drawing and three images show that the folded structure of the roof is an element that forms the interior of the building as well as its exterior appearance.

Ein Schnitt und drei Fotos zeigen, dass die gefaltete Dachkonstruktion ein Element darstellt, das den Innenbereich des Gebäudes ebenso wie sein äußeres Erscheinungsbild bestimmt.

Un plan de coupe et trois photos montrent que la structure pliée de la toiture forme également l'intérieur du bâtiment et lui donne son aspect extérieur.

P 262

The fractured appearance of the building is evident in images, but also in the plans below. These surprising forms of course do not keep the restaurant from being fully efficient.

Die aufgebrochene Gestaltung des Gebäudes ist auf den Fotos, aber auch in den Plänen unten erkennbar. Trotz dieser erstaunlichen Formen kann das Restaurant natürlich vollkommen effizient betrieben werden.

L'aspect fracturé du bâtiment est évident ici, comme dans les plans ci-dessous. Ces formes n'empêchent en rien le restaurant d'être pleinement fonctionnel.

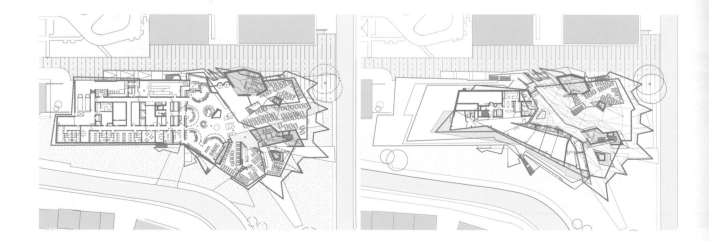

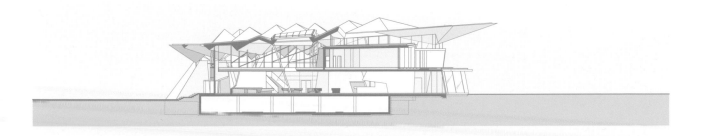

A night view confirms the spectacular appearance of the facility, seen above in a long section.

Eine Nachtaufnahme bestätigt, wie auch der Längsschnitt, das spektakuläre Erscheinungsbild der Anlage.

Une vue nocturne confirme l'aspect spectaculaire du restaurant. Ci-dessus : coupe dans l'axe de la longueur.

MATHIAS KLOTZ

Mathias Klotz
Los Colonos 0411
Providencia, Santiago
Chile

Tel: +56 2 233 6613
Fax: +56 2 232 2479
E-mail: estudio@mathiasklotz.com
Web: www.mathiasklotz.com

MATHIAS KLOTZ was born in 1965 in Viña del Mar, Chile. He received his architecture degree from the Pontificia Universidad Católica de Chile in 1991. He created his own office in Santiago the same year. He has taught at several Chilean universities and was director of the School of Architecture of the Universidad Diego Portales in Santiago (2001–03). His work has been exhibited at the GA Gallery in Tokyo (Japan); at MoMA in New York, where he was a finalist for the 1998 Mies van der Rohe Prize; and at Archilab (Orléans, France, 2000). He participated in the Chinese International Practical Exhibition of Architecture in Nanjing in 2004, together with such architects as David Adjaye, Odile Decq, Arata Isozaki, and Kazuyo Sejima. Recent work includes the Casa Viejo (Santiago, 2001); the Smol Building (Concepción, 2001); the Faculty of Health, Universidad Diego Portales (Santiago, 2004); the remodeling of the Cerro San Luis House (Santiago, 2004); the Ocho al Cubo House (Marbella, Zapallar, 2005); La Roca House (Punta del Este, Uruguay, 2006, published here); the Techos House (Nahuel Huapi Lake, Patagonia, Argentina, 2006–07); the 11 Mujeres House (Cachagua, 2007); 20 one-family houses in La Dehesa (Santiago); and the Buildings Department San Isidro (Buenos Aires, Argentina), all in Chile unless stated otherwise.

MATHIAS KLOTZ wurde 1965 in Viña del Mar, Chile, geboren und machte 1991 sein Architekturdiplom an der Pontificia Universidad Católica de Chile. Im gleichen Jahr gründete er in Santiago sein eigenes Büro. Er hat an mehreren chilenischen Universitäten gelehrt und war Direktor der Architekturabteilung an der Universidad Diego Portales in Santiago (2001–03). Seine Arbeiten wurden in der GA Gallery in Tokio, im MoMA in New York, wo er 1998 Finalist für den Mies-van-der-Rohe-Preis war, sowie bei Archilab (Orléans, Frankreich, 2000) ausgestellt. Er war Teilnehmer an der Chinese International Practical Exhibition of Architecture in Nanking 2004, neben so renommierten Architekten wie David Adjaye, Odile Decq, Arata Isozaki und Kazuyo Sejima. Zu seinen neueren Projekten zählen die Casa Viejo (Santiago, 2001), das Edificio Smol (Concepción, 2001), die medizinische Fakultät der Universidad Diego Portales (Santiago, 2004), der Umbau des Hauses Cerro San Luis (Santiago, 2004), das Haus Ocho al Cubo (Marbella, Zapallar, 2005), das Haus La Roca (Punta del Este, Uruguay, 2006, hier veröffentlicht), das Haus Techos (Lago Nahuel Huapi, Patagonien, Argentinien, 2006–07), das Haus 11 Mujeres (Cachagua, 2007), 20 Einfamilienhäuser in La Dehesa (Santiago) und das Bauamt San Isidro (Buenos Aires, Argentinien), alle in Chile, sofern nicht anders angegeben.

MATHIAS KLOTZ, né en 1965 à Viña del Mar au Chili, a obtenu son diplôme d'architecte de l'université catholique du Chili (1991) et a fondé son agence à Santiago du Chili la même année. Il a enseigné dans plusieurs universités chiliennes et dirigé l'École d'architecture de l'Universidad Diego Portales à Santiago (2001–03). Son travail a été présenté à la GA Gallery à Tokyo (Japon), au MoMA à New York lorsqu'il fut finaliste du prix Mies van der Rohe 1998, et à Archilab (Orléans, France, 2000). Il a participé à l'Exposition internationale pratique chinoise d'architecture à Nankin en 2004 en compagnie d'autres architectes comme David Adjaye, Odile Decq, Arata Isozaki et Kazuyo Sejima. Parmi ses réalisations récentes, toutes au Chili, sauf mention contraire : la Casa Viejo (Santiago du Chili, 2001) ; l'immeuble Smol (Concepción, 2001) ; la faculté de la santé, université Diego Portales (Santiago du Chili, 2004) ; la faculté de santé de l'université Diego Portales (Santiago, 2004) ; le remodelage de la maison Cerro San Luis (Santiago, 2004) ; la maison Ocho al Cubo (Marbella, Zapallar, 2005) ; la maison La Roca (Punta del Este, Uruguay, 2006, publiée ici) ; la maison Techos (lac Nahuel Huapi, Patagonie, Argentine, 2006–07) ; la maison des 11 Femmes (Cachagua, 2007) ; 20 maisons monofamiliales à La Dehesa (Santiago) et la Direction de l'equipement San Isidro (Buenos Aires, Argentine).

LA ROCA HOUSE

Punta del Este, Uruguay, 2006

Address: Punta de José Ignacio, 80 kilometers north of Punta del Este, Uruguay
Area: 300 m², Client: not disclosed, Cost: not disclosed
Collaboration: Baltasar Sánchez, Carolina Pedroni

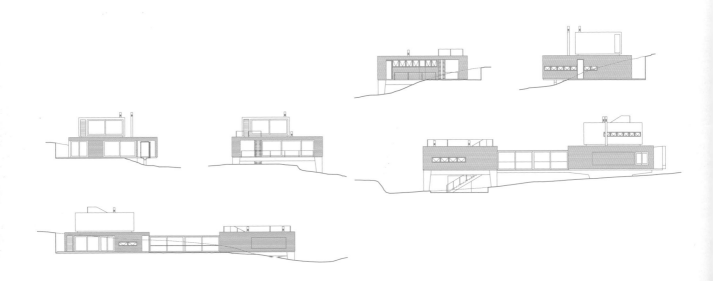

The exact location of this house is the village of José Ignacio, 80 kilometers north of Punta del Este on the Atlantic coast of Uruguay. The "public" and "private" spaces of the house are divided into two boxes of the same height with patios beneath and between the boxes. The architect states: "La Roca House is defined through a sequence of spaces, almost square in plan, which run entering from the most public to the most intimate, crossing terraces, patios, exterior, intermediate, and interior spaces and arriving finally at the master bedroom." Natural ventilation obviates the need for air conditioning, while roof gardens shield the roofs of the boxes from heat gain. Gray water from the house is recycled for garden irrigation. Ipe wood and exposed concrete are the most obvious material elements employed in the architectural design.

Der genaue Standort dieses Wohnhauses ist das Dorf José Ignacio, 80 km nördlich von Punta del Este an der Atlantikküste von Uruguay. Die „öffentlichen" und „privaten" Bereiche des Hauses sind in zwei gleich hohe Kisten mit Patios darunter und dazwischen aufgeteilt. Der Architekt erklärt: „Das Haus La Roca besteht aus einer Folge von – im Grundriss fast quadratischen – Räumen. Sie führt, vom Eingang ausgehend, über die weitgehend öffentlichen bis zu den absolut intimen Bereichen, über Terrassen, Patios, Außen-, Zwischen- und Innenräume und endet schließlich im Elternschlafzimmer." Natürliche Belüftung macht eine Klimaanlage überflüssig; Dachgärten verhindern, dass die Dächer der Kisten sich aufheizen. Das Brauchwasser des Hauses wird zur Bewässerung des Gartens wiederaufbereitet. Ipe-Holz und Sichtbeton sind die bestimmenden Materialien für diesen Entwurf.

Cette maison est située dans le village de José Ignacio, à 80 km au nord de Punta del Este sur la côte atlantique de l'Uruguay. Les parties « privées » et « publiques » se répartissent en deux boîtes de même hauteur. Des patios sont aménagés sous et entre ces deux éléments. « La maison La Roca se définit comme une séquence d'espaces suivant un plan presque carré, qui va de l'entrée et de la partie la plus publique jusqu'à la plus intime en franchissant les terrasses, des patios, l'extérieur, des espaces intermédiaires et intérieurs pour arriver finalement à la chambre principale », explique l'architecte. La ventilation naturelle rend la climatisation inutile et la végétalisation des toitures protège l'intérieur du gain thermique. Les eaux usées sont recyclées pour l'irrigation des jardins. Les matériaux utilisés les plus visibles sont le béton et le bois d'ipé.

Made of wood and concrete, the house is designed with a rectilinear vocabulary as the drawings above show. It is low and open to the ocean.

Das aus Holz und Beton errichtete Haus folgt einem rechtwinkligen Vokabular, wie die Zeichnungen oben beweisen. Es ist niedrig und offen zum Ozean.

Construite en bois et béton, la maison entièrement ouverte sur l'océan utilise un vocabulaire de lignes droites étirées, comme le montrent les dessins ci-dessus.

Opposite page: A bedroom offers a spectacular view of the terraces and the ocean beyond.

Gegenüberliegende Seite: Aus einem Schlafraum bietet sich eine spektakuläre Aussicht auf die Terrassen und den Ozean.

Page opposée : une des chambres bénéficie d'une vue spectaculaire sur les terrasses et l'océan.

Wooden terraces allow the residents to take in the view without going onto the beach directly. The design of these elements is open and simple.

Die hölzernen Terrassen bieten den Bewohnern die Aussicht, ohne dass sie zum Strand hinuntergehen müssen. Diese Elemente sind frei und einfach gestaltet.

De dessin très simple, les terrasses en bois permettent aux habitants de bénéficier de la vue sans devoir se rendre à la plage.

Plans of the house show the way it is composed with square elements.

Die Grundrisse des Hauses zeigen seine Zusammensetzung aus quadratischen Elementen.

Les plans de la maison illustrent sa composition à partir d'éléments de forme carrée.

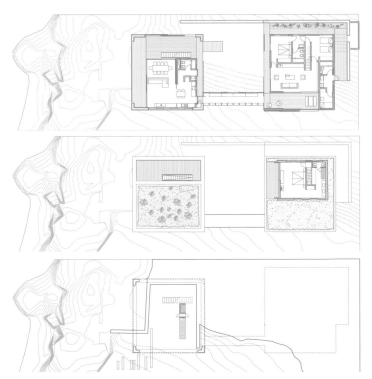

MARCIO KOGAN

*Marcio Kogan
Studio MK27
Alameda Tietê 505 – Cerqueira César
01417-020 São Paulo, SP
Brazil*

*Tel: +55 11 3081 3522
Fax: +55 11 3063 3424
E-mail: info@marciokogan.com.br
Web: www.marciokogan.com.br*

Born in 1952, **MARCIO KOGAN** graduated in 1976 from the School of Architecture at Mackenzie University in São Paulo. He received an IAB (Brazilian Architects Institute) Award for UMA Stores (1999 and 2002); Coser Studio (2002); Gama Issa House (2002); and Quinta House (2004). He also received the Record House Award for Du Plessis House (2004) and BR House (2005). In 2002 he completed a Museum of Microbiology in São Paulo and in 2003 he made a submission for the World Trade Center Site Memorial. He worked with Isay Weinfeld on the Fasano Hotel in São Paulo. He also participated with Weinfeld in the 25th São Paulo Biennale (2002) with the project for a hypothetical city named Happyland. Kogan is known for his use of boxlike forms, together with wooden shutters, trellises, and exposed stone. Amongst Kogan's recent residential projects are the Cury House (São Paulo, 2004–06); the Primetime Nursery (São Paulo, 2005–07); the E-Home, a "super-technological" house (Santander, Spain, 2007); an "extreme house" on an island in Paraty (Rio de Janeiro, 2007); Warbler House (Los Angeles, California, USA, 2008); a villa in Milan (Italy, 2008); House 53 (São Paulo, 2008); and two other houses in Brasilia, all in Brazil unless stated otherwise. His office is also working on a "green building" in New Jersey (USA, 2008–) and has recently completed Bahia House (Salvador, Bahia, 2010, published here).

Der 1952 geborene **MARCIO KOGAN** beendete 1976 sein Architekturstudium an der Universidade Presbiteriana Mackenzie in São Paulo. Er erhielt einen Preis des brasilianischen Architekturinstituts IAB für seinen Entwurf für die UMA Stores (1999 und 2002), das Coser Studio (2002), die Häuser Gama Issa (2002) und Quinta (2004). Für die Häuser Du Plessis (2004) und BR (2005) wurde ihm der Record House Award verliehen. 2002 stellte er ein Museum für Mikrobiologie in São Paulo fertig, und 2003 reichte er einen Vorschlag für das World Trade Center Site Memorial ein. Mit Isay Weinfeld plante er das Fasano Hotel in São Paulo. Ebenfalls mit Weinfeld nahm er an der 25. Biennale von São Paulo (2002) teil mit einem Projekt für eine hypothetische Stadt namens Happyland. Kogan ist durch seine Kistenformen mit Holzläden, Gittern und Naturstein bekannt geworden. Zu seinen neueren Projekten zählen das Haus Cury (São Paulo, 2004–06), eine Kindertagesstätte (São Paulo, 2005–07), das E-Home, ein „supertechnologisches" Wohnhaus (Santander, Spanien, 2007), ein „extremes Haus" auf einer Insel in Paraty (Rio de Janeiro, 2007), das Haus Warbler (Los Angeles, 2008), eine Villa in Mailand (Italien, 2008), Haus 53 (São Paulo, 2008) sowie zwei weitere Wohnhäuser in Brasília, alle in Brasilien, sofern nicht anders angegeben. Sein Büro arbeitet zurzeit auch an einem umweltfreundlichen Gebäude in New Jersey (USA, 2008–) und hat kürzlich das Haus Bahia (Salvador, Bahia, 2010, hier veröffentlicht) fertiggestellt.

Né en 1952, **MARCIO KOGAN**, diplômé en 1976 de l'École d'architecture de l'université Mackenzie à São Paulo, a reçu en 1983 plusieurs prix de l'IAB (Instituto de Arquitetos do Brazil) pour les magasins UMA (1999 et 2002), le Coser Studio (2002), la Maison Gama Issa (2002) et la Maison Quinta (2004), tous à São Paulo. Il a également reçu le prix Record House pour la maison Duplessis (2004) et la maison BR (2005). En 2002, il a réalisé le Musée de microbiologie de São Paulo et a participé au concours pour le mémorial du World Trade Center. Il a collaboré avec Isay Weinfeld sur le projet du Fasano Hotel (2001–03) et à l'occasion de la 25e Biennale de São Paulo (2002) pour laquelle ils ont proposé une cité utopique surnommée Happyland. Kogan est connu pour son recours aux formes en boîtes, aux volets en bois, aux treillis et aux pierres apparentes. Parmi ses projets résidentiels récents figurent la maison Cury (São Paulo, 2004–06) ; la crèche Primetime (São Paulo, 2005–07) ; la E-Home, une maison « super-technologique » (Santander, Espagne, 2007) ; une « maison extrême » sur une île face à Paraty (Rio de Janeiro, 2007) ; la maison Warbler (Los Angeles, Californie, 2008) ; une villa à Milan (2008) ; la maison 53 (São Paulo, 2008) et deux autres maisons à Brasília. Son agence travaille actuellement sur le projet d'un « immeuble vert » dans le New Jersey (États-Unis, 2008–) et a récemment achevé la maison Bahia (Salvador, Bahia, 2010, publiée ici).

BAHIA HOUSE

Salvador, Bahia, Brazil, 2010

*Area: 550 m². Client: not disclosed. Cost: $1.3 million
Collaboration: Suzana Glogowski and Samanta Cafardo (Coauthors) and
Diana Radomysler (Interior Design Coauthor)*

The architect explains that the design of this house comes close to traditional architecture in both plan and materials. "The **BAHIA HOUSE** makes use of the old popular knowledge that has been reinvented and incorporated throughout the history of Brazilian architecture. The house was considered for where it is, for the climate of where it is, for Bahia. And for this no 'green' software was used, no equipment and no calculations were made." Local houses with clay roofs and wood ceilings, or wooden mashrabiyyas—a type of Arab screen brought along with Portuguese colonial architecture—serve as an inspiration even as the architect achieves an obviously high degree of modernity. Natural airflow is encouraged through the creation of a central patio, another element frequently present in old, local houses.

Der Architekt gibt an, dass die Gestaltung dieses Hauses sowohl im Grundriss als auch in den Materialien traditioneller Architektur nahekomme. „Das **HAUS BAHIA** zieht Nutzen aus dem von alters her verbreiteten Wissen, das in der Geschichte der brasilianischen Architektur weiterentwickelt und angewendet worden ist. Das Haus wurde für seinen Standort und das dort herrschende Klima, eben für Bahia, geplant. Und dafür wurde keine ‚grüne' Software verwendet, wurde keine besondere Ausrüstung benötigt und wurden keine Berechnungen angestellt." Örtliche Häuser mit Lehmdächern und Holzdecken oder hölzerne Mashrabiyyas – eine Art arabische Gitterwand, die mit der portugiesischen Kolonialarchitektur ins Land kam – dienten als Inspiration, auch wenn dem Architekten eindeutig ein hohes Maß an Modernität gelungen ist. Natürliche Durchlüftung wird durch die Anlage eines zentralen Innenhofs verstärkt, ein weiteres Element, das häufig in alten Häusern vor Ort anzutreffen ist.

Pour l'architecte, la conception de cette maison se rapproche de celle d'une architecture traditionnelle tant pour son plan que pour ses matériaux. « La **MAISON BAHIA** utilise des connaissances populaires anciennes qui ont été réinventées et intégrées tout au long de l'histoire de l'architecture brésilienne. Elle a été pensée pour le lieu où elle se trouve, pour le climat dans lequel elle baigne, pour Bahia. Nous n'avons pas utilisé de logiciel 'vert', ni d'équipements spéciaux, ni de longs calculs. » Les maisons locales à toits d'argile, plafonds de bois et *mashrabiyyas* de bois – un type d'écran arabe importé par l'architecture coloniale portugaise –, ont servi d'inspiration même lorsque l'architecte atteint à un degré élevé de modernité. La circulation naturelle de l'air est encouragée par la création d'un patio central, autre élément fréquent dans les maisons anciennes de la région.

The long, low form of the house is marked by the geometrically disposed screen running along the entire façade.

Kennzeichen der gestreckten, niedrigen Form des Hauses ist die geometrisch aufgeteilte Gitterwand, die an der ganzen Fassade entlangläuft.

La forme longue et surbaissée de la maison est soulignée par l'écran de trame géométrique qui court tout le long de la façade.

The climate of Bahia allows for the house to be opened almost entirely to the exterior, especially given the emphasis on natural air flow.

Das Klima von Bahia gestattet es, das Haus fast völlig nach außen zu öffnen, wodurch ein natürlicher Luftaustausch gewährleistet wird.

Le climat de la région de Bahia permet de laisser la maison presque entièrement ouverte sur l'extérieur et donc de bénéficier d'une ventilation naturelle.

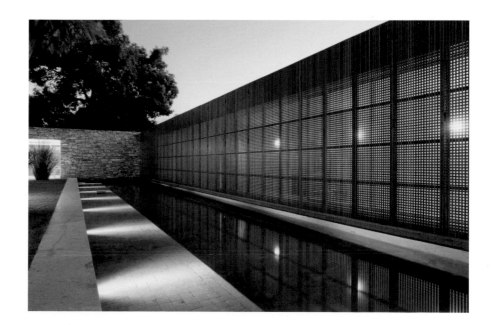

Wooden screens and open volumes
create an intimate atmosphere
enriched by luxuriant vegetation.

*Hölzerne Trennwände und offene
Volumen erzeugen eine intime
Atmosphäre, die durch die üppige
Vegetation bereichert wird.*

*Des écrans de bois et les volumes
ouverts créent une atmosphère intime
que vient enrichir la luxuriance
de la végétation.*

The plan of the house is square with an inner courtyard. Below, thin wooden terraces extend from the low, open spaces of the house.

Der Grundriss des Hauses ist quadratisch und umfasst einen Innenhof. Unten: Dünne Holzterrassen führen von den niedrigen, offenen Räumen des Hauses nach draußen.

Le plan de la maison est un simple carré qui contient une cour intérieure. Ci-dessous, des terrasses de bois juste posées sur le sol prolongent les espaces intérieurs ouverts de la maison.

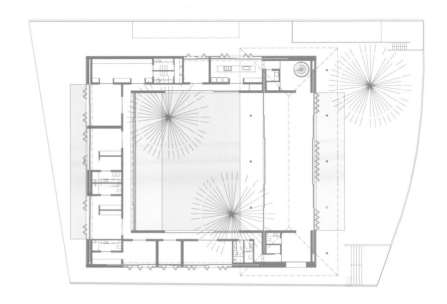

The walls of the house disappear to allow the interior spaces to be entirely open to the garden. Below, the architect contrasts a rough stone wall with a wooden ceiling and a polished floor.

Die Wände des Hauses verschwinden und öffnen die Innenräume vollständig zum Garten. Unten: Der Architekt setzte ein grobe Steinmauer in Kontrast zur hölzernen Decke und zum polierten Fußboden.

Les murs disparaissent pour permettrent aux volumes intérieurs de s'ouvrir entièrement sur le jardin. Ci-dessous: l'architecte fait contraster un mur de pierre brut avec un plafond de bois et un plancher vernis.

Rough stone surfaces are deliberately contrasted with the smooth floor or the screen wall seen above, right.

Raue Steinflächen bilden einen be-wussten Gegensatz zum glatten Boden oder zu der Trennwand oben rechts.

Les plans de pierre d'appareillage rustique contrastent délibérément avec les sols en bois poli ou le mur-écran (ci-dessus, à droite).

KIRSI KORHONEN
AND MIKA PENTTINEN

Arkkitehdit Kirsi Korhonen ja Mika Penttinen Oy
Meritullinkatu 4 B 8
00170 Helsinki
Finland

Tel: +358 9 856 34 564
E-mail: arkkitehdit@kp-ark.com
Web: www.kp-ark.com

MIKA PENTTINEN was born in 1951 and graduated from the Helsinki University of Technology in Finland (1976). He worked in various architectural offices including Penttinen & Tiensuu Arkkitehdit (1981–2002), before cofounding his current firm in 2002. **KIRSI KORHONEN** was born in 1958 and graduated from the Helsinki University of Technology in 1985. She was involved with Penttinen & Tiensuu Arkkitehdit (1986, 1993, 1998–2002) before the 2002 creation of Kirsi Korhonen and Mika Penttinen architects. **JULIUS JÄÄSKELÄINEN**, born in 1975, graduated from the Helsinki University of Technology in 2004, joining Korhonen and Penttinen the same year. Their work includes the Huvitus Terraced Housing (Helsinki, 2007–08, published here); Lontoonkatu 7 Housing (Helsinki, 2010–); Fenixinrinne Housing (Helsinki, 2010–); Leonkatu 16 and 20 Housing (Helsinki, 2010–); Sinisimpukka Housing (Helsinki, 2011–); and Saukonpaasi Housing (2011–), all in Finland.

MIKA PENTTINEN wurde 1951 geboren und beendete 1976 sein Architekturstudium an der Technischen Universität Helsinki. Er arbeitete in verschiedenen Architekturbüros, u. a. bei Penttinen & Tiensuu Arkkitehdit (1981–2002), bevor er 2002 mit Kirsi Korhonen ein gemeinsames Büro gründete. **KIRSI KORHONEN** wurde 1958 geboren und studierte bis 1985 ebenfalls an der Technischen Universität Helsinki. Bis zur Gründung des Architekturbüros Kirsi Korhonen und Mika Penttinen arbeitete sie in der Firma Penttinen & Tiensuu Arkkitehdit (1986, 1993, 1998–2002). **JULIUS JÄÄSKELÄINEN**, geboren 1975, studierte bis 2004 auch an der Technischen Hochschule Helsinki und trat im gleichen Jahr bei Korhonen und Penttinen ein. Zu den Arbeiten des Büros zählen die Reihenhäuser Huvitus (Helsinki, 2007–08, hier veröffentlicht), die Wohnbauten Lontoonkatu 7 (Helsinki, 2010–), die Wohnbauten Fenixinrinne (Helsinki, seit 2010), die Wohnbauten Leonkatu 16 und 20 (Helsinki, 2010–), die Wohnbauten Sinisimpukka (Helsinki, 2011–) und die Wohnbauten Saukonpaasi (2011–), alle in Finnland.

MIKA PENTTINEN, né en 1951, est diplômé de l'Université de technologie d'Helsinki (1976). Il a travaillé dans diverses agences dont Penttinen & Tiensuu Arkkitehdit (1981–2002), avant de fonder son agence actuelle en 2002. **KIRSI KORHONEN**, née en 1958, est diplômée de l'Université de technologie d'Helsinki (1985). Elle a d'abord travaillé pour Penttinen & Tiensuu Arkkitehdit (1986, 1993, 1998–2002) avant de créer en 2002 Kirsi Korhonen and Mika Penttinen architects. **JULIUS JÄÄSKELÄINEN**, né en 1975, est diplômé de la même université en 2004 et a rejoint Korhonen et Penttinen la même année. Parmi leurs réalisations, toutes en Finlande : les maisons en bande Huvitus (Helsinki, 2007–08, publiées ici) ; les logements Lontoonkatu 7 (Helsinki, 2010–) ; les logements Fenixinrinne (Helsinki, 2010–) ; les logements Leonkatu 16 et 20 (Helsinki, 2010–) ; les logements Sinisimpukka (Helsinki, 2011–) et Saukonpaasi (2011–).

HUVITUS TERRACED HOUSING

Helsinki, Finland, 2007–08

Address: Omenamäenkatu 7-27, Helsinki, Finland
Area: 1986 m². Client: City of Helsinki, Housing Department
Cost: € 4.5 million

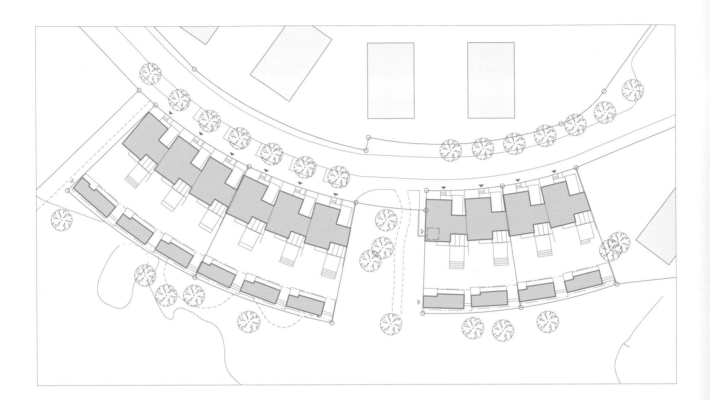

This three-story, wooden terraced housing was built on a sandy, pine-covered hill. The structure was partially factory-assembled and was brought to the site in wall-sized elements. The architects explain: "The laminated veneer lumber (LVL) ribs supporting the second floor have been left visible in the ceiling of the first floor. The ground floor is a concrete structure due to fire regulations." The wooden parts of the façades are painted in dark-colored tar paint, while red laminate cladding was used on the balconies and front doors. The housing units each have an area of 144 square meters and share a separate sauna building to the rear of the residence.

Diese dreigeschossigen Reihenhäuser aus Holz wurden auf einem sandigen, mit Kiefern bestandenen Hügel errichtet, zum Teil aus vorgefertigten, wandgroßen Elementen. Die Architekten erklären: „Die Rippen aus Schichtholz (LVL), die das zweite Obergeschoss tragen, sind in der Decke des ersten Obergeschosses sichtbar belassen. Das Erdgeschoss ist, den Brandschutzvorschriften entsprechend, eine Betonkonstruktion." Die Holzteile der Fassade haben einen dunklen Teeranstrich, für die Balkone und Eingangstüren wurde rote Laminatverkleidung verwendet. Die Wohneinheiten haben 144 m² Grundfläche; an der Rückseite der Anlage befindet sich ein separates Saunagebäude.

Ces maisons en bande de trois niveaux ont été édifiées sur une colline sableuse plantée de pins. La construction a été en partie assemblée en usine et livrée sur place sous forme d'éléments de la taille des murs. « Les nervures en lamibois (LVL) qui soutiennent le deuxième étage ont été laissées visibles au plafond du premier. Le rez-de-chaussée est une structure en béton pour se conformer à la réglementation sur l'incendie », expliquent les architectes. Les parties en bois des façades sont peintes de couleur goudron tandis que les balcons et les portes d'entrée sont habillés de bois lamellé rouge. Chaque unité d'habitation mesure 144 mètres carrés. Un sauna commun est aménagé à l'arrière de chaque résidence.

The housing structure is arrayed in an arc pattern, as seen in the site plan above. Right, the wooden structures are relatively austere, with their companion sauna structures, seen in the lower image.

Die Wohnhäuser sind, wie aus dem Lageplan oben ersichtlich, bogenförmig ausgelegt. Rechts: Die Holzbauten sind relativ streng gestaltet, ebenso wie das Sauna-gebäude im unteren Bild.

Les logements sont disposés selon un arc, comme le montre le plan ci-dessus. À droite, les constructions en bois semblent relativement austères. En bas à droite, la rangée des annexes consacrées aux saunas.

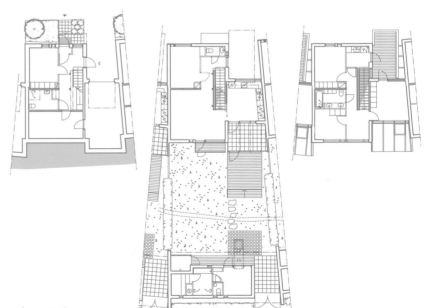

In contrast with their more severe exteriors, the houses are broadly glazed. The plans to the right show that the architect has flared out the rectangular forms on one end.

Im Gegensatz zu ihrem strengen äußeren Erscheinungsbild sind die Häuser großzügig verglast. Die Grundrisse rechts zeigen, dass der Architekt die rechtwinkligen Formen auf einer Seite aufgebrochen hat.

Par contraste avec leur aspect extérieur plus sévère, les logements sont largement vitrés. Les plans de droite montrent que l'architecte a évasé une extrémité de la forme par ailleurs rectangulaire.

Wood is quite present in the interiors and is contrasted in its colors, as is the case for the exterior cladding.

Holz in kontrastierenden Farben ist im Innern reichlich verwendet; das Gleiche gilt für die Außenverkleidung.

Le bois, assez présent à l'intérieur, est de couleurs contrastées, tout comme le bardage des façades.

NIC LEHOUX
AND JACQUELINE DARJES

Nic Lehoux Architectural Photography
555 West 17th Avenue
Vancouver BC V5Z1T6
Canada

Tel: +1 604 805 1811
E-mail: nic@niclehoux.com
Web: www.niclehoux.com

NIC LEHOUX was born in 1968 in Quebec, Canada. His presence in this book is unusual in that he does not have a background as an architect, but rather as a photographer, a profession for which he did not receive formal training aside from an apprenticeship. Lehoux has focused more specifically on architectural photography, subsequent to a decision at the age of 19 not to pursue a career as an architect. **JACQUELINE DARJES** was born in 1972 in Regina, Canada. She runs Nic Lehoux Architectural Photography. Lehoux's interest in contemporary architecture has clearly led him to imagine that he could actually build a small house, which he did for the first time, together with Jacqueline Darjes, with the Lilypad (Point Roberts, Washington, USA, 2008–09, published here and photographed by Nic Lehoux).

NIC LEHOUX wurde 1968 in Quebec, Kanada, geboren. Seine Aufnahme in das vorliegende Buch ist ungewöhnlich, da er kein studierter Architekt ist, sondern vielmehr Fotograf, wofür er, außer einer Lehre, auch keine professionelle Ausbildung absolvierte. Lehoux hat sich auf Architekturfotografie spezialisiert, nachdem er im Alter von 19 Jahren beschlossen hatte, auf eine Laufbahn als Architekt zu verzichten. **JACQUELINE DARJES** wurde 1972 in Regina, Kanada, geboren. Sie leitet die Firma Nic Lehoux Architectural Photography. Lehoux war aufgrund seines Interesses an moderner Architektur der Meinung, dass er auch selbst ein kleines Haus bauen könnte: Als erstes Projekt realisierte er, zusammen mit Jacqueline Darjes, das Lilypad (Point Roberts, Washington, USA, 2008–09, hier veröffentlicht mit Fotografien von Nic Lehoux).

NIC LEHOUX est né en1968 à Québec. Sa présence dans cet ouvrage peut surprendre puisqu'il n'a pas suivi de formation d'architecte mais est photographe, profession pour laquelle il n'a d'ailleurs pas suivi d'enseignement formel en dehors d'un apprentissage. Il s'est plus spécifiquement orienté vers la photographie d'architecture, après avoir renoncé à l'âge de 19 ans à poursuivre des études d'architecte. **JACQUELINE DARJES** est née en 1972 à Regina au Canada. Elle gère le studio Nic Lehoux Architectural Photography. L'intérêt de Lehoux pour l'architecture contemporaine l'a amené à penser qu'il pouvait se construire une petite maison, la Lilypad, ce qu'il a fait avec Jacqueline Darjes (Point Roberts, Washington, États-Unis, 2008–09, publiée ici et photographiée par Nic Lehoux).

THE LILYPAD

Point Roberts, Washington, USA, 2008–09

*Address: 936 Claire Lane, Point Roberts, Washington, USA
Area: 24 m². Client: Nic Lehoux and Jacqueline Darjes. Cost: $4500
Collaboration: Jacqueline Darjes (interiors)*

The basic structure of this house, set on a forested site amongst 400-year-old Douglas fir trees and western red cedar, measures just 16 square meters, plus an upper loft of eight square meters. It was built entirely by the two designers themselves, off the power grid and wholly of wood, above a 30-square-meter cedar deck lifted off the ground with sonotubes. The idea that this deck "floats" above the earth justifies the **LILYPAD** name. The house has recycled 80-year-old Douglas fir windows. The structure was built between November 2008 and October 2009. Glulam beams that support the upper loft were recovered from a construction site. The interior of this simple but convivial house is whitewashed. The actual construction cost was just $3000 or a total of $4500 including the decking.

Die Grundkonstruktion dieses Hauses auf einem mit 400 Jahre alten Douglastannen und amerikanischen Rotzedern bestandenen Grundstück misst nur 16 m², zuzüglich eines Lofts von 8 m². Der ganze Bau wurde von den Planern selbst errichtet, fern vom Energieversorgungsnetz und nur aus Holz, auf einer 30 m² großen Plattform aus Zedernholz, die auf Sonotube-Baurohren über dem Erdboden steht. Die Vorstellung, dass diese Plattform über der Erde schwebt, rechtfertigt den Namen **LILYPAD** (Seerosenblatt). Für das Haus wurden 80 Jahre alte Fenster aus Douglastanne wiederverwendet. Die Errichtung des Gebäudes dauerte von November 2008 bis Oktober 2009. Die das Loft tragenden, verleimten Holzbalken wurden von einer anderen Baustelle übernommen. Die Innenwände dieses schlichten, aber wohnlichen Hauses sind gekalkt. Die Baukosten betrugen nur 3000 US-Dollar, einschließlich der Plattform 4500 US-Dollar.

Cette petite maison de 16 mètres carrés au sol (plus une mezzanine de 8 mètres carrés) a été construite au milieu d'une forêt de sapins de Douglas et de cèdres rouges vieux de quatre siècles. Elle a été entièrement réalisée par ses deux concepteurs. À l'écart du réseau d'électricité, elle est totalement en bois, posée sur une terrasse de 30 mètres carrés surélevée du sol par des tubes de coffrage de poteaux. L'idée de cette terrasse « flottant » au-dessus du sol éclaire le nom retenu de **LILYPAD** (feuille de nénuphar). Les fenêtres de récupération en pin de Douglas sont vieilles de 80 ans. La construction a duré de novembre 2008 à octobre 2009. Les poutres en lamellé-collé qui soutiennent la mezzanine ont été récupérées sur un chantier. L'intérieur de cette maison simple mais conviviale est blanchi à la chaux. La construction a coûté 3000 $, ou 4500 en comptant la terrasse.

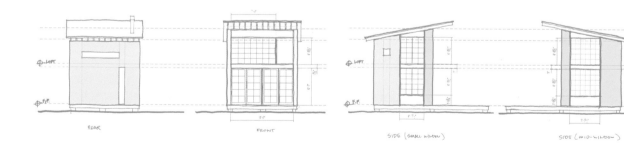

The elevations above make it clear that the Lilypad is indeed quite small, although the photographer's images show how open the space is.

Die Ansichten oben zeigen, dass das Lilypad wirklich sehr klein ist, auch wenn die Fotos die Offenheit der Räume bezeugen.

Les coupes montrent les faibles dimensions de la Lilypad, même si les photographies accentuent l'ampleur du volume intérieur.

The Lilypad is something of a "do-it-yourself" project since neither of the participants are professional architects.

Lilypad ist eine Art „Do-it-yourself"-Projekt, da keiner der Beteiligten ausgebildeter Architekt ist.

La Lilypad est un peu une maison de bricoleurs puisque ni l'un ni l'autre de ses créateurs n'est architecte.

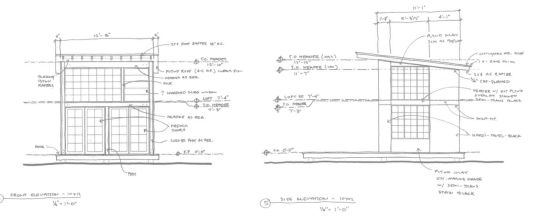

The placement of a bed on an upper mezzanine with the rest of the space open on two levels gives the house a more voluminous feeling than its actual floor area would imply.

Weil ein Bett ins obere Zwischengeschoss gestellt wurde, wobei der restliche Raum auf beiden Ebenen offen geblieben ist, wirkt das Haus geräumiger, als die tatsächliche Flächengröße vermuten ließe.

L'implantation du lit en mezzanine et le reste du volume ouvert sur toute sa hauteur, donnent une impression d'espace plus importante que la surface au sol ne pouvait le laisser penser.

NIALL MCLAUGHLIN ARCHITECTS

Niall McLaughlin Architects / 39–51 Highgate Road
London NW5 1RS / UK

Tel: +44 20 74 85 91 70 / Fax: +44 20 74 85 91 71
Email: info@niallmclaughlin.com / Web: www.niallmclaughlin.com

NIALL MCLAUGHLIN was born in Geneva, Switzerland, in 1962. He was educated in Dublin, Ireland, and received his architectural degree from University College Dublin in 1984. He worked for Scott Tallon Walker in Dublin and London between 1984 and 1989, before establishing his own practice in 1991. He won the Young British Architect of the Year award in 1998. He is a visiting professor of architecture at University College London. **EMMA GUY** was born in Yorkshire, UK, in 1974 and studied at Magdalene College, Cambridge, and the Bartlett, University College London. She joined Seth Stein Architects in 1999 and has been at Niall McLaughlin Architects since 2001. **TIM ALLEN-BOOTH** was born in Sheffield, UK, in 1974 and studied at the University of Nottingham. After graduating in 1996 he moved to London and joined Niall McLaughlin Architects in 2006. **ANNE SCHROELL** was born in Luxembourg in 1977 and studied architecture at the Bartlett, University College London. In her "year out" she worked for Bartenbach Lichtlabor, a lighting designer in Innsbruck, Austria. After graduating from the Bartlett, she joined Tonkin Lui and then worked for De Matos Storey Ryan Architects on several private houses. In 2006 she joined Niall McLaughlin Architects. Their recent work includes Castleford Forum Museum and Library (Wakefield, 2005); a House at Piper's End (Hertfordshire, 2006–08, published here); the Café-Bar on Deal Pier (Deal, Kent, 2008, also published here); a House at Anglesea Road (Dublin, Ireland, 2008); TQ2 Bridge (Bristol, 2008); Student Accommodation and Library Buildings, Somerville College, Oxford University (Oxford, 2010); and the Alzheimer's Respite Center (Dublin, Ireland, 2009), all in the UK unless stated otherwise.

NIALL MCLAUGHLIN wurde 1962 in Genf, Schweiz, geboren. Er wuchs in Dublin auf und machte 1984 seinen Abschluss in Architektur am University College Dublin. Danach arbeitete er von 1984 bis 1989 bei Scott Tallon Walker in Dublin und London; 1991 gründete er sein eigenes Büro. 1998 wurde ihm der Young British Architect of the Year Award verliehen. McLaughlin ist Gastprofessor für Architektur am University College London. **EMMA GUY** wurde 1974 in Yorkshire geboren und studierte am Magdalene College, Cambridge, und am Bartlett University College, London. Sie arbeitete ab 1999 bei Seth Stein Architects, seit 2001 ist sie bei Niall McLaughlin Architects tätig. **TIM ALLEN-BOOTH** wurde 1974 in Sheffield geboren und studierte an der University of Nottingham. Nach seinem Abschluss 1996 zog er nach London und trat 2006 bei Niall McLaughlin Architects ein. **ANNE SCHROELL** wurde 1977 in Luxemburg geboren und studierte Architektur am Bartlett University College, London. In einem Jahr „Auszeit" arbeitete sie bei Bartenbach Lichtlabor, einer Firma für Lichtplanung in Innsbruck. Nach ihrem Abschluss am Bartlett war sie bei Tonkin Liu und dann bei De Matos Storey Ryan Architects an der Planung mehrerer privater Wohnhäuser beteiligt. 2006 trat sie bei Niall McLaughlin Architects ein. Zu den neueren Werken dieses Büros zählen Castleford Forum Museum und Bibliothek (Wakefield, 2005), ein Wohnhaus in Piper's End (Hertfordshire, 2006–08, hier veröffentlicht), ein Café mit Bar am Deal Pier (Deal, Kent, 2008, ebenfalls hier veröffentlicht), ein Wohnhaus in der Anglesea Road (Dublin, 2008), die TQ2-Brücke (Bristol, 2008), Studentenwohnungen und Bibliothek des Somerville College, Oxford University (Oxford, 2010), sowie ein Pflegeheim für Alzheimerpatienten (Dublin, 2009), alle in Großbritannien, sofern nicht anders angegeben.

Né à Genève en 1962, **NIALL MCLAUGHLIN** a grandi à Dublin. Il sort diplômé du University College à Dublin en 1984. Il a travaillé pour Scott Tallon Walker à Dublin et Londres de 1984 à 1989, avant de créer son agence en 1991. Il a remporté le prix du Jeune architecte britannique de l'année en 1998. Il est professeur d'architecture invité au University College à Londres. **EMMA GUY**, née dans le Yorkshire (G.-B.) en 1974, a étudié au Magdalene College à Cambridge et au Bartlett, University College à Londres. Elle a rejoint Seth Stein Architects en 1999, puis Niall McLaughlin Architects en 2001. **TIM ALLEN-BOOTH**, né à Sheffield (G.-B.) en 1974, a étudié à l'université de Nottingham. Après son diplôme (1996), il s'est installé à Londres et est entré chez Niall McLaughlin Architects en 2006. **ANNE SCHROELL**, née à Luxembourg en 1977, a étudié l'architecture au Bartlett, University College à Londres. Pendant une année hors cursus, elle a travaillé pour Bartenbach Lichtlabor, un designer de luminaires d'Innsbruck en Autriche. Une fois diplômée du Bartlett, elle a rejoint Tonkin Lui puis De Matos Storey Ryan Architects, intervenant sur plusieurs résidences privées. En 2006, elle est entrée chez Niall McLaughlin Architects. Parmi leurs réalisations récentes : le musée et la bibliothèque du Castleford Forum (Wakefield, 2005) ; une maison à Piper's End (Hertfordshire, 2006–08, publiée ici) ; le café-bar sur Deal Pier (Deal, Kent, 2008, également publié ici) ; une maison à Anglesea Road (Dublin, 2008) ; le pont TQ2 (Bristol, 2008) ; des logements pour étudiants et une bibliothèque pour le Somerville College (Oxford University, 2010) et un Centre pour le traitement de la maladie d'Alzheimer (Dublin, 2009).

HOUSE AT PIPER'S END

Hertfordshire, UK, 2006–08

Address: not disclosed
Area: 175 m². Client: not disclosed. Cost: €600 000

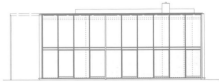

The unusual canopy poised above the house stands apart from the broadly glazed, wooden volume.

Das ungewöhnliche Vordach, das über dem Hause schwebt, hebt sich vom großzügig verglasten, hölzernen Baukörper ab.

Le curieux auvent dont la hauteur dépasse celle de la maison est détaché du volume en grande partie vitré de celle-ci.

The architects demonstrated that this house was more sustainable than refurbishing an existing building would have been. Built between an orchard and an open paddock, the structure is organized as a series of volumes: a "wooden box," a "vitrine" with the main rooms opening from a double-height space, and a steel canopy over a terrace contained by a concrete pool. The house is broadly glazed for the most part and is marked by the high, light canopy. The mixture of wood, steel, and glass makes for a very modern, transparent appearance, though shading from the sun is provided without reducing this openness.

Die Architekten haben gezeigt, dass dieses Wohnhaus zu einem viel nachhaltigeren Gebäude geworden ist, als wenn man ein bestehendes Haus modernisiert hätte. Der zwischen einer Obstplantage und einer freien Koppel errichtete Bau ist als Raumfolge angelegt: eine „hölzerne Kiste", eine „Vitrine", in der die wichtigen Räume Doppelgeschosshöhe haben, und ein Vordach aus Stahl über einer Terrasse mit dem Swimmingpool aus Beton. Das Haus ist zum großen Teil großzügig verglast, das hohe, leichte Vordach wird zu seinem Wahrzeichen. Die Verbindung von Holz, Stahl und Glas sorgt für ein sehr modernes, transparentes Erscheinungsbild, wobei ausreichend Sonnenschutz vorhanden ist, ohne diese Offenheit einzuschränken.

Les architectes ont démontré que réaliser cette maison était au final une démarche plus durable que de rénover une construction ancienne. Construite entre un verger et un paddock ouvert, la maison s'organise en une succession de volumes : « une boîte en bois », une « vitrine » organisée autour d'un volume double hauteur et un auvent en acier protégeant une terrasse bordée par une piscine en béton. La maison est généreusement vitrée dans sa plus grande partie et personnalisée par un auvent léger de grande hauteur. Le mélange de bois, d'acier et de verre lui confèrent un aspect moderne et transparent. Les protections solaires ne nuisent pas au sentiment d'ouverture.

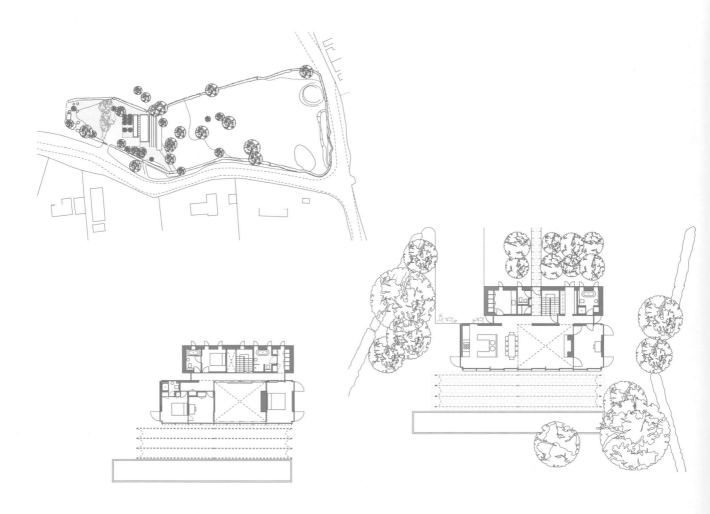

Seen in its site, and in plans, the house is composed of a staggered succession of rectangular volumes. The double-height living space has a wood-framed and fully glazed façade.

Lageplan und Grundrisse zeigen, dass das Haus aus einer gestaffelten Folge rechtwinkliger Baukörper besteht. Der doppelgeschosshohe Wohnbereich hat eine Holzrahmenkonstruktion und eine voll verglaste Fassade.

En plan, la maison se compose d'une succession de volumes rectangulaires décalés. Le séjour double-hauteur s'étend derrière une façade à ossature en bois entièrement vitrée.

CAFÉ-BAR ON DEAL PIER

Deal, Kent, UK, 2008

Address: Beach Street, Deal, Kent CT14 6HZ, UK
Area: 180 m². Client: Dover District Council. Cost: € 1.1 million

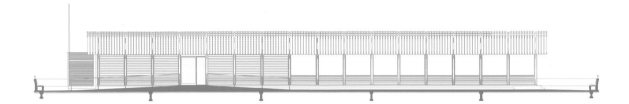

The café-bar is set on the end of the existing wood-columned pier, aligned perpendicular to its elongated form.

Das Café befindet sich am Ende einer Landungsbrücke auf Holzpfeilern, und folgt deren langgestreckter Form.

Le café-bar a été implanté à l'extrémité de l'axe de la jetée de bois.

The plan below shows the long pier and the café-bar at its end. Above, the new structure sitting on concrete pilings.

Der Lageplan unten zeigt die lange Landungsbrücke und das Café an ihrem Ende. Oben: Der Neubau steht auf Betonpfeilern.

Le plan ci-dessous montre la longue jetée et le café-bar à sa pointe. Ci-dessus, la nouvelle construction qui s'appuie sur des piliers de béton.

Deal developed as a seaport, where sailboats would wait for fair wind. When the town later became a resort, several piers were created. The most recent is a concrete pile structure built in 1957. The end of this pier was designed with three levels for viewing, boating, and fishing. The café-bar for this pier was commissioned in a RIBA competition. The architects state: "We wanted to make the building from a single material that would weather and improve with age. We hoped that it would eventually fade into the battered concrete on the pier." They created a laminated iroko structure with large glazed surfaces inspired to some extent by 19th-century industrial timber buildings. The structure is divided into two parts, an opaque section containing toilets, kitchens, and an entrance area. The other, glazed section contains a café "which is conceived as a single simple space open to the outside."

Deal war ursprünglich ein Seehafen, in dem Segler auf günstigeren Wind warteten. Als die Stadt sich später zu einem Seebad entwickelte, wurden mehrere Landungsbrücken errichtet. Die letzte von ihnen wurde 1957 als Pfahlkonstruktion aus Beton erbaut. An ihrem Ende gibt es drei Ebenen: eine zur Aussicht, eine als Anlände und eine zum Angeln. Das Café auf diesem Pier wurde vom Royal Institute of British Architects (RIBA) als Wettbewerb ausgeschrieben. Die Architekten erklären: „Wir wollten das Gebäude aus einem Material errichten, das mit der Zeit verwittert und dabei anschaulicher wird. Wir hoffen, dass es schließlich in den abgenutzten Beton des Piers aufgehen wird." Sie wählten eine verleimte Konstruktion aus Iroko-Holz mit großen, verglasten Flächen, die in gewisser Weise von den hölzernen Industriebauten des 19. Jahrhunderts beeinflusst wurde. Das Gebäude besteht aus zwei Teilen: einem undurchsichtigen Bereich, der Toiletten, Küchen und eine Eingangshalle enthält, und einem verglasten für das Café, „das als ein einziger, schlichter, nach außen geöffneter Raum konzipiert wurde".

Deal était à l'origine un port de mer dans lequel les bateaux attendaient les vents favorables. Lorsque la ville devint un lieu de vacances, plusieurs jetées furent créées. La plus récente est une construction en béton édifiée en 1957. L'extrémité de la jetée comportait trois niveaux : un pour l'observation, les deux autres pour l'accostage des bateaux et la pêche. Le café-bar est une commande obtenue à l'issue d'un concours organisé par le RIBA. « Nous voulions réaliser cette construction dans un matériau unique qui puisse se patiner et s'améliorer avec le temps, expliquent les architectes ; nous souhaitions qu'ils se confondent même avec le béton délabré de la jetée. » L'agence a dessiné une structure en lamellé d'Iroko à grandes baies vitrées inspirées dans une certaine mesure des bâtiments en bois du XIXᵉ siècle. L'ensemble est divisé en deux parties, une section fermée contenant les toilettes, les cuisines et une entrée, l'autre, vitrée, réservée au café « conçu comme un vaste et simple espace, ouvert sur l'extérieur ».

The café-bar uses wood like the pier itself but succeeds in taking on a modern appearance in the context of an old type of structure over the sea.

Wie auch für die Landungsbrücke wurde für das Café Holz verwendet. Den Architekten ist jedoch ein modernes Erscheinungsbild im Kontext der alten Konstruktion gelungen.

Le café-bar est en bois, comme la jetée, mais réussit à prendre un aspect contemporain dans le contexte d'un ouvrage d'art ancien.

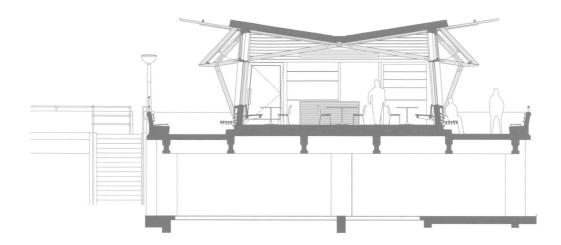

The sides of the café are fully glazed, giving patrons the impression of hovering above the sea. Above, a section drawing shows the X-shaped form and the placement of the facility on the pier.

Die Seitenwände des Cafés sind voll verglast und vermitteln den Besuchern den Eindruck, als schwebten sie über dem Meer. Oben: Eine Schnittzeichnung zeigt die kreuzförmige Gestalt und die Lage des Gebäudes auf dem Pier.

Les façades latérales du café sont entièrement vitrées, ce qui donne l'impression aux clients de se trouver en suspension au-dessus de la mer. Ci-dessus, une coupe montre l'ossature, la charpente en X et le positionnement de la construction sur la jetée.

With its wooden slat roof, the building is as open to its environment as the weather permits. Below, the concrete pilings and platform on which the café-bar is built.

Mit seinem hölzernen Lattendach ist das Gebäude so offen zu seinem Umfeld, wie es das Wetter gestattet. Unten: die Betonpfeiler und die Plattform, auf der das Café errichtet wurde.

Doté d'une toiture en poutrelles de bois, le café est aussi ouvert sur son environnement que le temps le permet. Ci-dessous les piliers de béton et la plate-forme sur laquelle il a été construit.

ANDREAS MECK

meck architekten
Kellerstr. 39
81667 Munich
Germany

Tel: +49 89 614 58 90
Fax: +49 89 614 58 979
E-mail: office@meck-architekten.de
Web: www.meck-architekten.de

ANDREAS MECK was born in 1959 in Munich, Germany, and studied architecture at the Technical University of Munich (TUM), obtaining his diploma in 1985. He attended the Architectural Association (London, 1987) and went to work for the firm of Professor M. Kovatsch (Munich, 1986–89). Since 1998 he has been the chair of Design and Structural Design at the Fachhochschule München. He created his own firm in 1989, which has been called meck architekten since 2001, and also worked in collaboration with Stephan Köppel (1998–2000). His work includes the Aufberg Holiday Home (Aufhausen, Austria, 2008); St. Nikolaus Community Center (Neuried, 2008); Dominikuszentrum (part of a diocesan youth center and a Caritas center, Munich, 2008); the Bundeswehr Memorial (Berlin, 2009); and the Slender House (Das schmale Haus, Munich, 2009, published here), all in Germany unless otherwise indicated.

ANDREAS MECK wurde 1959 in München geboren und studierte an der Technischen Universität München (TUM), wo er 1985 sein Diplom machte. Danach besuchte er die Architectural Association (London, 1987) und begann, im Büro von Professor M. Kovatsch (München, 1986–89) zu arbeiten. Seit 1998 ist er Lehrstuhlinhaber für Entwurf und Statik an der Fachhochschule München. Er gründete 1989 sein eigenes Büro, das seit 2001 unter dem Namen meck architekten firmiert, und arbeitete auch mit Stephan Köppel zusammen (1998–2000). Zu seinen ausgeführten Bauten zählen das Ferienhaus Aufberg (Aufhausen, Österreich, 2008), das Pfarrzentrum St. Nikolaus (Neuried, 2008), das Dominikuszentrum (Teil eines Jugendzentrums der Diözese sowie ein Zentrum der Caritas, München, 2008), das Ehrenmal der Bundeswehr (Berlin, 2009) und das „Schmale Haus" (München, 2009, hier veröffentlicht), alle in Deutschland, sofern nicht anders angegeben.

ANDREAS MECK, né en 1959 à Munich, a étudié l'architecture à l'Université polytechnique (TUM) de cette ville, dont il est sorti diplômé en 1985. Il a ensuite étudié à l'Architectural Association (Londres, 1987) et a travaillé dans l'agence du professeur M. Kovatsch (Munich, 1986–89). Depuis 1998, il dirige le département de Conception et de Conception structurelle à l'université des sciences appliquées de Munich. Il a créé son agence en 1989, qui s'appelle meck architekten depuis 2001, et a également collaboré avec Stephan Köppel (1998–2000). Parmi ses réalisations, la plupart en Allemagne : la maison de vacances de l'Aufberg (Aufhausen, Autriche, 2008) ; le centre paroissial St. Nikolaus (Neuried, 2008) ; le Dominikuszentrum (partie d'un centre de jeunesse diocésain et d'un centre Caritas, Munich, 2008) ; le mémorial de la Bundeswehr (Berlin, 2009) et la maison étroite (Das Schmale Haus, Munich, 2009, publiée ici).

THE SLENDER HOUSE

Munich, Germany, 2009

Address: not disclosed
Area: 273 m². Client: Gerhard and Katharina Matzig. Cost: not disclosed
Collaboration: Francesca Fornasier

This house for two architecture critics with three children is intended to be "black and clearly shaped on the outside," but with different heights and lighting effects inside. There is also a contrast between the use of concrete ("heavy") and wood ("light"). The architect explains that the house is "low and high, and surprisingly generous. What is all but impossible, becomes space. It is different but at the same time familiar… A house with an attitude; it wants to be treated with respect," concludes Andreas Meck. The black, vertical wood cladding emphasizes the rather austere simplicity of the shape of the house and contrasts with the more complicated, untinted wood structure inside.

Dieses Haus für zwei Architekturkritiker mit drei Kindern sollte „von außen schwarz und klar gestaltet" sein, innen jedoch verschiedene Höhen und Lichteffekte aufweisen. Es besteht auch ein Kontrast zwischen der Verwendung von Beton („schwer") und Holz („leicht"). Der Architekt sagt, das Haus sei „niedrig und hoch und erstaunlich großzügig. Raum ist an nahezu unmöglichen Stellen geschaffen worden. Es ist ungewöhnlich, aber vertraut zugleich … Ein Haus mit Haltung, es möchte mit Respekt behandelt werden", schließt Andreas Meck seine Beschreibung. Die schwarze, vertikale Holzverkleidung betont die strenge Schlichtheit seiner Form und bildet einen Gegensatz zur komplexeren, unbehandelten Holzkonstruktion im Innern.

Cette maison réalisée pour deux critiques d'architecture et leurs trois enfants se veut « noire et clairement inspirée de son environnement extérieur » mais bénéficiant à l'intérieur de hauteurs et d'éclairages différents. On note également un contraste entre le béton (« lourd ») et le bois (« léger »). L'architecte a expliqué que la maison est « à la fois traditionnelle et d'avant-garde, et étonnement généreuse. Tout ce qu'il était possible d'exploiter est devenu espace. Elle est différente et familière à la fois… Une maison qui a une attitude, elle veut être traitée avec respect », conclut Andreas Meck. L'habillage vertical en bois noirci met en valeur la simplicité de la forme et contraste avec la structure intérieure plus complexe en bois non teinté.

Although it fully adapts the typology of nearby houses, the Slender House is surprising in its contrast of black wood surfaces and white window frames.

Obgleich das „Schmale Haus" exakt der Typologie der benachbarten Bauten folgt, fällt es durch den Kontrast von schwarzen Holzflächen und weißen Fensterrahmen auf.

Bien qu'elle soit pleinement adaptée à la typologie de ses voisines, la maison étroite surprend par le contraste entre ses façades noires en bois et les châssis blancs de ses fenêtres.

Section drawings show the disposition of the volumes of the house, while the photo to the right emphasizes the austerity of the black wood façade.

Die Schnitte zeigen die Verteilung der Räume innerhalb des Hauses, während das Foto rechts die Strenge der schwarzen Holzfassade zum Ausdruck bringt.

Les coupes montrent la disposition des volumes de la maison. La photo de droite fait ressortir l'austérité de sa façade en bois teinté noir.

P 308

The vertical, black wood façade gives way to a natural wood coloring inside the house.

Die vertikale, schwarze Holzfassade geht in das in natürlichen Holzfarben gestaltete Innere des Hauses über.

À l'intérieur, le noir de la façade laisse place à des teintes de bois plus naturelles.

Drawings show the house in plan and section within its long narrow site, ending in a black wall.

Der Schnitt und die Grundrisse zeigen das Haus mit der schwarzen Außenwand und seine Lage auf dem langen Grundstück.

Plans et coupes de la maison édifiée sur un terrain en longueur finissant sur une petite construction annexe également en bois noir.

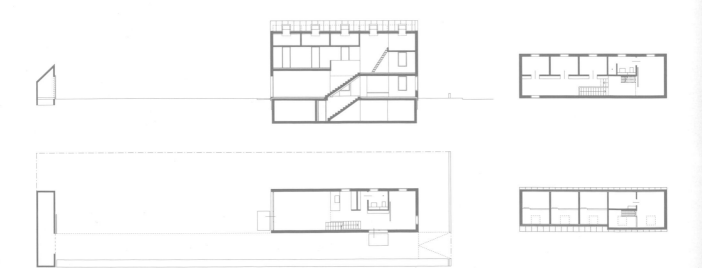

BEATRIZ MEYER

Beatriz Meyer Arquitetura
Rua Fidalga 787 no. 31
São Paulo 05432–070, SP
Brazil

Tel: +55 11 8476 2000
E-mail: beatriz@beatrizmeyer.com.br
Web: www.beatrizmeyer.com.br

BEATRIZ MEYER was born in São Paulo, Brazil, in 1977. She attended Mackenzie Presbyterian University in São Paulo (1996–2000) and worked for the following four years on scenography for the theater. From 2004 until 2009 she had her own office. Since 2009 she has been working in the office of Marcio Kogan (Studio MK27). In 2005 she participated in the International Biennial of São Paulo with the Open School project. She received a prize from IAB (Brazilian Architects Institute), the 8th Young Architect Award for her Chapel (Tatuí, São Paulo, 2006, published here). In 2008 she participated in the VI BIAU (Ibero-American Biennial of Architecture and Urbanism) in Lisbon with the Chapel project.

BEATRIZ MEYER wurde 1977 in São Paulo, Brasilien, geboren und studierte an der Universidade Presbiteriana Mackenzie in São Paulo (1996–2000). In den darauffolgenden vier Jahren arbeitete sie als Bühnenbildnerin am Theater. Von 2004 bis 2009 hatte sie ein eigenes Büro; seit 2009 arbeitet sie in der Firma von Marcio Kogan (Studio MK27). 2005 nahm sie mit dem Projekt einer „offenen Schule" an der Internationalen Biennale von São Paulo teil. Für ihre Kapelle (Tatuí, São Paulo, 2006, hier veröffentlicht) erhielt sie einen Preis vom brasilianischen Architektenverband IAB, den 8th Young Architect Award. 2008 beteiligte sie sich mit dem Entwurf für diese Kapelle an der VI. BIAU (Bienal Iberoamerican de Arquitectura y Urbanismo) in Lissabon.

BEATRIZ MEYER, née à São Paulo en 1977, a étudié à la Universidade Presbiteriana Mackenzie à São Paulo (1996–2000) et travaillé ensuite pendant quatre ans sur des projets de scénographies pour le théâtre. De 2004 à 2009, elle a dirigé sa propre agence et, depuis 2009, est entrée chez Marcio Kogan (Studio MK27). En 2005, elle a participé à la Biennale internationale de São Paulo avec le projet de l'École ouverte. Elle est titulaire du 8e prix du jeune architecte décerné par l'IAB (Institut des architectes brésiliens) pour une chapelle (Tatuí, São Paulo, 2006, publiée ici). En 2008, elle a participé à la VIe BIAU (Biennale ibéro-américaine d'architecture et d'urbanisme) à Lisbonne avec ce projet de chapelle.

CHAPEL

Tatuí, São Paulo, Brazil, 2006

Address: Tatuí, São Paulo, Brazil
Area: 60 m². Client: not disclosed. Cost: $100 000

The **CHAPEL** was commissioned by the owners of a ranch in the countryside of the state of São Paulo. It is set between two lines of pine trees and is surrounded by lush vegetation. "Their ultimate purpose," says the architect, "was to have a place where it would be possible to enjoy peace and be close to nature." The construction material was chosen because other structures on the ranch were in wood. Large glazed areas allow a closer communion with the natural setting. An Alwitra membrane roof was used to permit a low angle. A stone wall with a cruciform cutout stands behind the altar. Recuperated wood is used inside, and dry-sealed bricks are used for the exterior floor. The architect designed benches and the altar for the project. Inlaid, floor lighting marks the pillars and the path leading to the altar.

Die **KAPELLE** wurde von den Besitzern einer Ranch im Staat São Paulo in Auftrag gegeben. Sie steht zwischen zwei Reihen von Kiefern und ist von üppiger Vegetation umgeben. „Eigentlich war sie als ein Ort gedacht", sagt die Architektin, „an dem man den Frieden genießen und der Natur nahe sein kann." Das Baumaterial entspricht dem der anderen Holzbauten auf der Ranch. Durch große, verglaste Bereiche wurde eine engere Verbindung zur natürlichen Umgebung erreicht. Das Dach ist mit einer Alwitra-Membrane versehen, die eine leichte Neigung gestattete. Eine Steinmauer mit ausgeschnittenem Kreuz steht hinter dem Altar. Das Innere ist mit wiederverwendetem Holz ausgestattet, der Boden außen mit wasserabweisenden Ziegeln gepflastert. Die Architektin entwarf auch die Bänke und den Altar dieser Kapelle. In den Boden eingelassene Strahler beleuchten die Stützen und den Weg zum Altar.

Cette **CHAPELLE** est une commande des propriétaires d'un ranch de l'État de São Paulo. Implantée entre deux alignement de pins, elle est entourée d'une végétation luxuriante. « Le but ultime [des clients], explique l'architecte, était de disposer d'un lieu où il soit possible de profiter de la paix au plus près de la nature. » Le matériau de construction a été choisi, entre autres, parce que tous les autres bâtiments de la propriété sont en bois. De vastes murs vitrés assurent une communion étroite avec le cadre naturel. La toiture est recouverte d'une membrane en Alwitra, ce qui a permis de lui conserver une faible inclinaison. Un mur de pierre dans lequel est découpée une croix se dresse derrière l'autel. L'intérieur est en bois de récupération et les sols extérieurs en briques à joint de mortier sec. L'architecte a également dessiné les bancs et l'autel. Un éclairage intégré dans le sol signale les piliers et l'allée vers l'autel.

The full-height glazing of three sides of the chapel makes it particularly open. Wood is used everywhere aside from the rear stone wall.

Die auf drei Seiten in voller Höhe verglaste Kapelle wirkt besonders offen. Mit Ausnahme der rückwärtigen Natursteinwand wurde überall Holz verwendet.

Les murs de verre toute hauteur des trois côtés de la chapelle lui confèrent un aspect extrêmement ouvert. Le bois est partout présent, à l'exception du mur en pierre de l'autel.

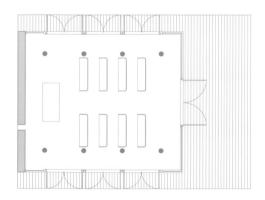

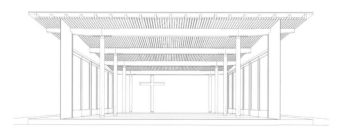

Seen in plan and elevation, the structure is simple, basically a square with carefully aligned pews and a simple table serving as an altar.

Im Grundriss und in der Ansicht gesehen, ist das Gebäude schlicht konzipiert, im Grunde als ein Quadrat mit überlegt platzierten Bänken und einem einfachen Altartisch.

Vu en plan et en élévation, le petit bâtiment est pratiquement carré. Il contient les bancs soigneusement alignés et une table simple qui fait office d'autel.

KEN SUNGJIN MIN

SKM Architects
SKM Building
60–15 Samseong-dong, Gangnam-gu
Seoul 135–870
South Korea

Tel: +82 2 543 2027
Fax: +82 2 548 2027
E-mail: skm@skmarchitects.com
Web: www.skmarchitects.com

KEN SUNGJIN MIN received his B.Arch degree from the University of Southern California, School of Architecture (1989), and his M.Arch in Urban Design (MAUD) from the Harvard GSD (1993). He created SKM in 1996. The recent work of the firm includes the Kumgang Ananti Golf & Spa Resort (Gangwon-do, North Korea, 2008, published here); Lake Hills Suncheon Country Club (Suncheon, JeollaNam-do, South Korea, 2008, also published here); Asiana Airlines Weihai Point Golf & Spa Resort (Weihai, China, 2009); Asiana Airlines Laolaobay Golf & Spa Resort (Saipan, Marianas, USA, 2009); Arumdaun Golf & Spa Resort (Chungcheongnam-do, South Korea, 2009); Cheong Pyeong Village, 70 prestigious single-family houses (Gyeonggi-do, South Korea, in preliminary design); and the Anmyeun Island Newtown Master Plan (Chungcheongnam-do, South Korea, in design phase).

KEN SUNGJIN MIN machte seinen Bachelor in Architektur an der University of Southern California, School of Architecture (1989), und seinen Master in Architektur und Städtebau (MAUD) an der Harvard Graduate School of Design (1993). 1996 gründete er das Büro SKM. Zu dessen neueren Werken zählen das Kumgang Ananti Golf & Spa Resort (Gangwon-do, Nordkorea, 2008, hier veröffentlicht), Lake Hills Suncheon Country Club (Suncheon, JeollaNam-do, Südkorea, 2008, ebenfalls hier veröffentlicht), Asiana Airlines Weihai Point Golf & Spa Resort (Weihai, China, 2009), Asiana Airlines Laolaobay Golf & Spa Resort (Saipan, Marianas, USA, 2009), Arumdaun Golf & Spa Resort (Chungcheongnam-do, Südkorea, 2009), Cheong Pyeong Village, 70 anspruchsvolle Einfamilienhäuser (Gyeonggi-do, Südkorea, in der Vorplanung), und der Masterplan für Anmyeun Island Newtown (Chungcheongnam-do, Südkorea, in der Planung).

KEN SUNGJIN MIN a obtenu son B. Arch. de l'École d'architecture de l'université de Californie du Sud (1989) et son M. Arch. en urbanisme (MAUD) de l'Harvard GSD (1993). Il a créé SKM en 1996. Parmi ses récentes réalisations figurent le club de golf et spa de Kumgang Ananti (Gangwon-do, Corée du Nord, 2008, publié ici) ; le *country club* des collines du lac de Suncheon (Suncheon, JeollaNam-do, Corée du Sud, 2008, également publié ici) ; le golf et hôtel de séjour de Weihai Point des Asiana Airlines (Weihai, Chine, 2009) ; le golf et spa de Laolaobay des Asiana Airlines (Saipan, îles Marianne, États-Unis, 2009) ; le golf et spa d'Arumdaun (Chungcheongnam-do, Corée du Sud, 2009) ; le Cheong Pyeong Village, 70 résidences privées de luxe (Gyeonggi-do, Corée du Sud, en phase de conception), et le plan directeur de la ville nouvelle de l'île d'Anmyeun (Chungcheongnam-do, Corée du Sud, en phase de conception).

KUMGANG ANANTI GOLF & SPA RESORT

Gangwon-do, North Korea, 2008

Address: Kumgang Mountain, Gangwon-do, North Korea, +52 2 22 61 33 88, www.emersonpacific.co.kr
Area: 13 210 m². Client: Emerson Pacific Group. Cost: $24 million

This rather spectacular structure is surely the first in the Architecture Now! books to be located in North Korea, not generally known for its contemporary architecture.

Dieses beeindruckende Gebäude ist sicher das erste in der Buchreihe Architecture Now!, *das in Nordkorea steht – einem Land, das im Allgemeinen nicht für moderne Architektur bekannt ist.*

Cette réalisation assez spectaculaire est certainement la première construction à paraître dans Architecture Now! *qui vienne de Corée du Nord, un pays qui ne s'est pas fait remarquer jusque-là pour la qualité de son architecture contemporaine.*

The architect makes use of an over-arching roof, as seen in the section below. The overall plan approaches an organic design, combining curves, straight lines, and skewed angles.

Der Architekt entschied sich für ein überhängendes Dach, wie der Schnitt unten zeigt. Der Gesamtplan folgt einer organischen Gestaltung, einer Kombination aus Kurven, geraden Linien und schrägen Winkeln.

L'architecte a dessiné une toiture en-veloppante qui s'appuie sur des arcs (coupe ci-dessous). Le plan d'ensem-ble évoque une approche organique dans sa combinaison de courbes, de lignes droite et d'angles aigus.

Kumgang Mountain is admired in Korea as a beautiful natural location. The architect explains: "The key design issue in the **KUMGANG ANANTI GOLF & SPA RESORT** was the panoramic view created by the well-preserved natural environment. Instead of designing a resort for short-term use, it was designed to uphold the comparison to worldwide resorts when the North and South are unified." The master plan for the site put an emphasis on the preservation of the natural setting and the adaptation of the architecture to the natural topography. The hotels on the site all face Kumgang Mountain; and a skylight on the eastern side of the clubhouse, at the center of the site, and condominium building also face the summit. The use of concrete was minimized and a wooden post-and-beam structure employed. An exterior canopy echoes the interior lobby with its glulam arches.

Die Bergregion Kumgang gilt in Korea als besonders schönes Naturgebiet. Der Architekt erklärt: „Das entscheidende Thema beim **KUMGANG ANANTI GOLF & SPA RESORT** war die Panoramasicht auf diese geschützte, natürliche Umgebung. Wir haben es nicht als Erholungsgebiet für kurzfristige Nutzung geplant, sondern so, dass es einem weltweiten Vergleich standhält, wenn Nord- und Südkorea einmal vereinigt werden." Der Masterplan für das Gelände legte das Schwergewicht auf die Erhaltung der natürlichen Umgebung und die Anpassung der Architektur an die gegebene Topografie. Alle Hotels auf dem Gelände sind zum Berg orientiert, ein Oberlicht an der Ostseite des Klubhauses im Zentrum des Geländes und die Wohnanlage geben auch den Blick auf den Gipfel frei. Ein äußeres Vordach nimmt die Form der Eingangshalle mit Schichtholzbögen auf.

Les monts Kumgang sont considérés en Corée comme un magnifique cadre naturel. Selon l'architecte : « L'enjeu essentiel du **GOLF & SPA HÔTEL KUMGANG ANANTI** était de conserver la vue panoramique de cet environnement naturel préservé. Au lieu de se contenter d'un *resort* pour séjours de brève durée, le projet a été conçu pour soutenir la comparaison avec les grandes installations touristiques internationales. » Le plan directeur du site met donc l'accent sur la préservation du cadre de la nature et l'adaptation de l'architecture à la topographie. Les hôtels font tous face aux monts Kumgang ainsi que l'immeuble d'appartements et la verrière sur la façade orientale du *club-house*. Le béton reste discret et la structure est à poutres et poteaux de bois. Un auvent à grands arcs de lamellé-collé fait écho à la structure du hall.

The elegant, asymmetrical arch of the dining area seen above allows for fully glazed walls on one side.

Die im Foto oben sichtbare elegante, asymmetrische Wölbung des Speisesaals ermöglichte die geschosshohe Verglasung auf einer Seite.

L'élégant arc asymétrique de la salle à manger (ci-dessus) a permis de créer un mur de façade entièrement vitré.

The laminated arches over the main space, seen to the right and on the left page, give a feeling of considerable space and openness.

Die rechts und auf der linken Seite sichtbaren laminierten Holzbögen über dem großen Raum lassen ihn sehr geräumig und offen erscheinen.

Les arcs en lamellé-collé du hall principal (à droite et page de gauche) créent un sentiment très fort d'ouverture et de volume.

Landscaped pond areas enrich the view from inside the building, while the wooden arches are continued on the exterior to form a canopy.

Landschaftlich gestaltete Bereiche mit Teichen machen den Blick nach draußen interessant. Die hölzernen Bogenbinder setzen sich außerhalb fort und bilden ein schützendes Vordach.

Des bassins paysagés agrémentent la vue à partir de l'intérieur du bâtiment. Les arcs se poursuivent à l'extérieur pour constituer un auvent.

LAKE HILLS SUNCHEON COUNTRY CLUB

Suncheon, JeollaNam-do, South Korea, 2008

Address: 54 Haengjeong-ri, Juam-myeon, Suncheon-si, JeollaNam-do, South Korea, www.lakehillssuncheon.com
Area: 16 311 m². Client: Lake Hills Golf & Resorts Group
Cost: $17 million

The architects explain that this complex is "inspired by the region's rolling hills as well as the history and traditions of the area." A division between the natural landscape and the architecture in the form of an earthen berm marks the perimeter of the design. Concrete elements are buried partially in the earth while prefabricated glulam post-and-beam buildings "reinterpret traditional Korean architecture, providing a light and spacious foil to the earthen structures beneath them." The main public spaces—including the lobby, restaurant, and lounge—are set in the wooden volumes. Skylights and curtain walls make "visual connections with the sky and surrounding hillside topographies."

Die Architekten erklären, dass diese Anlage „von der Topografie der hügeligen Region wie auch von ihrer Geschichte und Tradition inspiriert wurde". Eine Trennung der natürlichen Landschaft von der Architektur in Form eines umlaufenden Erdwalls kennzeichnet diese Planung. Ein Teil der Betonelemente wurde im Erdboden verborgen, während vorgefertigte Ständerkonstruktionen aus Schichtholz „die traditionelle koreanische Architektur neu interpretieren sowie eine leichte und großzügige Erweiterung der darunter im Boden verhafteten Strukturen bilden". Die wichtigen öffentlichen Räume – zu denen die Lobby, das Restaurant und die Lounge gehören – befinden sich in den hölzernen Volumen. Oberlichter und Vorhangfassaden bieten „visuelle Verbindungen zum Himmel und der Topografie des bergigen Umfelds."

Selon les architectes, ce complexe « s'inspire des vallonnements de la région mais aussi de l'histoire et des traditions du lieu ». Une berme de terre suit le périmètre du projet et marque la séparation entre le paysage naturel et l'architecture. Les éléments en béton sont en partie enterrés dans le sol. Les ossatures à poutres et poteaux en lamellé-collé préfabriquées « réinterprètent l'architecture traditionnelle coréenne, tout en offrant des espaces et un éclairage généreux aux parties enterrées ». Les principaux espaces collectifs – dont le hall d'accueil, le restaurant et le salon – sont répartis dans ces volumes en bois. Des verrières et des murs rideaux établissent des « connexions visuelles avec le ciel et la topographie des collines environnantes ».

An aerial view of the complex with its curving roofs visible in the mountain setting.

Luftaufnahme der Anlage mit ihren gekrümmten Dächern inmitten der bergigen Umgebung.

Vue aérienne du complexe et de ses toits incurvés dans son cadre de montagnes.

The curved roofs are seen in both the section drawings (below) and the image above. There is a hint of reference to tradition in this architecture without any sense of "pastiche," or imitation of the old.

Die gekrümmten Dächer sind in den Schnitten (unten) wie auch auf dem Foto oben sichtbar. Auch ist in dieser Architektur ein Bezug zum traditionellen Bauen erkennbar, ohne dass sie zu einem „Pastiche" oder einer Imitation des Alten geworden ist.

La courbure des toits vue à la fois dans les coupes ci-dessous et l'image ci-dessus. On note un soupçon de référence à la tradition dans cette architecture sans aucune tentative de « pastiche » ou d'imitation de l'ancien.

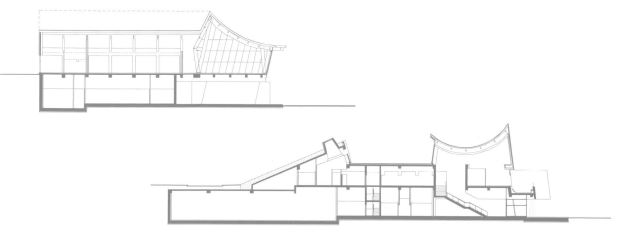

The curving arch of the roof
might bring to mind some temple
structures or even naval designs of
another era.

*Die Bogenkrümmung des Dachs
erinnert an Tempelbauten, sogar an
Schiffe aus einem anderen Zeitalter.*

*L'arc incurvé de la toiture peut rappe-
ler certains temples ou même des co-
ques de navires d'une autre époque.*

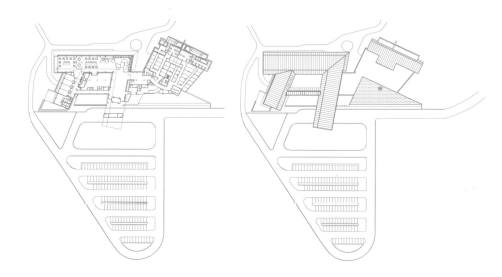

Windows allow light in at the top of the arching roof. Above, plans show the angled composition in its entirety.

Fenster im oberen Bereich des gekrümmten Dachs lassen natürliches Licht ein. Oben: Die Grundrisse zeigen die schräg ausgerichtete Gesamtkomposition.

Des fenêtres entre le sommet de la toiture et le mur de façade assurent l'éclairage. Ci-dessus, plan d'ensemble des installations.

MURMAN ARKITEKTER

Murman Arkitekter AB
Peter Myndes backe 12
11846 Stockholm
Sweden

Tel: +46 8 462 14 50
Fax: +46 8 462 14 89
E-mail: info@murman.se
Web: www.murman.se

HANS MURMAN was born in 1947 in Falun, Sweden. He graduated as an architect from KTH in Stockholm in 1975 and worked for 10 years at Hans Borgström Arkitektkontor, before creating his own practice. He founded his firm in 1985 with projects in Swedish ski resorts. The partners of Murman Arkitekter are Hans Murman, Ulla Alberts, Helena Andersson, and Wivian Eidsaunet. Based in Stockholm, the firm has a staff of 30 people (2010). **ULLA ALBERTS** worked with Hans Murman on the Tusen Restaurant (Ramundberget, 2007–08, published here). She was born in 1965 in Stockholm and graduated from the CTH/KTH in 1990, joining Murman Arkitekter in 1993. The firm won a 2005 competition for the Saimi Parliament Building (Kiruna, due to start construction). Other work includes a wooden office building for the Alpine World Championship (Åre, 2007); 300 student residences (Hammarby sjöstad, Stockholm, 2008); the Juniper House (Katthammarsvik, Gotland, 2008); and vacation houses in Ramundberget (1985–2010), all in Sweden.

HANS MURMAN wurde 1947 in Falun, Schweden, geboren. Er beendete 1975 sein Architekturstudium an der Kungliga Tekniska Högskolan (KTH) in Stockholm und arbeitete zehn Jahre bei Hans Borgström Arkitektkontor, bis er 1985 sein eigenes Büro mit Projekten in den schwedischen Skigebieten gründete. Partner der Firma Murman Arkitekter sind Hans Murman, Ulla Alberts, Helena Andersson und Wivian Eidsaunet. Das in Stockholm ansässige Büro hat 30 Mitarbeiter (2010). **ULLA ALBERTS** arbeitete mit Hans Murman am Restaurant Tusen (Ramundberget, 2007–08, hier veröffentlicht). Sie wurde 1965 in Stockholm geboren und beendete 1990 ihr Studium an der CTH/KTH; 1993 trat sie bei Murman Arkitekter ein. Das Büro gewann 2005 einen Wettbewerb für das Parlamentsgebäude Saimi (Kiruna, Baubeginn demnächst). Weitere Werke sind ein Bürogebäude in Holz für die alpinen Weltmeisterschaften (Åre, 2007), 300 Studentenwohnungen (Hammarby Sjöstad, Stockholm, 2008), das Juniper House (Katthammarsvik, Gotland, 2008) sowie Ferienhäuser in Ramundberget (1985–2010), alle in Schweden.

HANS MURMAN, né à 1947 à Falun (Suède), est architecte diplômé de KTH (Stockholm) depuis 1975. Il a travaillé pendant dix ans chez Hans Borgström Arkitektkontor avant de créer sa propre agence en 1985 à l'occasion de projets de stations de ski en Suède. Ses partenaires sont Hans Murman, Ulla Alberts, Helena Andersson et Wivian Eidsaunet. Basée à Stockholm, l'agence possède une trentaine de collaborateurs (2010). **ULLA ALBERTS** a travaillé avec Hans Murman sur le projet du restaurant Tusen (Ramundberget, 2007–08, publié ici). Née en 1965 à Stockholm, elle est diplômée de CTH/KTH (1990) et a rejoint Murman Arkitekter en 1993. En 2005, l'agence a remporté le concours pour l'immeuble du parlement de Saimi (Kiruna, construction prochaine). Parmi leurs autres réalisations, toutes en Suède, figurent un immeuble de bureaux en bois pour les Championnats du monde alpin (Åre, 2007) ; 300 logements pour étudiants (Hammarby sjöstad, Stockholm, 2008) ; la maison Juniper (Katthammarsvik, Gotland, 2008) et des résidences de vacances à Ramundberget (1985–2010).

TUSEN RESTAURANT

Ramundberget, Sweden, 2007–08

Address: Ramundbergets Fjällgård, 84097 Bruksvallarna, Sweden, +46 684 66 88, www.ramundberget.se
Area: 340 m². Client: Ramundberget Alpina AB. Cost: € 1 million.
Collaboration: Ulla Blomberg, Ylva Bäckström

Seen in its natural, wintery setting, the restaurant has something of the reminiscence of an ancient campsite.

Inmitten der winterlichen Landschaft erinnert das Restaurant an einen altertümlichen Lagerplatz.

Dans son cadre hivernal naturel, le restaurant évoque presque un campement.

The architects sought "a building in harmony with nature—all year round and day and night." Because birch is the only tree that grows at the altitude of the restaurant, they employed this wood. Full-height tree trunks frame the entrance. The architects point out that these trunks can be easily replaced, as required, and that they protect the underlying façade. "By choosing wooden construction," say the architects, "we achieved low weight. It is a prefabricated building with a small impact on the ground and this was also a way to minimize the building time." White birch plywood is on the interior. The architects conclude: "The interior is both spacious and intimate. Each window in the restaurant frames a unique view on both levels. The upper windows are intended to allow visitors to experience the stars and the northern lights. The interior colors are inspired by moss, lichens, and cloudberries." The restaurant has its own sewage treatment system and gets water from a ground spring. Air and water heat pumps are used, with outside electrical sources employed only on very cold days.

Die Architekten wollten ein Gebäude errichten, das „das ganze Jahr über sowie Tag und Nacht in Harmonie mit der Natur" ist. Weil die Birke der einzige Baum ist, der am hoch gelegenen Standort des Restaurants wächst, verwendeten sie dieses Holz. Baumstämme in ganzer Höhe umgeben den Eingang. Die Architekten weisen darauf hin, dass diese Stämme bei Bedarf leicht ersetzt werden können und dass sie die dahinter liegende Fassade schützen. „Durch die Wahl einer Holzkonstruktion", sagen sie, „erreichten wir ein geringes Gewicht. Es handelt sich um ein vorgefertigtes Gebäude mit geringen Auswirkungen auf den Boden, und das war auch ein Weg, um die Bauzeit zu reduzieren." Innen ist der Bau mit weißem Birkenfurnier verkleidet. Abschließend bemerken die Architekten: „Das Innere ist sowohl geräumig als auch intim. Alle Fenster auf beiden Ebenen des Restaurants bieten einzigartige Ausblicke. Aus den Fenstern im Obergeschoss können Besucher die Sterne und das Nordlicht beobachten. Die Farbskala im Innern wurde von Moos, Flechten und den Moltebeeren inspiriert." Das Restaurant hat eine eigene Wasseraufbereitungsanlage und erhält Wasser aus einer unterirdischen Quelle. Luft- und Wärmepumpen sind im Einsatz; nur an sehr kalten Tagen liefern andere Energiequellen Strom.

Les architectes voulaient créer un « bâtiment qui soit en harmonie avec la nature, toute l'année, de jour comme de nuit ». Ils ont choisi le bouleau, seule essence d'arbre à pousser à cette altitude. Des troncs entiers en encadrent l'entrée. Ils peuvent facilement être remplacés si nécessaire et protègent la façade. « En choisissant le principe d'une construction en bois, expliquent les architectes, nous avons pu réduire le poids de celle-ci. C'est un bâtiment préfabriqué qui n'exerce qu'un faible impact sur le sol et n'a demandé qu'une durée de chantier réduite. » L'intérieur est en contreplaqué de bouleau blanc. « L'intérieur est à la fois spacieux et intime », poursuivent-ils : « Chaque fenêtre cadre une vue spécifique à deux niveaux. Les fenêtres en partie haute donnent aux clients l'occasion de découvrir les étoiles et la lumière du Nord. Les coloris retenus pour l'intérieur sont inspirés par la mousse, les lichens et les ronciers. » Le restaurant dispose de son propre système de traitement des eaux usées et tire son eau d'une source naturelle. Le chauffage est assuré par des pompes thermiques à air et à eau et l'appoint de l'électricité n'est nécessaire que par les jours de grand froid.

Seen from a distance, the structure looks a bit like a hut that might not have been completed, but it fits, in any case, in the forested site.

Aus der Ferne betrachtet, wirkt der Bau fast wie eine Hütte, die nicht vollendet wurde, und passt auf jeden Fall in das bewaldete Gelände.

Vu de loin, le bâtiment fait penser à une hutte non encore achevée mais bien intégrée à son site boisé.

The plan of the structure is entirely circular with a broad opening on one side.

Der Grundriss des Gebäudes ist vollkommen kreisförmig mit einer weiten Öffnung auf einer Seite.

Le plan du bâtiment est circulaire, mais reste entièrement ouvert sur un côté.

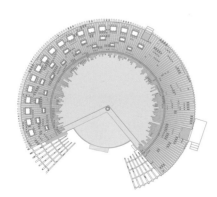 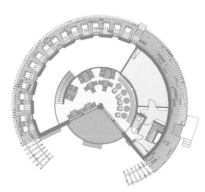 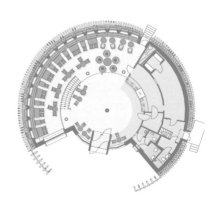

S House ▶

ROLF CARL NIMMRICHTER

Nimmrichter CDA Ltd.
Forchstr. 279
8008 Zurich
Switzerland

Tel: +41 44 262 0606
E-mail: rcn@nimmrichter.com
Web: www.nimmrichter.com

Born in 1968, **ROLF CARL NIMMRICHTER** received his diploma from the ETH in Zurich in 1996. After that he was a research and teaching assistant at the ETH, working with professors Paul Meyer and Marc Angélil. He also worked for Interbrand Zintzmeyer and Lux (Zurich), Bétrix & Consolascio (Erlenbach), and with Machado & Silvetti Associates (Boston). Since 1999 he has worked as an independent architect and corporate designer in Zurich. Recent work includes the S House (Dietlikon, 2008, published here) and the competition entry for the Werkhof St. Gallen (2009), both in Switzerland.

Der 1968 geborene **ROLF CARL NIMMRICHTER** machte 1996 sein Diplom an der Eidgenössischen Technischen Hochschule Zürich. Danach war er als Assistent der Professoren Paul Meyer und Marc Angélil an der ETH in Forschung und Lehre tätig. Er arbeitete auch bei Interbrand Zintzmeyer und Lux (Zürich), Bétrix & Consolascio (Erlenbach) und Machado & Silvetti Associates (Boston). Seit 1999 ist er selbstständiger Architekt und Designer in Zürich. Zu seinen aktuellen Arbeiten zählen das Haus S (Dietlikon, 2008, hier veröffentlicht) sowie der Wettbewerbsentwurf für den Werkhof St. Gallen (2009), beide in der Schweiz.

Né en 1968, **ROLF CARL NIMMRICHTER** est diplômé de l'ETH de Zurich (1996). Il a été assistant de recherche et d'enseignement à l'ETH, travaillant avec les professeurs Paul Meyer et Marc Angélil. Il a également travaillé pour Interbrand Zintzmeyer et Lux (Zurich), Bétrix & Consolascio (Erlenbach) et Machado & Silvetti Associates (Boston). Depuis 1999, il est architecte et designer indépendant à Zurich. En Suisse, il a récemment réalisé la maison S (Dietlikon, 2008, publiée ici) et a participé au concours pour le Werkhof de St. Gallen (2009).

S HOUSE

Dietlikon, Switzerland, 2008

*Address: Eichenbühlweg, 8004 Dietlikon, Switzerland
Area: 160 m². Client: not disclosed. Cost: not disclosed*

The house has slightly staggered or notched levels that make room for terraces. The horizontal wood siding gives a modern appearance.

Die Ebenen dieses Hauses sind leicht gestaffelt oder offen gelassen, um Platz für Terrassen zu gewinnen. Die horizontale Holzverkleidung gibt ihm ein modernes Aussehen.

La maison présente des niveaux légèrement décalés ou découpés qui permettent d'intégrer des balcons et des loggias. Le bardage horizontal en bois lui confère une apparence très moderne.

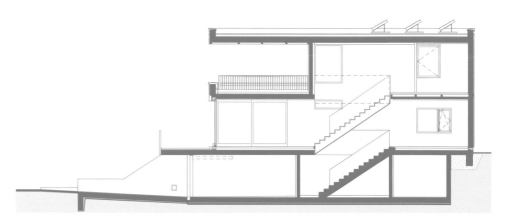

The plan of the house is slightly
inclined on the side of the small
swimming pool, seen above.

Der Grundriss des Hauses ist,
wie oben erkennbar, auf der Seite
des kleinen Swimmingpools leicht
abgewinkelt.

Le plan de la maison marque un
léger retrait devant une petite
piscine (ci-dessus).

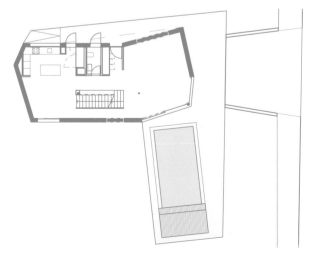

P 334

The architect states that the "box is the spatially defining element" for this detached house in Dietlikon on a site where there was already a house and pool. Rolf Nimmrichter was awarded this commission against the competition of a modular house manufacturer. The outside of the three-story house is faced in open-jointed cedar batten cladding. A garage is located in the basement, while the ground floor has a large living, cooking, and dining area. Three bedrooms and a recessed balcony are located on the upper floor. The architect also designed the interiors with their chestnut facing. The floor is finished in dark, rough concrete. The architect states: "The building is Minergie® certified, a registered quality label for low-energy buildings. The energy concept includes making use of the neighboring house's existing heating system and using solar panels to heat water for both houses."

Der Architekt erklärt, dass „die Kiste das raumbildende Element" dieses frei stehenden Hauses sei. Es wurde auf einem Grundstück in Dietlikon errichtet, wo sich bereits ein Haus und ein Swimmingpool befanden. Rolf Nimmrichter erhielt diesen Auftrag in Konkurrenz zu einer Fertigbaufirma. Außen ist das dreigeschossige Gebäude mit in Abständen verlegten Zedernlatten verkleidet. Im Untergeschoss befindet sich die Garage; im Erdgeschoss liegen ein großer Wohnraum, die Küche und der Essbereich, im Obergeschoss drei Schlafzimmer und eine Loggia. Nimmrichter entwarf auch die Innenausstattung mit Verkleidung aus Kastanienholz. Der Boden besteht aus rauem, dunklem Beton. Der Architekt erklärt: „Das Gebäude ist Minergie®-zertifiziert, eine eingetragene Qualitätsbezeichnung für Niedrigenergiehäuser. Zum Energiekonzept gehört die Nutzung der bestehenden Heizanlage des Nachbarhauses und von Solarzellen zur Warmwasserversorgung beider Häuser."

La « boîte est l'élément spatial qui définit » cette maison à Dietlikon, explique l'architecte. Le terrain était déjà occupé par une autre résidence et une piscine. Rolf Nimmrichter a remporté cette commande contre un fabricant de logements modulaires. L'extérieur de la maison de trois niveaux est habillé d'un bardage en lattes de cèdre à joint ouvert. Un garage occupe le sous-sol tandis que le rez-de-chaussée est réservé à un vaste séjour et une zone cuisine/repas. Les trois chambres et un balcon en loggia se répartissent l'étage. L'architecte a également conçu l'intérieur qu'il a habillé de noyer. Les sols sont en béton brut à finition de couleur sombre. « La maison est certifiée Minergie®, un label de qualité pour les constructions à faible consommation d'énergie. L'approche a consisté ici à se brancher sur le système de chauffage de la maison voisine existante et à utiliser des panneaux solaires pour la production d'eau chaude des deux résidences », précise l'architecte.

Contrasting surfaces and lighting enliven the interior appearance of the house.

Kontrastierende Oberflächen und Beleuchtung bereichern die Innenausstattung des Hauses.

Les surfaces contrastées et l'éclairage étudié animent l'atmosphère intérieure de la maison.

With its slightly irregular albeit rectilinear plan, the interior of the house provides for a number of spatial surprises, as seen in the stairway above, for example.

Mit seinem leicht unregelmäßigen, aber geradlinigen Grundriss bietet das Haus im Innern überraschende Raumwirkungen, wie z. B. im Treppenhaus (oben) erkennbar.

À travers son plan légèrement irrégulier bien que rectiligne, l'intérieur de la maison réserve un certain nombre de surprises spatiales, comme cet escalier par exemple.

VALERIO OLGIATI

Valerio Olgiati
Senda Stretga 1
7017 Flims
Switzerland

Tel: +41 81 650 33 11
Fax: +41 81 650 33 12
E-mail: mail@olgiati.net
Web: www.olgiati.net

VALERIO OLGIATI was born in Chur, Switzerland, in 1958. He studied architecture at the ETH in Zurich, and in 1986 he created his own architectural office in that city. From 1993 to 1995 he collaborated with Frank Escher in Los Angeles. Escher is a specialist in the work of the architect John Lautner (1911–94). Since 1998 he has been teaching at the ETH Zurich and has served as guest lecturer at the Architectural Association (AA) in London and at Cornell University (Ithaca, New York). Since 2002, he has been a full Professor at the Accademia di Architettura at the Università della Svizzera Italiana in Mendrisio (Switzerland). In 2009 he held the Kenzo Tange Chair at Harvard University (Cambridge, Massachusetts). He has built a number of private homes and participated in competitions for the National Palace Museum (Taiwan, 2004, finalist) and the Learning Center of the EPFL (Lausanne, Switzerland), among others. Three of his recent projects, the Peak Goernergrat, the University of Lucerne, and the Perm Museum XXI were competition-winning entries. He completed the Office in Flims (2007, published here), before opening his new office there in 2008, and completing the Swiss National Park Visitor Center the same year (Zernez, Switzerland, 2006–08).

VALERIO OLGIATI wurde 1958 in Chur, Schweiz, geboren und studierte Architektur an der Eidgenössischen Technischen Hochschule in Zürich. 1986 gründete er dort sein eigenes Büro. Von 1993 bis 1995 arbeitete er zusammen mit Frank Escher in Los Angeles. Escher ist Spezialist für die Bauten des Architekten John Lautner (1911–94). Olgiati lehrt seit 1998 an der ETH Zürich und war Gastdozent an der Architectural Association (AA) in London und an der Cornell University (Ithaca, New York). Seit 2002 hat er eine ordentliche Professur an der Accademia di Architettura der Università della Svizzera Italiana in Mendrisio (Tessin, Schweiz). 2009 hatte er den Kenzo-Tange-Lehrstuhl an der Harvard University (Cambridge, Massachusetts) inne. Er hat zahlreiche Einfamilienhäuser gebaut und an vielen Wettbewerben teilgenommen, z. B. (als Finalist) für das National Palace Museum (Taiwan, 2004) und das Lernzentrum der École Polytechnique Fédérale Lausanne (Schweiz). Drei seiner aktuellen Projekte, der Peak Gornergrat, die Universität Luzern und das Perm Museum XXI waren preisgekrönte Wettbewerbsentwürfe. Kürzlich ausgeführte Bauten sind das Bürogebäude in Flims (2007, hier veröffentlicht), worin er 2008 sein eigenes neues Büro eröffnete, sowie das Besucherzentrum im Schweizer Nationalpark (Zernez, 2006–08).

VALERIO OLGIATI, né à Chur (Suisse) en 1958, a étudié l'architecture à l'ETH de Zurich où il ouvre son agence en 1986. De 1993 à 1995, il collabore avec Frank Escher à Los Angeles, spécialiste de l'œuvre de l'architecte John Lautner (1911–94). Depuis 1998 il enseigne à l'ETH et comme conférencier invité à l'Architectural Association de Londres (AA) et à l'université Cornell (Ithaca, New York). Depuis 2002, il est professeur titulaire à l'Accademia di Architettura de l'Università della Svizzera Italiana à Mendrisio et a été nommé en 2009 titulaire de la Kenzo Tange Chair à l'université Harvard (Cambridge, Massachusetts). Il a réalisé un certain nombre de résidences privées et participé à des concours comme celui du musée du Palais national (Taïwan, 2004, finaliste) et du Centre d'apprentissage de l'EPFL à Lausanne. Trois de ses projets récents, le Pic de Gornergrat, l'université de Lucerne et le Museum XXI de Perm (Russie) ont été remportés à l'issue d'un concours. Il a achevé ses bureaux à Flims (2007, publiés ici) avant d'y ouvrir sa nouvelle agence en 2008 et d'achever le Centre d'accueil des visiteurs du Parc national suisse de Zernez la même année (Zernez, Suisse, 2006–08).

OFFICE
Flims, Switzerland, 2007

Address: Senda Stretga 1, 7017 Flims, Switzerland, +41 81 650 33 11, www.olgiati.net
Area: 165 m² (office); 40 m² (archives, storage). Client: Valerio Olgiati. Cost: not disclosed
Collaboration: Nathan Ghiringhelli (Project Manager), Nikolai Müller, Mario Beeli

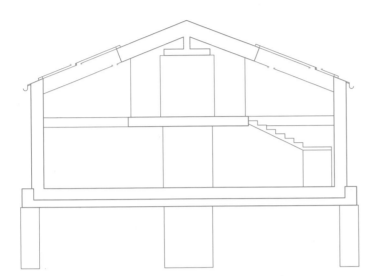
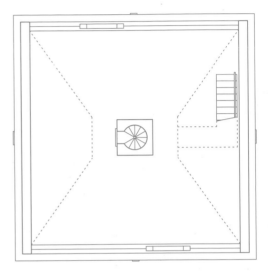

With its basic square plan and inclined roof, the office of Valerio Olgiati is not obviously in contrast with the historic environment of Flims.

Mit quadratischem Grundriss und geneigtem Dach bildet das Bürohaus von Valerio Olgiati keinen erkennbaren Gegensatz zu der historischen Bebauung von Flims.

De plan carré et logés sous un toit à double pente, les bureaux de Valerio Olgiati n'ont pas cherché le contraste avec l'environnement historique de Flims.

The basic materials of this structure, the architect's own offices, are black painted fir, concrete, and copper. The Olgiati family is from the Dado section of Flims. Rudolf Olgiati (1910–95), the father of Valerio Olgiati, acquired the main house, built in 1771, in 1931 and worked on it throughout his career. When Valerio Olgiati inherited the house at the death of his father, he built his own **ARCHITECTURAL OFFICE** on the site of the family barn. Lifted off the ground on concrete pillars, the office maintains the basic lines of local architecture and is made of dark wood, but otherwise assumes a modern presence and definition of space. Valerio Olgiati published both the new office space and the older residence in a very personal book, "Dado—Built and Inhabited by Rudolf Olgiati and Valerio Olgiati," in conjunction with an exhibition on the property at the Gelbe House in Flims (December 13, 2009–April 11, 2010).

Die Hauptmaterialien für dieses Gebäude, das eigene Büro des Architekten, sind schwarz gestrichene Fichte, Beton und Kupfer. Die Familie Olgiati stammt aus dem Stadtteil Dado in Flims. Rudolf Olgiati (1910–95), der Vater von Valerio Olgiati, erwarb 1931 das 1771 erbaute Haupthaus und baute sein ganzes Leben lang daran. Als Valerio Olgiati das Haus nach dem Tod seines Vaters erbte, errichtete er dort sein eigenes **ARCHITEKTURBÜRO** auf dem Grundstück der Scheune. Das auf Betonstützen aufgeständerte Gebäude folgt weitgehend den Formen der örtlichen Architektur und ist aus dunklem Holz, zeigt aber ansonsten ein modernes Erscheinungsbild und Raumgefüge. Valerio Olgiati veröffentlichte sowohl den neuen Bürobau als auch das alte Wohnhaus in einem sehr persönlichen Buch, „Dado – gebaut und bewohnt von Rudolf Olgiati und Valerio Olgiati", aus Anlass einer Ausstellung über das Anwesen im Gelben Haus in Flims (13. Dezember 2009–11. April 2010).

Les matériaux de base de cette construction – les propres bureaux de l'architecte – sont le sapin teinté en noir, le béton et le cuivre. La famille Olgiati est issue de ce quartier de Flims nommé Dado. Rudolf Olgiati (1910–95), le père de Valerio, avait acquis en 1931 une maison datant de 1771 et travaillé à son aménagement tout au long de sa carrière. Lorsque Valerio en a hérité, il a construit le **BUREAU DE SON AGENCE** sur le site de l'ancienne grange familiale. Suspendu au-dessus du sol sur des piliers de béton, l'ensemble respecte le style de l'architecture locale en bois sombre tout en affirmant une présence et une définition de l'espace très actuelles. Valerio Olgiati a présenté ses nouveaux bureaux et l'ancienne maison dans un livre très personnel : *Dado – Built and Inhabited by Rudolf Olgiati and Valerio Olgiati* en parallèle à une exposition sur le projet de la maison jaune de Flims (13 décembre 2009–11 avril 2010).

The dark wood space is enlivened
by skylights and large windows.

Der dunkle, holzverkleidete Raum
wird durch Oberlichter und große
Fenster belebt.

Le grand volume sombre est animé
par des verrières et de grandes
fenêtres.

There is a willful contrast inside the office between light and dark— between the opaque dark wood surfaces and the large bands of glazing.

Im Büro wurde bewusst ein Kontrast zwischen Hell und Dunkel, zwischen den undurchlässigen, dunklen Holzflächen und den langen Fensterbändern geschaffen.

À l'intérieur, le contraste est volontaire entre le clair et le sombre, les plans de bois foncés et les grands bandeaux d'ouvertures.

ONIX

Onix
Papiermolenlaan 3–15
9721 Groningen
The Netherlands

Tel: +31 50 529 02 52
E-mail: info@onix.nl
Web: www.onix.nl

ALEX VAN DE BELD was born in Leeuwarden, the Netherlands, in 1963 and graduated from the Academy of Architecture in Groningen in 1991. He was a project architect at Karelse van der Meer Architects (1987–94) and a cofounder of Onix, the Netherlands, in 1994. He was also a cofounder and partner of Onix Sweden (2005). **HAIKO MEIJER** was born in Appingedam, the Netherlands, in 1961. He also graduated from the Academy of Architecture in Groningen in 1991. From 1987 to 1994 he was a project architect at Gunnar Daan Architecture before cofounding Onix, the Netherlands, and Onix Sweden. Their work includes a Road Bridge (Sneek, an OAK project, Onix/Achterbosch Architecture, 2008); a Private School for Practical Training (Assen, 2009); Egenes Park (70 houses, kindergarten, garage, Stavanger, Norway, 2009); and the Plank Chimney House (Bosschenhoofd, 2009, published here), all in the Netherlands unless stated otherwise.

ALEX VAN DE BELD wurde 1963 in Leeuwarden, Niederlande, geboren und studierte bis 1991 an der Akademie für Architektur in Groningen. Er war Projektarchitekt bei Karelse van der Meer Architects (1987–94), 1994 Mitgründer von Onix Niederlande sowie 2005 Mitgründer und Partner von Onix Schweden. **HAIKO MEIJER** wurde 1961 in Appingedam, Niederlande, geboren und machte ebenfalls 1991 seinen Abschluss an der Akademie für Architektur in Groningen. Von 1987 bis 1994 war er Projektarchitekt bei Gunnar Daan Architecture, bevor er Onix Niederlande und Onix Schweden mitgründete. Zu ihren Werken zählen eine Straßenbrücke (Sneek, ein Projekt von OAK Architekten, Onix/Achterbosch Architecture, 2008), eine Privatschule für praktische Ausbildung (Assen, 2009), Egenes Park, eine Anlage mit 70 Häusern, Kindergarten und Parkhaus (Stavanger, Norwegen, 2009), sowie das Plankenhuis (Bosschenhoofd, 2009, hier veröffentlicht), alle in den Niederlanden, sofern nicht anders angegeben.

ALEX VAN DE BELD, né à Leeuwarden aux Pays-Bas en 1963, est diplômé de l'Académie d'architecture de Groningue (1991). Il a été architecte de projet chez Karelse van der Meer Architects (1987–94) et est l'un des deux fondateurs de l'agence Onix en 1994 aux Pays-Bas, puis d'Onix Sweden en 2005. **HAIKO MEIJER**, né à Appingedam (Pays-Bas) en 1961, est également diplômé de l'Académie d'architecture de Groningue (1991). De 1987 à 1994, il a été architecte de projet chez Gunnar Daan Architecture avant de participer à la fondation d'Onix, aux Pays-Bas et en Suède. Parmi leurs réalisations, la plupart aux Pays-Bas : un pont routier (projet Sneek an OAK, Onix/Achterbosch Architecture, 2008) ; une école privée de formation pratique (Assen, 2009) ; Egenes Park (70 maisons, jardin d'enfant et garage, Stavanger, Norvège, 2009) et la maison à la cheminée de planches (Plankenhuis, Bosschenhoofd, 2009, publiée ici).

PLANK CHIMNEY HOUSE

Bosschenhoofd, The Netherlands, 2009

Address: not disclosed
Area: 600 m². Client: not disclosed. Cost: not disclosed

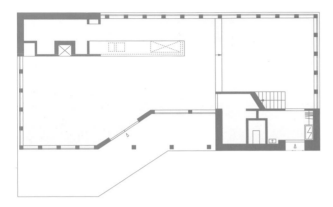

The basically rectangular plan is notched to allow for terraces or setbacks. Wood is present everywhere, although somewhat less near the ground-level, full-height glazing.

Der im Grunde rechtwinklige Grundriss hat Ausschnitte für Terrassen oder Rücksprünge. Holz ist überall vorhanden, wenn auch weniger im Erdgeschoss, das geschosshoch verglast wurde.

Le plan essentiellement rectangulaire est découpé pour laisser la place à des terrasses ou des retraits. Le bois est omniprésent, uniquement interrompu par de grandes baies vitrées toute hauteur.

A site plan and a general view of
the house show its terrace and
its somewhat unexpected vertical
wood cladding.

*Der Lageplan und die Gesamtansicht
des Hauses zeigen die Terrasse und
die etwas ungewöhnliche vertikale
Holzverkleidung.*

*Un plan du terrain et une vue
d'ensemble de la maison montrent
la terrasse et le bardage de bois
vertical assez inattendu.*

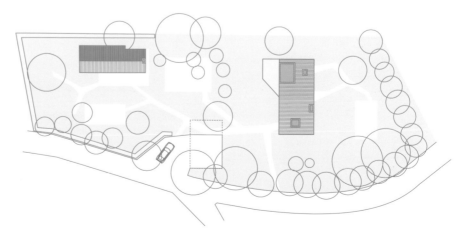

The site for this house is set between a wooded area on the south and agricultural land to the north. The architects explain the name of the house as follows: "The plank played an important role as the smallest element in the development of the house. Planks were used to make the shuttering into which concrete was poured. This concrete then acquired the imprint of the planks. The same planks were also used for the façade, for the finishing of the roof, and for the interior walls." The interior paneling was put in place by the clients themselves.

Das Grundstück dieses Hauses liegt zwischen einem Waldgebiet im Süden und landwirtschaftlich genutztem Gelände im Norden. Die Architekten erklären den Namen des Hauses wie folgt: „Die Planke, das Brett, spielte eine wichtige Rolle als kleinstes Element bei der Entwicklung dieses Hauses. Bretter wurden für die Schalung benutzt, in die der Beton gegossen wurde. Dieser nahm dann den Abdruck der Bretter auf. Die gleichen Bretter wurden auch für die Fassade verwendet, für den Dachausbau und für die Innenwände." Die Innenverkleidung wurde von den Bauherren selbst angebracht.

Le terrain de cette maison est situé entre une zone boisée au sud et des terres agricoles au nord. Les architectes expliquent ainsi son nom curieux : « Les planches ont joué ici un rôle important en tant que plus petit élément possible utilisé dans la mise au point de la maison. Elles ont servi à fabriquer les coffrages dans lesquels le béton a été coulé, béton qui a conservé l'empreinte de leur grain. Les mêmes ont aussi servi à la façade, au recouvrement de la toiture et aux murs intérieurs. » L'habillage de l'intérieur a été mis en place par le client lui-même.

Vertical planks are also used inside the house. The fireplace is made of rough concrete. The steps and floor are made of the same, but smoother, material.

Die vertikale Bretterverkleidung wurde auch innerhalb des Hauses verwendet. Der Kamin ist aus grobem Beton. Die Stufen und der Boden sind aus dem gleichen, aber glatteren Material.

On retrouve l'habillage de bois vertical à l'intérieur de la maison. La cheminée est en béton brut. Les escaliers et les sols sont traités dans un même matériau, mais plus lisse.

The concrete floor as well as the wood planks give an overall impression of a certain willful coarseness.

Der Betonboden und auch die Holzbretter vermitteln den Gesamteindruck einer gewissen beabsichtigten Derbheit.

Le sol en béton et la largeur des planches de bois laissent une impression de rudesse volontaire.

Lillefjord ►

PUSHAK

PUSHAK
Vidarsgate 4
0452 Oslo
Norway

Tel: +47 21 94 83 39
E-mail: post@pushak.no
Web: www.pushak.no

CAMILLA LANGELAND was born in Oslo, Norway, in 1975. She studied art history at Oslo University (1995), attended the University of Lund (1999), and received her degree in architecture from the Oslo School of Architecture (2001). She worked for Lund & Slaatto (1999–2000), and for div.A Architects (2002–04) before co-founding PUSHAK in 2004. **SISSIL MORSETH GROMHOLT** was born in 1974 in Oslo, studied at Bergen University (1999), and received an architecture degree from the Oslo School of Architecture (2001) before becoming a principal of PUSHAK in 2004. **MARTHE MELBYE** was born in 1973 in Oslo and received her degree from the Oslo School of Architecture in 2001 before becoming a partner of PUSHAK in 2004. **GYDA DRAGE KELIVA** was born in Oslo in 1972, received an architecture degree from the Oslo School of Architecture in 2000, and was also a founding partner of PUSHAK in 2004. The firm was created by all four partners in 2004 and has actually been called PUSHAK since 2006. The practice has completed Rest Stop Snefjord (Finnmark, 2005); Lillefjord (Måsøy, Finnmark, 2006, published here); Rest Stop Torskfjorddalen (Finnmark, 2007); Rest Stop Reinoksevatn (Finnmark, 2007); and Imagine Rommen (Rommen, Groruddalen, Oslo, 2008–). It is currently working on Vestfold Crematorium (Sandefjord, Vestfold, 2010); a Summer Cabin (Hvaler, 2010); Solstad Kindergarten (Stavern, Vestfold, 2010); and Rest Stop Storberget (Finnmark, 2011), all in Norway.

CAMILLA LANGELAND wurde 1975 in Oslo, Norwegen, geboren. Sie studierte Kunstgeschichte an der Universität Oslo (1995), besuchte die Universität Lund (1999) und beendete 2001 ihr Architekturstudium an der Oslo School of Architecture. Sie arbeitete im Büro Lund & Slaatto (1999–2000) und bei div.A Architekter (2002–04), bevor sie 2004 PUSHAK mitgründete. **SISSIL MORSETH GROMHOLT** wurde 1974 in Oslo geboren, studierte an der Universität Bergen (1999) und beendete 2001 ihr Studium an der Oslo School of Architecture. 2004 wurde sie Leiterin von PUSHAK. **MARTHE MELBYE** wurde 1973 in Oslo geboren und schloss 2001 ihr Studium an der Oslo School of Architecture ab. 2004 wurde sie Partnerin von PUSHAK. **GYDA DRAGE KELIVA** wurde 1972 in Oslo geboren, beendete 2000 ihr Studium an der Oslo School of Architecture und war 2004 ebenfalls Mitgründerin von PUSHAK. Die Firma wurde 2004 von allen vier Partnerinnen gegründet und heißt seit 2006 PUSHAK. Das Büro hat folgende Bauten ausgeführt: Raststätte Snefjord (Finnmark, 2005), Lillefjord (Måsøy, Finnmark, 2006, hier veröffentlicht), Raststätte Torskfjorddalen (Finnmark, 2007), Raststätte Reinoksevatn (Finnmark, 2007) sowie Imagine Rommen (Rommen, Groruddalen, Oslo, 2008–). Gegenwärtig arbeiten die Architektinnen am Krematorium Vestfold (Sandefjord, Vestfold, 2010), einem Ferienhaus (Hvaler, 2010), dem Kindergarten Solstad (Stavern, Vestfold, 2010) und der Raststätte Storberget (Finnmark, 2011), alle in Norwegen.

CAMILLA LANGELAND, née à Oslo en 1975, a étudié l'histoire de l'art à l'université d'Oslo (1995), puis à l'université de Lund (1999) et a reçu son diplôme d'architecte de l'École d'architecture d'Oslo (2001). Elle a travaillé pour Lund & Slaatto (1999–2000) et div.A Architekter (2002–04) avant de participer à la fondation de PUSHAK en 2004. **SISSIL MORSETH GROMHOLT**, née en 1974 à Oslo, a étudié à l'université de Bergen (1999), est diplômée de l'École d'architecture d'Oslo (2001) et a rejoint les partenaires de PUSHAK en 2004. **MARTHE MELBYE**, née en 1973 à Oslo, a suivi le même parcours, ainsi que **GYDA DRAGE KELIVA**, née à Oslo en 1972. L'agence fondée par ses quatre partenaires en 2004 a pris le nom de PUSHAK en 2006. L'agence a réalisé, toujours en Norvège : le Rest Stop Snefjord (Finnmark, 2005) ; Lillefjord (Måsøy, Finnmark, 2006, publié ici) ; le Rest Stop Torskfjorddalen (Finnmark, 2007) ; le Rest Stop Reinoksevatn (Finnmark, 2007) et Imagine Rommen (Rommen, Groruddalen, Oslo, 2008–). Elle travaille actuellement sur les projets du crématorium de Vestfold (Sandefjord, Vestfold, 2010) ; d'un chalet d'été (Hvaler, 2010) ; du jardin d'enfants Solstad (Stavern, Vestfold, 2010) et du Rest Stop Storberget (Finnmark, 2011).

LILLEFJORD

Måsøy, Finnmark, Norway, 2006

Address: Rv 889, Måsøy, Finnmark, Norway
Area: not applicable. Client: National Tourist Route Project. Cost: not disclosed

Part of a series of other projects, this installation in northern Norway involved benches, a shelter, and a toilet at the start of a trail to a mountain waterfall. PUSHAK proposed to create a steel-frame bridge with a wooden interior that leads visitors to an old trail. The architects state: "The steel frame was prefabricated, minimizing work on site in this rough climate. Materials were chosen to minimize maintenance."

Diese Anlage ist eines von mehreren Projekten im Norden Norwegens und umfasst Bänke, einen Schutzbau und Toiletten am Beginn eines Wanderwegs zu einem Wasserfall in den Bergen. PUSHAK schlug den Bau einer Brücke mit Stahlkonstruktion und einem Innenraum in Holz vor, die die Besucher zu einem alten Fußweg leitet. Die Architektinnen erklären: „Die Stahlkonstruktion wurde vorgefertigt, um die Arbeit vor Ort in diesem rauen Klima zu reduzieren. Es wurden Materialien gewählt, die nur minimaler Wartung bedürfen."

Élément d'une série de projets, cette installation mise en place dans le nord de la Norvège comprend des banquettes, un abri, des toilettes et le départ d'un parcours vers une cascade dans les montagnes. PUSHAK a proposé de créer une passerelle à ossature d'acier et tablier en bois qui oriente les visiteurs vers un ancien chemin. « La structure en acier est préfabriquée, ce qui a réduit la durée du chantier sous un climat difficile. Les matériaux ont été choisis pour minimiser la maintenance », ont expliqué les architectes.

The architects use pine planks and metal to create both a proximity to the natural setting and an intentional, manufactured distance, as seen in the frame.

Die Architektinnen wählten Kiefernholzbretter und Metall, um Nähe zur natürlichen Umgebung zu erreichen und – wie durch die Einfassung erkennbar – zugleich bewusst eine Distanz herzustellen.

Les architectes ont volontairement choisi des habillages en pin pour créer une proximité avec le cadre naturel et une ossature en métal pour installer une distance.

The elongated wooden structure seems to flow into and over the bridge, narrowing as it reaches the opposite bank of the stream.

Die langgestreckte Holzkonstruktion führt scheinbar in und über die Brücke und verengt sich auf der anderen Uferseite.

La superstructure en bois semble se projeter de la petite construction vers le pont qu'elle franchit en se rétrécissant lorsqu'elle atteint la rive opposée.

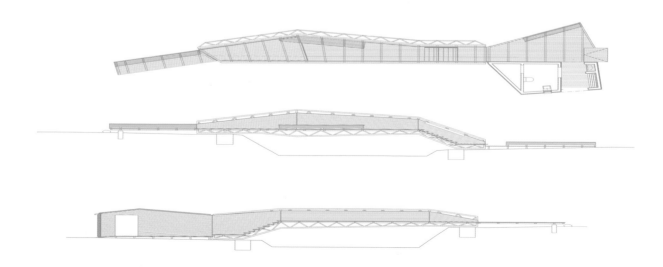

The horizontal planking and angled surfaces contribute to an impression of a flowing, almost mobile design that runs into the landscape itself.

Die horizontale Bretterverkleidung und die abgewinkelten Flächen tragen zur fließenden, beinahe mobilen Wirkung der Brücke bei.

Le bardage horizontal et les plans inclinés contribuent à donner une impression de fluidité, presque de mobilité.

ROOM 11

5th Floor, 50 Elizabeth Street
Hobart, Tasmania 7000
Australia

Tel: +61 3 6234 2847
Fax: +61 3 6234 7253
E-mail: thomas@room11.com.au
Web: www.room11.com.au

THOMAS BAILEY was born in 1977. He was a cofounder of Room 11 in 2003 and obtained his B.Arch degree the following year. He worked as a project architect for Morris-Nunn Associates (2005–07). **AARON ROBERTS** was also born in 1977 in Hobart, Tasmania. He received a bachelor of environmental design (University of Tasmania 1996–98) before working with Bush Park Shugg & Moon Architects (2000) and Maria Gigney Architect (2001). He cofounded Room 11 in 2003. They completed Little Big House (Hobart, Tasmania, 2008, published here) and Allens Rivulet House 2 (Allens Rivulet, Tasmania, 2009, also published here); while their current work includes Houses in Dodges Ferry, Lenah Valley, Sandy Bay, Sorrento, Fitzroy, and Longley as well as a Medical Center in Moonah, all in Australia, 2010. In conjunction with Scott Lloyd and Katrina Stoll, Room 11 was selected for the Australian Pavilion at the Venice Biennale (2010). Their speculative project concerns "linking Victoria and Tasmania via a hyper infrastructural spine."

THOMAS BAILEY wurde 1977 geboren. 2003 war er Mitgründer von Room 11 und machte im darauffolgenden Jahr den B.Arch. 2005 bis 2007 arbeitete er als Projektarchitekt bei Morris-Nunn Associates. **AARON ROBERTS** wurde ebenfalls 1977 in Hobart, Tasmanien, geboren und machte seinen Bachelor of Environmental Design (University of Tasmania, 1996–98), bevor er bei Bush Park Shugg & Moon Architects (2000) sowie Maria Gigney Architect (2001) arbeitete. 2003 war er Mitgründer von Room 11. Ausgeführte Bauten des Büros sind das Little Big House (Hobart, Tasmanien, 2008, hier veröffentlicht) und Allens Rivulet House 2 (Allens Rivulet, Tasmanien, 2009, ebenfalls hier veröffentlicht). Zu den aktuellen Arbeiten zählen Wohnhäuser in Dodges Ferry, Lenah Valley, Sandy Bay, Sorrento, Fitzroy und Longley sowie ein Ärztezentrum in Moonah, alle in Australien, 2010. Gemeinsam mit Scott Lloyd und Katrina Stoll war Room 11 mit der Planung des australischen Pavillons auf der Biennale von Venedig (2010) beauftragt. Ihr spekulatives Projekt befasste sich mit der „Verbindung von Victoria und Tasmanien durch eine hyper-infrastrukturelle Achse."

THOMAS BAILEY, né en 1977, cofondateur de Room 11 en 2003, a obtenu son diplôme d'architecte l'année suivante. Il a été architecte de projet chez Morris-Nunn Associates (2005–07). **AARON ROBERTS**, né en 1977 à Hobart (Tasmanie) est diplômé en design environnemental de l'université de Tasmanie (1996–98) et a travaillé pour Bush Park Shugg & Moon Architects (2000) et Maria Gigney Architect (2001). Il est cofondateur de Room 11 (2003). Ils ont réalisé Little Big House (Hobart, Tasmanie, 2008, publiée ici) et la maison Allens Rivulet 2 (Allens Rivulet, Tasmanie, 2009, également publiée ici) et travaillent actuellement sur des projets de maisons à Dodges Ferry, Lenah Valley, Sandy Bay, Sorrento, Fitzroy et Longley ainsi que d'un centre médical à Moonah, tous en Australie. En collaboration avec Scott Lloyd et Katrina Stoll, Room 11 a été choisi pour le pavillon australien de la Biennale d'architecture de Venise 2010. Leur projet portait sur une « liaison entre l'État de Victoria et la Tasmanie par un axe hyper-infrastructurel. »

LITTLE BIG HOUSE

Hobart, Tasmania, Australia, 2008

Address: 833a Huon Road, Fern Tree, Hobart, Tasmania, Australia
Area: 165 m². Client: Thomas Bailey, Megan Baines. Cost: $250 000

Thomas Bailey and Megan Baynes designed and built this house for themselves in Fern Tree on the eastern slope of Mount Wellington above Hobart. The location of the house takes this context into mind as well as such factors as a birch tree on the site. Set on a vacant lot between existing houses and gardens, the **LITTLE BIG HOUSE** is "defensive and diagrammatic" according to its architects, with a deliberately small footprint and a configuration intended to provide the owners with a maximum degree of privacy. Thomas Bailey writes: "It's just a box, a clean volume with two exceptions: a service core and an entry airlock." The designers have employed polycarbonate cladding on the eastern and western sides of the house to "render luminous shadow walls which enable the house to be concurrently light and contained." For other parts of the house, Tasmanian celery top pine from the Huon Valley, south of Hobart, was used with a "traditional vernacular 'batten-board' cladding technique common to the locale."

Thomas Bailey und Megan Baynes planten und bauten dieses Haus für sich selbst in Fern Tree über Hobart am Osthang des Mount Wellington. Der Entwurf für das Gebäude nimmt auf diesen Standort ebenso Rücksicht wie etwa auf eine auf dem Grundstück vorhandene Birke. Das auf einen freien Bauplatz zwischen bestehenden Häusern und Gärten gesetzte **LITTLE BIG HOUSE** ist, laut Aussage der Architekten, „defensiv und schematisch", mit bewusst klein gehaltenem Grundriss und einer Raumplanung, die den Bewohnern ein Maximum an Rückzugsmöglichkeiten bietet. Thomas Bailey schreibt: „Es ist nur eine Kiste, ein geschlossenes Volumen mit zwei Ausnahmen: einem Versorgungskern und einem Windfang am Eingang." Für die Ost- und die Westseiten des Gebäudes wählten die Architekten eine Verkleidung aus Polykarbonat, um „helle und schattenspendende Wände zu erzeugen, die das Haus licht und abgeschlossen zugleich machen". Für andere Bereiche wurde tasmanische Celery-Top-Kiefer aus dem Huon Valley südlich von Hobart für die „traditionelle, regional übliche Bretterverkleidung" verwendet.

Thomas Bailey et Megan Baynes ont conçu cette maison à Fern Tree sur la pente orientale du Mont Wellington au-dessus d'Hobart pour leur propre usage. L'implantation du projet prend en compte ce contexte de même que certains facteurs comme la présence d'un bouleau sur le terrain. Édifiée sur une parcelle vide entre des maisons et des jardins existants, **LITTLE BIG HOUSE** est « défensive et schématique » pour reprendre le descriptif des architectes. Son emprise au sol est délibérément réduite et sa configuration veut offrir à ses occupants le maximum d'intimité. Pour Thomas Bailey : « C'est juste une boîte, un volume net à deux exceptions près, le noyau de services et le sas d'entrée. » Les architectes ont utilisé un bardage en polycarbonate sur les faces est et ouest pour « rendre lumineuse l'ombre des murs qui permettent à la maison de paraître à la fois légère et compacte. » Les autres parties sont parées de pin de Tasmanie issu de la vallée d'Huon au sud d'Hobart et posé selon un principe vernaculaire de bardage à clins, technique traditionnelle commune dans la région. »

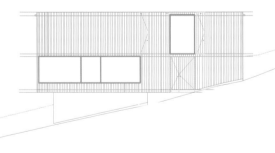

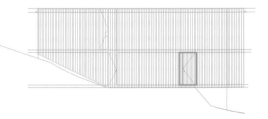

Like a box or a container, the house is cantilevered over its lower end and has contrasting façade treatments, dominated by vertical wood planking.

Dieses Haus in Form einer Kiste oder eines Containers kragt über seine untere Seite aus und zeigt unterschiedliche Fassadenbehandlungen, die von der vertikalen Holzverkleidung bestimmt werden.

En forme de boîte ou de conteneur, la maison est en léger porte-à-faux en partie inférieure. Ses façades sont composées d'éléments contrastants, même si le bardage vertical en bois domine.

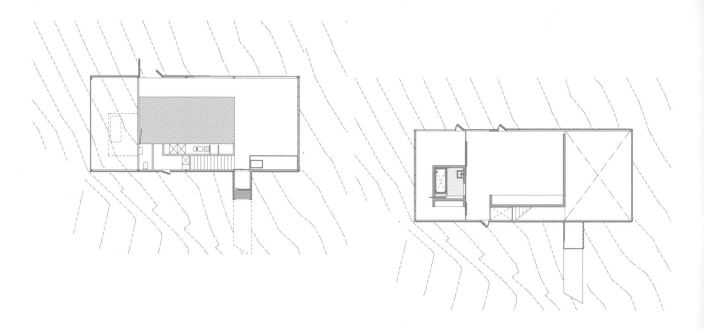

The plan is a simple rectangle. Interior volumes are quite strict, in keeping with the outside shapes of the house.

Der Grundriss ist ein einfaches Rechteck. Auch die Innenräume sind streng gestaltet, um der Außenform des Hauses zu entsprechen.

Le plan est simplement rectangulaire. Les volumes intérieurs sont assez stricts, mais en accord avec le style extérieur de la maison.

A long, glazed strip brings light into
the living and dining areas (above).
The side view (right) appears to show
the house in a perilous equilibrium
over the rocky site.

*Ein langes Fensterband lässt Tages-
licht in den Wohn- und Essbereich
(oben) einfallen. Die Seitenansicht
(rechts) zeigt das Haus in scheinbar
prekärem Gleichgewicht über dem
felsigen Gelände.*

*Un bandeau de fenêtres éclaire
le séjour et la salle à manger (ci-
dessus). Vue de côté, la maison
semble se tenir dans un équilibre
périlleux dans son site escarpé.*

ALLENS RIVULET HOUSE 2

Allens Rivulet, Tasmania, Australia, 2009

Address: not disclosed
Area: 233 m². Client: not disclosed. Cost: $500 000

This house appears to have an "angular and severe form" from the approach. It is described by the architects as "a toughened, abstract container, bracing itself against the robust Tasmanian landscape and weather." By way of contrast, the underside of the house provides shelter from the sun while allowing the residents to be outdoors. A roof deck allows for more exposure and views. The client's request to put the kitchen at the center of life in the house was a key to its layout. Rooms in the house deform its shape slightly to provide specific views, toward Mount Wellington for example. The architects state: "The compact plan is made to feel larger via the positioning of the voids and linked external areas. Internal and external spaces are blurred at one extreme and highly contained in others." Dark metallic cladding is contrasted with a timber lining. Natural ventilation and thermal mass provided by a suspended concrete slab reduce energy consumption.

Die Erscheinungsform dieses Haus wirkt „eckig und streng". Von den Architekten wird es als „abstrakter Behälter in der kargen Landschaft und widerstandsfähig gegen das raue Klima Tasmaniens" beschrieben. Im Gegensatz dazu bietet die Unterseite des Hauses Schutz vor der Sonne und den Bewohnern die Möglichkeit zum Aufenthalt im Freien; eine Dachterrasse dient als weitere Wohnfläche und zum Ausblick. Auf Wunsch des Bauherrn wurde die Küche im Zentrum des Hauses angeordnet und zum Ausgangspunkt des Grundrisses. Die Räume haben leicht unregelmäßige Formen, etwa um besondere Ausblicke auf den Mount Wellington zu bieten. Die Architekten erklären: „Der kompakte Grundriss wirkt größer durch die Anlage von Zwischenbereichen und miteinander verbundenen Freiräumen. Innen- und Außenräume greifen im Extremfall ineinander und sind in anderen Fällen sehr abgeschlossen." Die dunkle Metallverkleidung bildet einen Kontrast zur Holzverschalung. Natürliche Belüftung und die thermische Masse einer aufgehängten Betonplatte reduzieren den Energieverbrauch.

La maison peut paraître « anguleuse et sévère » quand on s'en approche. Les architectes la décrivent comme « un conteneur abstrait renforcé, qui fait face à la robustesse du paysage et au climat de la Tasmanie ». Par contraste, le dessous de la maison permet à ses habitants de s'abriter du soleil tout en restant dehors. Une terrasse en toiture offre d'autres possibilités de profiter du soleil et de la vue. Le plan exprime fidèlement le souhait du client de placer la cuisine au centre de la vie de la maison. Certaines pièces déforment légèrement l'enveloppe extérieure pour offrir des vues mieux cadrées sur le mont Wellington par exemple. Pour les architectes : « La compacité du plan est compensée par le positionnement des vides et des zones extérieures. Les espaces intérieurs et extérieurs sont confondus d'un côté et strictement contenus de l'autre. » Le bardage métallique sombre contraste avec l'habillage intérieur en bois. La ventilation naturelle et la masse thermique de la dalle de béton suspendue réduisent la consommation d'énergie.

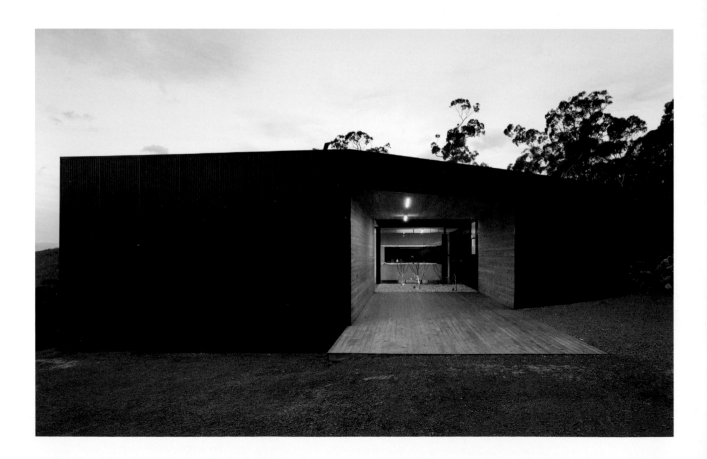

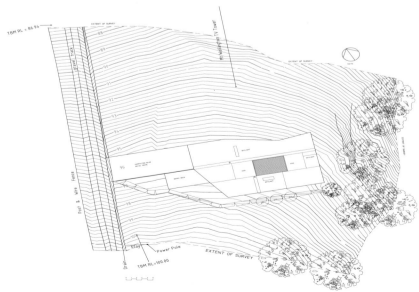

The notched and partially cantilevered volume is inscribed in the topography of the site, as seen in the
plan to the left. Timber cladding inside contrasts with the dark exteriors.

Die Baumasse mit Einschnitten und
Auskragungen ist in die Topografie
des Geländes eingefügt, wie auf dem
Plan links zu sehen. Die Holzverkleidung im Innern bildet einen Kontrast
zu den dunklen Außenwänden.

Le volume découpé et en partie
en porte-à-faux s'inscrit dans sa
topographie comme le montre le
plan de gauche. La couleur du
lambrissage intérieur contraste
avec celle des façades.

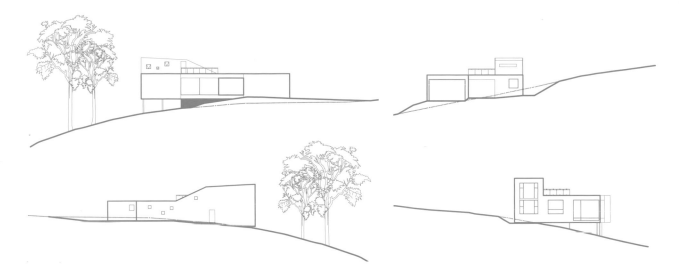

Elevations show the house on its sloped site. Below, a wooden dining table and benches contrast with the concrete floors, broad glazing, and the wood cladding around the fireplace.

Die Ansichten zeigen die Position des Hauses auf dem abfallenden Gelände. Unten: Esstisch und Bänke aus Holz im Kontrast mit dem Betonboden, der großzügigen Verglasung und der Holzverkleidung um den Kamin.

Élévations de la maison sur son terrain en pente. Ci-dessous, une table de repas et des bancs en bois contrastent avec le sol en béton, les grandes baies et l'habillage de bois autour de l'âtre.

Gravel and a stone mantlepiece
offset the rough wood surrounding
the fireplace. A view from the
opposite direction (right) shows the
fully glazed exterior wall.

Kies und eine steinerne Einfassung
ergänzen die Holzverkleidung um die
Feuerstätte. Ein Blick in umgekehrter
Richtung (rechts) zeigt die voll
verglaste Außenwand.

Du gravier et un avant-foyer en pierre
distraient le regard de l'habillage
en bois brut autour de l'âtre. Une vue
prise de l'autre direction (à droite)
montre le mur de verre donnant sur
le paysage.

HANS-JÖRG RUCH

Hans-Jörg Ruch
Via Brattas 2
7500 Saint Moritz
Switzerland

Tel: +41 81 837 32 40
Fax: +41 81 837 32 50
E-mail: info@ruch-arch.ch
Web: www.ruch-arch.ch

HANS-JÖRG RUCH was born in 1946 and received his diploma in architecture from the ETH in Zurich in 1971. He received his master's degree from the Rensselaer Polytechnic Institute (Troy, New York, 1973) with a thesis entitled "Towards an Architecture of Tourism." From 1974 to 1977 he worked in the office of Obrist und Partner, Saint Moritz, and then created a partnership with Urs Hüsler (Ruch + Hüsler, Architekten, Saint Moritz, 1977–88). He created his present firm in 1989. Widely traveled, Ruch has nonetheless made his career largely in the Engadine region of Switzerland, specializing in the renovation of the area's rich patrimony of old stone and wood houses. His delicate and knowing touch on these buildings provides an interesting answer to the question of how to modernize structures that may date, in some cases, from medieval times. Since completing the Hotel Saratz in Pontresina (1995); the Electrical Substation "Albanatscha" at the Julier Passroad (1996); and the Chesa Madalena in Zuoz (2001–02), he has realized numerous projects including the Palace Gallery in front of Badrutt's Palace Hotel (Saint Moritz, 2002); Hotel Castell (Zuoz, 2004, renovation project, undertaken with UNStudio); Not Vital House (Tschlin, 2004); Badrutt's Palace Hotel (Saint Moritz, south façade renovation, 2005); Chesa Albertini (Zuoz, 2006); a Vacation House (Sent, 2006, published here); and the reconstruction and extension of the Chamanna da Tschierva Hut for the Swiss Alpine Club (Saint Moritz, 2007), all in Switzerland.

HANS-JÖRG RUCH wurde 1946 geboren und machte sein Architekturdiplom 1971 an der Eidgenössischen Technischen Hochschule Zürich und den Master am Rensselaer Polytechnic Institute (Troy, New York, 1973) mit der Abschlussarbeit „Towards an Architecture of Tourism". Von 1974 bis 1977 arbeitete er im Büro Obrist und Partner, Sankt Moritz, und ging dann eine Partnerschaft mit Urs Hüsler ein (Ruch + Hüsler, Architekten, Sankt Moritz, 1977–88). Seine jetzige Firma gründete er im Jahr 1989. Trotz seiner weiten Reisen setzt Ruch den Schwerpunkt seiner Arbeit weitgehend auf das Schweizer Engadin und hat sich auf die Erneuerung des in dieser Region reichen Bestands an alten Naturstein- und Holzhäusern spezialisiert. Sein einfühlsamer und kenntnisreicher Umgang mit diesem Baubestand ist eine interessante Antwort auf die Frage, wie man Bauten modernisiert, die in einigen Fällen sogar aus dem Mittelalter stammen. Nachdem er das Hotel Saratz in Pontresina (1995), das Umspannwerk Albanatscha auf dem Julierpass (1996) und die Chesa Madalena in Zuoz (2001–02) fertiggestellt hatte, sind zahlreiche weitere Projekte realisiert worden: die Palace Gallery vor dem Hotel Badrutt's Palace (Sankt Moritz, 2002), das Hotel Castell (Zuoz, 2004, Modernisierung zusammen mit UNStudio), das Haus Not Vital (Tschlin, 2004), das Hotel Badrutt's Palace (Sankt Moritz, Erneuerung der Südfassade, 2005), Chesa Albertini (Zuoz, 2006), ein Ferienhaus (Sent, 2006, hier veröffentlicht) sowie der Umbau und die Erweiterung der Berghütte Chamanna da Tschierva für den Schweizer Alpen-Club (Sankt Moritz, 2007), alle in der Schweiz.

HANS-JÖRG RUCH, né en 1946, est diplômé en architecture de l'ETH à Zurich (1971). Il passe son mastère au Rensselaer Polytechnic Institute (Troy, New York, 1973) en soutenant un mémoire intitulé : *Vers une architecture du tourisme*. De 1974 à 1977, il travaille pour l'agence Obrist und Partner à Saint-Moritz, puis s'associe avec Urs Hüsler (Ruch + Hüsler, Architekten, Saint-Moritz, 1977–88). Il a créé son agence actuelle en 1989. S'il voyage beaucoup, il a néanmoins mène une grande partie de sa carrière en Engadine (Suisse), où il s'est spécialisé dans la rénovation du riche patrimoine local de maisons de pierre et de bois anciennes. Son approche délicate et savante de ces constructions est une intéressante réponse à la question de la modernisation d'un bâti datant, dans certains cas, de l'époque médiévale. Suite à la réalisation de l'Hôtel Saratz à Pontresina (1995) ; de la sous-station électrique Albanatscha sur la route du col de Julier (1996) et de la Chesa Madalena à Zuoz (2001–02), il a mené à bien de nombreux projets dont la Palace Gallery devant le Badrutt's Palace Hotel (Saint-Moritz, 2002) ; l'hôtel Castell (Zuoz, 2004, rénovation, avec UNStudio) ; la maison Not Vital (Tschlin, 2004) ; le Badrutt's Palace Hotel (Saint-Moritz, rénovation de la façade sud, 2005) ; la Chesa Albertini (Zuoz, 2006) ; une maison de vacances (Sent, 2006, publiée ici) et l'extension du refuge Chamanna da Tschierva pour le Club alpin suisse (Saint-Moritz, 2007).

VACATION HOUSE

Sent, Switzerland, 2006

Address: Via Sura, 7554 Sent, Switzerland
Area: 165 m². Cost: € 550 000. Client: not disclosed
Collaboration: Heinz Inhelder, Thorsten Arzet

Specialized in the restoration of old structures in the Engadine area of Switzerland, Hans-Jörg Ruch also creates modern buildings like this house, where wood cladding and a metal roof recall local structures.

Hans-Jörg Ruch hat sich auf die Restaurierung alter Bauten im Schweizer Kanton Engadin spezialisiert, plant aber auch moderne Gebäude wie dieses Haus, bei dem die Holzver-kleidung und ein Metall-dach auf die örtliche Bebauung Bezug nehmen.

Spécialisé dans la restauration de constructions anciennes en Engadine (Suisse), Hans-Jörg Ruch crée également des maisons modernes comme celle-ci, dans laquelle l'habillage de bois et le toit en tôle de métal rappellent les constructions locales.

This **VACATION HOUSE** is located to the east of the village of Sent on a sloping, south-facing site with a view toward local mountains such as the Piz Lischana. To profit from this view, and to maintain the terraced nature of the location, the architect set the house on the upper part of the site, making the three-story building as compact as possible. Sitting on a concrete base, the house is covered in locally harvested larch boards. An irregular arrangement of small and large windows accentuates the unexpected appearance of the house. An anthracite cement floor is contrasted with an interior cladding of larch in most areas, including bathrooms. The architect concludes: "Maintaining the continuity of the characteristic landscape of terraces in Sent was as important in this project as making a contemporary use of wood as a building material."

Dieses **FERIENHAUS** liegt östlich des Dorfs Sent auf einem nach Süden orientierten Hanggrundstück mit Blick auf die umgebenden Berge wie den Piz Lischana. Wegen dieser Aussicht und unter Berücksichtigung des terrassierten Geländes setzte der Architekt das Haus auf den oberen Teil des Grundstücks und plante das dreigeschossige Gebäude so kompakt wie möglich. Es steht auf einem Betonfundament und ist mit vor Ort gewonnen Lärchenbrettern verkleidet. Die unregelmäßig angeordneten, kleinen und großen Fenster setzen Akzente im ungewöhnlichen Erscheinungsbild dieses Hauses. Im Innern bildet der anthrazitfarbige Zementfußboden einen Kontrast zur Lärchenholzverkleidung fast aller Räume, einschließlich der Badezimmer. Der Architekt erklärt abschließend: „Die Kontinuität der charakteristischen terrassierten Landschaft von Sent zu bewahren, war bei diesem Projekt ebenso wichtig wie eine zeitgemäße Verwendung von Holz als Baumaterial."

Cette **MAISON DE VACANCES** est située à l'est du village de Sent sur une pente orientée au sud donnant dans le lointain sur les montagnes de la région dont le Piz Laschana. Pour profiter de cette vue et maintenir le caractère de l'aménagement en terrasses du site, l'architecte a implanté la maison en partie supérieure de la parcelle et a réussi à rendre cette construction de trois niveaux aussi compacte que possible. Reposant sur une base en béton, elle est habillée de planches de mélèze d'exploitation locale. Le positionnement irrégulier des fenêtres grandes et petites accentue l'aspect assez surprenant de l'ensemble. À l'intérieur, le sol en ciment anthracite contraste avec un habillage en mélèze présent dans la plupart des pièces, y compris les salles-de-bains. « Maintenir la continuité du paysage étagé caractéristique de Sent a joué un rôle important dans ce projet, de même que l'utilisation du bois comme matériau de construction contemporain, » conclut l'architecte.

SARC ARCHITECTS

SARC Architects
Tammasaarenlaituri 3
00180 Helsinki
Finland

Tel. +358 9 622 61 80
Fax: +358 9 62 26 18 40
E-mail: sarc@sarc.fi
Web: www.sarc.fi

ANTTI-MATTI SIIKALA was born in 1964 in Turku, Finland, and obtained an MS degree in architecture from the Helsinki University of Technology in 1993. He is a partner of SARC and a professor of building technology, Department of Architecture, Helsinki University of Technology / Aalto University (2002–). **SARLOTTA NARJUS** was born in 1966 in Turku. She obtained her MS degree in architecture from the Helsinki University of Technology in 1996. She worked with Heikkinen-Komonen Architects (1989–98) before becoming a partner of SARC in 1998. Their work includes Expo 2000 Finnish Pavilion (Hannover, Germany, 2000); University of Oulu, Faculty of Medicine, Main Building (Oulu, 2003); Metla, the Finnish Forest Research Institute (Joensuu; 2004, published here); Oulu City Hall (Oulu, 2008); and the Tapiola Headquarters (Espoo, 2010), all in Finland unless stated otherwise.

ANTTI-MATTI SIIKALA wurde 1964 in Turku, Finnland, geboren und machte 1993 seinen Master in Architektur an der Technischen Universität Helsinki. Er ist Partner von SARC und Professor für Bautechnik an der Architekturabteilung der Technischen Universität Helsinki/Aalto-Universität (seit 2002). **SARLOTTA NARJUS** wurde 1966 in Turku geboren und machte ihren Master 1996 an derselben Universität. Sie arbeitete bei Heikkinen-Komonen Architects (1989–98) und wurde 1998 Partnerin bei SARC. Zu den Werken dieses Büros zählen der finnische Pavillon auf der Expo 2000 (Hannover, 2000), das Hauptgebäude der medizinischen Fakultät an der Universität Oulu (Oulu, 2003), Metla, das finnische Institut für Waldforschung (Joensuu; 2004, hier veröffentlicht), das Rathaus Oulu (Oulu, 2008) und die Hauptverwaltung von Tapiola (Espoo, 2010), alle in Finnland, sofern nicht anders angegeben.

ANTTI-MATTI SIIKALA, né en 1964 à Turku en Finlande est M.Sc. en architecture de l'Université de technologie d'Helsinki (1993). Il est partenaire de l'agence SARC et professeur de technologie de la construction du département d'architecture de l'Université de technologie d'Helsinki / Université Aalto (2002–). **SARLOTTA NARJUS**, née en 1966 à Turku, est M.Sc. en architecture de l'Université de technologie d'Helsinki (1996). Elle a travaillé chez Heikkinen-Komonen Architects (1989–98) avant de devenir partenaire de SARC en 1998. Parmi leurs réalisations, presque toutes en Finlande : le pavillon finlandais pour Expo 2000 (Hannovre, Allemagne, 2000) ; le bâtiment principal de la faculté de médecine de l'University d'Oulu (Oulu, 2003) ; Metla, Institut finlandais de recherche forestière (Joensuu; 2004, publié ici) ; l'hôtel de ville d'Oulu (Oulu, 2008) et le siège de Tapiola (Espoo, 2010).

METLA, FINNISH FOREST RESEARCH INSTITUTE

Joensuu, Finland, 2004

Address: Joensuu Research Unit, Yliopistokatu 6, Box 68, FI-80101 Joensuu, Tel. +358 10 2111, www.metla.fi
Area: 7400 m². Client: Finnish Forest Research Institute. Cost: not disclosed

This building, an expansion of the existing Institute, intended for a staff of 150–170 employees, is located on the Joensuu University campus, near the city center. The Institute does applied forestry research and research on wooden materials. The architects explain: "The primary goal of the project was to use Finnish wood in innovative ways. Hence, wood is the main material used throughout the building, from the post-beam-slab system in the structural frame to the exterior cladding." The work areas are arrayed around a central courtyard and lobby. The walls of the entrance to the courtyard are made up of 100-year-old timber. Tall pines grow through the terrace in the courtyard. A conference space "resembles an overturned boat and fish-chest-inspired tilted wooden columns."

Dieses Gebäude, eine Erweiterung des bestehenden Instituts, bietet 150 bis 170 Arbeitsplätze und steht auf dem Campus der Universität Joensuu in der Nähe des Stadtzentrums. Das Institut führt angewandte Forschungen über Waldwirtschaft und über Materialien aus Holz durch. Die Architekten erklären: „Oberstes Ziel dieses Projekts war die Nutzung finnischen Holzes auf innovative Weise. Daher wurde Holz als Hauptbaumaterial für das gesamte Gebäude verwendet, von der Ständerkonstruktion des Tragwerks bis zur Außenverkleidung." Die Arbeitsbereiche sind um einen zentralen Innenhof und eine Lobby angeordnet. Die Wände des Eingangsbereichs zu diesem Innenhof bestehen aus 100 Jahre altem Holz. In diesem Hof wachsen hohe Kiefern durch die Terrasse. Die Form des Konferenzraums „ähnelt einem umgedrehten Boot und einer Fischkiste und wurde von den gebogenen Holzstützen bestimmt".

Ce bâtiment, qui est une extension de l'Institut installé sur le campus de l'université de Joensuu, près du centre-ville, a été conçu pour un personnel de 150 à 170 chercheurs et employés. L'Institut mène des recherches sur la forêt et les matériaux en bois. Selon les architectes : « L'objectif premier du projet est d'utiliser le bois finlandais selon des techniques novatrices. C'est pourquoi le bois est le principal matériau utilisé dans l'intégralité du bâtiment, du système d'ossature à poutres et poteaux sur dalle au parement extérieur. » Les zones de travail se répartissent autour d'une cour centrale et d'un hall d'accueil. Les murs de l'entrée qui donne sur la cour sont en bois de cent ans d'âge. De grands pins poussent dans la cour. On note un espace de conférences « ressemblant à une coque de bateau renversée et des colonnes en bois en forme de navettes inclinées ».

The Metla building demonstrates that wood can, indeed, be used to create an elegant, modern structure on a large scale.

Der Metla-Bau beweist, dass Holz in der Tat auch für elegante, moderne und großmaßstäbliche Bauten verwendet werden kann.

Le bâtiment du Metla montre que le bois peut servir à créer des constructions modernes et élégantes de grandes dimensions.

The basic plan of the building
(see below) is square with a notched,
interior courtyard. Splayed columns
made of wood connect the wood
ceiling to the tiled floor.

Die Grundform des Gebäudes
(unten) ist quadratisch mit einem
eingeschnittenen Innenhof. Schräg
gestellte Stützen aus Holz verbinden
die Holzdecke mit dem Fliesenboden.

Le plan du bâtiment décrit un carré
(ci-dessous) dans lequel a été découpée une cour intérieure. Des colonnes
inclinées en bois font le lien entre le
plafond de bois et le sol carrelé.

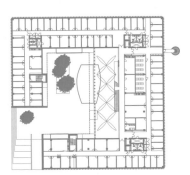
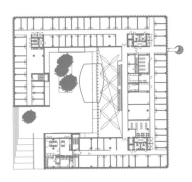
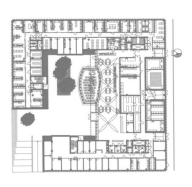

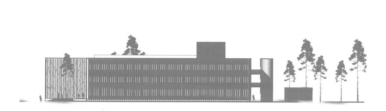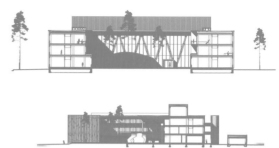

Glazed façades alternate with the more closed surfaces seen in the elevations above. Below, the space seen on the left page from a different angle.

Verglaste Flächen wechseln mit geschlossenen, wie die Ansichten oben zeigen. Unten: der auf der linken Seite dargestellte Innenraum aus einem anderen Blickwinkel.

Des façades vitrées alternent avec des plans plus fermés comme le montrent les élévations ci-dessus. Ci-dessus, l'espace de la page de gauche vu sous un angle différent.

RODRIGO SHEWARD

Rodrigo Sheward
Calle Simpson #80 depto. 32. Reñaca
Viña del Mar
Región de Valparaíso
Chile

Tel: +56 032 248 0031
E-mail: rodrigosheward@gmail.com
Web: www.ms-arquitectos.cl / www.grupotalca.org

RODRIGO SHEWARD was born in Chile in 1979 and attended the University of Talca (2000–07). Before obtaining his diploma in 2007, he worked on the Cudico House (Villarrica, 2003) and collaborated with the architect Fernando Montoya on the Sushi Home Restaurant (Viña del Mar, 2004). Recent projects include the Pinohuacho Observation Deck (Pinohuacho, Villarrica, 2006, published here); the Quincho Gorro Capucha, tourism facilities (Pinohuacho, 2009); and the Santa Fe Port service facilities (Las Ventanas, Valparaiso 2009), all in Chile.

RODRIGO SHEWARD wurde 1979 in Chile geboren und studierte an der Universidad de Talca (2000–07). Schon vor seinem Diplom 2007 arbeitete er am Haus Cudico (Villarrica, 2003) und mit dem Architekten Fernando Montoya am Sushi Home Restaurant (Viña del Mar, 2004). Seine neueren Projekte sind eine Aussichtsterrasse in Pinohuacho (Villarrica, 2006, hier veröffentlicht), die Tourismusanlagen Quincho Gorro Capucha (Pinohuacho, 2009) und Dienstleistungseinrichtungen im Hafen von Santa Fe (Las Ventanas, Valparaiso, 2009), alle in Chile.

RODRIGO SHEWARD, né au Chili en 1979, a étudié à l'université de Talca (2000–07). Avant d'obtenir son diplôme d'architecte en 2007, il a dessiné les plans de la maison Cudico (Villarrica, 2003) et collaboré avec l'architecte Fernando Montoya sur le projet du restaurant Sushi Home (Viña del Mar, 2004). Parmi ses projets récents figurent la plate-forme d'observation de Pinohuacho (Villarrica, 2006, publiée ici) ; les installations touristiques de Quincho Gorro Capucha (Pinohuacho, 2009) et des installations de service pour le port de Santa Fe (Las Ventanas, Valparaiso 2009), tous au Chili.

PINOHUACHO OBSERVATION DECK

Pinohuacho, Villarrica, Araucanía, Chile, 2006

Address: Pinohuacho, Villarrica, Araucanía, Chile, +56 9 9041 5230, www.pinohuacho.blogspot.com
Area: 78 m². Client: Pedro Vazquez, Miguel Vazquez. Cost: $3000

Access to this project requires an hour's walk along a winding path near forests and an old logging area. The logged area is being used for subsistence farming. Rodrigo Sheward's goal was to "bring architecture where there is none… creating a space to talk, and in order to do that manage, design, and build. An unpaved road for an architect who planned his *opera prima*." There are actually two volumes located 80 meters apart with a view toward the Villarrica Volcano. Each piece of wood was found and sawed on site: "gleaned at the scene, invented on the spot," as the architect says. He takes some pride in the fact that those cutting the wood worked with the same determination they once used to devastate the site. Sheward also points to his will to discuss the use of their own land with the local population.

Dieses Projekt ist nur nach einer einstündigen Wanderung auf einem gewundenen Pfad durch Wälder und einen alten Holzeinschlag erreichbar. Letzterer wird heute landwirtschaftlich genutzt. Rodrigo Shewards Ziel war es, „Architektur dorthin zu bringen, wo es keine gibt …, einen Ort zum Gespräch zu gestalten, ihn zu organisieren, zu entwerfen und zu bauen. Ein hindernisreicher Weg für einen Architekten, um seine opera prima zu planen." Es handelt sich eigentlich um zwei 80 m voneinander entfernte Bauten mit Blick auf den Vulkan Villarrica. Jedes Stück Holz wurde vor Ort gefunden und bearbeitet – „am Standort aufgelesen und dort verwendet", wie der Architekt es ausdrückt. Er ist stolz darauf, dass diejenigen, die einst das Gelände zerstörten, jetzt mit der gleichen Entschlossenheit das Holz bearbeiteten. Sheward verweist auch auf seine Bereitschaft, mit der örtlichen Bevölkerung über die Nutzung ihres eigenen Landes zu diskutieren.

Il ne faut pas moins d'une heure de marche sur un chemin qui serpente entre des forêts et une ancienne zone d'exploitation forestière aujourd'hui cultivée pour accéder à cette plate-forme. L'objectif de Rodrigo Sheward a été « d'apporter l'architecture là où il n'en existait pas … de créer un espace pour parler, et pour cela de gérer, de concevoir et de construire. Une voie difficile pour un architecte qui réalise sa première œuvre ». Le projet consiste en fait en deux volumes éloignés de 80 m l'un de l'autre qui donnent sur le volcan de Villarica. Chaque morceau de bois utilisé a été trouvé et scié sur place : « Glané sur les lieux, inventé sur place », comme aime à le dire l'architecte. Il fait remarquer que ceux qui ont découpé ce bois avaient participé avec la même détermination à la dévastation du site. Sheward insiste également sur sa volonté de discuter de l'usage du sol avec la population locale.

The roughness and simplicity of this structure is, of course, fully intentional. Looking like a closed wooden box from the side (left page), the building is, in fact, entirely open.

Die Grobheit und Schlichtheit dieses Bauwerks ist natürlich absolut gewollt. Von der Seite gesehen, wirkt es zwar wie eine geschlossene Kiste (linke Seite), tatsächlich ist es aber vollständig offen.

La simplicité rustique de cette construction est bien évidemment intentionnelle. Présentant un aspect de boîte fermée d'un côté (page de gauche), elle est en fait entièrement ouverte.

The edges of the viewing platform are irregular, and the wood is left rough, a product of this place assembled to allow visitors to appreciate the views.

Die Ränder der Aussichtsplattform sind ungleichmäßig und das Holz unbehandelt, ein Produkt dieses Standorts, der errichtet wurde, damit Besucher die Aussicht genießen können.

Les bords de la plate-forme d'observation sont irréguliers et le bois laissé brut, comme un produit issu du lieu que le touriste vient admirer.

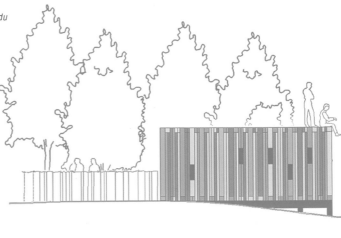

The deck seen on the left page is approximately 80 meters away from the shed, visible below and in the elevation drawing.

Das auf der linken Seite gezeigte Deck ist etwa 80 m vom Schuppen entfernt, der in der Ansichtszeichnung und unten zu sehen ist.

La terrasse (page de gauche) est située à 80 mètres environ de l'abri visible ci-dessous et sur l'élévation.

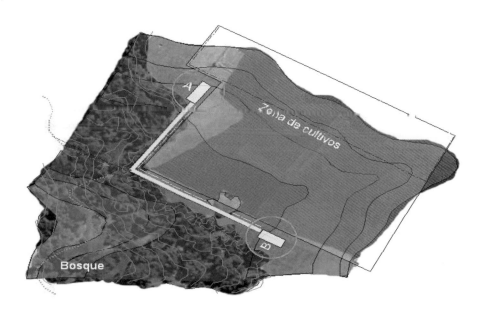

SIMAS AND GRINSPUM

Simas and Grinspum
Rua Fidalga 163, Casa 2
05432–070 São Paulo, SP
Brazil

Tel: +55 11 8299 3099
E-mail: marisimas@gmail.com

GABRIEL GRINSPUM was born in 1978 in São Paulo, Brazil, and attended the FAU-USP (Faculdade de Arquitetura e Urbanismo de São Paulo da Universidade de São Paulo, 1998–03). He has been working at Brazil Architecture since 1998, where he is currently developing a project for the new headquarters of the Shalom Community. He has had his own office since 2004, carrying forward the remodeling of apartments and houses; an Education Center linked to the Rainha da Paz School and a Community Center for the Christian Congregation, both located in Morro Grande (São Paulo); Pier House (Paraty, Rio de Janeiro, 2009, published here); and a Family House (Marumbi, São Paulo, 2010), all in Brazil. He works in partnership with **MARIANA SIMAS**, who is a collaborator of Marcio Kogan (Studio MK27).

GABRIEL GRINSPUM wurde 1978 in São Paulo, Brasilien, geboren und studierte von 1998 bis 2003 an der FAU-USP (Faculdade de Arquitetura e Urbanismo de São Paulo da Universidade de São Paulo). Er arbeitet seit 1998 bei Brazil Architecture, wo er gegenwärtig ein Projekt für das neue Hauptquartier der Gemeinschaft Shalom entwickelt. Sein eigenes Büro besteht seit 2004 und saniert Wohnbauten und Einfamilienhäuser, plant ein Ausbildungszentrum im Verbund mit der Schule Rainha da Paz, ein Gemeindezentrum für die christliche Ordensgemeinschaft, beide in Morro Grande (São Paulo), das Pier House (Paraty, Rio de Janeiro, 2009, hier veröffentlicht) sowie ein Wohnhaus (Marumbi, São Paulo, 2010), alle in Brasilien. Er arbeitet in Partnerschaft mit **MARIANA SIMAS**, einer Mitarbeiterin von Marcio Kogan (Studio MK27).

GABRIEL GRINSPUM, né en 1978 à São Paulo, a étudié à la FAU-USP (Faculdade de Arquitetura e Urbanismo de São Paulo da Universidade de São Paulo, 1998–03). Il travaille à Brazil Architecture depuis 1998, où il met actuellement au point un projet pour le nouveau siège de la communauté Shalom. Il a ouvert sa propre agence en 2004, avec laquelle il a réalisé la rénovation d'appartements et de maisons : un centre éducatif lié à l'école « Rainha da Paz » et un centre communautaire pour une congrégation chrétienne, tous deux à Morro Grande (São Paulo) ; la maison de la jetée (Pier House, Paraty, Rio de Janeiro, 2009, publiée ici) et une maison pour une famille (Marumbi, São Paulo, 2010). Il travaille avec **MARIANA SIMAS**, collaboratrice de Marcio Kogan (Studio MK27).

PIER HOUSE

Paraty, Rio de Janeiro, Brazil, 2009

Address: Saco do Mamanguá, Paraty, Rio de Janeiro, Brazil
Area: 60 m². Client: not disclosed. Cost: $100 000

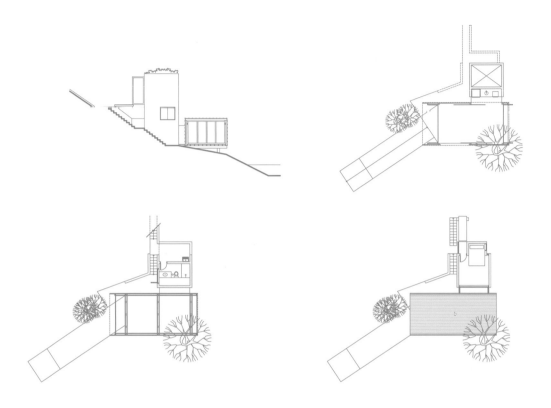

The Pier House assumes the typology of a boat house, with living space incorporated. As the drawings show, it is set on a slope.

Das Pier House folgt der Typologie eines Bootshauses mit darin enthaltenem Wohnraum. Wie die Zeichnungen zeigen, steht es auf einem Abhang.

La maison de la jetée reprend la typologie d'un hangar à bateaux à espace de vie intégré. Comme le montre le dessin, elle est implantée dans une pente.

This structure "was built to house a sailboat during the week and its owners during the weekends." One part of the house is made up of a solid, whitewashed box erected with construction methods inherited from colonial times, while the other part is made of prefabricated wood elements and metal tiles. The house had to be built near the water to allow the boat to be easily moved, a decision that also allowed the preservation of rainforest vegetation on the site. The architects explain that the "site is in the Saco do Mamanguá, a tropical fjord accessible only by boat without power, the very archetype of a lost paradise. In this context, the house brings together the idea of the 'noble savage' with the modern 'eulogy of the machine'."

Dieses Gebäude „wurde errichtet, um ein Segelboot während der Woche und seine Besitzer an den Wochenenden unterzubringen". Ein Teil des Hauses ist eine massive, weiß verputzte Kiste, die mit Baumethoden errichtet wurde, die aus der Kolonialzeit stammen. Der andere Teil wurde aus vorgefertigten Holzelementen und Metallplatten erbaut. Der Bau sollte dicht am Wasser stehen, um das Boot leichter manövrieren zu können – eine Entscheidung, die es auch ermöglichte, die Regenwaldvegetation auf dem Gelände zu erhalten. Die Architekten erklären: „Der Bauplatz liegt am Saco do Mamanguá, einem tropischen Fjord, der nur mit Booten ohne Motor anzufahren ist – einem wahren Urbild des verlorenen Paradieses. In diesem Kontext vereinigt das Haus die Vorstellung vom ‚edlen Wilden' mit der modernen ‚Verehrung der Maschine'."

Cette construction a été réalisée pour « abriter un voilier pendant la semaine et ses propriétaires pendant le week-end ». Une partie de la maison est une structure en forme de boîte fermée, passée à la chaux, édifiée à l'aide de techniques de construction héritées de la période coloniale; l'autre partie est en éléments de bois préfabriqués et dalles de métal. La maison devait évidemment se trouver à proximité de l'eau pour recevoir le bateau, décision qui permettait également de préserver la végétation de type forêt pluviale qui règne sur le site. Les architectes expliquent que « le site se trouve dans le Saco do Mamanguá, un fjord tropical accessible uniquement en bateau sans moteur, l'archétype d'un paradis perdu. Dans ce contexte, la maison réunit les concepts du 'noble sauvage' et de 'l'eulogie de la machine moderne' ».

Surrounded by dense vegetation, the
house can easily be opened on the
sides to create covered living spaces
that are close to the natural setting.

*Die Wände des von üppiger
Vegetation umgebenen Hauses
können geöffnet werden, sodass
ein überdachter Aufenthaltsraum
inmitten der Natur entsteht.*

*Entourée d'une végétation dense,
la maison peut facilement s'ouvrir
sur les côtés pour créer un espace
de vie couvert proche de la nature.*

A wooden boat ramp leads up to the house, as seen in these images. On the right page, sun flows into the small kitchen and dining area, with the shutters open to the forest.

Wie diese Bilder zeigen, führt eine hölzerne Bootsrampe hinauf zum Haus. Rechte Seite: Die Sonne scheint in die kleine Wohnküche; die Läden sind zum Wald geöffnet.

Une rampe à bateaux en bois conduit à la maison, comme le montrent ces images. Page de droite, le soleil inonde la petite cuisine et le coin des repas. Les volets ouvrent sur la forêt.

STUDIO WEAVE

Studio Weave
33 Saint John's Church Road
London E9 6EJ
UK

Tel: +44 79 03 03 19 76 / +44 79 40 32 50 80
E-mail: hello@studioweave.com
Web: www.studioweave.com

MARIA SMITH, born in 1982 in Edinburgh, Scotland, received her architectural education at London Metropolitan University (2006–09). She also studied at the Technical University of Delft and the University of Bath (2001–05) and was a founding member of Studio Weave in 2006. Her work includes "Freya's Cabin" and "Robin's Hut," two pavilions for Kielder Art and Architecture, Northumberland (of which one is published here). **JE AHN**, born in 1982 in Ulsan, South Korea, was also educated at London Metropolitan University, the Technical University of Delft, and the University of Bath. Je Ahn is also a director of MUSARC, an independent research and event platform based at the Department of Architecture and Spatial Design, London Metropolitan University, for "exploring the relationship between architecture, music, and sound."

MARIA SMITH, 1982 in Edinburgh, Schottland, geboren, studierte Architektur an der London Metropolitan University (2006–09), an der Technischen Universität Delft sowie der University of Bath (2001–05) und war 2006 Gründungsmitglied von Studio Weave. Zu ihren ausgeführten Bauten zählen Freya's Cabin und Robin's Hut, zwei Pavillons für das Programm Art and Architecture in Kielder, Northumberland (einer davon ist hier veröffentlicht). **JE AHN**, geboren 1982 in Ulsan, Südkorea, studierte ebenfalls an der London Metropolitan University, der Technischen Universität Delft und der University of Bath. Je Ahn ist auch Leiter von MUSARC, einer unabhängigen Forschungs- und Eventplattform am Department of Architecture and Spatial Design der London Metropolitan University, welche „die Beziehungen zwischen Architektur, Musik und Ton erforscht".

MARIA SMITH, née en1982 à Edimbourg en Écosse, a fait ses études d'architecture à la London Metropolitan University (2006–09), à l'Université polytechnique de Delft et à celle de Bath (2001–05) avant de participer à la fondation de l'agence Studio Weave en 2006. Parmi ses réalisations : Freya's Cabin et Robin's Hut, deux cabanes pour Kielder Art and Architecture (Northumberland, dont l'une est publiée ici). **JE AHN**, né en 1982 à Ulsan (Corée du Sud), a également étudié à la London Metropolitan University, à l'Université polytechnique de Delft et l'université de Bath. Il dirige par ailleurs MUSARC, une plate-forme de recherche indépendante et d'événements basée au département d'Architecture et de Design spatial de la London Metropolitan University qui « explore les relations entre l'architecture, la musique et le son ».

FREYA'S CABIN

Kielder Water, Northumberland, UK, 2009

Address: not disclosed
Area: not calculated. Client: Kielder Partnership. Cost: £45 000

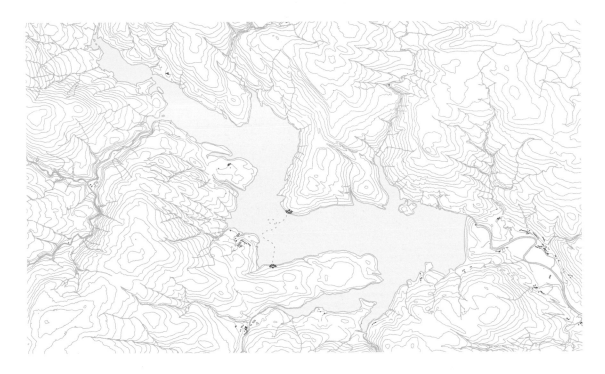

FREYA'S CABIN, together with Robin's Hut, is one of a pair of allegorical visitors' shelters by Studio Weave that overlooks Kielder Water, northern Europe's largest man-made lake. The designers write: "Their two structures have been imagined within a fairytale that the designers wrote specifically for Kielder, inspired by the two sites, mythology, and folklore. Within the story, Freya's Cabin and Robin's Hut are designed and built by the characters; the real structures offer visitors evidence of these characters and their adventures." Freya was inspired by the Norse goddess of love, beauty, and fertility who cried tears of gold. Built with "CNC-cut plywood layers pressed together, with each layer having a cutout shape like a stage set, the structure is held together with glue and tension rods that fit through pre-drilled holes in every layer." Some of the layers are made of clear acrylic to allow dappled light into the structure, creating a forest ceiling effect.

FREYA'S CABIN ist, ebenso wie Robin's Hut, einer von zwei allegorischen Schutzbauten für Besucher, die vom Studio Weave am Kielder Water, Nordeuropas größtem künstlichem See, errichtet wurden. Die Architekten schreiben: „Diese beiden Bauten wurden im Rahmen eines Märchens erdacht, das die Planer – inspiriert von den beiden Bauplätzen, von Mythologie und Folklore – speziell für Kielder verfassten. In dieser Geschichte werden Freya's Cabin und Robin's Hut von den Protagonisten entworfen und gebaut. Die realen Bauten vermitteln den Besuchern eine Vorstellung von diesen Charakteren und deren Abenteuern." Freya's Cabin wurde von der nordischen Göttin der Liebe, Schönheit und Fruchtbarkeit inspiriert, die Tränen aus Gold vergoss. Das Gebäude aus „mit CNC bearbeiteten, zusammengepressten Sperrholzlagen mit jeweils einem Ausschnitt als Kulisse wird durch Leim und Zugstäbe in vorgebohrten Löchern zusammengehalten". Einige dieser Lagen bestehen aus durchsichtigem Acryl, um gedämpftes Licht in das Gebäude einzulassen und eine Waldstimmung zu erzeugen.

FREYA'S CABIN (la cabane de Freya) comme Robin's Hut (la hutte de Robin) sont un couple d'abris allégoriques pour visiteurs conçus par Studio Weave. Ils donnent sur le Kielder Water, la plus importante retenue d'eau artificielle du nord de l'Europe. Comme l'expliquent ses concepteurs : « Ces deux structures ont été imaginées dans l'esprit d'un conte de fée que les designers avaient écrit spécialement pour Kielder, en s'inspirant de la mythologie et du folklore du site. Dans cette histoire, la cabane de Freya et la hutte de Robin sont dessinées et construites par les personnages. Leur construction offre aux visiteurs une sorte de preuve de l'existence de ces personnages et de leurs aventures. » Freya est inspirée de la déesse nordique de l'amour, de la beauté et de la fertilité qui pleurait des larmes d'or. Construite en « plaques de contreplaqué découpées par un outillage numérique et pressées les unes contre les autres, chaque plaque présente une découpe évoquant un décor de scène. La structure tient grâce à la colle et aux tiges de tension qui passent à travers les trous prépercés à travers chaque plaque ». Certaines sont en acrylique transparent pour laisser entrer une lumière tachetée qui crée un effet de forêt en plafond.

The unusual layered appearance of the cabin is made even more unexpected by the forest of rods that supports the structure.

Das ungewöhnliche, geschichtete Erscheinungsbild der Hütte wird zusätzlich betont durch einen Wald von Stangen, die den Bau tragen.

L'aspect de la cabane en plaques de contreplaqué découpé est rendu encore plus surprenant par la forêt de tiges qui la supportent.

An elevation of the structure shows
the rods that it is supported by and
its stylized leaf and branch design.

Diese Ansicht zeigt die Stangen,
von denen der Bau getragen wird,
und seine Gestaltung mit stilisierten
Blättern und Zweigen.

L'élévation montre les tiges de
soutien et les motifs stylisés de
feuillages et de branchages.

As befits the natural setting, the
complex cut-out forms of the wood
bring to mind an organic pattern.
Though it is a viewing platform,
the cabin might well be taken for
a chapel.

Passend zum natürlichen Umfeld
erinnern die komplexen, ausgeschnit-
tenen Holzformen an organische
Systeme. Obgleich es sich um eine
Aussichtsterrasse handelt, könnte
die Hütte für eine Kapelle gehalten
werden.

Les découpes complexes et
organiques des panneaux de bois
rappellent le cadre naturel. Plate-
forme d'observation, cette cabane
pourrait être prise pour une chapelle.

Although its exterior form is quite simple, the way the cabin sits on the inclined site above the water gives it a singular presence.

Obgleich die Außenform der Hütte sehr schlicht ist, verleiht ihr die Stellung auf abfallendem Gelände über dem Wasser eine ganz besondere Wirkung.

Bien que sa forme extérieure soit assez simple, la manière dont la cabane est implantée sur ce terrain en pente au-dessus de l'eau lui donne un aspect singulier.

TEZUKA ARCHITECTS

Tezuka Architects
1–19–9–3F Todoroki
Setagaya
Tokyo 158–0082
Japan

Tel: +81 3 3703 7056
Fax: +81 3 3703 7038
E-mail: tez@sepia.ocn.ne.jp
Web: www.tezuka-arch.com/

TAKAHARU TEZUKA, born in Tokyo, Japan, in 1964, received his degrees from the Musashi Institute of Technology (1987) and from the University of Pennsylvania (1990). He worked with Richard Rogers Partnership Ltd. (1990–94) and established Tezuka Architects the same year. He is currently a professor at Tokyo City University. Born in Kanagawa, Japan, in 1969, **YUI TEZUKA** was educated at the Musashi Institute of Technology and the Bartlett School of Architecture, University College of London. The practice has completed about a dozen private houses, and won the competition for the Matsunoyama Museum of Natural Science in 2001. Since then it has been based in Tokyo. Their work includes the Soejima Hospital (Saga-shi, Saga, 1995–96); Wood Deck House (Kamakura-shi, Kanagawa, 1999); Roof House (Hadano-shi, Kanagawa, 2000–01); Toyota L&F Hiroshima (Hiroshima-shi, Hiroshima, 2003); Echigo-Matsunoyama Museum of Natural Science (Tokamachi-shi, Niigata, 2002–03); Floating Roof House (Okayama, 2005); Fuji Kindergarten (Tachikawa, Tokyo, phase 1, 2006; phase 2, 2006–07); Temple to Catch the Forest (Yokohama, Kanagawa, 2006–07); Steel Sheet House (Tokyo, 2008–09); Pitched Roof House (Nagano, 2008–09, published here); and Woods of Net (Ninotaira, Hakone, Kanagawa / inside of the Hakone Open-Air Museum, 2009), all in Japan.

TAKAHARU TEZUKA, 1964 in Tokio geboren, studierte bis 1987 am Musashi Institute of Technology und bis 1990 an der University of Pennsylvania. Er arbeitete bei Richard Rogers Partnership Ltd. (1990–94) und gründete 1994 Tezuka Architects. Gegenwärtig ist er Professor an der Tokyo City University. Die 1969 in Kanagawa, Japan, geborene **YUI TEZUKA** studierte am Musashi Institute of Technology und der Bartlett School of Architecture, University College of London. Das Büro hat etwa ein Dutzend Privathäuser ausgeführt und 2001 den Wettbewerb für das Matsunoyama Museum of Natural Science gewonnen. Seitdem hat es seinen Sitz in Tokio. Zu seinen Projekten zählen das Soejima Hospital (Saga-shi, Saga, 1995–96), das Wood Deck House (Kamakura-shi, Kanagawa, 1999), das Roof House (Hadano-shi, Kanagawa, 2000–01), Toyota L&F Hiroshima (Hiroshima-shi, Hiroshima, 2003), das Echigo-Matsunoyama Museum of Natural Science (Tokamachi-shi, Niigata, 2002–03), das Floating Roof House (Okayama, 2005), der Kindergarten Fuji (Tachikawa, Tokio, 1. Bauabschnitt 2006; 2. Bauabschnitt 2006–07), Temple to Catch the Forest (Yokohama, Kanagawa, 2006–07), das Steel Sheet House (Tokio, 2008–09), das Pitched Roof House (Nagano, 2008–09, hier veröffentlicht) sowie Woods of Net (Ninotaira, Hakone, Kanagawa/im Hakone Open-Air Museum, 2009), alle in Japan.

TAKAHARU TEZUKA, né à Tokyo en 1964, est diplômé de l'institut de technologie Musashi (1987) et de l'université de Pennsylvanie (1990). Il a travaillé pour le Richard Rogers Partnership Ltd. (1990–94) et a fondé l'agence Tezuka Architects la même année. Il est actuellement professeur à l'université de la ville de Tokyo. Né à Kanagawa en 1964, **YUI TEZUKA** est diplômé de l'Institut de technologie Musashi et de la Bartlett School of Architecture, University College, à Londres. L'agence a construit une douzaine de résidences privées et remporté en 2001 le concours du Musée des sciences naturelles Matsunoyama. Installée aujourd'hui à Tokyo, elle a réalisé, entre autres et toujours au Japon : l'hôpital de Soejima (Saga-shi, Saga,1995–96) ; la Wood Deck House (Kamakura-shi, Kanagawa, 1999) ; la Roof House (Hadano-shi, Kanagawa, 2000–01) ; Toyota L&F Hiroshima (Hiroshima-shi, Hiroshima, 2003) ; le Musée de sciences naturelles Echigo-Matsunoyama (Tokamachi-shi, Niigata, 2002–03) ; la Floating Roof House (Okayama, 2005) ; le jardin d'enfants Fuji (Tachikawa, Tokyo, phase 1, 2006 ; phase 2, 2006–07) ; Le Temple qui capte la forêt (Yokohama, Kanagawa, 2006–07) ; la Steel Sheet House (Tokyo, 2008–09) ; la Pitched Roof House (Nagano, 2008–09, publiée ici) et Woods of Net (Ninotaira, Hakone, Kanagawa/à l'intérieur du Musée de plein air Hakone, 2009).

PITCHED ROOF HOUSE

Nagano, Japan, 2008–09

Address: not disclosed
Area: 107 m². Client: not disclosed. Cost: not disclosed
Collaboration: Hirofumi Ohno/OHNO JAPAN

Located on a 1059-square-meter site, this house employs what the architects call "an extremely simple pitched roof" that is unusual to the extent that only 40 percent of the space under the roof is enclosed as internal space. The cantilevered roof edge provides space extending out to the landscape. The architects writes: "The main theme of the house is the space under the eave. The existence of the internal space relies very much on the intermediate space. Every detail of this house is designed to achieve the columnless eave space. The folded shape of the pitched roof helps the very thin cantilevered roof to stretch almost six meters." Using full-height sliding doors for the enclosed space, it has been made possible to entirely open the interior when weather conditions permit. The architects conclude: "We believe the true nature of Japanese architecture lies in the intermediate space between outside and inside. The internal space exists, because the intermediate space exists. The client requested a simple house responding to the Japanese landscape. This is the attempt to amplify the Japanese-ness of the house to the limit that the latest technology allows."

Dieses auf einem 1059 m² großen Grundstück gelegene Haus hat ein, in den Worten der Architekten, „extrem einfaches, geneigtes Dach", was insofern ungewöhnlich ist, als nur 40 % des von ihm überdeckten Bereichs Innenräume sind. Das auskragende Dach bedeckt Flächen, die sich in die Landschaft erstrecken. Der Architekt schreibt: „Das Hauptthema dieses Hauses ist der Raum unter der Dachtraufe. Die Existenz der Innenräume beruht weitgehend auf den Zwischenbereichen. Jedes Detail dieses Hauses war darauf ausgerichtet, den stützenfreien Raum unter dem Dach zu ermöglichen. Die gefaltete Form des geneigten Daches trägt dazu bei, dass es über fast 6 m auskragen kann." Durch geschosshohe Schiebetüren können die Innenräume ganz geöffnet werden, sofern das Wetter dies zulässt. Die Architekten erklären abschließend: „Wir sind der Überzeugung, dass das eigentliche Merkmal der japanischen Architektur im Zwischenbereich zwischen außen und innen liegt. Der Innenbereich existiert, weil der Zwischenbereich existiert. Der Bauherr wünschte sich ein schlichtes Haus in Übereinstimmung mit der japanischen Landschaft. Dies ist ein Versuch, das Japanische des Hauses so weit zu führen, wie es die moderne Technik zulässt."

Implantée sur un terrain de 1059 mètres carrés, cette maison fait appel ce que les architectes appellent « un toit extrêmement simple à deux versants », d'aspect curieux dans la mesure où le volume intérieur habitable n'utilise que 40 % de la surface sous toiture. L'espace sous le porte-à-faux s'étend vers le paysage. Selon l'architecte : « Le thème principal de cette maison est l'espace sous le débord du toit. L'existence de l'espace intérieur dépend en grande partie de cet espace intermédiaire. Tout est conçu pour que cette zone protégée de dessous la toiture ne comporte pas de colonnes. Le pliage du toit en deux parties permet un porte-à-faux de chaque côté de près de six mètres. » Grâce à des portes coulissantes toute hauteur qui ferment l'espace intérieur, on peut entièrement ouvrir celui-ci quand le temps le permet. « Nous pensons que la véritable nature de l'architecture japonaise tient à l'espace intermédiaire entre le dedans et le dehors. L'espace interne existe parce que l'espace intermédiaire existe. Le client souhaitait une maison simple qui réponde aux caractéristiques du paysage japonais. C'est une tentative d'amplifier le caractère nippon de cette maison jusqu'aux limites permises par les plus récentes technologies. »

The very large roof of the house and its long, low form make it blend into the site in the image above.

Das sehr große Dach des Hauses und dessen lange, niedrige Form betten es gut in das Gelände ein (oben).

Le très grand toit surbaissé de la maison facilite sa fusion avec le paysage (ci-dessus).

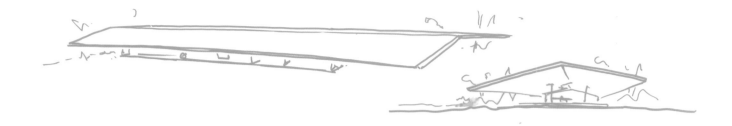

Drawings show the predominant shape of the roof. Below, the roof serves to cover living areas that can thus be exposed to the open air.

Die Zeichnungen zeigen die beherrschende Form des Dachs. Unten: Das Dach dient auch zur Überdeckung von Aufenthaltsbereichen im Freien.

Les dessins montrent la prééminence de la forme du toit. Ci-dessous, la toiture protège des zones du séjour qui peuvent ainsi rester ouvertes.

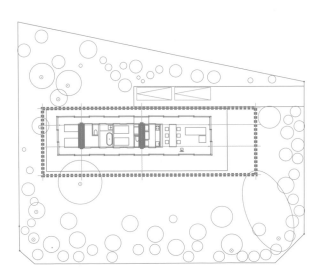

Wood dominates the relatively dark interior of this rectangular structure. On this page, the living areas, with their sliding screens, entirely open to the exterior.

Holz beherrscht die relativ dunklen Innenräume dieses rechtwinkligen Hauses. Auf dieser Seite ist der Wohnbereich durch die Schiebewände vollkommen nach draußen geöffnet.

Le bois domine l'intérieur relative-ment sombre de cette construction rectangulaire. Les différentes zones de vie s'ouvrent entièrement sur l'extérieur, protégées par des écrans coulissants.

TURNBULL GRIFFIN HAESLOOP

Turnbull Griffin Haesloop
1660 Bush Street, Suite 200
San Francisco, CA 94109
USA

Tel: +1 415 441 2300
Fax: +1 415 441 2385
E-mail: info@tgharchitects.com
Web: www.tgharchitects.com

MARY GRIFFIN worked in the Architecture Research Office, Harvard University (1973–74); Lyndon Associates (1978); James R. Grieves Associates (1979–80); Hartman-Cox Architects (1980–85); William Turnbull Associates (1985–97); and has been a partner of Turnbull Griffin Haesloop since 1997. **ERIC HAESELOOP** worked with Cesar Pelli and Associates (New Haven, 1981–84); and Spencer Associates (Palo Alto, 1984–85). He was an associate at William Turnbull Associates (1985–96) and then a principal of the same firm (1996–97), before forming Turnbull Griffin Haesloop in 1997. Recent projects of the firm include the Hornall Residence (Sebastopol, California, 2006–08, published here); a Private Residence (Sebastopol, California, 2008); Katherine Delmar Burke School (San Francisco, 2008); the Branson School (Ross, California, 2009); Hicks Mountain Ranch (Nicasio, California, 2010); Living Roof Hillside Residence (Kentfield, California, 2010); and a Private Residence (Point Reyes Station, California, 2010), all in the USA.

MARY GRIFFIN arbeitete im Architecture Research Office der Harvard University (1973–74), bei Lyndon Associates (1978), James R. Grieves Associates (1979–80), Hartman-Cox Architects (1980–85) sowie William Turnbull Associates (1985–97) und ist seit 1997 Partnerin von Turnbull Griffin Haesloop. **ERIC HAESLOOP** arbeitete bei Cesar Pelli and Associates (New Haven, 1981–84) und bei Spencer Associates (Palo Alto, 1984–85). Er war Gesellschafter bei William Turnbull Associates (1985–96) und danach Leiter dieser Firma (1996–97), bis er 1997 Turnbull Griffin Haesloop gründete. Zu den neueren Projekten des Büros zählen das Wohnhaus Hornall (Sebastopol, Kalifornien, 2006–08, hier veröffentlicht), ein privates Wohnhaus (Sebastopol, Kalifornien, 2008), die Katherine Delmar Burke School (San Francisco, 2008), die Branson School (Ross, Kalifornien, 2009), die Hicks Mountain Ranch (Nicasio, Kalifornien, 2010), das Wohnhaus Living Roof Hillside (Kentfield, Kalifornien, 2010) sowie ein privates Wohnhaus (Point Reyes Station, Kalifornien, 2010), alle in den USA.

MARY GRIFFIN a travaillé dans le Bureau de recherches architecturales de l'université Harvard, (1973–74), chez Lyndon Associates (1978), James R. Grieves Associates (1979–80), Hartman-Cox Architects (1980–85) et William Turnbull Associates (1985–97). Elle est associée de Turnbull Griffin Haesloop depuis 1997. **ERIC HAESLOOP** a travaillé pour Cesar Pelli and Associates (New Haven, 1981–84) et Spencer Associates (Palo Alto, 1984–85). Il a été associé de William Turnbull Associates (1985–96), puis directeur de la même agence (1996–97) avant de fonder Turnbull Griffin Haesloop en 1997. Parmi les récents projets de l'agence : la Hornall Residence (Sebastopol, Californie, 2006–08, publiée ici) ; une résidence privée (Sebastopol, Californie, 2008) ; l'école Katherine Delmar Burke (San Francisco, 2008) ; l'école Branson (Ross, Californie, 2009) ; le ranch de Hicks Mountain (Nicasio, Californie, 2010) ; la Living Roof Hillside Residence (Kentfield, Californie, 2010) et une résidence privée à Point Reyes Station (California, 2010).

HORNALL RESIDENCE

Sebastopol, California, USA, 2006–08

Address: not disclosed
.Area: 167 m² (main house); 34 m² (guesthouse)
Client: John and Loreta Hornall. Cost: not disclosed

The house is intimately integrated into its wooded environment, as can be seen in these photographs.

Wie diese Fotos beweisen, ist das Haus gut geschützt in seine bewaldete Umgebung integriert.

La maison s'intègre intimement à son environnement boisé, comme le montrent ces photographies.

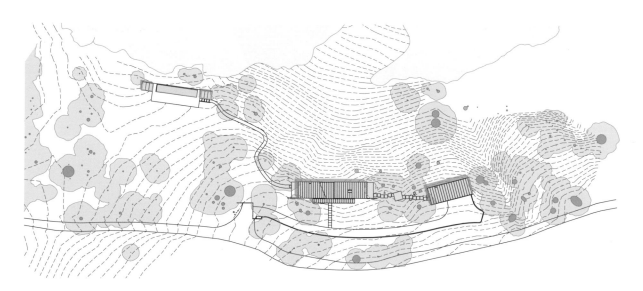

A site map shows the main house linked by paths to the pool on the left and to the guest house on the right.

Der Lageplan zeigt das Haupthaus, von dem Wege zum Pool (links) führen, und rechts das Gästehaus.

Un plan du terrain montre la maison principale reliée par un chemin à la piscine, du côté gauche, et à la maison d'amis, du côté droit.

Sebastopol is located in northern California. This house was built on a sloping site near redwood trees. The basic form of the house is rectangular, with a window wall facing the view. Decks at both ends of the house connect to paths leading to the guesthouse and pool. Aligned on the east-west axis, the house has operable windows on the northern and southern sides allowing for ventilation. The architects state: "Generous openings connect the spaces, and a bookcase arrayed along the southern wall houses the clients' wonderful art collection. The interior is finished with a Douglas fir ceiling and paneling, sheetrock walls, and ipe flooring. The exterior, clad in cedar siding with a metal roof, quietly blends with the surrounding landscape."

Sebastopol liegt im Norden Kaliforniens. Dieses Haus wurde auf einem mit Mammutbäumen bestandenen Hanggrundstück errichtet. Die Grundform des Gebäudes ist rechtwinklig; eine verglaste Wand bietet Ausblick in die Landschaft. Von Terrassen auf beiden Seiten des Hauses führen Fußwege zum Gästehaus respektive zum Swimmingpool. Das auf einer Ost-West-Achse angordnete Gebäude hat an der Nord- und der Südseite verstellbare Fenster zur natürlichen Belüftung. Die Architekten erklären: „Großzügige Öffnungen verbinden die Bereiche; ein an der Südwand angebrachter Schrank enthält die wunderbare Kunstsammlung der Bauherren. Innen ist das Haus mit Wandverkleidungen und Decken aus Douglastanne, Gipskartonwänden und Böden aus Ipe-Holz ausgestattet. Das außen mit Zedernholz verkleidete und mit einem Metalldach versehene Gebäude fügt sich unauffällig in die umgebende Landschaft ein."

La ville de Sebastopol est située en Californie du Nord. Cette maison a été édifiée sur un terrain en pente près d'une forêt de séquoias. Le plan de base est rectangulaire, un mur entièrement vitré faisant face à la vue. De chaque côté de la maison, des terrasses en bois relient les chemins conduisant à la maison d'amis et à la piscine. La maison construite selon un axe est-ouest est équipée au nord et au sud de fenêtres ouvrantes permettant la ventilation. Selon les architectes: «Des ouvertures généreuses relient les espaces et une bibliothèque disposée le long du mur sud accueille la superbe collection d'art du client. L'intérieur est habillé de plafonds et lambris en pin de Douglas, les murs sont plâtrés et les sols en ipé. L'extérieur, à parement de cèdre et toit métallique, se fond tranquillement dans le paysage environnant. »

The main façade of the house has full-height vertical glazing, allowing the residents to feel that they are very much part of the natural setting.

Die Hauptfassade des Hauses ist geschosshoch verglast und gibt den Bewohnern das Gefühl, selbst Teil der natürlichen Umgebung zu sein.

La façade principale est entièrement vitrée, ce qui donne à ses résidants l'impression de faire partie du cadre naturel.

Horizontal wood siding contrasts
with the large openings and vertical
windows. Below, the small pool with
its gravel terrace.

Die horizontale Holzverkleidung kon-
trastiert mit den großen Öffnungen
und vertikalen Fenstern. Unten: der
kleine Pool und die mit Kies gedeckte
Terrasse.

Le bardage en bois horizontal
contraste avec les grandes
ouvertures et les fenêtres verticales.
Ci-dessous, la petite piscine entourée
d'une terrasse de gravier.

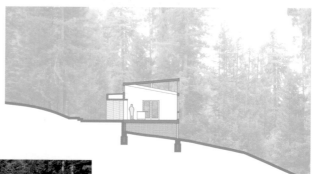

The interior of the house with its sloped roof is generous and column free. Wood is used for most surfaces, giving a warm feeling to the interior.

Das Innere des Hauses mit geneigtem Dach ist großzügig und stützenfrei. Holz, das für die meisten Oberflächen verwendet wurde, verleiht den Räumen eine warme Wirkung.

L'intérieur de la maison sous la pente de la toiture est à la fois généreux et dénué de toute colonne. Le bois est utilisé sur toutes les surfaces, ce qui crée une impression chaleureuse.

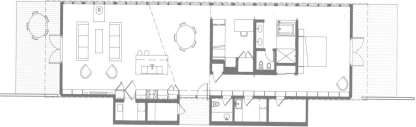

The glazing that rises up near the
round dining table seems to bring the
forest inside the house. The basic
plan of the house is rectangular.

*Die Verglasung um den runden
Esstisch holt den Wald scheinbar in
das Haus herein. Die Grundform des
Hauses ist rechtwinklig.*

*Le mur de verre qui s'élève près de la
table de repas ronde semble laisser
la forêt pénétrer dans la maison. Le
plan de la maison est rectangulaire.*

WINGÅRDHS

Wingårdh Arkitektkontor AB
Kungsgatan 10A
411 19 Göteborg
Sweden

Tel: +46 31 743 70 00
Fax: +46 31 711 98 38
E-mail: wingardhs@wingardhs.se
Web: www.wingardhs.se

Wingårdhs is one of the five largest architectural firms in Sweden. Founded in Göteborg in 1977, Wingårdhs has also had offices in Stockholm since 1985. Their staff numbers about 140. **GERT WINGÅRDH**, born in 1951 in Skövde, Sweden, is the owner, CEO, and manager of the firm. Wingårdh received his M.Arch degree from the Chalmers University of Technology (Göteborg, 1975). The office works on a variety of projects ranging from product development (Volvo stands at international car shows) to interior design (Filippa K store "Ease" in Grev Turgatan, Stockholm, 2006), city planning (Havneholmen in Copenhagen, Denmark), and large structures (Hyllie Center, Malmö, 2011). They completed the Swedish Embassy in Berlin (Germany, 1999) and have undertaken other projects such as a new 85-meter-high control tower at Stockholm Arlanda Airport (Runway 3 Project, Stockholm, 2001) and the Piano Pavilion (Lahti, Finland, 2007–08, published here).

Wingårdhs ist eins der fünf größten Architekturbüros in Schweden. Es wurde 1977 in Göteborg gegründet, hat seit 1985 auch eine Niederlassung in Stockholm und insgesamt etwa 140 Mitarbeiter. **GERT WINGÅRDH**, geboren 1951 in Skövde, Schweden, ist der Besitzer, Geschäftsführer und Manager der Firma. Er machte seinen Master in Architektur an der Technischen Hochschule Chalmers (Göteborg, 1975). Das Büro arbeitet an vielfältigen Projekten, die von Produktentwicklung (Volvo-Stände auf internationalen Autosalons) bis zu Innenausstattungen (Geschäft Filippa K „Ease" in Grev Turgatan, Stockholm, 2006), Stadtplanung (Havneholmen in Kopenhagen, Dänemark) und Großbauten (Hyllie Center, Malmö, 2011) reichen. Es baute die Schwedische Botschaft in Berlin (1999) und weitere wichtige Gebäude, z. B. einen 85 m hohen Kontrollturm auf dem Stockholmer Flughafen Arlanda (Projekt Startbahn 3, Stockholm, 2001) sowie den Piano-Pavillon (Lahti, Finnland, 2007–08, hier veröffentlicht).

Wingårdhs est l'une des cinq plus grandes agences d'architecture de Suède. Fondée à Göteborg en 1977, elle possède également des bureaux à Stockholm depuis 1985 et emploie environ 140 collaborateurs. **GERT WINGÅRDH**, né en 1951 à Skövde (Suède) en est le propriétaire, le président et le directeur général. Wingårdh a obtenu son M. Arch. à l'Université de technologie Chalmers (Göteborg, 1975). L'agence intervient sur des projets variés allant du développement de produits (stands pour Volvo dans les salons de l'automobile internationaux) à l'aménagement intérieur (magasin Filippa K « Ease » dans Grev Turgatan, Stockholm, 2006), en passant par l'urbanisme (Havneholmen à Copenhague) et de grandes réalisations architecturales (Hyllie Center, Malmö, 2011). Elle a réalisé l'ambassade de Suède à Berlin (1999) ; une tour de contrôle de 85 m de haut pour l'aéroport d'Arlanda à Stockholm (Projet piste 3, Stockholm, 2001) et le pavillon Piano (Lahti, Finlande, 2007–08, publié ici).

PIANO PAVILION
Lahti, Finland, 2007–08

Address: Börupinraitti 6, 15140 Lahti, Finland, +358 10 422 59 50, www.casseli.fi
Area: 147 m². Client: Wood in Culture Association. Cost: not disclosed

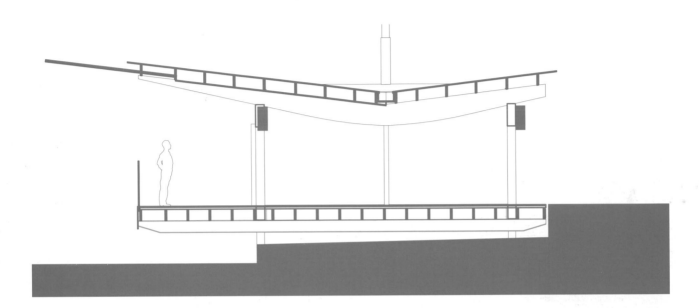

This Pavilion, commissioned by the Wood in Culture Association, is located near the Sibelius Hall in Lahti, Finland. Unexpectedly, the architect's firm declares of Gert Wingårdh: "His design echoes and celebrates the work of Italian Renzo Piano, recipient of the 2000 Spirit of Nature Wood Architecture Award." With steel foundation columns driven into the bedrock of the site, the structure has a glulam frame and steel beams. Glass walls give the impression that the roof is floating above the structure. The architect compares the building to a "ship about to be launched." Companies such as Finnforest supported the project, providing construction materials for example. The local UPM Lahti Mill provided the special plywood used for interior cladding, as they did the ProFi wood plastic composite employed for the terrace. Aspen staves used in the façade were trees felled in Artjärvi and Sysmä. Ash furniture in the café was designed by Tapio Anttila and manufactured at the joinery workshop of the ProPuu Association. The terrace furniture was designed by Kari Virtanen of Nikari Oy in Fiskars. In the summer, the Piano Pavilion serves as a 60-seat café; in winter it can be reserved for meetings and private functions.

Dieser vom Verein Wood in Culture in Auftrag gegebene Pavillon steht neben der Sibelius-Halle in Lahti, Finnland. Das Architekturbüro berichtet spontan über Gert Wingårdh: „Sein Entwurf wurde inspiriert von Renzo Piano und ist eine Hommage an das Werk des Italieners, dem 2000 der Spirit of Nature Wood Architecture Award verliehen wurde." Das Gebäude mit Gründungspfeilern aus Stahl, die in den Felsboden getrieben wurden, hat ein Tragwerk aus Schichtholz und Stahlträgern. Glaswände vermitteln den Eindruck, als würde das Dach über dem Bauwerk schweben. Der Architekt vergleicht den Pavillon mit „einem Schiff, das vom Stapel gelassen wird". Firmen wie Finnforest haben das Projekt subventioniert, auch Baumaterial geliefert. Die Firma UPM Lahti Mill vor Ort lieferte das spezielle Furnier für die Innenverkleidung sowie ProFi-Holz-Kunststoff-Verbundmaterial für die Terrasse. Die für die Fassade verwendeten Espenstäbe stammen von Bäumen, die in Artjärvi und Sysmä gefällt wurden. Das Mobiliar aus Eschenholz im Café wurde von Tapio Anttila entworfen und in der Schreinerwerkstatt der Vereinigung ProPuu hergestellt. Die Möbel für die Terrasse gestaltete Kari Virtanen von Nikari Oy in Fiskars. Im Sommer dient der Piano-Pavillon als Café für bis zu 60 Besucher, im Winter kann er für Sitzungen und private Veranstaltungen genutzt werden.

Ce pavillon, commandité par l'Association du Bois dans la culture, se trouve près du Hall Sibelius à Lahti en Finlande. De façon qui étonne un peu, l'agence déclare que « Le projet [de Gert Wingårdh] rappelle et célèbre l'œuvre de l'architecte italien Renzo Piano, récipiendaire en 2000 du prix d'Architecture Esprit de la nature. » Reposant sur des pieux de fondation en acier plantés dans l'assise rocheuse, la structure se compose d'une ossature en lamellé-collé et de poutres d'acier. Les murs de verre donnent l'impression que le toit flotte indépendamment. L'architecte le compare à un « bateau sur le point d'être lancé ». Des entreprises comme Finnforest soutiennent ce projet en fournissant par exemple les matériaux de construction. La scierie locale UPM de Lahti a offert le contreplaqué spécial utilisé pour l'habillage de l'intérieur ainsi que le matériau composite de bois et de plastique ProFi utilisé pour la terrasse. Les barreaux en peuplier proviennent d'arbres coupés à Artjärvi and Sysmä. Le mobilier en hêtre du café a été conçu par Tapio Anttila et fabriqué à l'atelier de menuiserie de l'association ProPuu. Celui de la terrasse a été conçu par Kari Virtanen de Nikari Oy à Fiskars. En été, le pavillon est aménagé en café de 60 places. En hiver, il est réservé à des réunions et des activités privées.

The Pavilion, with its asymmetric, upwardly inclined roof, is cantilevered over the water.

Der Pavillon mit seinem asymmetrischen, aufwärts gebogenen Dach kragt über das Wasser aus.

Le pavillon à toiture asymétrique en ailes de papillon se dresse en porte-à-faux au-dessus de l'eau.

The size of the roof allows for outdoor terraces to be fully covered. Full-height glazing allows patrons to view the harbor.

Aufgrund der Größe des Dachs sind die Außenterrassen voll überdeckt. Die Rundumverglasung bietet den Gästen Aussicht auf den Hafen.

Grâce à ses dimensions, le toit protège les terrasses. Les murs vitrés permettent aux clients de bénéficier de vues sur le port.

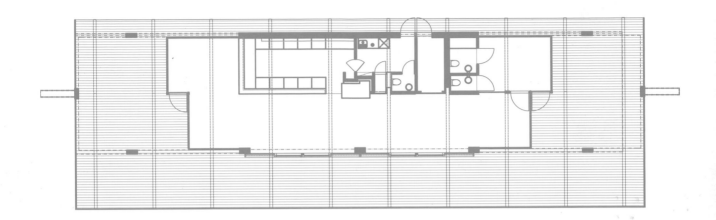

The terrace serves for outdoor
seating when weather permits.
Below, a drawing of the roof grid
of the structure.

Wenn das Wetter es zulässt, kann
auch die Terrasse genutzt werden.
Unten: eine Aufsicht der Dachkonstruktion.

Des tables sont dressées sur la
terrasse quand le temps le permet.
Ci-dessous, un dessin de la trame
de la structure du toit.

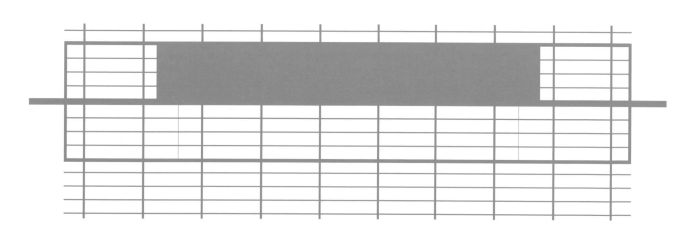

INDEX OF ARCHITECTS, BUILDINGS, AND PLACES

CREDITS